HEW STRACHAN is the Chichele Professor of the History of War and a Fellow of All Souls College at Oxford University. He is the author of several highly regarded books on military history, and is one of the world's foremost experts on the First World War.

D0540213

The First World War

Hew Strachan

SIMON &
SCHUSTER

London · New York · Sydney · Toronto · New Delhi

A CBS COMPANY

First published in Great Britain by Simon & Schuster UK Ltd, 2003
This edition published by Simon & Schuster UK Ltd, 2014
A CBS COMPANY

Copyright © Hew Strachan 2003, 2006, 2014

This book is copyright under the Berne Convention.
No reproduction without permission.
All rights reserved.

The right of Hew Strachan to be identified as author of this work has been asserted by him
in accordance with sections 77 and 78 of the Copyright, Designs and Patents Act 1988.

1 3 5 7 9 10 8 6 4 2

Simon & Schuster UK Ltd
1st Floor
222 Gray's Inn Road
London
WC1X 8HB

www.simonandschuster.co.uk

Simon & Schuster Australia, Sydney
Simon & Schuster India, New Delhi

Picture credits
Imperial War Museum: p. vi (3rd) (Q18593), p. vii (3rd) (Q5977), p. 1 top left (Q81794), p. 33 bottom left (Q49104), 10 (Q49104), p. 65 top left (Q115007), p. 65 right (Q18593), p. 65 bottom left (Q5104), 12 (Q115007), 13 (Q18593), 15 (Q5104), p. 95 left (Q45339), 16 (Q85953), 19 (Q13400A), p. 125 top left (Q23855), 21 (Q81539), 22 (Q23855), 26 (Q52339), p. 157 top left (Q49296), p. 157 bottom left (Q70773), 27 (Q6420), 28 (Q49296), 30 (Q53003), p. 193 top left (LC56), 33 (LC56), p. 225 right (Q8381), p. 225 bottom left (Q8381), 38 (Q5977), 39 (CO2250), p. 259 top left (Q29953), p. 259 bottom left (Q23964), 42 (Q29953), 43 (Q52803), 45 (Q55047), p. 293 top left (Q11086), 48 (Q72560), 49 (Q11086), 50 (Q9580). akg-images: 14. Österreichischen Staatsarchiv/Kriegsarchiv: p. vi (1st), p. 1 bottom left, p. 1 right, 1, 4, 5. L'Illustration: 41, 47. Corbis: p. vi (5th), p. vii (4th), p. vii (5th), 2, p. 33 top left, p. 125 right, p. 125 bottom left, p. 259 right, p. 293 right. Hulton Archive/Getty Images: p. vi (4th), p. 95 right. Stichting tot Beheer van Huis Doorn: 43, 11. Royal Army Museum Brussels: p. vi (2nd), p. 33 right, 6, 8. ullstein bild Berlin: 23. Historial de la Grande Guerre, Péronne: p. vii (1st), p. 157 right, 29, 46. Landesarchiv Berlin: p. vii (2nd), p. 193 right, 34. Roger-Viollet: 7, p. 293 bottom left, 51. Deutsches Marinemuseum: 17. Wallstein Verlag, Göttingen (Germany)/Deutsches Literaturarchiv: 18. Süddeutscher Verlag Bilderdienst: p. 95 bottom left, 20. Hoover Institution Archives: 24. USHMM Photo Archives/Jewish Historical Institute (ZIH): 25. National Archives and Records Administration: p. 193 bottom left, 35. Bibliothek für Zeitgeschichte, Stuttgart: 32. Archiv Zentner, München: 36. St. Petersburg Central Archive for Film and Photographic Documents: p. 225 top left, 37. Heeresgeschichtliches Museum, Wien: 40.

Inside cover picture credits
ECPAD France: centre back, bottom right front, top left front, bottom left back, centre front.
Archives photographiques, Centre des Monuments Nationaux, Paris: top right back, bottom left front, top right front, top left back, bottom right back.

Front cover image by C.J. Patterson

A CIP catalogue record for this book
is available from the British Library.

ISBN 978-1-47113-426-5
Ebook ISBN 978-1-47113-436-4

Typeset by M Rules
Printed and bound by CPI Group (UK) Ltd, Croydon, CR0 4YY

For Pamela and Mungo
Who may not have lived through the First World War
but have had to live with it

Contents

The Eastern Front

The Western Front
WINTER 1914–15

NETHERLANDS

N

R. Maas
(R. Meuse)

NORTH SEA

GERMAN

Antwerp

Brussels

BELGIUM

Passchendaele
Roulers
Ypres
Menin
R. Yser
R. Scheldt

Liège
R. Meuse

Namur
Stavelot

Neuve Chapelle
Loos
Lille
Vimy
R. Sambre

EMPIRE

ARTOIS

Arras
Doullens
Mailly
Flers
Cambrai
Albert
Longueval
Fricourt
R. Somme
Amiens
St Quentin

ARDENNES

LUXEMBOURG
• Luxembourg

F R A N C E

R. Oise
Soissons
R. Aisne
Rheims

R. Meuse

A R G O N N E

Fort Douaumont
Fort Vaux
Verdun
St Mihiel
• Metz

R. Seine
R. Marne

Paris
La Ferté-
sous-Jouarre

C H A M P A G N E

Toul
Nancy

P L A I N E

R. Seine

THE YPRES SALIENT
Spring 1915

• Bixschoote

Langemarck
• Pilckem
Passchendaele•

YSER CANAL

Zonnebeke•

Ypres
Polygon
Wood
MENIN ROAD
Gheluvelt

Zillebeke
Sanctuary
Wood
▲ Hill 60

Messines Ridge

• Messines

0 1 2 3 miles
0 1 2 3 4 5 km

.... The Front, Winter 1914–15
—·—·— International boundaries

0   50   100 miles
0   50   100   150 km

V O S G E S

A L S A C E

Belfort•

SWITZERLAND

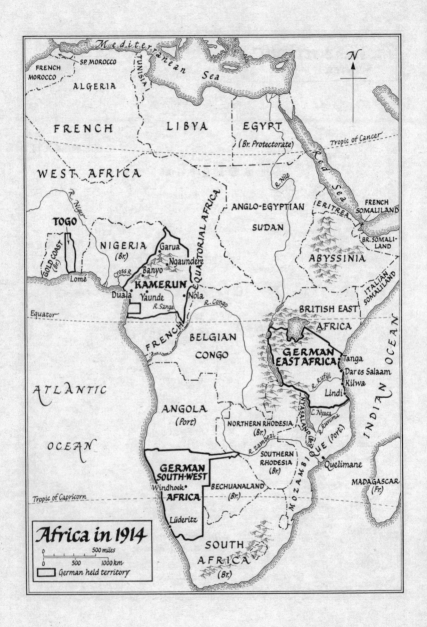

Africa in 1914

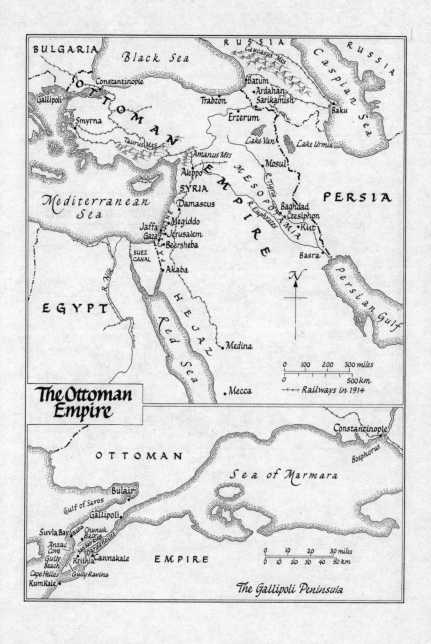

The Ottoman Empire

The Gallipoli Peninsula

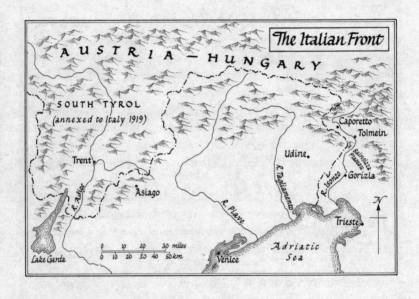

Introduction

Later in life those who were caught up in the First World War remembered with convincing accuracy what they were doing and where they were when they first heard the news of its outbreak. They knew that they confronted 'history in the making'. Nothing comparable had happened to them or had occurred in their lifetimes. As they struggled to put shape back onto their lives, they sought context. Many commentators cast around for parallels from the past. Just as Americans referred to Pearl Harbor after 9/11, so in 1914 Europeans cited the last great war, that against Napoleon, which had ended in 1815.

It soon became clear that too much had changed over the intervening century for the comparison to make much sense. Moreover, the First World War itself promoted dramatic change at a relentless pace. It was – literally – revolutionary, as events in 1917 in Russia confirmed.

Rather than look to the past, writers now looked to the future. The optimists (and especially radicals) said that this was 'a war to end all wars'. The pessimists considered the levels of national mobilisation that the war had brought forth, pondered the exponential effects of new technologies – the submarine, the tank, the aircraft – and turned the phrase 'total war'. The two were sides of the same coin: the possibility of total war meant that Europe and the world had to avoid another war like that of 1914–18.

In all this, one voice from the Napoleonic Wars not only retained his place but enhanced it. Carl von Clausewitz, the Prussian officer and writer on strategy, first saw action against France in 1792, and, over twenty years later, served in the Waterloo campaign. His great book, *On War*, is largely a reflection on war as he had experienced it, albeit leavened with other relatively recent historical examples. It was therefore founded on history. However, because his aim was to study war as a phenomenon, he could not avoid occasionally asking what war might look like in the future. Would it follow the pattern of the Napoleonic Wars? In that case war would be 'total', to use the vocabulary created by the First World War itself. Policy would march in step with war, whose natural tendency was to escalate to extremes. Or would it be more limited, as he argued the European wars of the eighteenth century had been?

Clausewitz did not answer his own question directly, but he clearly felt that it would be hard to put the genie of Napoleonic warfare back into its bottle. The combination of national mobilisation and overriding ambition made war a powerful and destructive tool whose own nature was inherently unconstrained.

On War was published, after Clausewitz's death, in 1832–4. Anyone reading it over the next three decades would have concluded that his expectations as to war's future character were wide of the mark. Although Europe experienced several wars, they were limited. The revolutions of 1848 affected most of the major capitals of the continent, but the wars that followed, notably in Hungary and Italy, were contained. The Crimean War of 1853–6, which involved the Ottoman Empire and Russia in the first instance, and in due course widened to include France, Britain and Piedmont, did not become a major war. The fighting at sea skirted Europe and Asia, and the war on land was overwhelmingly confined to the Crimean peninsula. Moreover, both the major powers of central Europe, Austria and Prussia, stood aloof.

After the First World War, however, *On War* was read very differently. Here was a book that anticipated much of what Europe had just experienced, and it provided a framework for its interpretation.

The British military theorist Basil Liddell Hart, who had served as a junior infantry officer at the Battle of the Somme in 1916, went even further. In lectures delivered at Cambridge University in 1932–3, he attributed to Clausewitz 'the principle of force without limit and without calculation of cost'.

He blamed Clausewitz for what he had been through. He said *On War* argued that 'the only true object of strategy' was 'the destruction of the enemy's armed forces'. At the heart of war was battle and the side with the greater numbers would prevail. 'By its grip on European thought, and the bias it gave to such thought,' Liddell Hart concluded, 'the philosophy of Clausewitz helped to bring about the World War'.

The point of all this is very simple. It is one about hindsight. How we see the events of the past depends on the place from which we do the looking. Those who read Clausewitz who had served in the Crimean War did so with very different lenses from those who served in the First World War. We claim that hindsight gives us the 20:20 vision that those caught up in the midst of events could not have. What we too often fail to acknowledge is how hindsight itself acts as a filter. Of course, we now know the basic contours of the First World War, which those who served in it could not. We know that it lasted over four years. We know that its aftermath spawned further wars, both within Europe and without, that lasted until 1923. We know that the war was responsible for the death of over 9 million military personnel. But many other questions we ask of the war today reflect less the basic facts, and more our present preoccupations and perspectives. Moreover, many of the answers we come up with can be as subjective and tendentious as many of the views expressed by the war's eyewitnesses.

Take the war's impact on civilian life. Liddell Hart wrote one of the very first general histories of the conflict. Called *The Real War* and published in 1930, it proved sufficiently successful and popular to be rebranded in subsequent editions as the 'history of the world war 1914–1918' and then the 'history of the First World War'.

At the end of the book Liddell Hart stressed the contribution of economic warfare, of naval power and blockade, to the achievement of final victory. This interpretation of the reasons for eventual allied success has dipped in and out of favour, especially in Britain, ever since. It grew in acceptance in the 1930s, as Britain sought to exercise influence in Europe without having once again to put a major army on the continent. It went out of fashion in the 1970s, as Britain confronted the fact that the bulk of its army was based in Germany, even in peacetime.

One of the reasons why Liddell Hart's belief in the efficacy of the blockade could be readily dismissed was his failure to adduce any evidence to support his case. He never addressed social and economic conditions in Germany, or in any of the other belligerent powers.

Today's historians are much more concerned with such topics. In doing so they are responding to one of the major themes in the history of war over the course of the twentieth century: that progressively more civilians than soldiers have been killed. The claim is that at its beginning one in ten of those who died in war was a civilian, but that at its end nine in ten were. The research behind these calculations is shoddy, not least because we have no secure hold on civilian death rates in war for the first twenty years of the twentieth century. That is especially true for war outside Europe, rather than within it. In 2000, given the absence of war within Europe, it was the comparison with non-European countries that mattered most.

More specifically, we have no idea how many civilians died as a consequence of the First World War. In October 2012, Prime Minister David Cameron, when announcing his proposals for the national commemoration of the centenary of the war's outbreak, said that, in all, 16 million people had died in the war. When allowance is made for more than 9 million military dead, simple arithmetic suggests that, therefore, more than 6 million civilians died. If that is true, did they die *in* the war, or *because* of the war? A fit, healthy young man, serving as a soldier at the front and killed by shell fire or a sniper's bullet, died *because* of the war. Attributing to the war the death of a civilian munitions worker who succumbed to tuberculosis is much more problematic. The influx of workers to cities in the war exacerbated an already poor housing situation, especially when the building trades declined over the course of the war. And what do we say of the soldier who died of influenza in 1918, while serving at home? He is included in most calculations of wartime losses, but he would not be if he had remained in civilian employment.

Immediately after the war, some Germans claimed that 1 million German civilians, many of them self-evidently noncombatants, died as a result of the allied blockade. This figure was disputed at the time: deaths directly caused by starvation were few to non-existent, and so the consequences of economic warfare for collective German health had to be indirect. Whatever figure we arrive at for German civilian deaths, it makes no allowance for blockade-related deaths in the other countries to which it was allied. In poor, peasant economies, which deaths are to be attributed to war and which to the natural cycles of weather and harvest yields? Within weeks of David Cameron's statement, some British newspapers were running with a total death rate for the First World War of over 30 million. Hindsight's hold on objective truth is a fragile thing. Did this higher total include the victims of the influenza epidemic that swept the world in 1918–19, and whose effect on global death rates outstripped that of the war? And, if it did, to what extent should we attribute the lethal effects of a disease that began in Asia to a war that began in Europe?

So very often the use of hindsight means less that we have objective answers to contentious issues, and more that we ask different questions of the past from those posed by our predecessors. After the Second World War, indubitably more lethal than the First, as well as both longer and closer in time, the memory of the war of 1914–18 faded from view. It re-emerged in 1964, fifty years on from its outbreak. The Cuban missile crisis, the near-escape from an all-out nuclear war, had occurred only two years before.

In 1962, John F. Kennedy, the American president, was reading Barbara Tuchman's Pulitzer Prize-winning account of the opening month of the First World War, *The Guns of August*, published in the same year. Tuchman's own verdict on the war was that it generated 'one single [result] transcending all others: disillusion'. That word caught the mood of the 1960s more than that of the 1920s. Given its experience by 1964 of an even greater war, and given its recent brush with obliteration, the world could be forgiven for regarding the First World War as a conflict over lesser objectives, which its original belligerents could and should have avoided, but which became, in Tuchman's, words 'a trap'.

At the fiftieth anniversary of its outbreak, Liddell Hart was still around to help shape public perceptions of the conflict. Even today, Liddell Hart's words, although written over eighty years ago, continue to find resonance in much that is written about the First World War. One of his Cambridge lectures went on to attribute to Clausewitz not only partial responsibility for the war's causation but, even more, blame for its conduct. The war's statesmen 'had to give way to "military reasons" that had no foundation in reason'. The former, Liddell Hart asserted, were handicapped by their own ignorance of war. 'The formula of war to the utmost was ceaselessly recited by their military advisers, and at each repetition of the sacred name of Clausewitz the statesmen bowed their heads. So they continued, rigid in their determination, to the point of common exhaustion.'

In 1998 one of Britain's best known military historians, the late Sir John Keegan, published his history of the war to mark the eightieth anniversary of its end. He followed a very similar line. Keegan was too young to have served in either world war (and, owing to his own experience of tuberculosis in wartime, was not fit for service even if he had been of age), but he was influenced by the experiences of his father and his father's two brothers, and of his father-in-law. All served in the British Army, as Liddell Hart had done. All of them came home, as Liddell Hart had done. Neither Keegan nor Liddell Hart noted the paradox in what they wrote: that they saw the war as extraordinarily wasteful, and yet their own direct experience of it was survival. Their experience was more typical than atypical. Of those British men who donned a uniform between 1914 and 1918, 12 per cent were killed in the war. Nearly 90 per cent returned. Of course, many of those who came back were marked by wounds, both physical and psychological. Of course, too, in some parts of the British army, the infantry and particularly the flying corps, service was much more dangerous than it was for the average. But the points remain: that hindsight can distort even if it illuminates, and that our judgements can say as much about our own concerns as about those of the past.

When the first edition of this book was published, over a decade ago, in 2003, I was at pains to make clear how immediate the First World War was, not how distant. As the impact of the Second World War itself became history, the reach of the earlier conflict came back into sharper focus. Revisionist historians had interpreted the Cold War as the product not of 1945 but of 1917. The Russian Revolution, and its call for a peace on the basis of the status quo ante, without annexations or indemnities, had prompted the President of the United States, Woodrow Wilson, to restate the principles for which the liberal democracies were fighting. Wilson set out the Fourteen Points to Congress on 8 January 1918. They had been anticipated by a speech on similar lines delivered by the British Prime Minister, David Lloyd George, three days before, but they were not overshadowed by it.

Wilson's progressive internationalism has found echoes in US foreign policy ever since. The First World War propelled the United States from the western hemisphere to the eastern. It ended the United States' isolation from the 'old world' of Europe. For all America's rejection of Wilsonianism in the 1920s, it found itself drawn back across the Atlantic in 1941, and it would stay in Europe after 1945. Nor was it just Franklin Delano Roosevelt who could sound Wilsonian: so too could George W. Bush.

It is a project in which Britain has participated under the rubric of the 'special relationship', most controversially when Tony Blair committed Britain to support the United States in its invasion of Iraq in March 2003. When this book appeared in August of the same year, the invasion seemed to have succeeded.

A decade on, the continuities from Wilson to the 'forward strategy of freedom' (Bush's phrase) are losing their force. The Soviet Union, given life during the First World War, ended in 1989–90, and with it so did the Cold War in Europe – even if it has taken longer for its intellectual superstructure to be demolished. In January 2012 Barack Obama described some states of Europe as 'net exporters of security', a far cry from what every American president had come to accept since Wilson. He announced that the United States would 'pivot' from the Atlantic Ocean to the Pacific. Meanwhile, the order established not least by Britain in western Asia and the Levant after the collapse of the Ottoman empire – itself, like Tsarist Russia, a casualty of the First World War – was challenged by the Arab Spring of 2011 and its consequences.

The tensions between Israel and Palestine are the products of the First World War, and the states of Iraq and Syria were given their present shape by the peace settlements that followed the war. All four countries still have bones to pick with the British. The conflicts that are being waged across the Arab world, in the case of Syria a civil war in name as well as reality, seem likely to revise the state structures put in place then. If these new structures are to have any link to the First World War, it may be through the rise of Recep Erdogan's Turkey, which Alan Little in a 2013 BBC Radio 4 documentary dubbed 'the new Ottomans', to become the pre-eminent regional power. This would be a return not to 1919, or even to 1914, when the empire was already in decline, but to an even older order.

So, a hundred years on from the First World War, are we reaching a point where in practice its influence on the world in which we live today is finally receding? Is it now as distant from us as the Napoleonic Wars seemed to those who fought in 1914–18? If we get to the stage where we can no longer point to the problems of the Middle East as symptoms of the First World War's ongoing legacy, then the answers to these questions may be affirmative. And yet there are three ways in which that is not the case.

First, there is the issue of how the war began. The assassination of the Austro-Hungarian heir apparent, Franz Ferdinand, looks typical of an old order. An aspirant absolute monarch, uniformed and addicted to blood sports, and largely devoid of any liberal sentiment, was killed in a backward part of Europe, the Balkans. The episode's

Ruritanian quality makes it the stuff of late-nineteenth- or early-twentieth-century boys' fiction. But it was an act of terrorism, carried out by young students, motivated by nationalist sentiment.

Today, it can be read as a cautionary tale against elevating a violent crime into an international incident, let alone treating it as an act of war. It therefore seems more modern to us now than it did on the war's fiftieth anniversary, when terrorism was rare. By then, in the 1960s, the independent south Slav state of Yugoslavia, which those students had wanted to see created, looked the most stable and yet most liberal of the elements of the communist bloc. In the 1990s its dissolution was to prove more violent than that of the Soviet Union.

Secondly, there is the issue of how the war ended. The collapse of the Austro-Hungarian and Tsarist empires created a raft of newly independent states in central and Eastern Europe, from Poland to Hungary, from Lithuania to Ukraine. Even if they were on the losing side in 1918, they emerged as victors from the peace settlement. In 1945, even if they were on the winning side, they lost their independence to Soviet rule. For them, the end of the First World War provides the moment of national birth, and so their current situations provide proximity to, not distance from, that war. Even Austria benefits from this connection with a Hapsburg past that can now be romanticised, and that can seem tolerant and benign compared with what was to follow it. So, while in the Arab world the end of continuity with the war may be the theme of the early twenty-first century, within parts of Europe the resumption of continuity is more obvious.

Thirdly, there is the issue of how the war was fought. It would be good if the peoples of the world took the centenary of the First World War as an opportunity to look forward, as did so many in 1919 – not just Woodrow Wilson. Most of what has been said above sees war as shaping the international order, for good or ill. But that is not how the war of 1914–18 is most often and popularly remembered today. Instead, not least because of the emotional force of what those who served rendered as poetry, fiction and memoir, we see it in terms of personal experience. That experience has been homogenised: it is trench warfare, it is shaped by artillery and machine-gun fire, it is wet and muddy, and it is overwhelmingly in Europe – and disproportionately in Western Europe.

There were many other experiences of the First World War. Those who commemorate the centenary between 2014 and 2018 are set to approach it through those of their own immediate forebears. The enthusiasm for genealogical research, access to the Internet and the readier availability of the materials for personal enquiry mean that most stories from this war will begin from the bottom up, in the trenches (at least metaphorically) and not in the command head-quarters or in the cabinet room.

Letters and diaries will be brought down from attics and posted on line. We shall valorise the personal as we elevate our ancestors. The challenge for us all is whether we shall enable this process to permit new interpretations. As we find out about grandparents or great-grandparents who did not fight, but who sat in government offices battling with paperwork, who brought up their children, who farmed or who profited from war-related industries, will we allow their contribution to reset our collective interpretations of the war? And, if they did fight, will we allow our presence – and therefore in most cases their survival in the war – to recast it in terms that are not shaped predominantly by cemeteries and war memorials?

This is going to be particularly difficult, because we no longer see the Second World War as a failure. Liddell Hart saw the commit-ment to a second major war in Europe as a disaster for Britain. Posterity has not been kind to that interpretation. His position flowed naturally from his interpretation of the First World War, as it did for those who were anxious to appease Hitler, but Liddell Hart persisted in it even when the concentration and extermination camps had been opened. He worked hard to absolve senior officers of the German army from blame for the atrocities committed by Germany and he remained extraordinarily blind to the titanic struggle on the eastern front. Today we acknowledge these things; we no longer exculpate the Wehrmacht, and Germany itself accepts a collective responsibility for what the Nazis did. But that was not why Britain went to war in 1939.

The Second World War was, like the First, the product of great power politics. Yet it, unlike the First, has been recast as a great crusade. For the British, partly because they have been influenced by the Americans, it has now become unequivocally the 'good' war fought by what America now calls the 'greatest generation'. It has become our benchmark for 'existential' war, the sort of war that has to be fought because it is necessary, that must be fought whatever the outcome and regardless of the cost. (That was also, as Hitler noted, how Clausewitz saw Prussia's need to fight France in 1812.) This is an overwhelmingly retrospective judgement, and one that has grown with the telling. It is fed by the Holocaust, despite the fact that none of the powers that declared war on Germany did so to save the Jews. Indeed, just as Europe was sucked into war by Serbia in 1914, so in 1939 war was precipitated by the needs of a small power in Eastern Europe. The effect of this moral elevation of the Second World War has been to depress or override the sense of moral purpose of those who fought and died in 1914–18. We gloss over too readily the last letters of those who were killed in the First World War, letters that tell their loved ones not to grieve because they have died in a just cause. History can involve empathy as well as judgement.

We need to be surprised by what the centenary of the First World War throws up, not to dismiss the uncomfortable and unfamiliar. We must not be so caught by the rhetoric set by the war's fiftieth anniversary that we shut out the messages contained in the rhetoric of a hundred years ago, and so exclude what for us may be new insights and fresh findings. If we are open to the evidence in all its diversity and complexity, then – like Clausewitz – we shall bring altered perspectives to the phenomenon that we call war, and that are, sadly, likely to stand us in good stead as we travel through another century.

1

TO ARMS

Austria-Hungary: An Empire under Threat

The weekend of 12–14 June 1914 was a busy one at Konopischt, the hunting lodge and favourite home of Archduke Franz Ferdinand. Here he could indulge his passion for field sports, and here he and his wife, Sophie, could escape the stultifying conventions of the Habsburg court in Vienna. Although he was heir apparent to his aged uncle, Franz Josef, the Emperor of Austria-Hungary, his wife was treated according to the rank with which she had been born, that of an impoverished Czech aristocrat. On their marriage, Franz Ferdinand had been compelled to renounce royal privileges both for her and for their children. At court dinners she sat at the foot of the table, below all the archduchesses, however young; at a ball in 1909, an Austrian newspaper reported, 'the members of the Imperial House appeared in the Ballroom, each Imperial prince with a lady on his arm according to rank, whereas the wife of the Heir to the Throne was obliged to enter the room last, alone and without escort'.[1]

Franz Ferdinand and Sophie were expecting two sets of guests, and got on well with both of them. The first, Kaiser Wilhelm II of Germany, treated Sophie with a warmness that provided a refreshing contrast with Habsburg flummery. He had been under thirty when he ascended the throne in 1888, and his youth and vigour had inspired the hopes of a nation which saw itself as possessed of the same qualities. Germany was younger even than its ruler, having united under Prussia's leadership in 1871. By 1914, however, the paradoxes of Wilhelm's character, at once both conservative and radical, seemed to be manifestations of inconsistency rather than innovation. Born with a withered arm and blighted by an uncertain relationship with his English mother, a daughter of Queen Victoria, the Kaiser was a man of strong whims but minimal staying power. Ostensibly, he had come to admire Konopischt's garden; in reality, he and Franz Ferdinand discussed the situation in the Balkans.

This, the most backward corner of Europe, was where the First World War would begin. The problems it generated, which pre-occupied Wilhelm and Franz Ferdinand, were not Germany's; they were Austria-Hungary's. Vienna, not Berlin, was to initiate the crisis that led to war. It did so with full deliberation, but the war it had in mind was a war in the Balkans, not a war for the world.

By 1914 Austria-Hungary had lost faith in the international order established at the Congress of Vienna in 1815, whose robustness had prevented major war on the continent for a century. For twenty years, between 1792 and 1815, Europe had been racked by wars waged at France's behest; they had challenged the old order, and they had promoted or even provoked nationalism and liberalism. For the Habsburg Empire, whose lands stretched from Austria south into Italy, and east into Hungary and Poland, and which claimed suzerainty over the states and principalities of Germany to the north, national self-determination threatened disintegration. In 1815 it therefore sponsored a settlement whose principles were conservative – which used the restoration of frontiers to curb France and elevated the resulting international order to suppress nationalism and liberalism. Rather than run the risk of major war again, the great powers agreed to meet regularly thereafter. Although formal congresses rapidly became more intermittent, the spirit of the so-called Concert of Europe continued, even when it transpired that the forces of nationalism and liberalism could be moderated but not deflected. After the revolutions that broke out in much of Europe in 1848, war occurred more often. Conservatives realised that liberals did not have a monopoly on nationalism, although for the multi-national Austrian Empire the effect of nationalism remained divisive. In 1859 it lost its lands in Lombardy to the unification of Italy. Seven years later, it forfeited control of Germany to Prussia after the defeat at Königgrätz, and in the aftermath it struck a deal with Hungary which acknowledged the latter's autonomy, recognising that the Emperor of Austria was also the King of Hungary. But, despite these challenges, the ideals of the Concert of Europe persisted. Wars remained short and contained. Even when Prussia invaded France in 1870 and emerged as the leader of a federal German state, the other powers did not intervene.

However, the writ of the 1815 system did not embrace Europe's south-eastern corner. At the beginning of the nineteenth century the entire Balkan peninsula, as far west as modern Albania and Bosnia and as far north as Romania, was part of the Ottoman Empire. From its capital in Constantinople, the Turks ruled the modern Middle East, with further territory in North Africa, Arabia and the Caucasus. As a result, many of the Balkan population were Muslim and therefore outside the purview of what the Tsar of Russia, in particular, had seen as a Christian alliance. Indeed, Russia itself had invaded the Balkans, and on the third occasion, in 1878, the representatives of the great powers convened in Berlin and recognised three independent Balkan states, Serbia, Montenegro and Romania, and expanded the frontiers of two more, Bulgaria and Greece. The Concert of Europe had put its seal on the decline of Ottoman power in the Balkans, but it had left a situation in which international order in the region depended on the forbearance and cooperation of two of its number: Russia and Austria-Hungary.

For Austria-Hungary the situation in the Balkans was as much a matter of domestic politics as of foreign policy. The empire consisted of eleven different nationalities, and many of them had ethnic links to independent states that lay beyond its frontiers. Austria itself was largely German, but there were Italians in Tyrol, Slovenes in Styria, Czechs in Bohemia and Moravia, and Poles and Ruthenes in Galicia. In the Hungarian half of the so-called Dual Monarchy, the Magyars were politically dominant but numerically in a minority, hemmed in by Slovaks to the north, Romanians to the east, and Croats to the south. In 1908 the foreign minister, Alois Lexa von Aerenthal, had annexed Bosnia-Herzogovina, still formally part of the Ottoman Empire, at the top end of the Balkan peninsula. He had hoped to do so without disrupting Austro-Russian cooperation in the area, but he had ended up compounding Austria-Hungary's problems in two ways. First, Russia had disowned the deal. Thereafter, the interests of the two powers in the region competed rather than converged, and this was an opportunity which the Balkan states were only too ready to exploit. Secondly, and relatedly, Bosnia-Herzogovina was populated not only by Bosnians but also by Croats and Serbs. Serbia took the view that, if Bosnia was not to be under Ottoman rule, it should be governed from Belgrade.

Serbia embodied the challenge that confronted Franz Ferdinand – or would do so when he eventually succeeded to the throne. Writ large, it said that nationalism outside the empire threatened the survival of the empire from within. Writ in regional terms, it said that Serbia had to be contained. In two Balkan wars, fought in rapid succession in 1912 and 1913, Serbia had doubled its territory and increased its population from 2.9 million to 4.4 million. Serbia's victories kindled the hopes not only of Serbs but also of some Bosnians and Croats, who aspired to create a new south Slav state in the Balkans. Those aware of the more unsavoury features of Serb government appreciated that such a state might mean not liberation but rather subordination to a greater Serbia. Indubitably, however, neither a south Slav state nor a greater Serbia could be created without considerable cost to Austria-Hungary – whether in its capacity as a Balkan power or as the ruler of other ethnic groups with nationalist ambitions elsewhere. Vienna had not intervened in either Balkan war. Austria-Hungary had paid a price for abstention. Its own interests had been ignored in the subsequent settlements, and the Balkan states had been rewarded rather than penalised for discounting international agreements. Since 1815 the great powers of Europe had kept the peace by being ready to broker deals among themselves; in 1914 it seemed to Austrians that the Concert of Europe could no longer be relied upon to protect Austria-Hungary's interests.

The discussions between Franz Ferdinand and Wilhelm at Konopischt did not just concern foreign policy. Like so many of Austria-Hungary's difficulties, the policy with regard to the Balkans carried significant domestic implications. Vienna needed an ally in the region and the obvious candidate seemed to be Romania. It had a wartime army of up to 600,000 men, a powerful consideration when Austria-Hungary's own peacetime military strength was only 415,000. Its king, Carol, was a member of the Hohenzollern family, the royal dynasty of Prussia. And it was, at least secretly, affiliated to the Triple Alliance of which not only Germany and Austria-Hungary were members but also Italy. However, Austria-Hungary's possible affections for Romania had little prospect of being reciprocated. The obstacle was Transylvania, ethnically Romanian but part of Hungary. Determined to hold on to power, the Magyars rejected constitutional reform for non-Magyars. They were a thorn in Franz Ferdinand's flesh in another way, too. The compromise between Austria and Hungary was subject to renewal every ten years. Franz Ferdinand had thought long and hard about the options for the future governance of the empire. He had entertained both federalism and trialism – a three-way split which would create a south Slav unit alongside those of Austria and Hungary. The latter might appease the Bosnians, Croats and even Serbs, but for the Magyars either solution would mean a loss of power. By 1914 his instincts were veering back towards centralisation under Austro-German domination.

The Kaiser was inclined to take a less jaundiced view of the Magyars. He had met their prime minister, István Tisza, in March, and had been sufficiently impressed to declare that the Magyars were honorary Teutons. What the Konopischt discussions boiled down to was whether Tisza could be persuaded to take a more enlightened approach to the Romanians, in the hope that Romania would then be induced to join an Austro-Hungarian Balkan league. What they were not – despite the presence in the Kaiser's entourage of the head of the German naval office, Alfred von Tirpitz – was a war council. Franz Ferdinand did not believe Austria-Hungary could wage war in the Balkans without triggering Russian intervention, but when he pressed Wilhelm for Germany's unconditional support the latter withheld it. The archduke was no warmonger himself: he recognised that an Austrian campaign against Serbia might push the suspect loyalties of the empire's south Slavs beyond breaking point.

The Kaiser left Konopischt on 13 June 1914. On the following morning, a Sunday, Aerenthal's successor as foreign minister, Leopold Berchtold, and his wife, Nandine, came for the day. Sophie and Nandine had been childhood friends. They, too, toured the garden and inspected the archduke's art collection. Meanwhile, their husbands reviewed Franz Ferdinand's discussion with the Kaiser. Both agreed that the time had come for a fresh initiative in the Balkans, designed to create an alliance favourable to Austria-Hungary and to isolate Serbia.

Berchtold returned to Vienna and entrusted the task of formulating this policy to Franz von Matscheko, one of a group of hawkish and thrusting officials in the Foreign Ministry. Aerenthal had tended to keep these men in check; Berchtold's more conciliar style gave them their head. Matscheko accepted that Romania might be Vienna's logical ally, but could see little hope of immediate progress on that front. He therefore concluded that the empire's most likely partner was Bulgaria. Tisza and the Magyars were supportive. Bulgaria had no joint frontier with the Dual Monarchy, but it did lie along Serbia's eastern border. It could also block Russia's overland route to Constantinople and the Dardanelles. Matscheko stressed Russia's aggression, its espousal of pan-Slavism, and its close relations with Serbia. The tone of Matscheko's memorandum was shrill, but its policy was to use diplomacy, not war. Its intended readership lay principally in Germany: the Kaiser had to be persuaded to favour Bulgaria rather than Romania as an ally, and, as Austria-Hungary lacked the floating capital, the German money market would have to provide the financial inducements to woo the Bulgarian government.

The July Crisis

The other potential recipient of Matscheko's memorandum was Franz Ferdinand himself. He never received it. Matscheko completed his labours on 24 June 1914. By then the archduke was en route for Bosnia, where he was due to attend the manoeuvres of the 15th and 16th Army Corps. He was joined there by his wife, and on Sunday, 28 June, a glorious summer day, the couple made a formal visit to Sarajevo. It was their wedding anniversary. It was also a day of commemoration for the Serbs: the anniversary of the battle of Kosovo in 1389, a terrible defeat redeemed by a single Serb, who had penetrated the Ottoman lines and killed the Sultan. Now, as then, security was lax. A private shopping visit two days earlier had passed without incident; indeed, the archduke had been well received and surrounded by dense throngs. But by the same token there was little secrecy about this occasion.

A group of students and apprentices, members of a revolutionary organisation called Young Bosnia, had crossed over from Serbia in order to assassinate the heir apparent. Although supplied with arms by Serb military intelligence, they were amateurish and incompetent. One of their number, Nedeljko Cabrinović, threw a bomb at the archduke's car. It rolled off the back and wounded those who were following and a number of bystanders. Franz Ferdinand and Sophie went on to the town hall and then decided to visit the injured officers. Thus the planned route was changed. The driver took the wrong turning at the junction of Appel quay and Franzjosefstrasse. One of the putative assassins, a nineteen-year-old consumptive, Gavrilo Princip, was loitering on the corner, having concluded that he and his colleagues had failed. He was therefore amazed to see the archduke's car in front of him and braking. He stepped forward and shot both the archduke and his wife at point-blank range. They died within minutes.

Matscheko's memorandum now took on a very different complexion from that in which it had been originally framed. The automatic reaction in Vienna, as in the other capitals of the world, was that Serbia was behind the assassination. 'The affair was so well thought out', Berchtold informed the German ambassador, 'that very young men were intentionally selected for the perpetration of a crime, against whom only a mild punishment could be decreed.'[2] Berchtold exaggerated. Serbia was in the middle of an election and its prime minister, Nikola Pašić, had enough domestic problems on his plate without compounding them. But principal among these were civil–military relations. The head of Serb military intelligence, Colonel Dragutin Dimitrijević, code-named Apis, was one of a group of officers who had murdered the previous king in 1903. An enthusiastic promoter of the idea of a greater Serbia and a member of a secret terrorist organisation, the Black Hand, he was 'incapable of distinguishing what was possible from what was not and perceiving the limits of responsibility and power'.[3] He resisted Pašić's attempts to subordinate the army to political control, and his sponsorship of Princip and his friends showed that he had been – in this respect, at least – successful. Pašić himself, caught between an enemy within and an enemy without, was dilatory in his response to the events in Sarajevo. The accusation of Serb complicity stuck.

In Austria-Hungary, the most powerful advocate of restraint, Franz Ferdinand, was dead. On 30 June Berchtold proposed a 'final and fundamental reckoning with Serbia'. Franz Josef, now almost eighty-four, agreed. His eyes were moist, less because of personal grief (like others, he had found Franz Ferdinand difficult) than because he realised the potential implications of the assassination for the survival of the empire. The issue was its continuing credibility, not only as a regional player in the Balkans but also as a multi-national state and a European great power. If it lacked the authority even to be the first, it could hardly aspire to be the second.

For the first time since he had taken up office in 1906, the chief of the general staff, Franz Conrad von Hötzendorff, found himself in step with the Foreign Ministry. Conrad had never fought in a war but he had studied it a great deal. As a social Darwinist, he believed that the struggle for existence was 'the basic principle behind all the events on this earth'.[4] Therefore Austria-Hungary would at some stage have to fight a war to preserve its status. 'Politics', he stated, 'consists precisely of applying war as method.'[5] In other words, state policy should be geared to choosing to fight a war at the right time and on the best terms. The Bosnian crisis in 1908–9 had been one such opportunity. Conrad had demanded a preventive war with Serbia. He went on to do so repeatedly, according to one calculation twenty-five times in 1913 alone. Both Aerenthal and Franz Ferdinand had kept Conrad in check, using his bellicosity when they needed it to send a diplomatic signal and marginalising him when they did not.

By the summer of 1914 Conrad thought the increasing tensions in his relationship with the archduke meant that his remaining time in office was likely to be short. This worried him for personal as well as professional reasons. He was deeply in love with Gina von Reininghaus, who was married and the mother of six children. In a country as devoutly Catholic as Austria, divorce seemed to be out of the question – unless Conrad could return victorious from a great war. Certainly Conrad's response to Franz Ferdinand's assassination was more visceral than rational. He favoured war, although he believed that 'It will be a hopeless fight'. 'Nevertheless', he wrote to Gina, 'it must be waged, since an old monarchy and a glorious army must not perish without glory.'[6]

The shift from certainty in the value of a preventive war against Serbia in 1909 to reliance on hazard in 1914 was the reflection of two considerations. The first was the poor state of the army Conrad led. For this both he and his erstwhile mentor, Franz Ferdinand, were wont to blame the Magyars. In 1889 the annual contingent of conscripts was set at 135,670 men. This fixed quota meant that the size of the joint Austro-Hungarian army did not grow in step with the expansion of the population or with the increase in size of other armies. But not until 1912 did Hungary approve a new army law, which permitted an addition of 42,000 men. It was too little too late: the lost years could not be made up. The trained reservists available to other powers in 1914, discharged conscripts who ranged in age from their early twenties up to forty, were simply not there in

Austria-Hungary's case. Its field army was half the size of France's or Germany's. Nor had it compensated for its lack of men with fire-power: each division had forty-two field guns compared with fifty-four in a German division, and the good designs to be found among some of the heavier pieces had not been converted to mass production. The two territorial armies, the Landwehr for Austria and the Honved for Hungary, had only twenty-four field guns per division, but the deficiencies of the regular army meant that they had to be used as part of the field army from the outset of the war. Austria-Hungary had no reserve if the war expanded or became protracted.

In military terms Austria-Hungary was already more a regional power by July 1914 than a European one. Its army was good only for a war in the Balkans, and it was not really capable of fighting more than one power at a time. Therefore Russia's attitude was crucial to Austro-Hungarian calculations. In 1909 Russia had not been a major player, as its humiliating acceptance of the Austro-Hungarian annex-ation of Bosnia-Herzogovina testified. It had been defeated by Japan in 1904, and revolution had followed in 1905. But the Bosnian crisis marked the point at which the resuscitation of the Russian army began. By 1914 it, too, was twice the size of the Austro-Hungarian army.

If Austria-Hungary was going to fight a Balkan war, it needed Germany to protect its back against Russia. German support could do two things: it could deter Russia from intervention on the side of Serbia and it could support Vienna in its pursuit of Bulgaria as its Balkan ally. The Matscheko memorandum was revised and sharpened for German consumption. The new version gave greater emphasis to Russia's aggressiveness, played on the uncertainties of Romania's position, and stressed the need for action as soon as possible. However, it still did not specify war, and neither did the personal letter from Franz Josef to the Kaiser that was drafted to accompany it.

On the evening of 4 July 1914 Berchtold's *chef de cabinet*, Alexander, Graf von Hoyos, boarded the train for Berlin. He carried both the latest version of the Matscheko memorandum and the

Emperor's letter to the Kaiser. Hoyos was another of the young hawks in the Foreign Ministry: convinced that Austria-Hungary must dominate the Balkans, he had been an advocate of armed intervention against Serbia in the First Balkan War. On his arrival in the German capital, he gave the Emperor's personal letter and Matscheko's memorandum to Count Szögyény, Austria's ambassador, who delivered them to the Kaiser over lunch in Potsdam on 5 July. Meanwhile, Hoyos briefed Arthur Zimmermann, the deputy foreign minister. The murders had triggered in Wilhelm both principled outrage and personal loss. He was uncharacteristically decisive. Of course, he declared, Austria-Hungary should deal quickly and firmly with Serbia, and certainly such action would have Germany's support. His only reservation was the need to consult his chancellor, Theobald von Bethmann Hollweg, a fifty-seven-year-old product of the Prussian bureaucracy, described by his secretary as 'a child of the first half of the 19th century and of a better cultivation'.[7] The latter duly attended a crown council, a meeting convened by the Kaiser, that same afternoon, as did Zimmermann and Erich von Falkenhayn, the Prussian minister of war. At last Berlin pledged its support for Vienna's determination to create a Balkan league centred on Bulgaria. What Austria-Hungary did with Serbia was its own affair, but it should be assured that if Russia intervened it would have Germany's backing. On the following morning, 6 July, Bethmann Hollweg conveyed the conclusions of the crown council to the Austrian representatives and Hoyos returned to Vienna.

Germany's support for Austria-Hungary has become known as the 'blank cheque'. Indubitably it was a crucial step in the escalation of the Third Balkan War into a general European war. But the Kaiser's crown council had formed no view that that was the inevitable outcome of a crisis which it had helped to deepen but which – at least for the moment – it did little to direct or control. Bethmann Hollweg, the key German player in the following weeks, was gripped by a fatalism which seems to have been the product of three factors: the recent death of his wife, the growing power of Russia, and the solidarity of the Triple Entente. In 1892 Russia had allied with France, a seemingly impossible combination of autocracy and republic. German frustration and incomprehension had deepened when Britain came to understandings with both powers, France in 1904 and Russia in 1907. Anglo-French hostility had been one of the givens of European international relations throughout all of the eighteenth century and much of the nineteenth. Anglo-Russian enmity was fuelled by competition in Central Asia and British sensitivities about the security of their hold on India. From Bethmann Hollweg's perspective the Triple Entente was therefore a brittle and friable compact. If he had a clear policy in July 1914, it seems to have been to disrupt the Entente.

He was, however, playing with the possibility of major war. All hinged on Russia's response. At their meeting the Kaiser had told Szögyény that 'Russia . . . was in no way ready for war and would certainly ponder very seriously before appealing to arms'.[8] The German ambassador in St Petersburg fed such optimism. Russia would stay out of any war between Austria-Hungary and Serbia because it had not yet recovered from the events of 1904–5 and it could not risk another revolution. Conservatives in St Petersburg were indeed arguing along these lines. But that thought reckoned without the open sore of the Bosnian crisis and the pressures of liberal nationalists, who saw Russia as the protector of all Slavs. The second line of argument accepted that Russia would indeed support Serbia, but that neither France nor Britain would, and that therefore the solidarity of the Triple Entente would be disrupted. That would be a major diplomatic coup. It would moreover trigger a Russo-German war sooner rather than later – a preventive war fought for reasons similar to those developed by Conrad in relation to Serbia. One of the assumptions of 1914 was that tsarist Russia was a sleeping giant about to awake. Its government had been liberalised in response to the 1905 revolution and its annual growth rate was 3.25 per cent. Between 1908 and 1913 its industrial production increased by 50 per cent, an expansion which was largely fuelled by defence-related output. Russia's army was already the biggest in Europe. By 1917 it would be three times the size of Germany's.

The irony of the crown council of 5 July is that Germany's

principal spokesman for preventive war, the chief of the general staff, Helmuth von Moltke the younger, was taking the waters in Baden-Baden. Moltke was the nephew of the military architect of the victories in 1866 and 1870, but, a theosophist, he possessed a more artistic and less decisive temperament than his forebear. Many observers expected him to be replaced in the event of war. One man canvassed as his successor was the senior soldier present at the meeting, the minister of war, Erich von Falkenhayn. Falkenhayn wrote to Moltke to tell him not to hurry back, as he was not convinced 'that the Vienna government had taken any firm resolution'. What it had in mind seemed not to be war but '"energetic" political action such as the conclusion of a treaty with Bulgaria . . . Certainly in no circumstances will the coming weeks bring a decision.'[9] Falkenhayn himself promptly went on leave. Moltke did not return until 25 July and Falkenhayn until 27 July.

Falkenhayn's judgement and Bethmann Hollweg's readiness to gamble were fed more by their knowledge of the recent past than by an awareness of Vienna's fresh resolve. The immediate significance of the 'blank cheque' was not in what it said about German assumptions but in the use made of it by Hoyos when he returned to Austria's capital. He played both sides off against each other. On 7 July, as soon as he arrived, he attended a ministerial council and presented what he had heard in Potsdam as pressure from Germany for action. In 1913 Austria-Hungary had been treated as of no account because it did not enjoy Germany's backing; it should therefore act while it could. The main doubter was Tisza. The Hungarian leader was opposed to any strike on Serbia, ostensibly for fear of Russian intervention but above all because the defeat of Serbia would jeopardise the existing Austro-Hungarian balance: the pressure for a tripartite solution, which recognised a south Slav entity, would be irresistible. But the south Slav challenge to Magyar supremacy was real enough whether there was war with Serbia or not, and popular feeling over the assassinations was running as high in Budapest as in Vienna. By 14 July his fellow Magyar Stephan Burian had won Tisza round to the idea of an Austrian strike on Serbia.

Vienna still did not act. Much of the army was on leave, its peasant soldiers released to help bring in the harvest. Their labours would, of course, be vital in feeding the army and its horses when it mobilised. As the date for the latter Conrad suggested 12 August, but he was persuaded to accept 23 July. The president of France, Raymond Poincaré, and his prime minister, René Viviani, were due to make a state visit to Russia which would end on that day. The French Third Republic, the outcome of Napoleon III's defeat at the hands of Prussia in 1870, was notorious for the instability of its ministries, and hence for the inconsistencies of its policies. But Poincaré, a Lorrainer, who served as prime minister and foreign secretary before beginning a seven-year term as president, gave direction to France's foreign policy. He firmly believed that the solidarity of the alliance system in Europe helped create a balance which prevented war. In the diplomatic machinations that had accompanied the First Balkan War in the autumn of 1912, he had more than once affirmed France's support for Russia's position in the Balkans. But what he intended as a solidification of the Entente could be interpreted by the Russians as a promise of backing should they find themselves at war with Austria-Hungary over Serbia. Berchtold took the view that it was best not to precipitate a crisis when the leaders of the two states would have the opportunity of direct conversation to concert their plans. When Poincaré heard the news of the Austrian ultimatum to Serbia he was already on the way home, aboard the *France* in the Baltic Sea.

By then any stir caused by the killings in Sarajevo in the rest of Europe had begun to die down. It was the summer, and Falkenhayn and Moltke were not alone in going on holiday. In France and Britain domestic events dominated the newspaper headlines. The trial of Madame Caillaux, wife of the former radical prime minister Joseph Caillaux, began on 20 July. She had shot the editor of *Le Figaro*, who had published the love letters exchanged between herself and her husband: on 28 July the gallant French jury acquitted her on the grounds that this was a *crime passionel*. In Britain, the cabinet was preoccupied with the threat, rather than the actuality, of violence: the commitment of the Liberal government to home rule for Ireland promised to drive Ulster loyalists into rebellion. By comparison with the situation at home, that abroad looked more peaceful than for some years. On 18 May 1914, Sir Arthur Nicolson, permanent under-secretary at the Foreign Office, and a former ambassador to St Petersburg, wrote: 'I do not myself believe there is any likelihood of an open conflict between Russia and Germany.'[10] And for those who considered the implications of a possible Austro-Hungarian response to the murder of their heir apparent, the general feeling was that the Serbs were a bloodthirsty and dangerous crew. Even on 31 July the British prime minister, H. H. Asquith, told the Archbishop of Canterbury that the Serbs deserved 'a thorough thrashing'.

By then Austria-Hungary and Serbia were at war. At 6 p.m. on 23 July, the Austro-Hungarian ambassador to Serbia delivered an ultimatum, demanding that the Serb government take steps to extirpate terrorist organisations operating from within its frontiers, that it suppress anti-Austrian propaganda, and that it accept Austro-Hungarian representation on its own internal inquiry into the assassinations. The Austro-Hungarian government set a deadline of forty-eight hours for Serbia's reply, but the ambassador had packed his bags before it had expired.

Germany's role on 24 July was to work to contain the effects of the ultimatum. Given the widespread perception that Austria-Hungary was in the right and Serbia in the wrong, that should not have been too difficult. But it rested on a fundamental miscalculation. Nobody in the Triple Entente was inclined to see Austria-Hungary as an independent actor. Vienna had taken a firm line because it was anxious to capitalise on Germany's backing while it had it. Those on the opposite side took account of that weakness in Austria-Hungary and rated Austro-German solidarity somewhat higher than Vienna itself was inclined to. If Austria-Hungary wanted Germany to cover its back, it could not so easily escape the imputation that it was Germany's stalking horse. The conflict with Serbia would not be localised because by July 1914 the experience of earlier crises had conditioned statesmen to put events in the broader context of European international relations.

Serbia, moreover, played its hand with considerable adroitness. It disarmed criticism by professing its readiness to go as far in its compliance with Austria-Hungary's demands as was compatible with its status as an independent country. It therefore could not accept Austria-Hungary's participation in any internal inquiry, as this would be in 'violation of the Constitution and of the law of criminal procedure'. By accepting all the terms save this one, Pašić swung international opinion his way. He needed all the help he could get.

Militarily Serbia had been weakened by the two Balkan wars, which had depleted the army's munitions stocks and inflicted 91,000 casualties. Although its first-line strength on mobilisation rose to 350,000 men, there were only enough up-to-date rifles (ironically, German Mausers) for the peacetime strength of 180,000, and in some infantry units a third of the men had no rifles at all. On 31 May 1914 the minister of war had embarked on a reconstruction programme phased over ten years, and the Austro-Hungarian military attaché in Belgrade concluded that it would take four years for the Serb army to recover. But Pašić had to act. Weakness on the international stage might have severe domestic consequences, not least on his election campaign. He was clear in his own mind that Austria-Hungary was squaring up for a fight. On the afternoon of 25 July he ordered the army to mobilise.

Serbia had therefore moved to a military response before the diplomatic tools had been exhausted. But it was not the first power in the July crisis to do so. On receipt of the ultimatum, Prince Alexander of Serbia immediately appealed to the Tsar of Russia. The Russian council of ministers met on the following day, 24 July. Sergey Sazonov, Russia's foreign minister and a career diplomat, 'a man of simple thought' and an anglophile,[11] said that Germany was using the crisis as a pretext for launching a preventive war. The minister of the interior confounded those in Berlin and Vienna who believed that Russia would be deterred from responding by the fear of revolution: he declared his conviction that war would rally the nation. And the ministers for the army and navy, the recipients of so much funding over the previous five years, could hardly confess the truth: that their services were not yet ready. The council approved orders for four military districts to prepare for mobilisation.

Mobilisation

Mobilisation was not, of course, the same as war. It had been used in previous crises as a buttress to diplomacy, a form of brinkmanship rather than a step in an inevitable escalation. But in those earlier confrontations developments had been spread over months. In 1914 the key decisions were taken in the space of one week. The pace of events was such that there was no time to clarify the distinction between warning and intent.

Serbia therefore knew it would not face Austria-Hungary alone. But over the next few days Conrad seemed reluctant to absorb that point. His was not an army capable of fighting Russia as well as Serbia if the former decided to support the latter. In 1909, during the Bosnian crisis, Conrad had sought clarification as to what the German army would do in such an eventuality. Moltke had told him that if Germany faced a two-front war, against Russia and France simultaneously, the bulk of the German army would concentrate against France first. However, he reassured Conrad with regard to the latter's principal worry: he said that the German 8th Army in East Prussia would draw in the Russians, who would be committed by their alliance with France to attack Germany.

What this reassurance hid was Moltke's own worries about the security of East Prussia. The German general staff planned to use the shield of the Masurian Lakes to enable it to fight an offensive-defence against the Russians, who would be forced by the lakes to advance in two eccentric directions. The effect would be to use German territory as a battlefield, and if the 8th Army was not quickly reinforced from the west it might have to fall back as far as the line of the River Vistula or even of the Oder. The German army would have abrogated its principal duty: the defence of the fatherland. Moltke therefore sought a quid pro quo for his reassurance of Conrad: he wanted an Austrian attack into Poland from Galicia, directed between the Bug and the Vistula. Moltke added the carrot that the Germans, once they were reinforced from the west, would push into Poland from the north and the River Narew. This idea – of enveloping Russian Poland – appealed to the strategic imaginations of generals educated through the histories of Napoleon's campaigns and of the wars of German unification. Envelopment on this scale was deemed likely to produce decisive success in short order. To Conrad the theorist, the idea was irresistible. The two armies would link at Siedlitz, east of Warsaw.

The plan was no plan – and whatever rationality it had in 1909 was forfeit by 1914. First, it assumed that the Germans would be sufficiently free from the campaign in France to despatch reinforcements to the east in a matter of weeks. To keep Conrad quiet Moltke suggested three to four weeks would be needed to defeat the French, and ten days to redeploy to the east, although these were not the planning assumptions of the German general staff. Second, no joint operational studies were conducted by the two armies in advance of hostilities. By 1913 and 1914 Moltke was more cautious in his promises to Conrad, but the latter did not hear him: each was reassured by the thought that the other would take the major burden against Russia. And, third, the idea took no account of the transformation effected in the capabilities and intentions of the Russian army in the intervening five years.

Conrad had assumed that it would take Russia thirty days to mobilise, but in February 1914 Moltke warned him (accurately enough) that two-thirds of the Russian army would be mobilised by the eighteenth day. Thus the Austrians and Germans were losing time. They also lost space. Given its need to face Asia as well as Europe, Russia adopted a system of territorial mobilisation: the army's higher formations – or corps – would be stationed in their recruiting areas and would mobilise by incorporating the reservists from those areas. This was exactly the model adopted in Germany and France.

But its effect – given Russia's geographical configuration in the west – would be to forfeit its defence of Poland. There would be nothing for the Austro-German scheme of envelopment to envelop.

To all intents and purposes Conrad had abandoned the fiction of the Siedlitz manoeuvre by 1914. This did not stop him later using it as a stick with which to beat his German ally when trying to transfer blame for his own failings. His first obligation, as he saw it, was to deal with Serbia. He reckoned that he needed eight divisions to hold the Austro-Serb frontier but twenty divisions to invade and defeat Serbia. This left a minimum of twenty-eight divisions to face the Russians in Galicia. He therefore created a reserve of twelve divisions which could go either to Serbia and be added to the eight already holding the frontier, or to Galicia if Russia supported Serbia and so increase the force there to forty divisions. This reserve, the 2nd Army, would not be mobilised and deployed in Galicia until between the twenty-first and twenty-fifth days of mobilisation. Given the increasing speed of the Russians' mobilisation and the growing volume of intelligence suggesting that their first priority would be to attack Germany so as to give direct aid to France, Conrad decided not to try to anticipate the Russian concentration but to hold his Galician force back, refocusing his plans for the Russian front to the north and west, and forcing the Russians to come further before making contact. The effect would be to blunt the Austrian offensive from Galicia. The difficulty inherent in the whole conception was that Austrian railway construction over the previous three decades had been predicated on a deployment to east and south. If the 2nd Army were shifted from Serbia to Galicia, the railway communications would place it on the Austrian right, not on the left.

The difficulty of redeploying troops from Serbia to Galicia was evident by 1909. But nothing was done to improve the situation as neither Austria nor Hungary would accept responsibility for the cost of new track. In 1912–13 the railway department of the general staff assured Conrad that he could replace a decision to mobilise against Serbia by one for mobilisation against Russia. What he could not do was to mobilise against both simultaneously.

On 25 July Franz Josef ordered mobilisation against Serbia only, to begin on 28 July. On that day Austria-Hungary declared war on Serbia. The guns mounted in the fortress of Semlin fired across the Danube, and from the river itself monitors of the Austro-Hungarian navy lobbed shells into the Serb capital. The hospital was hit. 'Windows were shattered to smithereens', Dr Slavka Mihajlovič reported, 'and broken glass covered many floors. Patients started screaming. Some got out of their beds, pale and bewildered. Then there was another explosion, and another one, and then silence again. So, it was true! The war had started.'[12]

In Vienna the previous night, Josef Redlich, a professor of law and later a government minister, went out to a restaurant. 'We heard the band, which played patriotic songs and marches without real spirit. There were not many on the streets and the mood was not really enthusiastic: on the other hand the loud sounds and tones of the national anthem carried through the warm summer night from the Ringstrasse and the city centre, where enormous crowds were demonstrating.'[13] This was not the euphoria that many later remembered, but nor was it a rejection of war. What enthused the Viennese crowds was the promise of a quick victory over Serbia; what restrained them was the fear of a great European war. Their wishful thinking reflected Conrad's: this was to be the Third Balkan War, not the First World War.

Their hopes were misplaced. On 28 July the Tsar responded to this Balkan crisis as Russia had responded to earlier ones: with the mobilisation of the four military districts facing Galicia. But this was nonsensical both to the military, since the reorganisation of the army meant that each district drew on the resources of others, and to Sazonov, who remained convinced that Germany – not Austria-Hungary – was the real danger. Over the next two days it was to be his counsels which prevailed, not the exchange of cousinly telegrams between the Kaiser and the Tsar. On 30 July the Russian army was ordered to proceed to general mobilisation.

Germany was now facing a general European war. However, right up until 28 July itself Bethmann Hollweg believed that the policy of limitation and localisation might work. On 26 July Sir Edward Grey, the fly-fishing British foreign secretary, tried to reactivate the Concert of Europe by proposing a conference. But, believing the Germans to be the key players, he made the suggestion to Berlin, not Vienna. By the time the Austro-Hungarians knew of it they had opened hostilities. In any case, the Germans were by then as unconvinced as the Austrians of the value of congresses. On 29 July Grey, 'entirely calm, but very grave', warned the German ambassador in London that, if the Austro-Serb war were not localised, 'it would not be practicable' for Britain 'to stand aside'. 'If war breaks out', he concluded, 'it will be the greatest catastrophe that the world has ever seen.'[14] Both the Kaiser and Bethmann Hollweg were appalled, and at 2.55 a.m. on 30 July Bethmann Hollweg telegraphed Vienna to urge mediation on the basis of a halt in Belgrade. But the Austrians feared another diplomatic defeat and Conrad insisted on the need to settle with Serbia once and for all.

In any case the messages from Berlin to Vienna were now mixed. Moltke had returned to his desk on 25 July, and the minister of war, Falkenhayn, did so on 27 July. The latter was alarmed by Moltke's lack of resolution, and felt that by 29 July the point had been reached when military considerations should override political. Given the indications of mobilisation elsewhere in Europe, and aware of how crucial time would be because of the dangers to Germany of a two-front war, he wanted the preliminary stages of German mobilisation to be put in hand. Moltke was aware that for Germany, if not for the other powers, mobilisation would mean war. At first, therefore, he respected the chancellor's wish to await Russia's response. But by 30 July he was prepared to hold on no longer. Then the Germans heard of the Russian decision to mobilise.

What now worried Moltke was that the Austro-Hungarian army would become so embroiled in Serbia as to be unable to play its part in tying down Russia in the east. So on 30 July, the very day when Bethmann Hollweg was telling the Austrians to halt in Belgrade, Moltke was urging Conrad to mobilise against Russia, not Serbia. Conrad refused to be deflected. However, he asked the Railway

Department to find a way to continue the movement of the 2nd Army to Serbia while beginning the mobilisation of the three armies – the 1st, 3rd and 4th – facing Russia. It said it could do so only if the mobilisation against Russia was delayed until 4 August. On 31 July Conrad agreed, but under further pressure from Germany asked that the 2nd Army be redirected to Galicia. He was told it was too late. The movement of the 2nd Army to Serbia would have to be completed or chaos would ensue.

Conrad later blamed the Railway Department for the delayed arrival of the 2nd Army in Galicia. In fact, he had already forfeited any advantages over the Russians in terms of speed by his decision consistently to focus on Serbia and to downplay the Russian front. Given the thrust of Austrian policy, a defensive on the Serbian front was not a political option. On 1 August, the day on which Germany declared war on Russia, he explained his position to Moltke: 'We could, and must, hold fast to the offensive against Serbia, the more so since we had [sic] to bear in mind that Russia might merely intend to restrain us from action by a threat, without proceeding to war against us'.[15] By postponing the commencement of mobilisation against Russia until 4 August, Conrad still ensured that the 2nd Army would arrive in Galicia within twenty-four days of mobilisation, on 28 August.

The Third Balkan War

Thus the Austro-Hungarian army was committed to a far larger war than it had bargained for, and found itself fighting over two fronts when it struggled to be strong enough on one. Moreover, the 2nd Army was so mishandled as to be valueless in both Serbia and Galicia. The military operations of the First World War began with defeats of Austria-Hungary so shattering that the empire would indeed have collapsed there and then but for the support of its ally.

In 1909 Conrad had said he could deal with Serbia in three months.

But that assumed he could deploy the entire Austro-Hungarian army. In 1914, with its greater bulk in Galicia, Conrad could hope to defeat Serbia only if he had the backing of a Bulgaria-led Balkan alliance. This was a chicken-and-egg problem: politically, Austria had first to defeat Serbia to woo Bulgaria. Politically, too, it could not now adopt the defensive against Serbia that its manpower and strength favoured.

Conrad himself set up his headquarters at Przemysl, today in Poland but then the citadel guarding the north-eastern extremity of the Austro-Hungarian empire. He therefore accepted the fact that Galicia had become the major front. Oskar Potiorek, the governor of Bosnia, was given command of the Serb theatre. He had been in the car with Franz Ferdinand on 28 June, and some held him responsible for the lax security. He had his eye on Conrad's job as chief of the general staff. When Conrad had told him on 30 June that he was 'working with all conviction for a final action against Serbia',[16] Potiorek had assumed that he was to have the chance not only to revenge the assassinations but also to outshine his professional rival.

The quickest route into Serbia was from the north, crossing the Danube and attacking Belgrade. It kept the lines of communication short and it could open two lines of advance into Serbia: the Morava valley to Niš and the Kolubara valley to Valjevo. An attack on Šabac across the River Sava could converge on Valjevo from a different direction.

The danger was that the Serbs would trade space for time, abandoning Belgrade and falling back south. Moreover, they could attack to the west, into Bosnia, stoking insurrection there – a consideration which bore heavily on Potiorek. He therefore proposed to direct the 6th Army from Višegrad across the upper Drina river in the direction of Užice. The area was mountainous and it lacked road or rail communications. The 5th Army was to support the 6th on its northern flank, by crossing the lower Drina and following the River Jadar in the direction of Valjevo. Envelopment was the key note here – both on the wider canvas of Serbia as a whole and in the more defined battlefield of the Drina. For the latter, Potiorek hoped that the Serbs would be drawn in to attack the 5th Army, so allowing the 6th to cut across their rear. For the larger manoeuvre to work the Serbs had to be pinned in the north. Therefore the thrust from the west still assumed an attack from the north by the 2nd army.

Then, on 6 August, Potiorek was told that he had the use of the 2nd Army only until 18 August, and that it was not to cross the Danube or the Sava. But the 6th Army would not be able to concentrate near Sarajevo until 13 August, so the pressure in the north would lift before that to the west could take effect. The Austrians were down to 290,000 men in the region, many of them garrison troops, while the Serbs mustered 350,000. For all their problems of recovery after the first two Balkan wars, the Serb army had recent combat experience, and they had French 75mm quick-firing field guns as well as better field howitzers. Radomir Putnik, Serbia's hero in the first two Balkan wars and the chief of the general staff, was taking the waters at Gleichenberg when the war broke out. He had with him the keys to the safe in which the war plans were stored, and it had to be blown open. The Austrians chivalrously, if misguidedly, allowed him to return to Serbia, where the ailing general deployed his three armies in a central position, ready to face west or north.

The Austro-Hungarian 5th Army led the way across the Drina, an operation for which it lacked sufficient bridging equipment. On 15 August it ran into the Serb 2nd and 3rd Armies on the Cer plateau. The Austrians were not equipped for mountain warfare, and the temperature soared as they toiled uphill. Potiorek was desperate to use the 2nd Army to support the 5th. It was allowed to establish bridgeheads at Mitrovica and Šabac, but Conrad – still clinging to his 18 August deadline – would release only one corps to support the 5th Army on 19 August. Conrad then ordered it to break off its attack. The 2nd Army began its move to Galicia on 20 August. It had not acted decisively enough to help the 5th Army on the Drina, and its position at Šabac had been too far from Belgrade to force Putnik to disperse his forces. The job of the 6th Army – in action at Višegrad and Priboj by 20 and 21 August – was to support the 5th Army, not vice versa. But it fell back, and as it did so it allowed the Serbs to push into Bosnia.

Potiorek had dreaded this possibility. He had predicted massive unrest in the province in the event of war with Serbia. But he had available a powerful tool, the war service law passed in 1912 at the time of the First Balkan War. In the event of a national emergency the rights of private citizens were forfeit to the army. Military government was established in Bosnia-Herzogovina and Dalmatia on 25 July, and was progressively extended throughout the empire. A War Surveillance Office to coordinate all the agencies responsible for the internal control of the state was created under the aegis of the army. Trial by jury was suspended. Over 2,000 Bosnians were deported or interned, some of them Muslims who had fled to Bosnia to escape the Orthodox Serbs. Bosnia remained quiet. But the Austro-Hungarian army clearly regarded the war as having had two immediate consequences: first, it had usurped all distinctions between civilian and soldier, and second, it had rendered the army accountable to no one but itself.

It applied these principles to Serbia as well. Having seen Serbs within Bosnia as potential enemies, Potiorek had little difficulty in seeing all Serbs within Serbia as hostile – regardless of age or sex. An order to one corps of the Austro-Hungarian army declared that: 'The war is taking us into a country inhabited by a population inspired with fanatical hatred towards us, into a country where murder, as the catastrophe of Sarajevo has proved, is recognised even by the upper classes, who glorify it as heroism. Towards such a population all humanity and all kindness of heart are out of place; they are even harmful, for any consideration, such as it is sometimes possible to show in war, would in this case endanger our own troops.'[17]

The army took civilian hostages in Serbia from mid-August 1914, destroying the homes of those who lived in areas where it encountered resistance. A report by a Swiss doctor, commissioned by the Serbs in 1915, reckoned that up to 4,000 civilians were killed or disappeared in the opening invasion. He described it as systematic extermination. To the north, the same happened in Galicia. The army dealt with the enemy without according to criteria similar to those which it applied to the enemy within, as traitors deprived of the protection of the laws of war. Austria-Hungary had not ratified the Hague Convention of 1907 but it instructed its army to observe it. It therefore justified its actions as reprisals. There were sectors in which guerrillas were operating, but the victims included old women and small children. The collapse of the invading army's supply arrangements fostered looting and that set it at odds with the civil population. 'Our troops', one soldier serving with the Honved reported, 'have struck out terribly in all directions, like the Swedes in the Thirty Years War. Nothing, or almost nothing, is intact. In every house individuals are to be seen searching for things that are still useable.'[18]

These frustrations were born of operational failure. In Serbia, Potiorek renewed the attack across the Drina in September, but he had difficulty in breaking out beyond his bridgeheads and he had too few men to support his thrusts from the west with attacks from the north. Although drained of munitions and increasingly short of regular officers, Potiorek refused to retreat. At the end of the month both sides established fixed positions. 'The war', wrote an officer with the Austrians at the beginning of November, 'is adopting in its present course ever more the character of a stubborn wrestling match, in which in the end success will be awarded to the side – given similar personal and moral qualities – whose material resources endure longer.'[19]

None the less Potiorek tried once more, setting Valjevo as his objective. The Austrians made slow progress towards the Kolubara valley. The river itself was in flood, and when the snow eased the sun turned the roads to mud. Potiorek finally bludgeoned his way to the south-west of Belgrade, which he was able to capture on 2 December. But then the weather hardened, aiding the observation of the Serb artillery and deepening the Austro-Hungarians' supply problems. By now, the 6th Army was shattered and to save the 5th, which had occupied Belgrade, the Serb capital had to be abandoned on 13 December. Within days Potiorek's military career was over.

For his rival, Conrad, the priority had long since been Galicia. But the tug-of-war between the two commanders kept the Austrian forces in Serbia stronger than they needed to be for pure defence, while those in Galicia were inadequate for the task that they faced. Such realities could not curb Conrad's ambition for long. All the news in August was depressing. Romania did not honour its alliance obligations, and so exposed Conrad's southern flank; German efforts were concentrated in East Prussia, so robbing him of security to the north. The decision to deploy further to the west therefore looked increasingly prudent. But, having deployed to defend, Conrad was lured back to the attack by the ambition of the Siedlitz manoeuvre. On 3 August Moltke told Conrad that the Germans would fight defensively in East Prussia. On 20 August Conrad responded that he would advance on Lublin and Cholm nevertheless. He did not get the first two of the 2nd Army's corps from Serbia until 28 August, and the third not until 4 September; the fourth would never arrive. He would then have thirty-seven divisions against – he reckoned – about fifty Russian. Moreover, by advancing from deep he was inflicting on his troops those same punishing movements that he had planned to inflict on the Russians. Nor did he know where the Russians were. Reports that two armies were advancing on him from the east were discounted; he wanted to place them to the north, as that was the direction in which he proposed to direct his thrust.

The Austro-Hungarian 3rd Army was deployed around Lemberg (or Lvov, as it is today) to face east, while the 4th and 1st Armies pushed north-east. The total Austrian front was 280 km, and it widened as the armies began their advance in divergent directions on 23 August. The Russians deployed four armies against Galicia, two from the north and two from the east. They had decided that the Austrians were concentrated around Lemberg, facing east. They therefore underestimated the strength of Conrad's northern thrust, and confused fighting between 23 and 29 August left Conrad on the verge of success. But on 26 August the Austrian 3rd Army sallied forth from Lemberg to meet the Russian 3rd Army – one of the two advancing from the east. Conrad now paid the penalty of stretching his forces too thinly. His 3rd Army was routed and it abandoned Lemberg on 2 September without a fight.

Conrad called on the Germans four times to implement the Siedlitz operation over this period, but they were themselves desperately engaged in East Prussia. From 2 September he had to abandon his Polish schemes to save Galicia. But typically he now plotted a massive envelopment of the Russians from north and south with forces he did not have. He was unable to coordinate his movements in space and time. On 11 September Conrad ordered a retreat to the Dniester river and then to the San. The Austrians had lost 350,000 men; some divisions were at one-third of their strength; the transport collapsed, as 1,000 locomotives and 15,000 wagons were abandoned. The roads turned to mud and were crowded with refugees. Conrad acknowledged that if Franz Ferdinand had been alive he would have been shot.

Russia set about making its conquest permanent. Reactionaries saw Galicia as part of Russia, and persuaded the governor-general appointed to run it that it should be subject to Russification and racial cleansing. This meant that Russian was to be the only language in schools, that the churches should convert to Orthodoxy, and that the Russian army was licensed to loot. The ingrained anti-Semitism of the Russian army meant that Jews were driven from their homes, either forward towards Austria-Hungary or back to the Russian interior.

Przemysl became the rallying point for the Austrians. Its fortifications proved to have greater worth than pre-war critics had allowed. As Conrad's headquarters it had been given seven new defensive belts, with trenches and barbed wire. On 16 September the garrison of 100,000 was ordered to hold out until the end. The siege began on 21 September. The 3rd Army fought forward to its relief, and for six days in mid-October kept open the railway line to enable supplies to be stockpiled. But provision had been made for a garrison of only 85,000, and by now it had swelled to 130,000. Furthermore, there were still 30,000 civilians within the city. When the 3rd Army fell back, the siege resumed, dragging on throughout the winter. Desperate fighting in the winter snows of the Carpathians failed to relieve it.

But the fortress bought Austria-Hungary time. It sucked in the Russians and slowed them, just at the point where they too were reaching the end of their logistical reach. The line of the Carpathians, running south-east to north-west, shouldered them towards Kraków and away from the Hungarian plain. By November the Russian 8th Army, which faced Przemysl, had – like the armies of other belligerents on other fronts – lost its pre-war cadres. Its commander, A. A. Brusilov, complained that it 'was literally unclad. Their summer clothing was worn out; there were no boots; my men, up to their knees in snow and enduring the most severe frosts, had not yet received their winter kit.'[20] The garrison of Przemysl held out until 22 March 1915.

By the end of 1914 stalemate had therefore set in on both Austria-Hungary's fronts. It had effectively lost the Third Balkan War that it – and Conrad in particular – had so ardently pursued. Within four months Austria-Hungary's casualties totalled 957,000, more than twice the army's pre-war strength. It sought scapegoats within, many of them ethnically similar to the enemies without, Bosnians or Ruthenes. But some, like the Czechs, were not.

It turned, too, on its ally. 'The Germans', Conrad complained in early September, 'have won their victories at our expense; they have left us in the lurch'.[21] But, thanks to Germany, Conrad had not yet lost the wider European war to which the empire was now committed. Logically Germany needed to direct all its attention to this wider war. But in practice Austria-Hungary could not on its own sustain the two fronts for which it was responsible, and therefore the Germans would have to provide help. The humiliation implicit in this dependence meant that Vienna could never show the gratitude to which Germany felt it was entitled. Germany, for its part, concluded that it was 'shackled to a corpse'.

2

UNDER THE EAGLE

Germany's Guilt?

From the moment the First World War began, the belligerents began publishing their own accounts of how the conflict had been caused. They did so because the issue of responsibility was the key element in the propaganda battle. Neutral opinion had to be won over. Within Europe, neither Bulgaria nor Romania had yet committed itself, and the search for allies in the Balkans was to preoccupy the chancelleries of both sides well into 1916. Outside, the United States was the world's premier industrial power, and, although nobody thought it likely that it would itself enter the war, access to its production might be vital to the war's outcome. At this stage of the war, opinion at home could be largely taken for granted. The war was justified because it was interpreted as a war of national self-defence. Before the war socialists had threatened to oppose war and disrupt mobilisation. However, the war they had vilified was a tool of imperialism and conquest. In 1914 every belligerent on the continent of Europe portrayed itself as the subject of direct attack. The working-class populations of all the powers may not have welcomed the war but they did not reject the duties and obligations it imposed. Phrases were coined – the '*union sacrée*' in France and the '*Burgfrieden*' in Germany – to institutionalise this new-found domestic unity.

There was a paradox in the flood of government white books, black books and yellow books produced in 1914–15 to buttress these perceptions. Their focus was on the events of July 1914 itself, but their central debate concerned the issue of whether or not Germany was guilty of causing the war. The paradox was this: Austria-Hungary, not Germany, was the power that at the beginning of July 1914 planned to use war as an instrument of policy. Admittedly, the conflict it sought was designed to be short, localised and fought between single powers, whereas the war that resulted was none of those things. For this Germany was blamed, both then and since. Even Austria-Hungary cast aspersions on its ally, holding Germany responsible for getting it into a war which was bigger than it could handle. For the Entente, the foreign ministers of Russia and Britain, Sergey Sazonov and Sir Edward Grey, were convinced that Vienna would never have acted as it had done unless Berlin had pushed it. But if they were right, the causes of the war were not short-term but long-term. Sazonov and Grey brought to the events of July 1914 assumptions formed before the assassination of Franz Ferdinand, and reckoned that their opposite numbers in Germany and Austria-Hungary had done so too.

They were right in one respect. Germany had played the key role in changing the tempo of international rivalries. When Germany was united in 1871, its chancellor, Otto von Bismarck, set out to reassure the powers of Europe about the ambitions of the powerful new political entity that had emerged in its centre. And those powers directed their competitiveness to fields beyond Europe. When Britain and France confronted each other in Africa they did not resort to war. Indeed, the original purpose of the Anglo-French Entente of 1904 was not to create a united front against Germany, but to settle the two powers' long-standing imperial rivalries in North Africa. The deal left the French free to expand westwards from Algeria into Morocco. Germany, however, saw the Entente as creating a new diplomatic constellation in Europe itself. The independence of Morocco was guaranteed by an international convention of 1880. On 31 March 1905 the Kaiser landed in Tangiers and declared his support for the Sultan of Morocco. He had little interest in Morocco but he was anxious to disrupt the Anglo-French Entente. Germany's heavy-handedness had precisely the opposite effect. The Entente hardened, and Britain as well as France began to see Germany as a potential enemy. This, the first of two crises over Morocco, showed that regional rivalries could no longer be handled by diplomats in a self-contained fashion, but were liable to be both 'Europeanised' and 'militarised'.

The Kaiser's action made clear that Germany had cut loose from Bismarck's inheritance. Germany was no longer posing as an upholder of the existing order; instead, it aspired to carve a fresh path. Bernhard von Bülow, foreign minister in 1897–1900 and chancellor from 1900 until 1909, promoted a 'world policy' or *Weltpolitik*. This rested on the premise that the unification of Germany under Prussian leadership was not a culminating point in the history of the nation, but a new departure – a beginning, not an end. The political theorist Max Weber declared in his inaugural lecture at the University of Freiburg in 1895: 'We must understand that the unification of Germany . . . would have been better if it had never taken place, since it would have been a costly extravagance, if it was the conclusion rather than the starting-point for German power politics on a global scale'.[1]

Weltpolitik was not a policy to use war for the fulfilment of German objectives; it did not make Germany responsible for the outbreak of the First World War. But it did challenge the status quo in three ways: colonial, naval and economic.

Of these the colonial was the least significant, and it roused little tension with the world's largest empire, Britain. By 1914, the German colonies attracted one in a thousand of Germany's emigrants, absorbed 3.8 per cent of Germany's overseas investment, and accounted for 0.5 per cent of its overseas trade. Territorial expansion was not a high priority for Germany, and it was not a cause of the First World War. Britain was more worried by the growth of the German navy, which began in 1897. From 1905 the German fleet replaced the French and Russian navies as the benchmark for British naval strength. But even here the rivalry proved containable. Agitation for increased naval spending on both sides of the North Sea aroused public awareness of the competition, but in their calmer moments both Tirpitz, the head of the German naval armaments office, and Jackie Fisher, the First Sea Lord between 1905 and 1910, recognised that their fleets were above all deterrents. Britain managed to maintain its naval supremacy in quantitative terms, and in the crisis of July 1914 both fleets were able to go onto alert without accelerating the plunge into war. The mobilisation of armies did not prove so politically neutral.

More important to *Weltpolitik* were its economic dimensions. Germany industrialised late but very rapidly. The value of its output increased well over six times between 1855 and 1913. In 1870 Britain, with 32 per cent of the world's manufacturing capacity, was the largest industrial power in the world. By 1910 it had been overtaken by the United States, which had 35.3 per cent of the world's manufacturing capacity, and Germany with 15.9 per cent: Britain now had 14.7 per cent. But Britain was still the dominant power in the world's banking, insurance and shipping markets. Its invisible exports therefore compensated for its relative decline in the manufacturing sector. Moreover, Germany's rapid industrialisation damped down its liquidity: it invested so heavily domestically that it could not use overseas investment to gain influence abroad. The key need of *Weltpolitik*, therefore, was to open world markets to German products. This was an aim which an open door in world trade would secure – an objective favoured by Britain's own historical commitment to free trade. As those engaged in commerce in both Britain and Germany recognised, war would only disrupt this growth and limit it.

Despite its title *Weltpolitik* also carried a domestic and internal purpose. The chancellor of Germany held office because he was the Kaiser's choice, not because he enjoyed a majority in the Reichstag. His success as chancellor largely depended on his ability to manage the Reichstag despite the lack of a party base. *Weltpolitik* was Bülow's solution to this problem – an effort to use foreign policy to appeal to different constituencies within Germany. But the funding of the navy undermined the internal coalition on which Bülow relied. He planned to increase inheritance tax to pay for warships but this

challenged the interests of conservative landowners. The conservatives and the Catholic Centre Party crushed the proposal in favour
of a tax on mobile capital, which of course struck at business and urban
interests. Confronted with domestic discord, Bethmann Hollweg,
Bülow's successor as chancellor, therefore abandoned *Weltpolitik* and
attempted to curb naval spending. He aimed at detente with Britain,
using the idea of an Anglo-German naval agreement to do so. This,
too, was not without domestic problems, as both Tirpitz and the
Kaiser were bound to oppose him. But it might appease the socialists,
who became the largest single party in the Reichstag in the 1912
elections.

Foreign policy and domestic policy were therefore linked, as they
were in Austria-Hungary, but in the German case the connections
were not as immediate and, if they did contribute to the outbreak of
war, they did so indirectly. The foreign policy that Bethmann
Hollweg pursued up to, and including, the crisis of July 1914 stood
in its own right. He wanted to disrupt the Entente, and so relieve
Germany of the encirclement into which the alliance system had
drawn it. This was the subtext of the proposed Anglo-German naval
agreement: what the Germans wanted in exchange for a limit on
warship construction was Britain's neutrality in relation to Europe.
Britain rejected the proposal not only because the trade-off was
unequal but also because its strategic interests bound it to the
Entente. It could not afford to reopen rivalries outside Europe. Its
need to neutralise the Low Countries, in order to leave the main sea
route from London to the wider world unfettered, bound it to maintain the balance of power within Europe: geography and economic
necessity determined that it would back the weaker power against the
stronger on the Continental seaboard.

German efforts in the same vein, to loosen the ties of the Entente
by pursuing bilateral deals with the Russians and the French in relation to issues outside Europe, were designed to reawaken the old
rivalries between Britain and its Entente partners. Bethmann Hollweg
had some success with Russia in relation to the construction of the
railway from Berlin through eastern Anatolia to Baghdad: tensions

between Britain and Russia in Central Asia had resurfaced by 1914, especially in Persia. But the policy backfired when it came to France.

On 17 April 1911 the French pushed troops into Morocco, ostensibly to police Fez, where riots had been directed against the Sultan. Under the terms of the Algeçiras conference, hammered out in 1906 after the first Moroccan crisis, France should not have acted without consulting the other signatories, including Germany. The French prime minister was Joseph Caillaux, the man whose wife did so much to distract the French in the key days of the July crisis: he was sufficiently conscious of the weakness of the French position to encourage the German Foreign Ministry to believe that Germany might be recompensed with concessions elsewhere in Africa. On 1 July 1911 a German warship, the *Panther*, appeared in the Atlantic port of Agadir.

Three weeks later, on 21 July 1911, David Lloyd George delivered the customary annual speech of the chancellor of the exchequer to the City of London. Lloyd George was a radical influence within the Liberal government of Herbert Asquith, promoting old age pensions and national insurance. At the beginning of the century he had been a 'pro-Boer', opposing Britain's policy in the South African war. But he did not use the opportunity of the Mansion House speech to counsel disengagement from the foreign relations of the powers of Continental Europe. Instead he sent a clear warning that war might be imminent. He went on: 'I am also bound to say this – that I believe it is essential in the highest interests, not merely of this country, but of the world, that Britain should at all hazards maintain her place and her prestige amongst the Great Powers of the world. Her potent influence has many a time been in the past, and may yet be in the future, invaluable in the cause of human liberty. It has more than once in the past redeemed continental nations, who are sometimes too apt to forget that service, from overwhelming disaster, and even from national extinction . . . If a situation were to be forced upon us in which peace could only be preserved by the surrender of the great and beneficent position Britain has won by centuries of heroism and achievement, by allowing Britain to be treated, where her interests were vitally affected, as if she were of no account in the Cabinet of nations, then I say emphatically that peace at that price would be a humiliation intolerable for a great country like ours to endure.'[2]

What had been a Franco-German dispute about colonial ambitions, designed to be resolved by diplomacy, now became an issue of vital national interest to Britain. Germany had deployed sea power beyond the purlieus of its immediate geographical waters; this was a direct threat to the premier navy in the world. Moreover, by doing so Germany had challenged the strength of the Anglo-French Entente as an alliance. Lloyd George's speech – for all that its words emphasised Britain's sense of honour and its status as a great power – was not, therefore, simply about prestige. Britain saw both the defence of its maritime supremacy and its alliances as matters of vital national interest.

The first of these hardly surprised the Germans. The second did. As a Protestant nation, ruled by a monarch with blood ties to most of the royal families of Europe, including that of Germany, Britain seemed temperamentally a more natural ally of Germany than of France. But what this calculation left out of account was the British Empire. Between 1902 and 1907 Britain entered into three alliances, all of them designed to ease the burden of imperial defence. The first, with Japan, relieved it of naval responsibilities in the Pacific and gave it a counterweight to its principal Asiatic rival, Russia. The second, the 1904 entente with France, effectively allocated the eastern end of North Africa (including the Suez Canal, the all-important link to the Far East) to Britain. And the third, in 1907, promised to lessen the rivalry with its most persistent challenger in the Near East and Central Asia, Russia. In combination, these alliances both secured the heart of the empire, India, and protected the routes to it.

The second Moroccan crisis confirmed the consequences of the first: that imperial and colonial rivalries could no longer be divorced from foreign policy in Europe itself. Britain supported France despite the technical strength of the Germans' case. Army staff talks between the two powers, which had originally begun during the first

Moroccan crisis but had then lapsed, were renewed, and in 1912 the two navies divided responsibilities, with the French taking on the Mediterranean and the British the North Sea and the Channel. There was still no formal alliance in terms of an automatic commitment to aid France if it found itself at war with Germany, but Lloyd George's audience – and it went far beyond the Mansion House – could be forgiven if it thought there was.

These tensions – colonial, naval and coalition – were the underpinnings of the crisis in July 1914. But none of them in any direct sense related to the Balkans or to Austria-Hungary. The war did not begin over another clash between Germany on the one hand and Britain and France on the other, and, if there had been such a clash, it would – on past form – have been a prolonged crisis and resolved by negotiation not force of arms. On 30 July 1914, Jean Jaurès, the French socialist leader, remarked to his counterpart in Belgium, Emil Vandervelde: 'It will be like Agadir. There will be ups and downs. But it is impossible that things won't turn out all right.'[3]

The principal link between the long-term and short-term origins of the First World War is the First Balkan War. The Germans saw it as a war fought by Russia by proxy, and on 2 December 1912 Bethmann Hollweg announced in the Reichstag that, if Austria-Hungary was attacked by a third party while pursuing its interests, Germany would support Austria-Hungary and fight to maintain its own position in Europe. Britain responded on the following day: it feared that a Russo-Austrian War would lead to a German attack on France and warned the Germans that if that happened it would not accept a French defeat. The Kaiser was furious, and summoned a meeting of his military and naval chiefs on 8 December. He said that, if Russia came to Serbia's aid, Germany would fight. He assumed that in such a war Bulgaria, Romania, Albania and Turkey would all side with the Triple Alliance, and take the main role against Serbia, so leaving Austria-Hungary to concentrate against Russia.

War Plans

Bethmann Hollweg was the key player in July 1914, but he was not present on 8 December 1912. What the meeting focused on was the armament programmes of the navy and the army. Tirpitz declared that the navy was not ready for war, and given that the Kaiser's ire was directed against Britain a large navy bill would have been its logical outcome. But that did not happen: Bethmann Hollweg was anxious both to pursue detente with Britain and to head off further naval spending. The army was increased by a total of 136,000 men in 1912 and 1913. But these additions were already in train before the First Balkan War, and were not due to be assimilated until 1916. They marked the inauguration of a land arms race. In the first decade of the twentieth century the budgets of European armies were too taken up with the procurement of quick-firing field artillery to allow room for expansion; that changed in the years immediately preceding the outbreak of the First World War. The increases in the German army were driven by its size in comparison with those of its neighbours, France and Russia, not by some notion that the German army itself would be deployed to the Balkans. Cooperation between Germany's general staff and Austria-Hungary's remained as rudimentary as it had been before the crisis, and certainly inferior to that between Britain and France, and France and Russia. The crisis therefore revealed how the Balkans might become a flashpoint for wider European tensions.

At the meeting of 8 December Moltke had expressed himself in terms similar to those used by Conrad: 'I believe war is unavoidable and the sooner the better'.[4] His thinking on preventive war accustomed the Kaiser and Bethmann Hollweg to the idea of war, but his arguments hardly constituted a case for seeking war as a definite policy objective. When he had been canvassed as chief of the general staff in succession to Alfred von Schlieffen at the beginning of 1905, he had told the Kaiser that a future war 'will be a national war which will not be settled by a decisive battle but by a long wearisome struggle with a country that will not be overcome until its whole national force is broken, and a war which will utterly exhaust our own people, even if we are victorious'.[5]

Moltke was not unusual among professional servicemen in anticipating that any future European war would be long, nor uncharacteristic among his own class in fearing that such a war would have revolutionary domestic consequences. Moreover, what he had described to the Kaiser was the war of one state against another. During his tenure of office it became progressively clearer that any war would be fought by coalitions. The creation of alliances reduced to vanishing point the chances of a quick and decisive victory. If one power defeated another in short order, the victory would not end the war. The conquered power would be bailed out by its ally.

Moltke's advice, though both sensible and accurate, showed how his realism could slide into pessimism: the former was a desirable attribute in a supreme commander in war, the latter not. Many German soldiers, particularly after the First World War, were wont to compare him unfavourably with his predecessor, Schlieffen. But, although the two were very different personalities, their thinking on the nature of future war was similar. Schlieffen, like Moltke, saw that war in Europe might become protracted and indecisive. In an essay on 'War Today', written in 1909 after he had retired, Schlieffen described the extension of the battlefield, and concluded that the war would be made up of several related battles, not one decisive victory. 'The total battle as well as its parts, the separated as well as the contiguous battles, will be played out on fields and across areas that dwarf the theatres of earlier martial acts.'[6]

The extension of the battlefield, and its apparent emptiness, was a direct consequence of Europe's industrialisation. The principles of breech-loading and rifling in firearms and artillery were finally allied to mass production in the last third of the nineteenth century. In 1815, at Waterloo, the infantry soldier's musket had a maximum effective range of 150 yards and a rate of fire of two rounds a minute; a century later, the infantry rifle could range almost a mile, and – fed by a magazine – could discharge ten or more rounds in a minute. A machine-gun, firing on a fixed trajectory, could sweep an area with

400 rounds a minute. The adoption of smokeless powder in the 1880s protected the location of the firer and guaranteed that visibility on the battlefield was subject only to the influences of nature (cloud, mist and night) but no longer to smoke. And in 1897 the French developed the first really effective quick-firing field gun, the 75mm. By placing the barrel on a slide and by absorbing the recoil with buffers, the 75mm could fire up to twenty rounds per minute without being relaid after each round. To protect himself from the volume of long-range fire the infantry soldier either dug trenches or erected field fortifications. Advances in artillery made permanent fortifications vulnerable, and their modernisation with reinforced concrete was costly. But in 1914 they were still used, as at Przemysl, to block the likely routes for a would-be invader and to defend high-value objectives. The strength of the defensive and the probability that attacks would soon get bogged down in a form of siege warfare led soldiers to warn against any exaggerated expectation of quick, decisive victory.

But such conclusions, drawn from tactics and technology, left Schlieffen and Moltke in a quandary. Strategically, Germany could not embark on a long war against an alliance which, even if it consisted of only France and Russia, outnumbered it. If Britain joined the French and the Russians, the arguments against accepting the inevitability of a long war were even greater. Both Schlieffen and Moltke reckoned that the British army was likely to be deployed to the Continent in the event of war, but that was not the major consideration. As a professional force shaped primarily for colonial warfare, its numerical contribution – about 100,000 men – would be paltry alongside armies which in peacetime approached one million men and on mobilisation for war would rise to three times that. The real threat posed by Britain was the Royal Navy, which could cut Germany off from overseas trade, and especially from the raw materials vital to its war industries in a long war. Until 1914 Germany relied on Chile for imports of saltpetre, from which it produced fixed nitrogen. Nitric acid was needed for explosives, and nitrogen for fertilisers and therefore for food production. Schlieffen and

Moltke had to find a short war solution precisely because they recognised the dangers of a long one. In a bid to secure a quick victory Schlieffen scouted an advance on France via the Low Countries, including Holland. But what made sense in operational terms did not do so in economic. In 1911 Moltke dismissed the idea: 'it will be very important to have in Holland a country whose neutrality allows us to have imports and supplies. She must be the windpipe that enables us to breathe.'[7]

The invasion of Holland formed part of a memorandum which Schlieffen finalised at the end of his tenure as chief of the general staff, or just after, and which has been handed down to posterity as 'the Schlieffen plan'. This recognised that the strength of France's defences on its eastern frontier, from Verdun down through Toul and Nancy to Belfort, prevented a frontal attack and demanded that the Germans swing into France from the north past the Belgian fortresses of Liège and Namur, and through Dutch territory around Maastricht. This was not the plan with which Germany went to war in 1914, not least because each year the general staff went through a cycle of revision and analysis which meant that what was posited in 1905 would be automatically superseded in 1906. Moreover, the evidence of exercises conducted in 1904 and in 1905 shows that Schlieffen was considering a number of different scenarios. The most important was the possibility that the German army would have to fight either first or simultaneously against Russia in the east. In 1905 itself that was in fact not too worrisome, as the Russian army was still reeling from its defeat at the hands of the Japanese and from the revolution: Germany was not so secure thereafter. Schlieffen also recognised in 1905 that he would probably not be free to swing right through Belgium and then bear down west of Paris, but might well have to react to what the French army did as it turned to meet the Germans. This would probably entail encounter battles close behind the French fortress barrier. The Germans upgraded their own fortifications at Metz as the pivot for these manoeuvres. 'The Schlieffen plan' was therefore no more a definitive statement of thinking in the German general staff in 1905 than it was in 1914. And what demonstrates this point most conclusively of all is its approach to man-power. 'The Schlieffen plan' assumed that Germany had ninety-four divisions available; in fact in 1905 it had barely sixty.

Between 1905 and 1914 the relative manpower position grew worse. France was only too aware that its population – 40 million to Germany's 60 million – confronted it with the danger that its army would be outnumbered on the battlefield. In 1911 it therefore con-scripted 83 per cent of its eligible adult males, to Germany's 57 per cent, and in 1913 it extended its period of regular service from two years to three. In 1914 the size of its army was comparable with that of Germany, and its ally, Russia, had recovered from the debacle of 1905. On the other hand, Austria-Hungary had failed to expand its army with sufficient urgency and both Italy and Romania failed to honour their obligations to the Triple Alliance. When war broke out the Entente could put 182 divisions into the field against 136 of the two Central Powers.

As a result, the increases of 1912 and 1913 were deemed inad-equate by the German general staff. Moltke had asked for 300,000 but got 136,000, and his chief of operations, Erich Ludendorff, wanted full conscription so that all able-bodied males received mil-itary training. It was reckoned in 1912 that 540,000 adult males in Germany avoided any form of military service. Schlieffen's and Moltke's need for a bigger army for operational reasons had to be balanced by the concerns of the Kaiser and of the minister of war. The former was of course the supreme commander of the army, the one person in whom the strands of military and political power were united, and it was to him that all the generals commanding the twenty-one corps districts (excluding three additional corps in Bavaria) were directly responsible. Many of them were stationed in areas where the rapidity of industrialisation and its corollary, urban-isation, threatened the conservative constitution of the Reich. Strike-breaking seemed a more imminent military duty than war against a foreign opponent. The Kaiser, too, thought that the army's first use might be to quell internal insurrection. When he addressed recruits to the Guards regiments at Potsdam on 23 November 1891, he told them that they must be prepared 'to shoot and cut down your own relatives and brothers'.[8] The more inclusive the embrace of military service, the greater the likelihood of this happening. Internal policing was therefore a constraint on the army's size. In 1914 only 5.84 per cent of German reservists came from big cities; as a result the army was comparatively untouched by the socialism that seemed to threaten the Reich from within.

The argument about quality over quantity was not driven solely by the fear of revolution. In peacetime the minister of war, a general who had to manage the army's budget and answer to the Reichstag on military issues, was as influential as the chief of the general staff. Karl von Einem, minister of war from 1898 until 1909, preferred more machine-guns to more men, and rated command as more decisive in war than mass armies. A sudden increase in the recruit intake adversely affected training levels. Charles à Court Repington, military correspondent of *The Times*, attended the manoeuvres of the German army in the autumn of 1911. 'No other modern army', he wrote, 'displays such profound contempt for the effect of modern fire'. And that was before the increases of 1912 and 1913 worsened the ratios of officers and guns to men.

Repington's charge is one more frequently directed at the French army. But all armies in the decade before the First World War confronted the problem of how to mount an attack across a fire-swept battlefield. It was not sufficient to say that the defensive was the stronger form of warfare – nor was it necessarily true, as the First World War was itself to show. To win, an army had eventually to attack. The general solution was for the attacking troops to approach under cover, to close by breaking into small groups, advancing in bounds, and then to build up fire superiority before the final rush. It was this last and most difficult phase that dominated so much military thought before 1914, as well as generating a great deal of wishful thinking. If an attacker could not believe that he was going to be successful, he was unlikely to have the resolve and determination to advance under fire. Good morale and the will to win were essential attributes of infantry soldiers, not the semi-mystical incantations of military theorists blind to the effects of the transformation of fire-power.

The attack across a fire-swept battlefield was a tactical problem. The issue of whether the French war plan should revolve around the offensive was of a totally different order – a matter of strategy. The French knew that the Germans would come through Belgium, but they also knew that they had major forces facing them in Alsace-Lorraine, and that German railway communications to the eastern frontier had received as much attention as those to the Belgian. Joseph Joffre, an engineer, possessed of a large and contented belly and an imperturbable temperament, became chief of the general staff in 1911. He could not see how the German army could cover both fronts adequately, given its size. This was hardly surprising when it was an issue the Germans had not resolved, either. The French had to do three things in their war plan. First, they had to mobilise as fast as the Germans, avoiding the chaos into which their army had been thrown by mobilisation in the Franco-Prussian war of 1870. They managed it so well that in 1914 they mobilised ahead of the Germans. Second, they had to deploy their forces to allow them to concentrate to either north or east, depending on where the main weight of the German attack came. Plan 17, the final version of France's war plan, posted ten corps on the eastern frontier and five on the Belgian, with a further six behind Verdun ready to go in either direction. Formally speaking, Plan 17 made no provision for the British Expeditionary Force, but in the years before the war the expectation had developed that its two corps would be added to and extend the French front facing Belgium. The third task was to provide for advance guards to make contact with the enemy and identify the thrust of the attack. This was where things came unstuck. On 1 August France mobilised in support of its Russian ally, and on 3 August Germany declared war on France. Three days later Sordet's cavalry corps set off into Belgium, following the line of the Meuse to within nine miles of Liège. It covered nearly forty miles a day, giving the horses no rest on the metalled roads, and getting through 15,000 horseshoes by 10 August. The cavalry continued the hectic pace over the next five days, ranging through the Ardennes and as far west as Charleroi. Sordet found no evidence that the Germans had come west of the Meuse. Joffre's expectations that the Germans lacked the strength to make more than a limited incursion into Belgium, that they would stay east of the Meuse, seemed confirmed.

Gallant Little Belgium

On 6 November 1913 Albert, King of the Belgians, visited Berlin. He was taken on one side by both the Kaiser and Moltke and warned that Belgium should throw in its lot with Germany in the coming war. Albert was no more blind to the drift of German war planning than were the general staffs of France and Germany. He recognised that his country was likely to be invaded. The Belgian military attaché in Berlin reported that Moltke had been enquiring what Belgium would do if a large foreign army crossed its territory. The answer, if that army were German, would be a defence on the Meuse based on the fortresses of Liège and Namur. But Belgium was not decided that the invader would be German. Right up until the war's outbreak it continued to espouse a policy of pure neutrality, treating all its neighbours as potential enemies. To enable all-round defence, the main field army would be massed in central Belgium, with the fortified port of Antwerp to its rear. Thus Belgium would be as ready to strike against the French and British as against the Germans. The fact that the British showed so much concern for the protection of Belgium's neutrality was seen as evidence of the self-interested nature of their policy, and a reason for Belgium distancing itself from the Entente as international tension mounted, not aligning itself with it.

As Catholics, many Belgians felt sympathy for Austria-Hungary even after 23 July. They suffered a tremendous shock on 2 August. The Germans presented Belgium with an ultimatum, demanding passage for its army through Belgian territory and a reply within twelve hours. It was the occasion, if not the cause, for Britain's entry to the war. Belgium's neutrality was guaranteed by all the great powers acting collectively, and they included Germany as the successor state to Prussia. Legally Britain was under no obligation to act. But the threat to Belgium fused British strategic self-interest with liberal morality. It united the government and it rallied the nation. Britain responded with an ultimatum of its own, demanding that Germany respect Belgian neutrality. It expired at midnight on 4 August.

For the Belgians, the issue now was not religious fellow-feeling but national identity. The manifestations of popular support for resistance surprised and gratified the King. His problem was that the army was in the throes of a reorganisation not due for completion until 1926. A field army of 117,000 was improvised, and 200,000 were left to man the fortifications. In theory all remaining able-bodied males were liable for service in the Garde Civique. In reality only those who resided in towns and fortified places were active and possessed the Garde Civique's rather unmilitary uniforms: in 1913 it had 46,000 members. In the enthusiasm of early August 1914 about another 100,000 joined the non-active Garde Civique based in rural areas.

The Hague Conventions of 1899 and 1907 had attempted to codify the laws of war. They had recognised the rights of an invaded people to rise up in resistance, provided they formed themselves in organised bodies and were identifiable as belligerents. As the Belgian representative at the 1899 conference said: 'If warfare is reserved exclusively for states and if the citizens are mere spectators, does one not thus lame the force of resistance, does one not thus deprive patriotism of its effectiveness? Is it not the first duty of the citizen to defend his fatherland?'[9] The Germans opposed this interpretation. They argued that war on land was a matter for large standing armies only, and that the international recognition of the levée en masse and of guerrilla war would remove limits on war and lead to barbarism. Their field service regulations published the relevant articles of the Hague convention in an appendix, but the body of the text made clear that the general staff did not recognise the right of civilians to resist invasion.

Germany was fearful of '*francs tireurs*' – irregular combatants or literally 'free shooters' – because of its experiences in the Franco-Prussian war in 1870–71. The war had been prolonged by France adopting the levée en masse. The Germans had responded by taking hostages, by organised and collective reprisals, and by increasingly random violence. They feared a recurrence when they invaded France again. In reality there was very little – and possibly no – civilian resistance to the German invasion. But the German army killed 5,521 civilians in Belgium and 896 in France. Citing the Germans' suppression of the Herero uprising of 1904–5 in their colony in south-west Africa (modern Namibia), allied propagandists damned such practices as 'colonial'. Stories of the atrocities focused on the rape of young girls, the cutting off of infants' hands, and the execution of priests and nuns. The destruction of buildings – including the university library of Louvain and the cathedral of Reims – confirmed that anti-Catholicism was an element in the Germans' motivations.

The first wave of outrages clustered around the Germans' attack on the fortresses of Liège. The siege began on 4 August and was not completed until Krupp 420mm and Skoda 305mm heavy mortars were brought up. But the frustrations of the advance were also self-inflicted. When the main German advance began, on 18 August and long after Sordet had reconnoitred the area, Alexander von Kluck's 1st Army on the German right wing was expected to march an average 23 kilometres a day for three weeks. The railways were disrupted by Belgian and French sabotage, and the roads were cluttered with refugees. Lorry transport was in its infancy, so the supply systems of the armies once they were beyond their railheads were predominantly horse-drawn. Kluck's army had 84,000 horses and much of its supply effort was devoted to the fodder – 2 million lb a day – needed to feed them. Most of the transport formations were newly formed on mobilisation, with both men and horses new to the rigours and demands of military supply in war. Thus tired and exhausted infantrymen, having marched all day and perhaps having fought as well, had to set off in search of food before they could settle down for the night. The local civilian population, itself worried about its own food supply, was hardly disposed to be cooperative.

Discipline was on a knife-edge. But the killing of civilians was not the product simply of alarmed and nervous reservists losing control. It was condoned and promoted from above. Conscious of both the need for speed and the threat of insurrection in their rear, army and corps commanders endorsed repression of imagined civilian resistance. One Saxon soldier, named Philipp, entered Dinant on the Meuse at 10 p.m. on 23 August, and found fifty civilians, 'shot for having treacherously fired on our troops. In the course of the night many more were shot, so that we could count over 200. Women and children, with lamps in their hands, were forced to watch the horrible spectacle. Then we ate our rice among the corpses, as we had eaten nothing since the morning.'[10] In all, 674 civilians were killed in Dinant by the Saxons on the orders of their corps commander. Conceived as a pre-emptive strike against anticipated *franc-tireur* activity, the massacre was justified by German claims that they had indeed been fired upon. The shots probably came from French soldiers on the other bank of the Meuse.

The Shock of Battle

The German army was not the only army to find that the strains of war caused discipline to collapse and buckle. Joffre began his campaign by pushing the French 1st and 2nd Armies against the German left, into the provinces of Alsace and Lorraine, forfeited as part of the peace settlement in 1871. By 18 August he realised that the German right was swinging north of the Meuse. He deemed his 5th Army sufficient to counter the threat. The 5th Army was supported on its left by the British Expeditionary Force. It had been decided on 5 August that the BEF should go to France, but initially it deployed only five divisions, or about 100,000 men, the largest body that the diminutive professional British army could put into the field. With the Germans strong on their left and on their right, Joffre concluded that they must be weak in their centre, and so he directed his 3rd and 4th Armies to attack into the Ardennes, aiming to hit the German right wing on its left flank. In fact the German 4th and 5th Armies were also pushing into the Ardennes and a series of bloody encounter battles took place in the forested and steep ground on 21–22 August.

The 'battles of the frontiers' were the first occasion on which most French, German and British soldiers came face to face with modern firepower, and they were devastated and disorientated by the effects. Lieutenant Ernst von Röhm, on coming under heavy French fire in Lorraine, thought that at last he would see the enemy and got out his field glasses, 'but there is nothing to recognise and nothing to see'. As the fire of his own unit slackened, he stood up and called on his comrades to do likewise. 'I want to see how many are still fit to fight. The bugler, who has remained by my side like a shadow, says to me sadly: "Herr Leutnant, there is nobody there any more!" And in truth nobody is standing on the whole front line. Only three men are still unscathed, everybody else is dead or wounded.'[11] On the other end of the line, at Mons on 23 August, the British army found itself holding ground against the main weight of Kluck's 1st Army. Aubrey Herbert recalled that 'It was as if a scythe of bullets passed directly over our heads about a foot above the earthworks. It came in gusts, whistling and sighing . . . It seemed inevitable that any man who went over the bank must be cut neatly in two.'[12]

Over a period of three days the allies were defeated along the entire length of the front. Forty thousand French soldiers were killed, and by 29 August their casualties totalled 260,000. They retreated. Rumour now fed panic. The 2nd Army had been shattered by the Germans in defensive positions on the Morhange heights, and fell back on the Grand Couronné de Nancy. On the morning of 24 August, *Le Matin* described the state of its 15th Corps: 'Companies, battalions passed in indescribable disorder. Mixed in with the soldiers were women carrying children in their arms or pushing little carts in front of them, girls in their Sunday best, old people, carrying or dragging a bizarre mixture of objects. Entire regiments were falling back in disorder. One had the impression that discipline had completely collapsed.'[13] Within four days the gossip in a village in central France reported that in one of the 15th Corps' regiments, 'the men had reversed arms in front of the enemy. The colonel, out-raged, killed six of his men with a revolver. So the soldiers had massacred their officers, then had taken to their heels, turning their backs to the enemy, and throwing into panic the army of Lorraine, which had been obliged to retreat 75 kilometres.'[14]

The French army's use of summary justice was more severe at this than at any other stage of the war. On 1 September the Ministry of War instructed the army to carry out death sentences within twenty-four hours. Soldiers were executed without trial. Joffre emphasised that requests for clemency were to be exceptional: 'Men have been recovered in bivouacs or in the rear without packs and without rifles. It is indisputable that most of them have abandoned their posts in the terms defined by the code of military justice . . . We must be pitiless with the fugitives.'[15] France executed about 600 soldiers in the First World War, and the majority were shot in the first year of the war. The British pattern was similar to the French. They executed 346 soldiers between 1914 and 1920, almost all for desertion in the face of the enemy. Although the absolute numbers rose as the war progressed, that was because the army itself became bigger. When judged in relation to the size of the army, both convictions for desertion and executions peaked in the first year of the war.

These British soldiers were regulars. Previous combat experience was not necessarily proof against a loss of nerve in this sort of fight-ing. Commandant Wolff, a veteran of France's colonial campaigns, was executed on 1 September after he had raised a white flag and called on his men to retreat in the fighting on 25 August at Meurthe-et-Moselle. On the same night a British veteran of the South African war, Douglas Haig, commanding one of the two British corps as they fell back from Mons, panicked when one of his brigades clashed with German advance guards. It was an uncharacteristic response, probably the result of the fatigue that gripped the entire British force. Haig's career prospered, but those of the two regimental commanding officers, who decided to surrender their exhausted battalions at St Quentin on 27 August, did not. Like Haig, both colonels had served in the South African war. They did not in fact surrender, but they were court-martialled and cashiered. One of them, J. F. Elkington of the Royal Warwickshire Regiment, joined the French Foreign Legion, was badly wounded and awarded the Croix de Guerre, and was then reinstated in the British army in his old rank and given the DSO.

Joffre asserted his authority. By 6 September he had purged his army of fifty-eight generals who had failed to meet the demands of war. But there were tactical solutions as well. His instructions repeatedly insisted that infantry attacks should not be launched from too great a distance or prematurely. He emphasised the role of the artillery, not only in support of the attack but also in its preparation. Backed by their 75mms, the French infantry dug in. The battle of the Marne, fought between 6 and 9 September 1914, checked the German advance. One of the truly decisive battles of history, it is remembered as a battle of manoeuvre, but the fighting extended from Paris on the French left all the way across France to Verdun and then turned south to the French right resting on the Swiss frontier. On 6 September the sector from Verdun to Switzerland, 280 km, was already stable; by the 9th the sector from Verdun to Mailly, another 100 km, was also fixed. On that day only the 105 km from Mailly to La Ferté-sous-Jouarre was really fluid; the rest was dominated by a dogged defensive battle. French corps commanders, like Ferdinand Foch in the marshes of St Gond, continued to use the rhetoric of the offensive, but the key point was that their lines held fast. On 5 September the French had 465,000 75mm shells in reserve; by the 10th the reserves had slumped to 33,000. Free to choose their ground, the French gunners had good fields of fire. Employing delayed-action fuses for ricochet fire, a 75mm battery was able to sweep an area of 4 hectares, 400 metres deep, in 40 to 50 seconds. Its four guns, firing ten rounds of shrapnel a minute, discharged 10,000 balls. This was far more effective against advancing infantry than machine-guns.

The Kaiser's son, Crown Prince Wilhelm, commanding the

German 5th Army, later said of Moltke's intentions, 'The plan of the supreme command was simply to overrun the enemy's country on as broad a front as possible.'[16] This is accurate on two counts. First, if the French line had broken anywhere – particularly between Verdun and Toul or south of Nancy – the battle of the Marne would have been lost as surely as if things had miscarried round Paris: Moltke was looking for victory where he could get it, not where some grand design of envelopment suggested. Second, Moltke was in no position to exercise hands-on command in this battle. With his headquarters in Luxembourg, he was too far from the fighting, and used only one officer, his head of intelligence, Richard Hentsch, to go forward to seven separate army headquarters scattered over a massive front. Wireless communications were slow and often overloaded; they could take twenty-four hours in transmission, and by then had often been intercepted by the French.

Posterity has seen the German invasion of France somewhat differently. It emphasises the strong right wing aiming to envelop the French army round Paris. But the right wing was not strong enough. It had detached forces to carry on operations to its rear – especially around Antwerp, behind whose fortifications the bulk of the Belgian army had withdrawn – and it had to occupy conquered territory. The army as a whole had lost 265,000 men killed, wounded and missing by 6 September. Meanwhile the French, holding their positions in the east defensively, were able to redeploy troops to the west, using their own railway system. On 23 August the 24.5 divisions of the three armies of the German right wing faced 17.5 allied divisions. But between 27 August and 2 September an average of thirty-two trains travelled westwards every twenty-four hours. Joffre created a new army, the 6th, around Paris and outside the German envelopment. By 6 September the German right wing confronted a total of forty-one allied divisions.

As Kluck's 1st Army turned to face the threat to its flank from the 6th Army a gap opened between it and its neighbour, the 2nd Army under Karl von Bülow. Sir John French, the British commander-in-chief, had taken the British Expeditionary Force out of the line, planning to give it a rest behind the Seine and west of Paris. On 4 September the French realised – thanks not least to the use of aircraft for reconnaissance purposes – that the moment for a counter-stroke had arrived. Joffre stressed to the British that the BEF would be supported by the French 6th Army on its left and the 5th Army on its right, and pleaded with Sir John for it to enter the gap and strike Kluck's exposed left flank. In reply, Sir John 'tried to say something in French. For a moment he struggled with his feelings and with the language, then turning to an English officer . . . he exclaimed: "Damn it, I can't explain. Tell him that all that men can do our fellows will do."'[17]

On 6 September the allies' retreat ended as they turned to attack. Kluck remained focused on his battle with the 6th Army, and so in Bülow's mind the threat from the BEF was primarily to his right flank, not Kluck's left. On 8 September he pulled back his exposed right wing, reorientating his army more on a north–south line – and thus widened the gap. None of Kluck, Bülow or Moltke knew what the others were doing or intended to do. On the morning of 8 September Moltke sent Hentsch to establish what the situation was. He was authorised to order a retreat on the part of the right wing only if this was the only way to close the gap between the 1st and 2nd Armies. Hentsch visited the 5th, 4th and 3rd Armies first, travelling along roads clogged with troops and transport, and did not reach the 2nd Army until 7.45 p.m. Bülow had already decided that the 1st and 2nd Armies should retreat on converging lines. Whereas he was preoccupied with the dangers presented by an enemy breakthrough, Kluck was focused on the opportunities for victory presented by envelopment: the one was the obverse of the other, since Kluck's pursuit of envelopment was what opened the opportunities for an allied breakthrough. When Hentsch at last arrived at Kluck's headquarters after a five-hour drive on crowded roads on the morning of the 9th, Kluck himself was out of contact, pushing the attack on the French 6th Army. Hentsch and Kluck's chief of staff therefore took the responsibility for ordering the 1st Army's retreat. Kluck liked to maintain that he was on the verge of defeating the 6th army, but such an argument leaves out of account any effects that the BEF's advance would have had as it hit his army on its left and rear. The Germans fell back to the heights overlooking the Aisne valley, where they entrenched.

After the First World War was over the German army claimed that it had been 'stabbed in the back' – that the war had been lost because of the collapse of the home front. According to this argument, the army itself had been undefeated in the field. But such assertions ignored the events of 1914. France had been saved. In its eyes, the Marne was a miracle and Joffre a new Napoleon. The battle was seen in traditional terms, confirming the expectation that manoeuvre would bring operational success. Pre-war staff exercises seemed still to be relevant. They were not: the efforts that had enabled that manoeuvre, the lines of trenches and the dogged defensive battle to the east of Paris, were. Opinion among neutrals and waverers, including Germany's nominal ally, Italy, hardened against the Central Powers. Germany had failed to secure a quick victory in the west, and was now committed to a long war on two fronts – a war it could not win. The Marne was a decisive battle, and its consequences were strategic. But German press releases between 6 and 16 September presented the withdrawal as tactical. The full truth was not divulged and a false prospect of continued military success generated – one which fed German domestic reporting right up until August 1918. In its own internal post-mortems the German army blamed individuals – Moltke, Hentsch, Bülow, and Kluck – rather than reviewing its own approach to strategy or its own institutional weaknesses.

Germany had, however, made two significant gains, even if both were incidental. First, it had overrun almost all Belgium as well as the industrial heartlands of north-eastern France, including 74 per cent of its coal production and 81 per cent of its pig iron. Second, it held so much French territory, and did so along positions which in many cases were so extraordinarily well adapted for fighting defensively, that it retained the advantages of an offensive strategy. The allies would have to attack across the fire-swept battlefield just to regain what was rightfully theirs. And it would seem that they had little choice in the matter: their own strategy had been forced into a strait-jacket.

The Ideas of 1914

The comparatively static nature of the front line in the west for much of the war meant that, after the first three months, most of France and Belgium was not directly in the fighting zone. But for those trapped in the areas of German occupation the war took on another meaning. Some were interned in concentration camps and others held as hostages. For the remainder, the pattern of the day was set by German time; they required passes in order to go about their daily business; family life was disrupted as women were deported as labourers; class was reversed as bourgeois families found themselves short of food and humiliated by the invaders. Many of these indignities were little different from those suffered as the result of wartime necessities in the rest of France, but those who were suffering them did not know that. Nor did those from whom they were divided. In 1916 Henri Barbusse published one of the most famous novels of the war, *Le Feu* (Under Fire). It won the Prix Goncourt and became a bestseller. The book focuses on the life of a squad. One of its members manages to get behind enemy lines to his home in Lens. He arrives at night and stands outside his home, looking into the lighted house. There is his wife: 'She was smiling. She was contented. She had a look of being well-off, by the side of the Boche non-com . . . I could see my baby as well, stretching her hands out to a great striped simpleton and trying to climb on his knee.'[18]

France and Belgium had been invaded, and their soldiers were fighting either to protect their homes and hearths or to liberate them. The purpose of the war was clear: it was not a war of dubious morality but a struggle for basic freedoms. In the minds of some it was even more. Jean-Richard Bloch, a socialist, wrote to a friend, the pacifist Romain Rolland, on 2 August 1914, as he went off to enlist:

'The war of the Revolution against feudalism is reopening. Will the armies of the Republic assure the triumph of democracy in Europe and perfect the work of [17]93? That will be more than the unavoidable war for home and hearth, that will be the awakening of liberty.'[19]

Germany, too, was invaded, even in the west, for all that it was the aggressor there. French troops entered Mulhouse in Alsace and posed a danger to Freiburg. In southern Bavaria the wives of some reservists, left at home without their men, killed themselves rather than confront vengeful French soldiers. To the east, in August the Russians threatened to overrun East Prussia up to the line of the Vistula. The image of the Cossack, ruthless, unprincipled, and above all uncivilised, had a pedigree which stretched back to the Russian army's occupation of Paris at the conclusion of the Napoleonic wars. Germany was not just defending itself against invasion but defending Europe against barbarism. Bloch's correspondent, Rolland, saw the German point of view. In October he declared that Prussian imperialism was 'the worst enemy of liberty' and a 'barbaric despotism'. But he acknowledged the glories of German culture and appreciated that tsarism could be construed as a threat to it. Recognising his own desire for an Entente victory, he retired to Switzerland rather than compromise his objectivity.[20]

Thus, as men adjusted to the idea of war, their nations became vehicles for broader ideologies. Britain, alone of the original belligerents, was not invaded. In a speech at the Guildhall in London on 9 November 1914, the prime minister, Asquith, explained his country's involvement in the war not in terms of its own strategic and imperial interests, but through the German invasion of Belgium and the protection of France from aggression. Britain was fighting to uphold international law and the rights of small nations; its enemy was Prussian militarism, embodied in the Kaiser himself. The French government used the vocabulary of the French Revolution and the Terror to mobilise the nation: it was fighting for the legacy of the revolution in terms of democracy and political rights. But, in doing so, it incorporated the right and the Catholic Church. Joan of Arc became an icon for all France. God would protect France as He had

guided Joan. Before the war the socialist Jean Jaurès had been criticised by the radical right for his internationalism and his advocacy of
a pure citizen army. But when he was assassinated by a solitary mav-
erick on 31 July 1914, his death became symbolic for the right as well
as the left. This was a Jaurèsian war: a war of national self-defence.

Both Britain and France were defenders of the status quo.
Germany said it stood for progress and change. On 16 October 1914
over 4,000 German academics signed a manifesto identifying
German culture with Prussian militarism. The outbreak of the war
in 1914 marked the end of the 'long' nineteenth century, which had
begun with the French Revolution in 1789. In its stead would be
erected a set of values which elevated the heroic spirit over the ma-
terialism of capitalism and the mediocrity of political liberalism.
A German Jew, Nachum Goldmann, in *Die Geist der Militarismus*
(1915), described the military spirit as the means to human progress
because it combined equality of opportunity with the advantages of
a meritocracy. On 9 August 1914 another Jew, Walther Rathenau, of
the German electronics firm AEG, was put in charge of organising
raw materials for the purposes of war production by Falkenhayn, the
minister of war – an extraordinary step for a Prussian officer to take.
Rathenau postulated a new form of economic organisation which
would combine the best features of capitalism with those of collectivism in a managed economy. 'The German eagle', Paul Natorp
wrote in 1915, 'is not like the bird of Minerva, which, according to
Hegel, first begins its flight at dusk. We signify the morning chorus
of a new day not only for Germany, but also for mankind.'[21] The
sociologist Werner Sombart wrote a book called *Händler und Helden*
(Traders and Heroes) in 1915 in which he interpreted man as living
two lives – one superficial and the other spiritual – and described life
as a continuing struggle to pass from one to the other: his heroes, the
Germans, were those who freely responded to the call of duty and
willingly sacrificed self.

This was a great war because it was a war fought over big ideas.
What had begun in the Balkans and had been originally driven by
issues of ethnicity and nationalism was now clothed with principles

whose force lay precisely in their claims to universality. In due course these ideologies became the basis of propaganda, but that could only happen because they expressed convictions with which the belligerent populations could identify. They were deemed to be so fundamental that they sustained the war despite both its length and its intensity. The peoples of Europe fought the First World War because they believed in – or at least accepted – the causes for which their nations stood. It was emphatically not a war without purpose.

The photographs of August 1914 suggest a party mood. But those were brave faces put on for the cameras. Most reservists called up on mobilisation in August 1914 left their families and jobs with reluctance. They went because it was their duty. They consoled themselves that they would be back home soon: before the leaves fell as winter set in, and certainly in time for Christmas. It is here – in the fantasies of peasants and clerks, shoe-horned into uniform once more – that the idea that the First World War would be short took hold.

It was a fantasy which helped sustain the front-line soldier for far longer than rationality suggested was likely. On Thursday, 1 January 1915, New Year's Day, Heinrich Woebcken – who was not a conscript but a twenty-eight-year-old schoolmaster who had volunteered for military service – wrote home to his family from Champagne: 'This year the decision will certainly come. It is taking a long time, but it's getting there.'[22] In other words the 'short war' illusion was being recycled: the war would end within a recognisable time-span, but – because no one could see how – the victory had to be located at a point which was in the middle distance rather than immediate. On the same day but a bit further south and on the French side of the line, Alexis Callies, a regular artillery officer in his mid-forties, wrote: 'We don't doubt that this war – already five months long – will end in the coming year. But how will it end?'[23]

3

GLOBAL WAR

War for the World

> Think of lying on the ground where the hot sun is beating directly on your backs; think of yourself buried in a hole with only your head and hands outside, holding a gun. Imagine yourself facing this situation for several days, no food, no water, yet you don't feel hungry; only death smelling all over the place. Listen to the sound of exploding bombs and machine guns, smoke all over and the vegetation burnt and of course deforested. Look at your relatives getting killed, crying and finally dead.[1]

This was how Fololiyani Longwe of the King's African Rifles recalled his First World War service. His memories were not very different from those of veterans of the war in Flanders and France. And yet one title used for the war as it was being waged was the Great European War. Some subsequent interpretations of the war have been similarly negligent. According to this view, the war was an unnecessary conflict waged between states whose similarities were more marked than their differences – a sort of European civil war. As a result of its self-destructive folly Europe forfeited its collective position as the leader of the Western world, a status assumed – eventually – by the United States of America. Moreover, if the Great European War was truly a global war, it became so only after the United States entered it in April 1917. Fololiyani Longwe's testimony corrects such arrogant uses of hindsight. He was one of over 2 million Africans who served in the war as soldiers and labourers: 10

per cent of them died, and among the labourers the rate may have reached 20 per cent. These were casualty rates comparable with those on the western front.

Longwe served because Malawi, then Nyasaland, was part of the British Empire. In 1914 the entire continent of Africa with the exception of Liberia and Ethiopia was under the rule of European powers, principally Britain, France, Belgium and Germany. Of the other colonial powers in Africa, Spain, Italy and Portugal, only Spain remained neutral throughout the war, and Portugal entered the conflict in 1916 principally in order to secure international support for its shaky authority in Africa. On this reading Portuguese soldiers took the first shock of the second German spring offensive in Flanders in April 1918 because of Portugal's anxieties about its holdings in Angola and Mozambique. That was not typical. In the same month and year German and British black troops were campaigning across Portuguese East Africa in order to further their conduct of the war in Europe. That was more typical. In 1914 conflict spread from the European centre to the periphery, and it did so because the states of Europe were imperial powers. War for Europe meant war for the world.

Some colonial administrators in 1914 hoped that would not be the case. The local units they commanded were designed not to fight each other but to maintain internal order. To many whites it seemed self-evident that the use of colonial troops to topple other European powers could only be self-destructive in the long term. War would rekindle the very warrior traditions that colonialism had been designed to extirpate, and ultimately the black trained to use a rifle against a white enemy might turn his weapon on his own white ruler. For such men the civilising and progressive, if paternalist and culturally supremacist, attributes of colonialism were the conditioning factors in 1914. They hoped that they might be exempt from developments in Europe. In Africa they pinned their hopes on the Congo Act. In 1884–5 Bismarck, acting in his capacity as the reassuring broker of Europe, had hosted a conference in Berlin to orchestrate the partition of Africa. The Berlin Congress had settled that all nations would have complete freedom to trade in the basin of the River Congo, and permitted any one of them to declare itself neutral in the event of war. In 1914 Belgium controlled not only the eastern bank of the river but also its estuary, and was also – given its situation in Europe – keen to uphold the principle of neutrality. The implications for one German central African colony, the Cameroons, were direct: French forces could not approach it from the south if France adhered to the Congo Act. The protection the Act gave to the others, Togoland and German East Africa (modern Tanzania), could only be indirect. But after the war the Germans cited the Congo Act both to support their claim to the restitution of their colonies and to argue that they were not the only power that breached international law in 1914.

The idea that war in Europe – or at least one involving Britain and Germany – would not spread beyond Europe was a later construct. In 1906, F. H. Grautoff, a newspaper editor and naval writer, published, under the pseudonym 'Seestern', *Der Zusammenbruch der alten Welt* (the Collapse of the Old World), a fictional account of a future war, translated into English as *Armageddon 190–*. It contained a real warning: 'They [Britain and Germany] had not stayed to consider that a war in Europe, with its manifold intricate relations with the new countries over the seas, the millions of whose populations obeyed a handful of white men, but grudgingly, must necessarily set the whole world ablaze'.[2] Grautoff's account of the war's origins began in Samoa, one of a clutch of German possessions in the south Pacific, and the name Grautoff gave its governor, Dr Solf, was the same as that of Germany's colonial secretary when the real war did break out. Grautoff's fictional war was naval and imperial in its origins. It was a corollary of *'Weltpolitik'*, the basis of German foreign policy at least until 1911.

The word *'Weltpolitik'* therefore gave rise to another word, *'Weltkrieg'* (world war). It was not only popular writers who prefixed their descriptions of future war in this way; responsible politicians like Bethmann Hollweg did so, too. They used it for three reasons. The first was of course for effect: they were not being geographically precise. It was not necessarily clear that Europe and the world were different. After all, to their Eurocentric eyes any war involving two alliance blocs would be massive, and in many contexts that was all '*Welt*' meant. The second reason related to Germany's challenge to the status quo. Britain had a vested interest in peace, because the existing order confirmed its own domination. In 1907 Henry Campbell-Bannerman, the Liberal prime minister, combined pacifism with navalism in a logic which was self-evident to British liberals but nonsensical to Continental powers: 'The sea power of this country implies no challenge to any single State or group of States. . . . Our known adhesion to those two dominant principles – the independence of nationalities and the freedom of trade – entitles us of itself to claim that, if our fleets be invulnerable, they carry with them no menace across the waters of the world, but a message of the most cordial good will.'[3]

Campbell-Bannerman emphasised Britain's subscription to universal principles for a pragmatic reason. The military value of the Royal Navy lay above all in its ability to protect the United Kingdom; its capacity to defend Britain's far-flung possessions and their trading routes was much less assured, and relied to a large extent on the acceptance by other powers of the Pax Britannica. If Germany found itself at war with Britain, the latter's overseas possessions were more vulnerable to attack than Britain itself; its trade and its financial markets were more sensitive to danger than were its forces in the field. Germany therefore had an interest in taking the war beyond Europe if it could find the means to do so. Although Germany – like the other powers of Europe – had a vociferous colonial lobby, its enthusiasm for widening the conflict was not principally a form of covert imperialism. It was a way of fighting the war.

This was the third reason underpinning Germany's use of *Weltkrieg*. By the same token Britain had an imperative need to close the war down. On 5 August 1914 the Committee of Imperial Defence, an advisory body of the British cabinet, convened a sub-committee to consider 'combined operations in foreign territory'. Its cardinal

Franz Ferdinand went to Bosnia in June 1914 to attend the manoeuvres of two corps of the Austro-Hungarian army. As well as giving consideration to the map, he was also thinking about sacking the bellicose chief of staff, Conrad von Hötzendorff.

A third of the Serb army had to march to its deployment positions, rather than go by train. This soldier is sensibly taking some additional supplies as well as his wife. But at least he has been issued with a rifle: many were not.

Mobile operations at the start of the war meant that the pillage and destruction, wrought by all armies, were widespread. Austro-Hungarian infantry, convinced that Serb civilians were as hostile as combatants, were particularly harsh in the Balkans.

Smiling for the camera because – rather than in spite – of the gallows was a common reaction on the Eastern Front in both world wars. In 1914 the Austro-Hungarian army was vested with the authority to reach its own conclusions with regard to treason.

The Carpathian mountains, which in the east rose to 4,000 feet and more, were pierced by the Dukla pass. This wounded Austrian, being helped through the pass in February 1915, might yet escape the freezing death which confronted many of the 800,000 casualties.

On 4 August 1914 Belgian civilians had not yet learned to fear German soldiers. These young men pose alongside each other at Stavelot, just across the German border in the Belgian Ardennes.

The French 75mm field gun was the artisan of the victory on the Marne. Able to fire up to twenty shells a minute, it was deployed with good fields of fire in direct support of the infantry. During the course of the battle French ammunition stocks fell by 432,000 rounds.

Polishing boots in the Place Rogier in Brussels may have been how this Belgian woman made her living in 1914, but her actions symbolise her nation's subordination to German militarism.

The British and the French invaded the German Cameroons from all four points of the compass. In September 1914, the so-called Cross River Column, from Nigeria to the north, hit strong German defences and was repulsed.

Trenches were built from the outset of the war but by the winter of 1914–15 they were its dominating feature. Mud and rain meant that they required constant maintenance, especially in Flanders. The 2nd Battalion Royal Scots Fusiliers takes a rest from its labours.

The war confirmed the Lutheran church as the religious bedrock of the German state, and the army as defender of both. In Potsdam on 9 August 1914, the Kaiser and his family join the 1st Garde-Reserve-Regiment in a field service before it departs for the front.

12

War enthusiasm in Tokyo: on 12 December 1914 crowds welcome the Japanese victors on their return from the capture of Tsingtao. Of all the belligerents, Japan best showed that it was possible to use the war for the successful pursuit of policy.

In 1914 coal powered almost all ships, which bunkered every eight or nine days. This gave Britain two advantages: it possessed a network of bases for coaling, and Welsh anthracite burned more slowly and with greater heat than other coal.

13

The German *Schütztruppen* were intended for internal policing, not for fighting foreign powers. Although professional soldiers, their loyalty was not as unconditional as post-war German propagandists, anxious to regain Germany's African territories, claimed.

Africa comes to Europe: Smuts, the former Boer commando but now member of the British Imperial War Cabinet, inspects the South African Native Labour Contingent in France in April 1917.

16

The Kaiser was as strong a supporter of the Turkish–German alliance as was Enver. But Wilhelm's belief in monarchy made him suspicious of a man who had challenged the powers of the Sultan.

In March 1916 August von Mackensen, fresh from his conquests of Poland and Serbia, was fêted in Constantinople. He inspects the German crews of the *Goeben* and *Breslau*, now in Turkish service.

objective was that nothing should be undertaken which might prej-
udice the conduct of the war in Europe. The principal task outside
Europe was defensive, to secure Britain's sea routes against German
attack: these were the links that would enable Britain to tap the
resources of both its empire and its neutral trading partners. The
targets of offensive operations were to be the naval bases and wireless stations that supported the German navy. The sub-committee
laid down two guiding principles. It renounced the conquest of
territory, and it declared that any land forces used should be local
formations only.

These principles proved mutually incompatible. Those dominions
and allies on whom Britain called to provide forces for local operations proved ready to do so. But their motives were shaped less by
the needs of the war in Europe than by territorial ambitions in their
own regions. Britain did not see the outbreak of the First World War
as an opportunity to acquire German colonies; however, others on
whom it relied did. British imperialism may have been dormant
between 1914 and 1918, but so-called 'sub-imperialism' flourished.

War in the Far East

This conundrum became immediately evident. The biggest of
the German overseas naval bases was Tsingtao on the Shantung
peninsula in China. Acquired in 1897, it was the most obvious
manifestation of *Weltpolitik* in action. The East Asiatic Squadron,
which was based there, consisted of two armoured cruisers, *Scharnhorst*
and *Gneisenau*, and three light cruisers, all under the command of
Graf von Spee. It was numerically comparable and qualitatively
superior to the British ships based on Hong Kong. The dominions
of both Australia and New Zealand had begun the creation of their
own navies just before the outbreak of the war, and each had built a
battle cruiser, but neither ship was available for use against Spee.
HMS *New Zealand* was not even in the Pacific: she had been deployed
to the North Sea to improve the naval balance against the main

German fleet. HMS *Australia* was in the right ocean, but the Common-
wealth of Australia was determined that she would be used for the
close defence of its own territory.

In the minds of Australians the danger of invasion lay not just with
Germany. Japan was seen as a threat which was as great and more
immediate. Racism underpinned the fear. But Japan was Britain's ally.
The Anglo-Japanese alliance of 1902 was designed by the British to
deal with the balance of power in the Far East. It had never been
intended as a weapon against Germany. However, in August 1914
the Admiralty's anxiety about the defence of British trade in the
Pacific caused it to change tack: the Japanese navy included fourteen
battleships, among them the *Kongo*, laid down in 1912 and at the
time the most powerfully armed and largest battleship in the world.
On 6 August the British foreign secretary, Sir Edward Grey, asked
the Japanese for limited naval assistance in hunting down German
armed merchantmen. This was a lifeline for the Japanese navy. It had
designs on the islands of the north Pacific as the base for a Japanese
empire. It was therefore engaged in a major funding battle with the
army, whose ambitions focused on the mainland of China. Entry to
the war gave both services, and their political lobbies, an opening to
further their own interests.

The war in Europe was, in the words of Inoue Kauro, an elder
statesman, 'divine aid ... for the development of the destiny of
Japan'.[4] Like many others in Japan, as in Australia, Inoue interpreted
international relations in racial terms. Just as the current war in
Europe could be seen as a conflict between Teuton and Slav, so a
future war would pit the yellow races against the white. Grey's invi-
tation was therefore a 'one in a million chance'[5] to establish Japanese
suzerainty in China, and therefore in Asia, while the European
powers were engaged elsewhere. Most of these elder statesmen and
service chiefs believed that the Anglo-Japanese alliance had outlived
its usefulness. In 1902 it had given Japan great power status and
provided a foil to Russia in the Far East. By 1914 Russia seemed
the more logical ally in a regional context, and Germany the more
obvious role model in terms of constitutional development.

Crucially, these were not the views of Kato Takaaki, the foreign minister, who had served as ambassador in London and who was an ardent anglophile. He wished to exclude the elders from government, to assert the cabinet's control over the armed forces and to put parliamentary politics on a secure footing. Of all the world's statesmen in 1914, Kato proved the most adroit at using war for the purposes of policy. Domestically he exploited it to assert the dominance of the Foreign Ministry and of the cabinet in the making of Japan's foreign policy. Internationally he took the opportunity to redefine Japan's relationship with China. In doing so he was not simply outflanking the extremists opposed to him; he was also honouring his own belief that Japan should be a great power like those of Europe. An essential aspect of that status was imperialism, as Britain itself showed.

On 23 August Japan declared war on Germany. It had every intention of keeping its involvement limited: it never seriously entertained the idea of sending troops to Europe, although it did deploy a squadron of ships to the Mediterranean in 1917. But, equally, it was not going to conform to the constraints on its actions suggested by the British. It immediately set about the capture of Tsingtao by means of an amphibious assault. Germany had presumed that the principal threat to Tsingtao would come from the sea; its landward fortifications had been designed to check the Boxers, a secret society which had orchestrated an anti-foreigner rebellion in 1900. An overland approach from the sea breached China's neutrality. The British contributed two battalions to a Japanese force of 60,000 and therefore colluded (not for the last time in this war) in the infringement of the rights of neutrals – a principle which they had ostensibly got into this war to defend. On 7 November the German garrison surrendered.

Japanese troops were home by Christmas, and their total losses in the First World War were less than 2,000. The Tsingtao campaign was sufficiently short and decisive to ensure that Kato retained the initiative in policy. On 18 January 1915 he presented China with the so-called 21 Demands, divided into five groups. The first four groups sought to extend Japanese direct control over Shantung, southern Manchuria and eastern Inner Mongolia, and to buttress its trading position elsewhere; the fifth group were dubbed 'wishes' rather than 'demands', and aimed to secure for Japan the sort of privileges already accorded to the other great powers. Kato's aims were economic rather than annexationist. But the objectives of the army, of big business and of pan-Asiatic nationalists were more directly political and military. Kato miscalculated the effects of his own success, and by 1916 the elders and the army had reasserted their hold on government. Admirers of German rather than British styles of government, they began to orientate themselves for what they saw as the coming struggle with the United States.

The Japanese navy also used the opportunity of the war to seize the German Pacific islands north of the equator. Britain could hardly protest too strongly when its own dominions similarly seized the opportunity to further their colonial ambitions. New Zealand had occupied Samoa by 30 August 1914, and Australia laid claim to New Guinea and the Solomon Islands. But British anxieties were focused on the activities of the Japanese army on the continent of Asia. China was already in chaos, following the revolution in 1911 and the fall of the Manchu dynasty in 1912. The 21 Demands deepened China's domestic turmoil. The president of the Chinese republic, Yuan Shih-kai, claimed the credit for moderating the humiliation of the 21 Demands and suggested that he become emperor, seeking the backing of the Entente for his bid. The military governors of south China turned against Yuan, and the Japanese army encouraged their rebellion by supplying them with military advice. Internal division within China created Japan's opportunity to advance its indirect control over the remainder of China. The Japanese economy boomed in the First World War, not least on the back of Japanese investment in China and exploitation of China's labour and raw materials. On 14 August 1917 China abandoned its neutrality. Its declared enemy was Germany, but the real danger came from Japan. Its purpose was not to fight the war but to attend the peace conference in order to regain Shantung and reassert its sovereignty.

Germany's loss of Tsingtao left the East Asiatic Squadron without a base. But Spee had never intended to contribute directly to its defence. The basic presumption of cruiser warfare was that cruisers should retain their freedom of manoeuvre as long as possible. Spee's ships should therefore have dispersed. Individual ships were easier to supply and coal, particularly with so many bases around the Pacific littoral in British control. By scattering he would force a superior enemy to follow suit. He would be free to direct his attacks against vulnerable targets, such as merchant ships and harbours, and he would avoid a battle in which the enemy could concentrate strength against weakness.

But in mid-August, with Japan not yet in the war, Spee's quandary was that his squadron was not – in local terms – the inferior force. As a professional sailor and as an admiral, Spee's temperamental preference was to keep his squadron united and under his own control, and to exercise maritime dominance while he could. On 12 August he received a signal warning him of Japan's probable entry to the war, but he did not revise his intentions. He had already resolved to direct his squadron south-east towards Chile. Chile was neutral, but was reported to be well disposed towards Germany and could provide coal. The Entente naval chain was weakest in this quarter of the Pacific.

When Spee told his captains what he intended, Karl von Müller of the *Emden* disagreed. Spee's scheme would keep his command intact, but it would do so at the price of the principles of cruiser war, and it would not threaten Britain's commerce at its most vulnerable points. Spee agreed to the extent that he allowed Müller to detach the *Emden* from the squadron and to make for the Bay of Bengal. Over two months, beginning on 10 September, the *Emden* raided Madras and Penang, captured twenty-three vessels, and sank a Russian cruiser and a French destroyer. Müller applied the principles of cruiser warfare to brilliant effect. Although his exploits created chaos in British trade in the Indian Ocean, he was lionised as much by the British press as the German. On 9 November the *Emden* was surprised and sunk by an Australian light cruiser as she was raiding the wireless station on the Cocos Islands. Even then the *Emden*'s exploits were not over. Müller had put a landing party ashore on Direction Island. It seized a schooner and sailed to the Yemen. After crossing to the Red Sea, it braved the desert, despite attacks by hostile Arabs, and reached Damascus and then Constantinople. A German journalist greeted the party on its arrival by asking its commander, Hellmuth von Mücke, which he would prefer, a bath or Rhine wine: 'Rhine wine,' replied von Mücke.[6]

Spee's squadron set a course for the Marshall Islands, so eluding both the Japanese navy, which was confined to the north Pacific, and the British and Australian vessels, which focused on the defence of the trade routes from the Far East to Europe. The swift destruction of the German wireless stations in the Pacific forced Spee to observe radio silence, and so helped him hide in the vastness of the ocean. Having learnt via an American newspaper of the fall of Samoa, Spee called at Apia in the hope of finding enemy warships there – a clear indication of his abandonment of cruiser warfare. Luckily for him there were no major targets. As he left Samoa he made course for the north-west to fool any pursuers, but then doubled back towards Tahiti as darkness fell. At Tahiti his good fortune deserted him. He bombarded Papeete on 22 September. Papeete had no wireless of its own, but a French steamer was able to report the attack, and so confirmed what some of his pursuers were beginning to realise: that Spee was aiming for South America.

Sir Christopher Cradock, commanding the Royal Navy's Western Atlantic Squadron off South America, was one of those who had suspected as much since early September. It was a rare flash of intuition: a brave man, he was not particularly intelligent, and believed that 'a naval officer should never let his boat go faster than his brain'.[7] To cover both the western Atlantic and the eastern Pacific, Cradock was obliged to divide his command, taking four ships only round the Horn. The Admiralty intended to reinforce them, but the attacks of the *Emden* and Spee's north-westerly course after the attack on Apia persuaded it that it must have been mistaken about Spee's destination. Only an ageing pre-Dreadnought, HMS *Canopus*, arrived. Her

12-inch guns gave Cradock the firepower if he could lure Spee's faster-moving ships into range. But the engineer on *Canopus* said that she could not make more than 12 knots and that she needed four days' overhaul after the long voyage to the Falklands. If Cradock waited for the *Canopus*, he risked losing track of Spee, and so he left her behind: in reality, the engineer was mentally unhinged and the ship could do 16 knots.

The Admiralty's orders to Cradock were ambiguous – the consequence of an offensive-minded First Lord of the Admiralty, Winston Churchill, who could not resist the temptation offered by the wireless to direct operations from London on the basis of outdated intelligence. The Admiralty certainly told Cradock that it was his job to seek out the enemy, and only by leaving *Canopus* did it seem that he would have the speed to do so. The trouble was that he now lacked the firepower to be effective when he found Spee.

Spee used only one vessel, the light cruiser *Leipzig*, to transmit wireless signals. Cradock heard the signals and fancied that he might catch the *Leipzig* in isolation. In fact, Spee's squadron had rendezvoused with two cruisers, including the *Leipzig*, off Easter Island. Cradock used HMS *Glasgow* in exactly the same way. The Germans heard the *Glasgow*'s signals and closed with her off Coronel at about 4.30 p.m. on 1 November. Cradock could still have escaped. He did not. He closed up to the *Glasgow*. While the setting sun was in the Germans' eyes, his ships had a temporary advantage, but as soon as it sank over the horizon the British ships were silhouetted against a reddening sky. Spee kept his distance until the light was right, and then at 7 p.m. opened fire. His theoretical broadside was 4,442 lb to the British 2,875 lb. In practice, the British guns were mounted lower on the ship than the Germans', and the rough seas meant that water flooded the casemates, so up to half of them could not be used. Cradock's flagship, *Good Hope*, was hit before she opened fire and sank within half an hour; HMS *Monmouth* followed two hours later.

It was a crushing victory, but Spee was realistic about his options. When he called at Valparaiso on 3 November to bunker, he told an old friend: 'I cannot reach Germany; we possess no other secure harbour; I must plough the seas of the world doing as much mischief as I can, till my ammunition is exhausted, or till a foe far superior in power succeeds in catching me.'[8] After an uncharacteristic delay he set course for Cape Horn and the Atlantic. He was now in the one quarter of the globe not reached by the German wireless network. He therefore did not know, as those in Germany did, that the British had responded to the news of Coronel by detaching two battle cruisers, *Inflexible* and *Invincible*, from the Battle Cruiser Squadron in the North Sea. Commanded by Sir Doveton Sturdee, they reached the Falkland Islands on the morning of 7 December 1914.

Spee could have given the Falklands a wide berth, but once again his propensity for action got the better of him, even though his shell stocks were running low. As the *Gneisenau* closed on Cape Pembroke, its senior gunnery officer spotted the three-legged tripod masts characteristic of Dreadnoughts, the all-big-gun battleships pioneered by the British in 1905. Spee turned away, confident that he had the speed to outdistance battleships – if indeed they were there. But battle cruisers had been developed by Jackie Fisher, the First Sea Lord, for action exactly like this. They combined the hitting power of the battleship with the manoeuvrability of the cruiser. Not only did they mount 12-inch guns, but they could make speeds of up to 25 knots (as opposed to the Dreadnought battleship's 21 knots). They forfeited deck armour to do so, but when on the oceans, with plenty of manoeuvring space, the risk was – it seemed – neutralised by their ability to engage at great ranges and at great speed.

In fact, the British ships managed 26 knots, while the German light cruisers, their hulls befouled by the long cruise, made 18. *Inflexible* opened fire at 16,500 yards, although her guns were calibrated for 12,000 yards. Sturdee avoided closing beyond about 14,000 yards, the maximum range for the Germans' 8.2-inch main guns. Spee looked for a break in the weather, knowing that the British had the afternoon and evening of a South Atlantic summer to deal with their foe. *Scharnhorst* was sunk at 4.17 p.m. Aboard the *Gneisenau*, 'debris and corpses were accumulating, icy water dripped in one place and in another gushed in streams through panels and shell-holes, extinguishing fires and drenching men to the bone'.[9] Out of ammunition, at 6.02 she, too, went down.

One of Spee's two sons, Heinrich, drowned with the *Gneisenau*. The other, Otto, was on the light cruiser, *Nürnberg*. She was overhauled and sunk, as was *Leipzig*. Only *Dresden* escaped: she was not run down until 14 March. By the end of 1914 the German cruiser threat to Britain's maritime trade was all but eliminated. So large was Britain's merchant fleet that the achievements of Spee, Müller and others were in statistical terms insignificant. By January 1915 German surface vessels had accounted for 215,000 of the 273,000 tons of merchant shipping sunk, but that was only 2 per cent of British commercial tonnage.

War in Africa

However, one German cruiser continued her operational effectiveness beyond the year's end. SMS *Königsberg* began the war attacking trade off the coast of German East Africa. She abandoned her base at Dar es Salaam for exactly the same reasons as Spee's cruisers left Tsingtao. Instead she established herself in the Rufiji delta about two hundred miles to the south. By November she was blocked in, but as she drew up the river the overhanging branches protected her from aerial observation. Having consumed the efforts of a blockading squadron of twenty-five vessels for over half a year, she was finally sunk on 11 July 1915 by two shallow-draught monitors. Even then her war continued. Her crew and her guns, dismounted from the ship, joined the forces of Colonel Paul von Lettow-Vorbeck in the longest campaign in Germany's global war.

Lettow-Vorbeck became a legend. Forty-four years old when the war broke out, he was physically tough and extremely aggressive. He did not surrender until 25 November 1918, two weeks after the armistice in Europe. Here, at least, was a German commander who had never been defeated. But he became a legend to his enemies as well. Lettow-Vorbeck led them the length of East Africa from Uganda to the Zambezi, but they never caught him up. Their incompetence played a large part, but it suited them better to believe that he had conducted a guerrilla campaign. That was nonsense. Lettow-Vorbeck was a Prussian general staff officer, with all the preconceptions that that implies. His African soldiers, or askaris, were organised in independent field companies, and were trained in bush fighting, but his inclination was to seek battle, not shun it. Cut off from Germany, he was almost entirely reliant on what he could get from within the colony: fighting for fighting's sake both depleted his ammunition stocks and endangered his irreplaceable European officers and non-commissioned officers. As with Spee and his cruisers, Lettow's strength lay in dispersal and in striking against weakness, forgoing the temptation to concentrate for battle. Like Spee, Lettow could not resist the pressures of the traditions in which he had been brought up.

A true guerrilla strategy would have rested the defence of German East Africa on the opportunities for fomenting revolution in the adjacent colonies of the enemy. The British colonial service was depleted by the need for its younger officials to join the armed forces, and the Belgians to the west and the Portuguese to the south had the reputation of being the most bloodthirsty and tyrannical of all the European colonial powers. Lettow-Vorbeck did not exploit this chance: he saw the fighting as a matter between armies in the field and the territories as simply ground over which they operated.

By the same token, he never acknowledged – and perhaps never realised – how much he owed to the civil administration of German East Africa. Although there were certainly areas of the colony which gave support to the British forces, the Germans never had to cope with insurrection in their rear. The German governor, Heinrich Schnee, was not enthusiastic about the war, which he saw as under-mining the progressive effects of colonisation. Initially, he embraced the Congo Act. For Lettow-Vorbeck, German East Africa fulfilled a purely military function: to draw British troops off from the main theatre in Europe. This could never be accomplished by neutrality. Lettow-Vorbeck therefore saw himself as constantly at odds with Schnee. In reality, he could never have lasted as long in the field as he did without the efforts of the civil administration.

Primarily this was a matter of logistics. British naval supremacy meant that the Germans in Africa sustained the war very largely on the basis of their own resources. But it was also a matter of men. Many of them were soldiers procured through the agencies of colonial government. France enlisted over 600,000 soldiers in its colonies, the vast majority in West and North Africa. It even used its African soldiers in the war in Europe. The Germans took strong exception to what they interpreted as the barbarisation of war, although the performance of the French Senegalese was not as effective as their reputation. While European soldiers were citizens of the states on whose behalf they were fighting, Africans were – in general – pressed men or mercenaries. Some served on both sides in the course of the war. Kazibule Dabi, a German askari, was captured by the British:

> They said that we should become soldiers . . . We asked them how much they would pay us if we enlisted. They said one pound, one shilling, and fourpence [a month]. We told them that we would not accept that. We told them that when we were on the German side we used to receive three pounds and ten shillings. We refused and there was great talk about it. When they saw that we were not willing to give way, they decided not to give us food. . . . As a result we ended up by enlisting.[10]

However, the majority of the Africans who served were not soldiers but labourers. Sub-Saharan Africa had few roads or railways, and pack animals fell prey to the tsetse fly. Supplies were therefore carried by human beings. The British recruited over a million carriers for the East African campaign, drawn from the Belgian Congo, Ruanda, Uganda, Kenya, Northern Rhodesia, Nyasaland, and Mozambique. At the end of the war, the British district commissioner in what had been German East Africa, an area where both sides had recruited labour, reported that a third of the male taxable population had been taken. Mobile operations demanded at least two or three carriers for every soldier, and the demands grew exponentially as the line of communications lengthened. The longer the line of march, the more likely that the carriers themselves would consume the loads they carried. Assuming an average ration of 3 lb per day and a load of 60 lb, a line of communications of ten daily marches needed as many porters as there were soldiers in the front line. A march of three weeks and the porter consumed the entire load himself. Thus there was a trade-off between the nutritional needs of the porters and those of the troops. Porters in British pay in West Africa were given daily rations on two scales – either 2,702 or 1,741 calories – but in East Africa in 1917 porters were getting less than 1,000 calories a day. Natives were assumed to be more resistant to the effects of the climate and its local diseases, but very often they had been marched out of their own localities and their resistance to disease had been undermined by changes in diet, by poorly cooked food and, above all, by its insufficiency. Among East and West Africans employed as carriers the death rate was 20 per cent over the war as a whole: this was higher than the death rate for British soldiers in the war.

On 15 September 1918, with the campaign reaching its conclusion, a doctor with Lettow-Vorbeck's force, Ludwig Deppe, wrote: 'Behind us we leave destroyed fields, ransacked magazines and, for the immediate future, starvation. We are no longer the agents of culture; our track is marked by death, plundering and evacuated villages, just like the progress of our own and enemy armies in the Thirty Years War.'[11] For Schnee German colonialism was an end in itself; for Lettow-Vorbeck it was a means to an end. Both were defeated. Germany lost its colony: its active defence did not begin until March 1916 and it was overrun by November 1917. Thereafter German troops fought largely on Portuguese territory. In doing so, they did not draw off troops which could have been deployed in Europe. The British decision at the outset of the war, that only local forces should be used in the elimination of German colonies, broadly interpreted, remained good. Although about 160,000 troops, both British and Belgian, were deployed against Lettow-Vorbeck in the course of the East African campaign, few of them would have been available for the western front. Indeed, the fact that the campaign was not allowed to detract from the British army's effort in France and Flanders was one reason why it was so protracted.

The other British decision at the outset of the war, that the objectives of operations outside Europe were naval, created – unbeknown to them – an almost perfect symmetry between their objectives and the Germans'. Precisely because of British maritime supremacy, the Germans had little intention of defending the coast, and planned instead to withdraw inland so as to use the interior in order to prolong their resistance. Germany's cruisers were to put to sea and use alternative bases for coaling and supplies. Thus the British secured several quick successes but were then baffled as to why the fighting continued. The mutual incomprehension prevailed throughout the war and even after.

The first speedy victory for the British was also the most important. By 25 August the wireless station in Togoland at Kamina, which linked Germany's other African stations with Nauen in Germany itself, was destroyed, following a British invasion by the Gold Coast Regiment. The war in Africa lasted four more years but the principal objective had been achieved within three weeks of its outbreak.

In East Africa, the principal port, Dar es Salaam, was a long way from the nearest British colony, Kenya. Moreover, the activities of the *Königsberg* revealed to the Admiralty that the coastline contained several bases from which a cruiser could operate. The Admiralty therefore wanted mastery of the whole coast. The King's African Rifles had been designed for internal colonial policing and were not strong enough for such a task. Two conclusions followed: the principal garrison of the British empire, India, was asked to provide the troops, and Tanga, because it was in the north, was chosen as the first target. It stood at the foot of the Northern Railway, and an attack on it could be combined with a thrust on the other end of the line which reached into the foothills by Mount Kilimanjaro.

On 2 November 1914 Indian Expeditionary Force B went ashore at an undefended beach close to Tanga. The town was held by a single company, and Lettow-Vorbeck's attention was focused on the danger to the other end of the railway. But the preparation of IEF B had not been a high priority for the Government of India, which had already diverted its best troops to other theatres – France, Mesopotamia and Egypt. 'They constitute the worst in India, and I tremble to think what may happen if we meet serious opposition', the expedition's intelligence officer, Richard Meinertzhagen, wrote in his diary. 'The senior officers are nearer to fossils than active, energetic leaders of men.'[12] They had been at sea for the best part of a month, and they were not trained in bush warfare. Moreover there was no attack from the other end of the northern line until 3 November. Lettow-Vorbeck could have suffered a major defeat at the very outset of the campaign; instead he was able to snatch a crucial victory. IEF B's dilatory and demoralised approach gave him time to concentrate seven companies by the morning of 4 November, with two more due to arrive that day. Deprived of effective artillery support by a decision not to disembark its guns, and confused by the thick bush, IEF B none the less fought its way into Tanga by late afternoon on 4 November. At this juncture some German company commanders instructed their buglers to sound the recall in order to regroup. But the signal was mistaken as one for a general retreat. On the British side, Meinertzhagen recognised the call for what it was, but others insisted it was the charge. For a second time the Germans were given a chance to recover an apparently irredeemable situation. Tanga was empty and, as British naval gunfire at last began to take effect, Lettow-Vorbeck prepared to continue the fight to the west of the town. But the British commander, A. E. Aitken, had decided to give up. IEF B had completed its evacuation by 3.20 p.m. on 5 November. Tanga was only the first of Britain's amphibious expeditions to fail because of divided ministerial authority, lack of army and navy cooperation, and confused and irresolute command.

Lettow-Vorbeck was now given a breathing space of over a year. This was the product not of his own efforts but of those of the men defending Germany's colonies in other parts of Africa. Given the inadequacies of the Indian forces in East Africa, the British had two alternative sets of 'local' troops to turn to. One was the South

African Defence Force, and the other was the West African Frontier Force. But both were fully committed, the former in South-West Africa until July 1915, and the latter in the Cameroons until January 1916. Although Lettow-Vorbeck never acknowledged it, the conduct of the second campaign in particular stands comparison with his own achievement – and indeed underpinned it.

Just as Australia and New Zealand harboured 'sub-imperialist' designs in the south Pacific, so South Africa – particularly its defence minister, Jan Smuts – wanted to push the frontier of the Union to the Zambezi river. By securing the ports of Delagoa Bay and Beira, South Africa could open up the Transvaal and further the interests of the Afrikaner population, many of whom were still smarting from defeat at the hands of the British in the Boer War of 1899–1902. The war in Europe threatened to deepen their feeling of grievance: the most obvious contribution South Africa could make to the British war effort would be to overrun German South-West Africa (modern Namibia) – a move which would hit a power which had been pro-Boer and which would benefit the status of the English-dominated Cape Town as a port. Smuts's scheme could mollify Afrikaner senti-ment, but it had a big hurdle to overcome: the territory up to the Zambezi was already part of Portuguese Mozambique. Smuts's solu-tion was to conquer German East Africa, keep the northern part for Britain, give the southern part to Portugal, and ask the Portuguese to give the southern part of its existing colony to South Africa.

To achieve this the South Africans were prepared to provide troops to conquer East Africa. But in 1914 and 1915 the South African forces were not free. First, they had to deal with rebellion in their own territory. The idea that Britain was engaged in a war for the defence of small nations did not convince those who had been on the receiving end of the British army in 1899–1902. Second, Britain had asked the Union to seize the harbours and wireless stations of German South-West Africa. The commandant-general of the defence forces opposed the invasion of German territory, and he and other senior officers resigned. Open rebellion flared in October, but the Germans could not give it effective support from across the frontier and it was suppressed by early December. Thereafter the conquest of South-West Africa was carried through in six months.

The South Africans' opening experience of the First World War, in a territory adjacent to their own, was sufficiently like the Boer War to leave intact too many of the assumptions that they had inherited from that war. Smuts had led a commando of about 400 men in the Boer War and in South-West Africa he commanded a column of three brigades. Both campaigns were fought in comparable climates, with the horse as the pivot of manoeuvre. When Smuts took over the East African command at the beginning of 1916, he had a ration strength of 73,300 men deployed for the conquest of a tropical colony, much of it barely mapped. He was a fine leader on a personal level, a man of courage and intelligence, but he had limited command experience and no staff training. None the less, his first step was to dismantle the professional staff that had been put in place and bring in men like himself – South Africans without proper training and devoid of local knowledge. His second was to manoeuvre the Germans out of their colony rather than fight them: 'he told me', Meinertzhagen wrote, 'that he could not afford to go back to South Africa with the nickname "Butcher Smuts".'[13]

The key to his approach was the use of mounted infantry on the lines favoured by the Afrikaners in both their previous campaigns. But horses in East Africa inevitably succumbed to the tsetse fly. The British knew which were the worst regions for fly, because German veterinarians had obligingly supplied them with maps before the war, but this information was not incorporated in the campaign plan. Basic procedures to prolong the horse's life were not observed. Equine wastage ran at 100 per cent per month in 1916.

Smuts's transport services had assumed that he would not begin his advance until after the March–May rainy season was over. They were wrong. Humans succumbed to disease caused by malnutrition as supply collapsed. The medical services were no more integrated in Smuts's organisation than were the veterinary. For men the principal problems were dysentery and malaria, which tended to be debilitating rather than fatal. The 2nd Rhodesia Regiment had an effective strength of 800 men, but with a wastage rate of 20 per cent per month it was often reduced to 100 men. Between March 1915 and January 1917 it deployed 1,038 all ranks in East Africa, and suffered only 68 deaths – 36 in action and 32 from disease. But it had 10,626 cases of sickness, one-third of them from malaria, a largely preventable disease.

By the beginning of September 1916 the results of Smuts's efforts looked impressive on the map. He had reached and overrun the central railway and he had control of Dar es Salaam. But he put no effort into establishing the German port and its communications infrastructure as the base for his push into the south of the German colony. His administrative staff remained at Tanga, and his principal base was still in Uganda, at Mombasa. When he was recalled to London in January 1917 to represent South Africa at the Imperial War Cabinet his forces stood on the Mgeta and Rufiji rivers. He claimed victory, presenting the war in East Africa as all but finished, the result of a great South African feat of arms. In reality, the advance had eventually stalled. The December rains, which Smuts had attempted to ignore, had turned the area between the Mgeta and the Rufiji into a continuous swamp. The Rufiji itself was a torrent hundreds of yards across. The nearest railhead was Mikese, 255 km away. The troops were sodden, hungry and sick. His successor, A. R. Hoskins, postponed any further action until April 1917.

Smuts was determined that his campaign was going to prove the invincibility of the white man. The South-West African campaign had been an affair of whites only. When in 1915 mixed-race Africans had offered to rise in revolt in support of the South Africans, the latter rejected their cooperation for racial reasons. On arrival in East Africa the Boers had dubbed the German askaris 'damned Kaffirs'. Over the course of 1916 Smuts had had to change his tune, at least privately. Africans seemed to have greater resistance to local diseases than Europeans. By the time Smuts left the East African theatre, it was clear that the only way to carry the fighting forward was to use African soldiers. But, by claiming that the campaign was all but over, and by implying that all that remained was to mop up the vestiges of resistance in the colony's remotest corner, Smuts kept the self-esteem of the white man intact.

The Africanisation of the East African campaign was also dependent on the completion of the conquest of the Cameroons. This had taken far longer than anybody on the British side expected – eighteen months – because nobody had appreciated the true nature of German intentions. The British wanted to secure Douala on the coast, the Cameroons' principal port and wireless station, an objective entirely consonant with their original policy of August 1914. By 27 September 1914 they had done so, without a shot being fired. The French in French Equatorial Africa had meanwhile embarked on their own campaign in the south, without approval from Paris. They had two objectives: to recover territory ceded to the Germans in settlement of the 1911 Moroccan crisis, and to take the war into German territory. In the main the Germans in the south of the colony had no forewarning of hostilities, so these initial objectives, too, were soon achieved.

Neither Paris nor London had any desire to conquer the German Cameroons. The problem for both governments was that they did not know how to stop what they had begun. The Germans still controlled the bulk of their colony, and their forces were intact. In 1913 they had drawn up a plan to defend the colony not from its periphery but from its interior. Its focus was Ngaundere in the northern highlands, well defended by nature and agriculturally productive. In the Cameroons, as opposed to East Africa, the German civil authorities remained paramount. So the Cameroons did not become simply a battlefield, sacrificed to the greater struggle in Europe, but was held because its defenders believed in the merits of colonisation, and especially German colonisation, as an end in itself. These assumptions had two implications. First, the Germans could rely on local support, and this in turn gave their defence greater resilience. Second, the initial losses at Douala and elsewhere were not of major strategic significance.

The French and – more particularly – the British never appreciated the underpinnings of German strategy. As a result, their conquest lacked direction and purpose, too often hitting the Germans hard where it did not hurt them. On 10 March 1915 London, in conformity with the original policy of August 1914, told the British commander in the Cameroons, Charles Dobell, to go over to the defensive. But a month previously the governor-general of French Equatorial Africa, M. Merlin, had convened a meeting in Brazzaville designed to wrest control of the French side of the campaign from its column commanders on the spot and impose an overall plan. It adopted Yaounde as the focus of the different advances, so that the columns' efforts should have mutually supporting effects. Merlin's plan was not lacking in sense, but it did of course completely neglect the fact that the Germans' pivot was not Yaounde but Ngaundere. The allies intercepted a signal which revealed Ngaundere's importance on 4 February, but the intelligence was dismissed by Merlin.

Dobell's initial attempt to reach Yaounde failed. The French attacked from two directions, the south, where progress was slow and disjointed, and the east, where it was not. By June 1915 the Germans, cut off from resupply from Germany, were running low on ammunition. Rounds for the 1898-pattern rifle were restricted to use in machine-guns only, and the askaris had to employ older models firing bullets made from spent cases collected from the battlefield, percussion caps fashioned from brass ornaments, and black powder. The smoke gave away their position and the bullets themselves – if they did not get stuck in the breech – rarely ranged more than twenty yards. Even more serious for the Germans was the decision of their commander, Zimmerman, to reduce the garrison at Garua, in the north, so as to reinforce that at Banyo, protecting Ngaundere's western flank. The British operating out of Nigeria were meant to be supporting Dobell's advance by tying down Germans, but they now had an overwhelming superiority and were able to capture Garua on 10 June. The British did not know what to do next. They still assumed that Yaounde was the key to the German defence, not Ngaundere. But Colonel Brisset, commander of a French column in the north-east, persuaded the British to push on to Ngaundere.

None of the British appreciated what had been achieved, any more than did Brisset's French superiors: all saw him as insubordinate and bloody-minded.

Now allied plans and German intentions fell into step for the first time in the campaign. The Germans could no longer use the northern highlands as their lifeline; instead they had to switch to the Spanish colony of Muni (today Equatorial Guinea), and neutral territory. At last Yaounde became the axis of the German line of communications. Forced to pause during the rains, the British and French resumed their converging movement on Yaounde from the west and east on 15 November and 15 October respectively. Movement was also resumed in the north at the beginning of November. Although the columns moved in ignorance of each other, their effects were now reciprocal and on 8 January the British from the north and French from the east linked at the Nachtigal rapids, to the north of Yaounde.

The allies' attention had been focused on the north. They had neglected the south. The Germans' route to neutral territory lay open and they took it. The allied columns were exhausted by their advance: when the French reached Yaounde they were 700 km from their intermediate base at Nola on the Sanga. Short of supplies, their pursuit was dilatory. About 6,000 askaris and 7,000 families and followers followed 1,000 Germans into Muni. From here, the Germans kept alive their hopes that the defeat was only temporary and that German colonialism could be revived.

The allies' victory in the Cameroons released black troops from West Africa for service in East Africa. The Gold Coast Regiment arrived there in July 1916. The four Nigerian regiments of the West African Frontier Force were delayed by worries about possible rebellion within Nigeria, but sailed in November 1916. In East Africa itself, the King's African Rifles, composed of three battalions at the outset of the war, had risen to thirteen by January 1917 – and reached twenty-two by the war's end. Britain never considered using these African troops in Europe, although the French did: in this the British reflected the difficulties their Indian soldiers had encountered from the cold on the western front in the first winter of the war. So Lettow-Vorbeck's contribution to the wider war was undermined.

Lettow-Vorbeck aimed to hold the line of the Rufiji until the crops ripened in April 1917. The supply position of the Germans to his left, to the north of Songea, was also desperate. They split, one column under Georg Kraut going south and the other, under Max Wintgens, going north. Setting off at the end of January 1917 Wintgens led his column clean across the allied lines of communications, and up to the central railway near Tabora. Wintgens, sick with typhus, surrendered on 21 May, but Heinrich Naumann, his successor, held out until 2 September. By then he was right back in the north of the colony. This was a classic guerrilla operation. Naumann's men marched 3,200 km between February and September; they had found a population which was passively supportive; and they had drawn up to 6,000 men away from the main battle.

Lettow-Vorbeck never appreciated what had been achieved: such independence smacked of insubordination not initiative. His own instinct still was to give battle not to adopt guerrilla methods. The British resumed their advance at the end of May, after the rainy season, but under the command of another Afrikaner. Hoskins's delay – given that Smuts had said that the campaign was over – had exhausted London's patience, and he was replaced by 'Jap' van Deventer. The frontal push was supported by thrusts from the coastal ports of Kilwa and Lindi. Lettow met the Kilwa column with head-on battles – at Narungombe on 19 July and at Nahungu in an eighteen-day struggle beginning on 19 September. In the battle of Mahiwa, begun on 15 October and extended over four days, the Lindi force faced eighteen out of Lettow's total of twenty-five available companies. Ground was won and lost up to six times. The British suffered 2,700 casualties out of 4,900 men engaged. Although the German losses were comparatively light (about 600), the battle – the fiercest of the campaign so far – broke Lettow-Vorbeck's force as a combat-ready formation. All its smokeless ammunition was expended, machine-guns had to be destroyed, and only twenty-five rounds remained for each of the older-pattern rifles. However, Mahiwa enabled Lettow-Vorbeck to break contact with the British and on 25 November he crossed the Ruvuma river into Portuguese East Africa (today Mozambique). In July his rifle strength had been 800 Europeans and 5,500 askaris; on 25 November he took with him 300 Europeans and 1,700 askaris. Over 1,000 soldiers had to be left behind because there were no longer the weapons or munitions for them. The last of the *Königsberg*'s guns was destroyed.

Lettow-Vorbeck carried on fighting and marching for a whole year longer. His column, a self-contained community with 3,000 women, children and carriers, was able to exploit the weakness of Portugal's hold on its colony and the incompetence of its forces. Portugal's greater concern was with internal order: the northern parts of the colony had never been properly pacified, and in the south the Makombe in Zambezia rose in revolt in March 1917. The Portuguese turned Ngoni auxiliaries on the Makombe, and suppressed the rising by the end of 1917 by condoning inter-tribal terrorism and slavery. However, Lettow-Vorbeck did not fan these flames for his own ends. He paid for goods with worthless paper currency, and the German doctors attended to the sick – albeit without medicines – but he continued to regard Africa and Africans as neutral bystanders in a wider conflict. Lettow-Vorbeck marched straight through Portuguese East Africa and reached Quelimane on the coast. At Namakura on 1–3 July he defeated a Portuguese–British garrison and plundered large quantities of food and ammunition. He then set off north again, skirted the top of Lake Nyasa, and was in Northern Rhodesia when the war ended. Some of his party had favoured making for Angola, others for Abyssinia or even taking ship for Afghanistan.

In the eighteenth century Britain and France had fought each other in India and America for the control of continents. This was not why war came to Africa in 1914. The powers did not fight to take territory. Indeed, the most obvious immediate effects were to loosen the holds of empires. Most whites in the colonies feared that the sight of Europeans fighting each other would promote rebellion and resistance. Those fears could only grow as local administrators joined up, and as local forces turned from their policing function to that of confronting an external enemy. But such fears proved exaggerated. Where colonial authority collapsed, anarchy was more likely than revolution. In the Cameroons German pastors were interned and German doctors fled to Muni: the French took over much of the colony in 1916 but were in no position to provide replacements. Education collapsed and witchcraft revived. In South-West Africa, the South Africans wisely left the German settlers in place – at least until the peace settlement in 1919.

That settlement completed the last stage of the partition of Africa, allocating the German colonies to the victorious powers. Although it was not an intention at the outset, the war promoted imperialism – even if the ambitions of South Africa were in the end thwarted. Moreover, it was not only the peace settlement that had this effect. Where the campaigns were conducted, white men penetrated areas which they had never entered before. Soldiers spread the cash econ-omy and the market; they mapped; and they created the rudiments of a communications network. Above all, they conscripted men. Traditional patterns of authority were broken down as adult – and not-so-adult – males were taken for the army and for labour. Particularly for those who left Africa, and who were treated with respect in Europe, the war could open the door to political aware-ness: 'We were not fighting for the French', Kamadon Mbaye, a Senegalese, recalled; 'we were fighting for ourselves [to become] French citizens.'[14] The long-term consequences would be the emergence of modern resistance movements to colonialism. But immediately colonial rule was deepened and extended in order to serve the war efforts of the belligerents.

The Entente powers wished to stabilise their hold on their empires by closing down the global war outside Europe. But the demands of the war within Europe meant that instead they had to mobilise overseas resources almost as much as domestic resources in order to wage it. That in turn was more a reflection of Germany's success in extending its own frontiers within Europe, rather than outside it. In 1916 the South Africans went to France, and reports of Senegalese cannibalism were propagated to terrify the Germans at Verdun. The efforts of Spee and Lettow-Vorbeck may have been contained, but Germany's idea of weakening the Entente by widening the war did not stop there. Through an alliance with the Ottoman empire, Germany aspired to lead Muslims to war not just in Africa but across the Middle East and Central Asia.

4

JIHAD

The German–Ottoman Alliance

> O Muslims, who are the obedient servants of God! Of those who go to the *Jihad* for the sake of happiness and salvation of the believers in God's victory, the lot of those who remain alive is felicity, while the rank of those who depart to the next world is martyrdom. In accordance with God's beautiful promise, those who sacrifice their lives to give life to the truth will have honour in this world, and their latter end is paradise.[1]

In Constantinople, capital of the Ottoman Empire, the Sheikh-ul-Islam declared an Islamic holy war against Britain, France, Russia, Serbia and Montenegro on 14 November 1914. He spoke on behalf of the Caliphate, a combination of spiritual and temporal authority claimed by the Sultan, and justified by the fact that the holy cities of Mecca and Medina fell within the purlieus of his rule. But the reach of the Ottoman Empire, which at its height in the sixteenth century had extended from the Persian Gulf to Poland, and from Cairo to the gates of Vienna, was contracting. In 1914, of 270 million Muslims in the world in 1914, only about 30 million were governed by other Muslims. Almost 100 million were British subjects; 20 million were under French rule, most of them in North and Equatorial Africa; and another 20 million were incorporated in Russia's Asian empire. Those Muslims in the British, French and Russian empires who opposed the Ottoman Empire's summons to holy war were promised 'the fire of hell'. The Muslims in Serbia and Montenegro, who were likely to commit the lesser offence of fighting Austria-Hungary, would merit only 'painful torment'.

This was a call to revolution which had, it seemed, the potential to set all Asia and much of Africa ablaze, forcing the Entente powers to forget the war within Europe as they struggled to hold on to their empires outside it. The message was translated into Arabic, Persian, Urdu and Tatar. It was carried to the Crimea and Kazan, and through Central Asia to Turkestan, Bokhara, Khiva and Afghanistan; it went to India and China; it extended south-east to the Shi'ite Muslims of Iran; and in Africa its call was heard in Nigeria, Uganda, the Sudan, the Congo and as far south as Nyasaland. But its reverberations were minimal. The First World War may have been a war in which men were motivated by big ideas, but that of Islam failed to override the loyalties of temporal rule.

For many the true author of holy war was not the Sheikh-ul-Islam but Kaiser Wilhelm II of Germany. In 1898 Wilhelm had visited Jerusalem and Damascus. His love of uniforms and military ceremonial, which looked faintly ridiculous to the cynics of the liberal West, struck a chord in the East. He was dubbed 'Haji' Wilhelm, implying that he was a 'saint' who had made the pilgrimage to Mecca. His reaction when he heard of Britain's warnings to Germany on 30 July 1914 was to write angrily: 'Now this entire structure must be ruthlessly exposed and the mask of Christian peacefulness be publicly torn away . . . Our consuls in Turkey and India, our agents, etc., must rouse the whole Muslim world into wild rebellion against this hateful, mendacious, unprincipled nation of shopkeepers; if we are going to shed our blood, England must at least lose India.'[2] Moltke, the chief of the general staff, agreed with him. On 2 August he wrote to the Foreign Ministry calling for revolution in India, the heart of the British Empire, and in Egypt, which connected Britain's eastern empire to London via the Suez Canal.

Here was the articulation of Germany's strategy for world war: it would weaken the Entente powers by attacking them indirectly through their empires. Moltke's problem was that the German army and German weapons were all fully committed to the war in Europe.

He had no rifles he could send to those who might rise against British, French or Russian rule, and certainly no troops. And, even if he had had them, British naval supremacy meant that he could not send them by sea. The Ottoman Empire could confer two strategic benefits on Germany: its army could provide the troops for overseas deployment and its land mass could open the overland routes to Central Asia and Africa.

In some respects the Ottoman Empire bore a superficial resemblance to its western neighbour, Austria-Hungary. Like it, it was a multi-national concern in an age of nationalism, and it also possessed a monarchy in need of reform. In 1914, the empire was still geographically extensive, running from the Caucasus in the north to the Persian Gulf in the south, and from Iraq in the east right across North Africa in the west. For practical purposes, however, it had lost its grip west of the Sinai Desert, except in the case of Libya, where it was actively supporting the local population in their continued resistance to the Italian invasion of 1911. In Europe the Balkan wars had left it with no more than a toe-hold in Macedonia. It seemed that before long this once-mighty multi-national empire would be shorn of its outlying possessions and reduced to the Anatolian heartlands that constitute modern-day Turkey. None of the great powers necessarily wished to initiate this final collapse, but all were preparing themselves for the eventuality.

Germany, Britain, Holland, France, Italy and Austria-Hungary were represented on the Ottoman Public Debt Commission, an attempt to consolidate Turkey's overseas borrowing, which by 1878 consumed 80 per cent of Turkish state revenues. But none of the powers intended to be marginalised from other forms of profiteering within the Ottoman Empire through this process. The privileges given to foreign businessmen in the days of Ottoman might – exemptions from Turkish law and taxation, called 'capitulations' – prevented any increase in tariffs to protect nascent Turkish industries from cheaper imports or the generation of state wealth from exports. Between them Britain and France controlled most of the Ottoman Empire's banking and financial system as well as its debt.

While the great powers exploited the empire, they also staked out their claims in anticipation of its demise. France jockeyed for position in Syria and Palestine. Britain had interests in Iraq, both as a buffer for India and because of the discovery of oil: its first oil-fired battleship, HMS *Queen Elizabeth*, was laid down in 1912. Italy had already taken the opportunity of Turkey's troubles in the Balkans to seize Libya and the Dodecanese in 1911–12. And although Rome's hold in North Africa was shaky, its actions were condoned by Britain and France for fear of driving Italy back into the embrace of Germany and the Triple Alliance. Turkey's most inveterate enemy, Russia, with which it had gone to war three times since 1828, lacked economic and maritime clout, but because it, too, was now linked into the security system of Europe through the Entente neither France nor Britain was likely to oppose it in its Ottoman policy. It wanted control of the Dardanelles, through which a third of its exports (and three-quarters of its grain) passed, and it seemed to sponsor the nationalisms not only of the Balkans but also of the Caucasus. Georgians, Armenians and Tatars straddled the frontier and threatened the stability of both empires: Russia's solution, Russification, was defensive, but that was not how it looked to Turks, concerned for the survival and even promotion of Turkish culture.

Each of the main actors, with the exception of Russia, had managed to secure a holding position. The British became advisers to the Turkish navy in 1908, and the French administered the gendarmerie. The Germans had a military mission, although the defeats in the Balkans had dented its – and its parent army's – reputation. But in the desperate circumstances of the Balkan wars, the Turks could not afford a change of style and ethos, and in 1913 they invited Germany to send a fresh military mission. Its head, Liman von Sanders, had been passed over for the command of a corps in Germany, but was determined that he would enjoy in Turkey the status and pomp which such an appointment would have conferred on him at home. Initially, he was not disappointed. He was asked to command Ottoman I Corps in Constantinople. The Kaiser told him to Germanise the Ottoman army, and to make Turkey an instrument of German foreign policy and a counterweight to Russia. The Russians were outraged. But they mistook the Kaiser's rhetoric for the substance of German foreign policy. The purpose of the mission was to recoup the German army's image of professional excellence and to secure the market for arms sales, especially Krupp's quick-firing artillery. It was not to prepare the ground for Turkey's entry to a European war as Germany's ally. Hans von Wangenheim, Germany's ambassador in Constantinople, saw an accommodation with Russia as a more important priority than an alliance with the Ottoman Empire. On 18 July 1914 – with the German foreign ministry all too aware of the Austrians' designs for war in the Balkans – Wangenheim reported that, 'without doubt, Turkey is still an unsuitable alliance partner. They only want their allies to take on their burdens, without offering the slightest gains in return . . . The policy of the Triple Alliance must be to shape relations so that, if the Turks should after years finally become a major power, the threads will not have been cut.'[3]

If Turkey had any appeal as an ally it lay in its military prowess. The Janissaries had taken Islam into Europe and North Africa, but military excellence now seemed, on the evidence of the defeats in the Balkans, to be firmly in the past. Only weeks before the outbreak of the war, on 18 May 1914, Moltke concluded that 'any expectation that Turkey will be of value to the Triple Alliance or Germany in the foreseeable future must be counted as entirely wrong'. Germany's ambassador had just reported that recovery from the last Balkan war and the completion of the reforms required would take a decade to effect: a new war before then could only put the whole programme in jeopardy.[4]

Germany did not want Turkey as an ally, but Turkey desperately needed an ally somewhere, to reconstruct its position in the Balkans, and it sought an alliance with Bulgaria in order to isolate Greece. It could not hope to achieve that without the patronage of one of the great powers. There was no obvious candidate. Each increasingly tended to subordinate its Turkish policies to its perceptions of the needs of the alliances of which it was a member. The French and

British were pro-Greek, and yet the King of Greece was a Hohenzollern and so related to the Kaiser. Austria-Hungary was interested in establishing a new Balkan league around Bulgaria, to the extent that it risked war with Serbia to achieve it. Therefore Austrian and Turkish interests in the Balkans might converge. But Germany was opposed to Bulgaria. The fact that Russia did not possess a viable Black Sea fleet (not a single up-to-date battleship was ready to take to the water) did give Turkey some freedom of manoeuvre. It even sounded the Russians out as possible allies in May 1914. Sergey Sazonov, the Russian foreign minister, was so taken aback that he did not know how to respond. In July 1914, the Turkish naval minister, Ahmed Cemal, attended the French naval manoeuvres off Toulon, and took the opportunity to float an alliance with France. But the French were too conscious of Russian sensitivities to respond. Thus, in the months immediately before the war the Turks were more open to an alliance with a member of the Entente than of the Triple Alliance. Britain was not approached largely because Turkey had proposed the idea three times in recent years – in 1908, 1911 and 1913 – and been rebuffed on each occasion.

Germany now began to look less unattractive than anybody else. Germany was not a major player in Asia Minor; it could not threaten Turkey's coastline or its interior; and it had no Muslim colonies to create a clash of interests with Islam – at most about 2 million Muslims lived under German rule. Thus the initiative for a Turco-German alliance came from Turkey, not Germany, and the fact that the offer was made on 22 July 1914 – the day before Austria-Hungary delivered its ultimatum to Serbia – was fortuitous. It had no connection to the July crisis proper but it did have one feature in common with it: the driving force was the situation in the Balkans. The Ottoman Empire hoped that an alliance with Germany would boost its appeal to Romania and Bulgaria, and so provide the basis for a new Balkan bloc.

If Turkey's aims were long-term, regional and unrelated to the war that was about to engulf Europe, Germany's response most emphatically was not. Again, Wilhelm was the driving force. A Balkan grouping of the sort to which Turkey aspired would transform the position of Austria-Hungary and the balance of forces on the eastern front. Moltke's military nonentity suddenly became capable of attacking Russia. Liman von Sanders reckoned that the Ottoman Empire would soon have four or five corps ready to take the field. On 2 August a deal was struck. But Turkey did not enter the war.

In 1908 a group called the Young Turks had staged a revolution in Turkey which in many respects was no revolution: the Sultan had stayed on his throne, and the Young Turks did not themselves seize power. They were in origin a group of westernisers and liberals, many of them émigrés, but within Turkey they were mostly army officers and civil servants. The two elements united under the umbrella title of the Committee of Union and Progress. The professional grievances of the army officers, motivated particularly by promotions from the ranks, were deepened in 1909 when a battalion based in Constantinople mutinied. The officers dressed up the rising as a counter-revolution. Under the guise of restoring order, the army, orchestrated by Mustafa Kemal (the future Atatürk), declared martial law, consolidated the hold of the Committee of Union and Progress, and replaced the Sultan.

The Committee of Union and Progress was an amorphous body, and the course of Turkish politics ran no more smoothly after 1909. By 1912 the Unionists seemed to be a spent force. They were saved by the crisis of the First Balkan War. As the army fell back towards Constantinople in December, it seemed that the government would accept the loss of Adrianople (modern Edirne) in a bid to get peace. On 23 January 1913 a thirty-one-year old officer, Enver Pasha, stormed into a cabinet meeting at the head of a group of soldiers. The minister of war was shot dead and the grand vizier forced to resign. Enver asked the Sultan to form a coalition government under a senior general, Mahmut Şevket. An attempted counter-coup and Şevket's assassination in June allowed the Committee of Union and Progress to consolidate its hold on power. Adrianople, which had been lost in March, was recovered in July. Even success in foreign affairs seemed to flow from the Unionists' assumption of power.

America's ambassador, Henry Morgenthau, described Enver as 'almost dainty and feminine ... but always calm, steely, imperturbable'.[5] In January 1914 he became minister of war. During the course of the year he expanded the ministry's responsibilities by placing under it the Committee of National Defence, which had interests in the state's social and economic mobilisation, and ranged from industry to education. Enver had made his reputation in organising Libyan resistance to the Italian invasion, and from that experience he forged a secret service, the Teşkilât-i Mahsusa, answerable only to him. It engaged in propaganda, subversion, sabotage, and terrorism. It was the agent of political conformity to his will at home and of revolution abroad. Enver joined Cemal and Mehmed Talât in government; these three constituted the triumvirate that took the Ottoman Empire into the First World War and guided its destiny during it.

The immediate beneficiary of the Unionists' grasp on power was the army. The appointment of Liman von Sanders's mission was part of a wider package of reform. Older officers were forced out in a major purge, and political unity imposed. New equipment was ordered from Germany. German methods were also evident in the adoption of a regional corps organisation and a new recruitment law which widened the obligations of military service to embrace all non-Muslims who did not pay taxes; in the past only Muslims had been required to serve. The size of the army was now projected to rise to 1.2 million. But this was a long-term programme: in February 1914 Enver reckoned it would take five years before the army was fit for war. And he meant a Balkan war, not a world war. The army lacked a common language and was short of 280 guns and 200,000 rifles. It lacked horses for its cavalry and pack animals for its transport. It was mobilised in August, following the alliance with Germany, but the process was still not complete in October. Reservists were sent home again because they could not be fed. But in the latter month the British military attaché, Francis Cunliffe-Owen, filed a report which suggested that Enver's reforms had begun to take effect: 'There is no doubt that very considerable progress is being made in [the Ottoman army's] efficiency, and that it will be far superior to that in existence before the Balkan war. The continuous training . . . and the time which has elapsed for the deliberate organisation of mobilisation and administrative arrangements must cause the Turkish forces to be now regarded as a factor . . . to be taken seriously into account.'[6]

What worried the British more than the Ottoman Empire's army was its navy. The absurdity of Britain's naval mission in Turkey was that, if it were successful, it would create a body to counter the Greeks and the Italians in the Aegean, and the Russians in the Black Sea. The former may not have been allies, but the British rather wished they were, and the latter most certainly were. The British advised the Turks to acquire torpedo boats for coastal defence, but, after the humiliations at the hands of the Italians and Greeks in 1911 and 1912, the Turks wanted super-Dreadnoughts. They ordered two from British yards. Legally, the terms of the contract allowed the British to take over the vessels, and they did so on 29 July 1914. Strategically the decision was the right one; politically the outcome was a gift to Young Turk propaganda, because the purchase of the ships had been funded by a high-profile public subscription.

The significance of the British action was compounded by British naval incompetence. When the war broke out, Germany had two cruisers, *Goeben* and *Breslau*, under the command of Wilhelm Souchon, in the Mediterranean. The Mediterranean Fleet detached four armoured cruisers under Rear-Admiral Ernest Troubridge to track the Germans, but Troubridge's guns could not match those of the *Goeben*, and, in tears, Troubridge broke off an action round Cape Matapan. He had instructions from the Admiralty not to engage 'superior force', which almost certainly meant not the *Goeben* but the Austro-Hungarian navy in case it sallied out from its Adriatic base to shepherd the German cruisers to safety. In the same vein the remainder of the Mediterranean Fleet failed to support Troubridge, but guarded against the Germans breaking back to the Adriatic or even the western Mediterranean. Only the light cruiser HMS *Gloucester*, although out-gunned, continued the pursuit. *Goeben's* boilers gave her problems; 'the coal-dust, irritating, penetrated the nostrils, caking the throat. The lungs only inhaled with great difficulty under the pressure of the frenzied effort. A crust of coal formed in the throat causing a dry cough.'[7] Boiler tubes burst, sending scalding water over the stokers, and killing four of them. But as the German vessels entered the Aegean, *Gloucester* gave up. She was running out of coal, her crew was exhausted and the Greek archipelago provided too many opportunities for a German ambush. In London both the Admiralty and the Foreign Office knew by now that the eastward course plotted by the German cruisers was not a feint, but they did not correct the misapprehensions of their vessels in the Mediterranean. At 5 p.m. on 10 August the two German ships anchored off the Dardanelles and were then ushered into the safety of Constantinople.

Their arrival should have forced Turkey out of its neutrality. That was what the Germans hoped, not least because in some senses they replaced the two Dreadnoughts due from Britain. In practice the replacement was almost too direct, as they became Turkish ships and the German crews were taken into the Ottoman navy. The crew struck the German flag, put on fezes, and observed Friday, not Sunday, as their day of rest. Churchill, as First Lord of the Admiralty, felt humiliated and treated the Turks as enemies henceforth. He told Troubridge to sink the *Goeben* and *Breslau*, whatever flag they sailed under. Britain's respect for international law and for neutrality had its limits. It blockaded Turkey, which given the latter's reliance on coastwise communication deepened its economic woes. The foreign secretary, Sir Edward Grey, tried to build a pro-Entente Balkan alliance around Greece, and its implicit enemy could only be Turkey. And the India Office worried about the Persian Gulf, where Arab revolution threatened the status quo and therefore the outer ramparts of the defence of India. An Indian division, or Indian Expeditionary Force D as it became, was readied for Mesopotamia from late September, ostensibly to secure the Admiralty's oil supplies.

Ideally, Britain would still have preferred to keep the Ottoman

Empire out of the war rather than push it in, but nothing it did served that aim. Those in Turkey's government who espoused neutrality found little to support their policy. Although outnumbered in the cabinet, the triumvirate was eventually able to engineer hostilities. On 29 October the Turkish fleet, including the German ships, and commanded by Souchon, attacked the Russian Black Sea ports in obedience to secret orders from Enver. The Ottoman Empire had entered the First World War.

The Caucasus

The Germans thought it had done so in order to pursue their agenda; in reality it had its own. The Young Turks, as remodelled and refined by Enver and his ilk, were modernisers. Their goals were administrative efficiency. What attracted them to Islam was not religion but expedience. The summons to holy war did not call on the Muslims under German or Austro-Hungarian rule to rebel; Italy, whose invasion of Libya and the Dodecanese had given the greatest recent offence to Ottoman interests, was not mentioned, in the hope that it would still honour its obligations to the Triple Alliance. Politics were more important than faith, and nationalism than Ottomanism. The loss of territory had modified the multi-nationalism of the Ottoman Empire. As Anatolia became more obviously the heartland of the state, so pan-Turkism flourished. Pan-Turkism defined nationalism in terms of culture and sentiment more than ethnicity or even geography. So a movement whose origins were linked to the contraction of frontiers became a voice for their expansion. Turkic peoples were identified in the Caucasus, Azerbaijan, Turkestan, Persia and Afghanistan. 'For the Turks', wrote Ziya Gokalp, professor of sociology at the University of Istanbul, 'the fatherland is neither Turkey nor Turkestan; their fatherland is a great and eternal land: Turan.'[8]

The rhetoric of pan-Turkism pulled the Ottoman army towards the Caucasus. Across the mountain range lay a polyglot population of Georgians, Armenians and Tatars, whose shifting loyalties had generated Russia's most persistent frontier problem throughout the nineteenth century. Russia's solution was both military and political: conquest had been accompanied by Russification and by the forced repatriation of Osman Turks. Here the Ottoman army could pose as both the liberator of oppressed Turkic peoples and the instrument of jihad. Moreover, it would not only unite these ideological strands but would also fulfil its alliance obligations. Offensive operations here would prevent Russia redeploying its three Caucasian corps to the Central Powers' eastern front.

In reality divisions between the allies were evident from the outset. The Germans sponsored Georgia's independence, not its incorporation in the Ottoman Empire, and favoured a limited attack, not the advance on Afghanistan and India about which Enver was grandiloquently speaking by the end of November. 'In December', according to Felix Guse, a German staff officer with the Ottoman 3rd Army in the Caucasus, 'there are heavy falls of snow, which last three to seven days, and which leave behind snow one to two metres deep in the valleys and three to four metres deep on the mountains, totally blocking many roads.'[9] The Ottoman base for operations was Erzurum, almost 100 km from the frontier and ten times that from the railhead linking it to Constantinople. Guse favoured short leaps after careful preparations; Enver decided on deep envelopment with immediate effect. He argued that the more exposed the route, the more it would be swept clear of snow. His aim was to encircle the Russians at Sarikamish on Christmas Day 1914, and he directed his left hook on Ardahan, almost 100 km further on. His units were short of boots and groundsheets, and those with the deepest snow to traverse were instructed to leave their packs and greatcoats behind. The mildest temperature in the entire operation was −31°C. The Turks' supplies ran out on 25 December. The Russians held Sarikamish and then counterattacked in the first week of the new year. The 3rd Army was shattered. Its total casualties were at least 75,000 men, and some estimates rise as high as 90,000. The majority fell not in battle but to the terrain, the climate, the supply situation and the lack of medical care. The blow to the notion of holy war, at least in this quarter of the Ottoman area of operations, was devastating, and that to pan-Turkism scarcely less so.

By 23 January 1915 the 3rd Army mustered 12,400 effectives, or possibly 20,000 in all. The Turks tried to recoup the situation by striking out to the east, towards Persian Azerbaijan and Tabriz, hoping to provoke the Kurds into rising against the Russians. But they, not their enemies, were to prove more susceptible to the uncertain loyalties of the region.

Russian intentions for the spring were limited: to push from Kars in a southerly direction, west of Lake Van, and so secure their Persian flank. Six provinces of eastern Anatolia contained populations which were Armenian and therefore Christian, although in none of them were they in a majority. Indeed, the forced migration of Turks from Russia had reduced their profile proportionately, while at the same time elevating the affront they presented to both militant Islam and pan-Turkism. In 1894–6 Armenian revolutionary activity had culminated in violence which had been bloody and protracted. Moreover, it was a movement which enjoyed Russian patronage. In 1914 both Sazonov, the foreign minister, and the governor-general of the Caucasus sketched out plans to foment revolt. At least 150,000 Armenians who lived on the Russian side of the frontier were serving in the Tsar's army. Enver persuaded himself that his defeat at Sarikamish had been due to three units of Armenian volunteers, who included men who had deserted from the Ottoman side. The Ottoman 3rd Army knew of the Russian intentions and anticipated problems as early as September. Its soldiers began murdering Armenians and plundering their villages in the first winter of the war. On 16 April 1915, as the Russians approached Lake Van, the region's Ottoman administrator ordered the execution of five Armenian leaders. The Armenians in Van rose in rebellion, allegedly in self-defence. Within ten days about 600 leading members of the Armenian community had been rounded up and deported to Asia Minor.

In the confused and uncertain situation on the ground, the issue of immediate responsibility for what followed is now almost impossible to unravel. The Ottoman army's discipline, already weak, was not best served by defeat on the battlefield and inadequate supply arrangements. Looting and pillaging were aids to survival as well as instruments of terror. It was operating in conjunction with Kurds, who were as ready to spill Armenian blood as any Anatolian Turk. On the other hand, any fears they may have had of an enemy in the rear, not uniformed and ready to operate in an underhand way, did not lack foundation. The best that could be said of the Armenians' loyalty to the Ottoman Empire was that it was conditional. The responses of their community leaders in 1914 were characterised by *attentisme*, and the possibility of a rising in the Turkish rear was one which the Russians were ready to exploit. Significantly, the first note of international protest was prepared by Sazonov as early as 27 April, although it was not published until 24 May. In it he claimed that the populations of over a hundred villages had been massacred. He also said that the killings had been concerted by agents of the Ottoman government.

This became the crux. On 25 May 1915, Mehmed Talât, the minister of the interior, announced that Armenians living near the war zones would be deported to Syria and Mosul. His justifications for the decree were rooted in the needs of civil order and military necessity, and it was sanctioned by the Ottoman council of ministers on 30 May. The latter included provisions designed to safeguard the lives and property of those deported. But three days earlier the council had told all senior army commanders that, if they encountered armed resistance from the local population or 'opposition to orders ... designed for the defence of the state or the protection of public order', they had 'the authorisation and obligation to repress it immediately and to crush without mercy every attack and all resistance'.[10]

It is impossible to say precisely how many Armenians died. Part of the problem is uncertainty as to how many were living in the Ottoman Empire in 1915 in the first place. Calculations range from 1.3 million to about 2.1 million. The difficulty of dispassionate analysis is compounded, rather than helped, by the readiness of Armenians and others to use the word 'genocide'. In terms of scale of loss such a word may be appropriate: estimates approaching a million deaths are probably not wide of the mark. In terms of causation the issue is more complex. The initial violence was not centrally orchestrated, although it was indirectly sanctioned by the pan-Turkish flourishes of Enver and others. Once it had begun, it did, however, provoke the very insurrection that it had anticipated. The violence of war against the enemy without enabled, and was even seen to justify, extreme measures against the enemy within. By this stage – late May 1915 – the Turkish leadership was ready to give shape to the whole, to Turkify Anatolia and to finish with the Armenian problem. It defies probability to suppose that those on the spot did not take the instructions from the council of ministers as *carte blanche* for rape and murder. The hit squads of the Teşkilât-i Mahsusa set the pace. This was most certainly not a judicial process, and it did not attempt to distinguish the innocent from the guilty or the combatant from the non-combatant. The American consul in Erzurum, Leslie Davis, reported from Kharput, the principal transit point, in July that 'The Turks have already chosen the most pretty from among the children and young girls. They will serve as slaves, if they do not serve ends that are more vile'.[11] He was struck by how few men he could see, and concluded that they had been killed on the road. Many thousands of Armenians also succumbed to famine and disease. Mortality among the 200,000 to 300,000 who fled to the comparative safety of Russia rose to perhaps 50 per cent, thanks to cholera, dysentery and typhus. The Ottoman Empire, a backward state, unable to supply and transport its own army in the field, was in no state to organise large-scale deportations. The Armenians were put into camps without proper accommodation and adequate food. Syria, whither they were bound, was normally agriculturally self-sufficient, but in 1915 the harvest was poor and insufficient to feed even the Ottoman troops in the area. The situation worsened in the ensuing years of the war, the product of the allied blockade, maladministration, hoarding and speculation. By the end of 1918 mortality in the coastal towns of Lebanon may have reached 500,000.

Moreover, in 1915 eastern Anatolia was not the only area of the Ottoman Empire subject to invasion. Indian Expeditionary Force B had moved beyond Basra in a push up the Tigris towards Baghdad, and in the west the capital itself was under threat as the Entente mounted an attack on the Dardanelles. Suspect peoples were moved from other potential combat zones: the Armenian population in Cilicia, which was canvassed as the target of an Entente amphibious operation, and the Greeks along the Bosphorus were also deported. The Turkish army was engaged in a desperate defensive battle on three fronts. Ostensibly it had the strategic advantage of interior lines. Its enemies were approaching from different points of the circumference, were a long way from their home bases, and were having to operate on sea lines of communication. The Turks, by contrast, could move troops and supplies along the chords within the circle. But such logic assumed that the Ottoman Empire had a satisfactory system of internal transport. It did not. The Berlin-to-Baghdad railway was not complete. It had still to cross the Taurus and Amanus mountains in southern Anatolia, and the track from Aleppo to Baghdad had barely been begun. The Mesopotamian front was even more isolated than the Caucasian, and insurrection any-where in the interior could only result in the collapse of the entire system. Desperate situations begat desperate responses.

Gallipoli

As the battle of Sarikamish had reached its crisis, on 1 January 1915, the Russians appealed to the British to launch a diversionary oper-ation against the Turks. Lord Kitchener, the British secretary of state for war, was not optimistic, not least because the small British army, depleted by the fierce fighting at Ypres on the western front in November, was fully committed in France. But he recognised that if such an operation were to be mounted its best choice of target would be the Dardanelles, 'particularly if . . . reports could be spread at the same time that Constantinople was threatened'.[12] Kitchener had opened a door wide enough for his counterpart at the Admiralty to force entry.

Winston Churchill had been chafing at the bit since the war's beginning. Wireless telegraphy had enabled him to intervene in operational matters, not always with the happiest of results, as the fates of Cradock and Troubridge testified. But it had not abated his thirst for battle. To his chagrin, more action had come the army's way than the navy's, and he felt particularly keenly the humiliation the senior service had suffered at the hands of the Turks. Here was an opportunity to right the situation. In its pre-war planning, the navy had considered the possibility of amphibious assaults against Germany on the Baltic coast; to apply these principles to Turkey and the Dardanelles seemed logical not only to him but also to Jackie Fisher, restored in August 1914 as First Sea Lord.

In operational terms the project was guided by a great deal of wishful thinking. When he was commander-in-chief in the Mediterranean in 1904, Fisher had concluded that storming the straits was 'mightily hazardous'. In 1906 the army's general staff had studied the problem and the then war minister, Richard Haldane, had reported that 'there would be a grave risk of a reverse, which might have a serious effect on the Mohammedan world'.[13] And in 1911 Churchill himself wrote that 'it is no longer possible to force the Dardanelles, and nobody should expose a modern fleet to such peril'.[14] Neither the navy nor the army held the key to success. The navy would depend on a sizeable landing – estimates ran between 75,000 and 100,000 men – to deal with the shore defences and so open up the narrower part of the channel, and the army would be reliant on the navy's big guns to provide it with the fire support it would need to effect a lodgement in the first place.

The operational difficulties did not, however, invalidate the powerful attractions of the scheme in terms of grand strategy. It was an undertaking suited to Britain's military capabilities – a large navy and an army ill adapted to the mass warfare being played out in western Europe. Kitchener was right: for a diversion to have maximum effect, the Gallipoli peninsula was the place. It was home to the Ottoman

1st Army, essentially the empire's strategic reserve, and a landing would prevent those troops' redeployment elsewhere. Moreover, his suggestion that success might open the way to Constantinople with further wide-ranging consequences was not as far-fetched as some of the campaign's critics have contended. Grey, the British foreign secretary, thought military action might provoke a coup d'état in the Ottoman capital: given the instability of Turkish politics in the years preceding the war, as well as the divisions on the issue of entry to the war itself, this was hardly a unreasonable expectation. British intelligence offered a bribe of £4 million. Offering cash was not in itself misplaced: the Ottoman public debt was evidence of that. The real difficulty was that the Germans had just handed over £5 million.

Moreover, success at Gallipoli might have repercussions in two directions. Both the Central Powers and the Entente were actively competing for allies in the Balkans. Indeed, the possibility that Greece might side with the British in August 1914, and that therefore its army would be available for use against Turkey, was what had first triggered the Gallipoli idea in Churchill's mind. Victory in the region would give substance to British approaches to Bulgaria and possibly Romania. For the first time in the war, therefore, the Western allies would give real succour to the hard-pressed Serbs. To the east, forcing the straits would open a warm-water route to Russia. Both the British and the French were convinced of the latent power of the 'Russian steam-roller'. It seemed to them that Russia had the men to mount the more effective challenge to the Central Powers if only it had the arms with which to equip them. Britain could either provide munitions direct or use its credit in the international market to buy them overseas. Little wonder, then, that many Germans thought the Dardanelles campaign was the most important of the war in 1915. The Foreign Ministry was particularly concerned that its ambitions in the Balkans and Germany's route to the wider world via the Ottoman Empire would be forfeit. But its worries were shared by some members of the army, even if their focus was more Eurocentric: 'It seems to me', Wilhelm Groener wrote in his diary on 9 March 1915, 'not impossible that the Dardanelles question could give the whole war a different direction.'[15] Groener was the general staff's head of railways. He thought that, if the allies' supply route to Russia was opened, Romania would join the Entente, and Russia would defeat Austria-Hungary.

These ends outstripped the means the Entente had available. The Anglo-French alliance of 1904 was predicated on an acceptance of the two powers' respective spheres of influence in the Mediterranean and North Africa. The Dardanelles expedition threatened to undermine this delicate balance by re-establishing British predominance in the Mediterranean, especially given French long-term designs on Syria should the Ottoman Empire implode. The French navy shared the view that the scheme was impracticable, but neither the naval minister nor the French government as a whole was disposed to be left behind if the British were going ahead. The real constraint was the attitude of Joffre, who, as commander-in-chief in France itself, argued that he needed every available soldier, French or British, for the western front. Théophile Delcassé, the architect of the Entente and the French foreign minister, wanted to delay until troops were available, but Churchill would not. The upshot was that the efforts of the navy and the army were conducted in succession, not in combination.

The Turks had plenty of warning that a naval attack up the narrows might be a possibility, and with German help had done much to improve their defences. 'My first impression', the American ambassador, Henry Morgenthau, recorded of a tour of the defences, 'was that I was in Germany. The officers were practically all Germans and everywhere Germans were building buttresses with sacks of sand and in other ways strengthening the emplacements.'[16] As British and French warships entered the straits, they were vulnerable to mines. Therefore the mines had to be swept first, but minesweepers had to cope with the fire from the batteries and a fast current flowing from the direction of the Black Sea into the Mediterranean. The result of these interlocking problems was that naval enthusiasm for the scheme waned, particularly that of Fisher and of the naval commander on the spot, Admiral Sackville Carden.

However, Churchill remained determined and on 18 March an attempt was made to 'rush through' the straits using warships in daylight. Carden fell sick on the morning of the attack, and his deputy, Admiral John de Robeck, described what happened as a disaster. Three ships – two British and one French – were sunk by mines. Churchill maintained – as have others – that if the attack had been renewed on the next day it would have succeeded, because the Turks were running low on munitions. They were not. In any case, de Robeck had not abandoned the idea of a naval operation; gales prevented any action over the next five days. What de Robeck did accept was that the navy should operate in conjunction with the army – so that the batteries could be attacked from the landward side.

The landings on the Gallipoli peninsula on 25 April 1915 were therefore not seen as the cue for the navy to hand over the attack to the army. The army relied on ship-based artillery support, but the navy confronted considerable technical difficulties in providing it. The maps it was using were inaccurate; the ground itself steep and intersected; and observation of fire inadequate. There were too few aeroplanes in the theatre, and the orders to the navy's shore-based observers specifically instructed them to direct fire at targets a safe distance from allied soldiers. Despite all this, naval gunfire could be enormously effective. But the Turks learnt to neutralise it by attacking at night or at first light, when observation was difficult, or by keeping their trenches close in to the allied positions to maximise the risk to the British from 'friendly fire'. On 25 May German submarines sank HMS *Triumph* and on 27 May HMS *Majestic*. All capital ships were withdrawn to port, and only destroyers with 4-inch guns remained to support land operations. The navy's major contribution thereafter was also submarine – sinking the Turkish merchant vessels supporting the troops on the peninsula; the Turks lost half their merchant fleet in the campaign.

Sir Ian Hamilton, the British general given charge of the British, French and imperial forces, was a sixty-two-year-old protégé of Kitchener, who had seen extensive service in colonial wars. He later attributed his failure to insufficient manpower and material. The impression was created that his small force was taking on the might of the Turkish army in its own backyard. But Hamilton did not complain about the manpower situation at the time, and he would not really have been justified if he had.

The Dardanelles area was commanded by Liman von Sanders. He expected a landing at Bulair across the neck of the peninsula. But Hamilton had rejected this option precisely because the aim was to open the passage for the ships, and Bulair was both a long way from the Dardanelles batteries and a difficult place for the navy to give fire support. He therefore chose to put his main forces ashore along the tip of Cape Helles. The French mounted a diversionary attack on Kum Kale on the Asiatic side of the straits. Further north, on the Aegean side of the peninsula, the Australian and New Zealander Army Corps went ashore behind Hamilton's immediate target, the Kilid Bahr range. Originally slated for Europe, they had stopped in Egypt for training when the war with Turkey was declared. There they earned a reputation for mayhem and indiscipline, mingled with combativeness and high morale, which was to last throughout the war.

Gallipoli has been defined as the moment when Australia came of age as a nation. This was largely the work of C. E. W. Bean, who managed to get himself accepted as Australia's war correspondent, rather than as the representative of an individual newspaper. Bean was born in Britain and was educated at the same English public school, Clifton, as Douglas Haig. In being a first-generation Australian he was little different from most of the Anzac soldiers on whom he reported. They fought not for Australia or New Zealand but for the 'old country', with which they still had strong ties of kinship and sentiment. Moreover, most of them were city-dwellers, not the bronzed 'diggers' from the outback of popular legend. Nor were they necessarily more natural soldiers than any other troops in this war. Morale came close to collapse on 25 April. The landings at Z beach were poorly managed, with too many troops clustering towards the north, in what became known as Anzac Cove. The result was congestion and administrative chaos. Moreover, here the

Turkish reaction was vigorous and swift. Disregarding Liman von Sanders's orders to wait until he could be sure about the direction of the main attack, Mustafa Kemal committed his whole division to holding the high ground above the beaches. 'I knew – I don't know how, but one guessed from the way those guns were firing at all of ours, that the troops were being very severely tried', Bean wrote in his diary of that afternoon's fighting. 'It was sickening to hear it.'[17] Many unwounded Anzacs were making their way back to the beaches, and both the corps' divisional commanders favoured re-embarkation. They were overruled, not least because the navy said evacuation was impossible. There were tensions, too, at lower levels of command. A New Zealand lieutenant-colonel, William Malone of the Wellington Battalion, thought that the Australian commanding officer commanding the unit alongside his should have been court-martialled and that his men were 'a source of weakness'. When the Australians were relieved on 28 April, he wrote: 'It was an enormous relief to see the last of them. I believe they are spasmodically brave and probably the best of them had been killed or wounded. They have been, I think, badly handled and trained. Officers in most cases no good.'[18]

The problems at Anzac Cove were not reproduced at most of the main beaches at Helles. Against their expectations, the British got ashore with comparative ease, except at V beach. The Turks were in disarray, held back by Liman von Sanders's orders. But the failure to exploit the opportunity with a rapid follow-up to the landings condemned the allied advance to a stalemate comparable with that which had now established itself on the western front. Successive attacks on Krithia, a village on the forward slopes of the high ground of Achi Baba which dominated the peninsula, failed. As the Turks built up their defences, so trench warfare asserted itself. The differences from the western front were the products of the terrain and the climate. The narrow and steep foothold on the shore meant that the positions had little depth, and that the only relief was to go for a swim in the sea. But the heat that made that an attractive option also brought flies and then disease, particularly dysentery; water supplies were a constant headache. Only 30 per cent of British casualties in the campaign were sustained in battle.

The allies' forward bases were on the islands of Imbros and Lemnos, and those further back in Egypt and Malta. On the hospital ships the nurses were women. One, a New Zealander called Lottie LeGallais, wrote in September, 'it was dreadful, and what with fleas and crawlers my skin at present is nearly raw, but we all scratch – scratch – except the men patients poor devils, they are used to them'. In November a transport was torpedoed, and LeGallais reported on the fate of the nurses. 'Fox they say her back was broken, another nurse both legs; Rattray had two nurses keeping her up for hours, they were holding on to spars & with hands crossed these girls kept Rattray up until she became mental & died of exhaustion.'[19]

The respect that built up between the allies and the Turks should not be exaggerated. There were armistices to collect the dead. But snipers when captured were regularly shot out of hand, as were other prisoners. One French officer, Jean Giraudoux, wrote on 13 June 1915, 'The Australians massacre all the Turks: the Australian's national enemy, one of them said to me, is the Turk'.[20] Nor could British prisoners necessarily expect any better treatment. Some Ottoman soldiers, uprooted from inner Anatolia, thought they were off to fight Greece, a traditional enemy, but others were like Hasan Ethem, who wrote to tell his mother that he had prayed: 'My God, all that heroic soldiers want is to introduce thy name to the French and English. Please accept this honourable desire of ours and make our bayonets sharper so that we may destroy our enemy! . . . You have already destroyed a great number of them so destroy some more.'[21]

On 6 August Hamilton tried to relaunch the campaign with a thrust from the Anzac positions designed to secure the high ground of the Sari Bair ridge. Only Chunuk Bair was captured, by Malone's Wellington Battalion, but it could not hold the forward slope and Malone himself was killed by friendly naval fire. Simultaneously a landing to the north at Suvla Bay was designed to support the attack on Sari Bair by capturing the high ground adjacent to it, and by establishing a new port for the navy to use. When the Anzac attacks miscarried, Hamilton presented the Suvla thrust as the principal one and found a scapegoat for his setback in its dilatory corps commander, Sir Frederick Stopford.

The idea of evacuation had been bruited before the Suvla landings; after their failure it grew in force. 'Raining tonight', Bean wrote in his journal on 26 August. 'I think our hardships will really begin with the winter – though I must say that, by the way in which the Tommies, who come here from elsewhere compare their lot as enviable, I am not sure that we haven't been greater heroes than we were inclined to think of ourselves.'[22] The story of the evacuation at the end of 1915 is traditionally told as one of excellent staff work and successful deception, an effort to salvage some relic of self-respect from defeat. But, for all the difficulties of disengaging from an enemy in the field, the key point remains that it was hardly in the Turks' interests to prolong the allies' departure or to incur further losses needlessly. The Turks had 86,692 dead; the French suffered 10,000 more than the Australians, whose deaths totalled 8,709, a low number by the horrific standards of this war; the French dead were less than half those of the British. New Zealand's losses were smaller still, 2,721.

It was not only Australian and New Zealand national identity that was forged at Gallipoli, it was also Turkey's. This was a major victory, less for the Ottoman Empire than for the ethnically and geographically more defined state that emerged from the First World War. Moreover, although many of the architects of the defensive battle were German, it produced a Turkish hero who became the founder of that state, Mustafa Kemal. It was he who was accorded the credit for rallying the Turks at Anzac on 25 April, and it was he whose men had checked Malone's New Zealanders at Chunuk Bair on 8 August.

Mesopotamia

In Entente counsels what militated against evacuation from Gallipoli was not the effects within Turkey but the wider political ramifications within the Muslim world. In Mesopotamia, too, the British forces had overreached themselves. Easy victories at the outset had spurred on the ambitions of Sir John Nixon, the commander on the spot. Grandiose notions of a converging movement linking with the Russians coming down through Persia and Azerbaijan did not help. But the real difficulty was that Nixon was not subject to firm direction. In London, the general staff at the War Office was cautious, anxious not to overcommit itself so far from the main theatre of operations in Europe. But the campaign was less the responsibility of the War Office and more that of the Government of India: it provided the bulk of the troops. Indian official opinion was divided. On the one hand, it was attracted to control of Mesopotamia in order to secure India. Moreover, a major victory against the Turks would settle Muslim sentiment in the subcontinent, an argument which grew in force as the setbacks on the Gallipoli peninsula mounted. On the other, this argument cut two ways: another setback in the war against the Turks would be disastrous for British prestige in the Islamic world.

Ambition overrode caution. The British general staff estimates of 60,000 troops being sent to reinforce the Ottoman 6th Army were grossly exaggerated, even after the Turks had cleared the threat to the Dardanelles. The Turks had about 17,000 men in Mesopotamia at the outset of the war. By the winter of 1915–16, the 6th Army mustered 25,000 men. It had no heavy artillery and it was four to six weeks' march from Constantinople. In March 1915 Nixon enjoyed at least a two-to-one superiority, and he was authorised to occupy the whole province of Basra up as far as Kut al-Amara, a town on a bend of the Tigris, and at its confluence with the Shatt al-Hai. With Kut secured by the end of September, Nixon now pressed for an advance on Baghdad itself. His forward divisional commander, Sir Charles Townshend, had become a national hero in 1895, when he was besieged in Chitral on the North-West Frontier of India. Townshend was reluctant to go on. He had reached the limit of his logistical capabilities. His medical arrangements were inadequate and the navigation of the Tigris down to Basra was impeded by low water. But most important of all he was doubtful of the quality of his Indian troops.

In July 1914 the government of India said it could provide two divisions and one cavalry brigade for use outside India. In the event Nixon's command was one of four expeditionary forces it sent overseas. India enlisted over a million men during the course of the war, but in so extending itself it strained both its infrastructure and its recruiting base. When Townshend reached Ctesiphon (or Selman Pak) on 22 November 1915 his units were one-third below their establishment. The Turks fought a successful defensive action. However, Townshend's decision to fall back on Kut was a reflection of his waning confidence rather than of any Turkish superiority. At Ctesiphon almost half his British officers were sick or wounded, and the lack of officers had two direct consequences for his force, as well as for its relief when it found itself besieged in Kut. First, staff work collapsed. Townshend himself failed to form a proper estimate of his food position or of how long he could hold out. Back at Basra, a divisional staff could not be formed for the three brigades that arrived in January 1916. Second, junior leadership declined and morale with it. Townshend was reluctant to breach religious scruples regarding diet for fear of worsening the spirit of his troops, but he could not prevent 147 of them deserting during the course of the siege. Rather than fight his way out, he waited for relief which did not arrive. The winter rains now raised the water level of the Tigris, so aiding navigation but rendering operations along its banks extraordinarily difficult: 'the entire surface of the land', Abdul Rauf Khan, serving with an Indian field ambulance, wrote, 'becomes a quagmire in which the slush is knee deep'.[23] The relieving force could not envelop the Turks in its path: it was tied on one flank to the river that provided its transport, and it lacked the manpower to stretch out into the slush to get round the other. Four attempts resulted in 23,000 casualties, almost twice the strength of the Kut garrison.

For Nixon the siege of Kut was a means to other ends: the British forward base for its advance into Mesopotamia and the pivot of a massive allied envelopment involving the Russians swinging through Persia. It similarly acquired a dual significance for the Turks and Germans. In October 1915 the septuagenarian German general

Colmar von der Goltz was given the command of the 6th Army. His mission, Enver told him, was 'to prepare an independent war against India'.[24] Von der Goltz's primary objective was not to re-establish Ottoman control of lower Mesopotamia but to keep the route open through Persia and Afghanistan. He was to carry the holy war to the heart of the British Empire. It was a task which revealed the dependence of the Turkish–German alliance on achieving pragmatic congruities despite divergent aims. Berlin promoted Persia's independence; Constantinople sought its subjugation. The capture of Kut provided a short-term priority which glossed over the differences in long-term strategy.

Kut fell on 29 April 1916. Townshend and 13,000 men went into a captivity from which very few of them returned. Townshend was an exception, living in comfort overlooking the Bosphorus for the remainder of the war. Britain's humiliation in the Middle East and Central Asia was complete. Its worst fear, that of resurgent Islam in the empire, seemed to be about to be realised. 'For me', von der Goltz had written home, '. . . the hallmark of the twentieth century must be the revolution of the coloured races against the colonial imperialism of Europe.'[25] In 1916 the novelist John Buchan produced *Greenmantle*, one of the best-known of what he called his 'shockers'. In some ways its plot seems far-fetched and unconvincing; in reality it was very close to the truth. At the time Buchan was working for the War Propaganda Bureau, the press arm of the British Foreign Office. In his novel, the hero, Richard Hannay, is briefed by Sir Walter Bullivant: 'There is a dry wind blowing through the East, and the parched grasses wait the spark. And the wind is blowing towards the Indian border. . . . We have laughed at the Holy War, the Jehad that old von der Goltz prophesied. But I believe that stupid old man with the big spectacles was right. There is a Jehad preparing.'[26]

Buchan's novel concerns spies and skulduggery. So did German methods and British counters. Fiction and fact were closely intertwined. A German expedition crossed Persia to reach Kabul, in a bid to persuade the Emir to raise an army for the invasion of India. German consuls in the United States bought arms for shipment to

Indian revolutionaries. Their agents penetrated nationalist movements throughout North Africa and Central Asia, and their propaganda was disseminated from locations in Constantinople and neutral Bern. And yet there was no holy war. The Muslim soldiers of India remained loyal to the British. Moreover, the defeats at Gallipoli and Kut overshadowed a far more significant albeit limited victory, the successful defence of the Suez Canal against Turkish attack in February 1915 and July 1916. The key waterway linking the British Empire to the east with that in the west was held, and the threat of revolution in Egypt was contained. Germany's global strategy was checked.

One explanation for the Central Powers' failure was that ideologies were on the cusp. The force of religion, on which holy war relied, was declining, while that of nationalism was not yet as developed or as powerful outside Europe as it was within. The Young Turks played both cards, as did the Germans, but in doing so they sent a message that was contradictory. Islam was universal in its appeal, while nationalism was particular. Moreover, the nationalism of the Young Turks translated into imperialism when carried beyond the frontiers of Anatolia. It therefore conflicted with the message of genuine independence that the Germans wished to convey. But Wilhelmine Germany was tied to the coat-tails of Turkey. It could never become a force to undermine overseas imperialism when it itself lacked the military clout to translate promises into deeds. The British, as well as the French and Russians, were right to take the danger seriously. In doing so, they warded it off – at least for the time being.

5

SHACKLED TO A CORPSE

East Prussia

> The religion of Muscovite imperialism is primitive and medieval, literally half barbaric. Its peasant and national culture belong overwhelmingly to the same inferior category – if they are not wholly and purely Asiatic . . . Not only the perceptions of law, but also all morality and all social feeling belong to a backward west and central Asian type, not a European one . . . Therefore France's and Britain's alliance with Russia against Germany and Austria-Hungary is an alliance not only against Germany and Austria-Hungary, but also against the inseparable joint life interests of all Europe.[1]

These words, published in 1915, are those not of a German but of a Swede, not of a conservative but of a socialist. However, in 1914 they were sentiments which both rallied Germans of all political persuasions and convinced them that they were in the vanguard of civilisation. Socialists and trade unionists might feel beleaguered in Germany, but they knew that they would suffer far more under the heel of tsarist autocracy. The defence of what they had gained for the working class, both politically and materially, now required them to protect the nation. When the German Socialist Party met on 3 August 1914 to discuss its stance on the war, the time for prevarication was past. Germany was already at war with Russia and France. It resolved to vote in the Reichstag in favour of war credits. It hoped that, by opting for collusion rather than confrontation with the Reich, it would secure constitutional reform, but its decision was unconditional.

The plight of peasants in East Prussia justified the socialists' stance. Although the Russian cavalry proved inept in its reconnaissance, in mid-August its leading formations pushed into German territory. One of its officers, Vladimir Littauer, later admitted, 'The scene on the German side of the border was . . . frightening. For miles, farms, haystacks, and barns were burning . . . Like every army under the sun, we looted and destroyed, and later hated to admit it.'[2] On 23 August Max Hoffmann, chief of operations with the German 8th Army, wrote in his diary: 'There has never been such a war as this, and never will be again – waged with such bestial fury'.[3] On the same day refugees arrived in Berlin with reports 'of heads being cut off, children being burned, women raped'.[4] As in the case of atrocities in Belgium, rumour and then propaganda ran ahead of reality, but the reports from East Prussia rested on less secure foundations. After the war the Germans' official history claimed that within four weeks the Russians had killed 1,620 civilians, but in 1915 they themselves had put the figure as no higher than 101. Moreover, there is no evidence that, in this invasion, unlike those of Belgium and Serbia, the high command deliberately used terror in a preemptive strike against civilian resistance. 'The wish of the Tsar of all the Russias', the commander of the Russian 1st Army, Paul Rennenkampf, instructed, 'is to take care of the peaceful inhabitants'.[5] However, the supply arrangements of the Russians had been neglected before the war and collapsed as soon as they started their advance. They subsisted by plundering, and what they could not take with them they destroyed. As elsewhere, mobile warfare generated its own horrors.

The Bosnian crisis of 1908–9 had convinced the Russians that the Austrians would not go to war without German support. But this belief did not resolve the issue of how to deploy their forces. When the Russians had first allied themselves with France, in 1890, they anticipated that the Germans would strike east first, before turning west. The French alliance would therefore guard Russia's back while it dealt with Austria-Hungary. Russia's defeat at the hands of Japan in 1904–5 and the subsequent revolution had two effects. First, it encouraged Russia to concentrate its forces in the heart of the country, so that it could confront threats in Asia as well as in Europe: Poland, Russia's westernmost territory and vulnerable to envelopment by Germany from the north and by Austria-Hungary from the south, was abandoned. Second, Russian weakness permitted the German general staff to plan on striking France before it turned east to face Russia. The result was that the boot was now on the other foot: France needed Russia to hit Germany from the east as soon as possible so as to relieve the pressure in the west.

In 1911 the French general staff had asked the Russian army to attack the German army by the fifteenth day of mobilisation. The request was problematic. Russia had insufficient railway track in relation to its vast size to complete its mobilisation so quickly, especially given its abandonment of Poland. Moreover, the war plan it had adopted in 1910, although it was certainly weighted towards Germany rather than Austria-Hungary, was primarily defensive in orientation. Between 1910 and 1914 Russia increased the number of trains it could send westward from 250 a day to 360, but by the fifteenth day of the war only half the infantry was mobilised and no more than twenty-seven out of 114 divisions were concentrated. In 1912 the chief of staff of the Kiev military district, M. V. Alekseyev, pointed out that the army of Austria-Hungary in Galicia was more beatable than that of Germany, and that Poland provided the opportunity to attack across the upper reaches of the Vistula against its flank and rear. But that assumed that the French would bear the strain against Germany. The result was compromise. The 1912 Russian war plan had two variants, Case A for Austria-Hungary using three armies (but in the event four) and Case G for Germany employing two armies. In 1914 both were implemented. Two more armies were kept in reserve, and in due course they gave rise to a third variant. Successes to the south against Austria-Hungary in Galicia and to the north against Germany in East Prussia would secure the flanks of Russia's Polish salient. A thrust from Poland to Posen would open the most direct route to Berlin. This second stage was what would give unity to Case A and Case G, and it exerted a powerful pull on the Tsar's lanky uncle, Grand Duke Nikolay, when he assumed the command of the armies on the outbreak of the war.

Geography intended the Russo-German frontier for defensive warfare, not offensive, and both sides had worked on that assumption. Russian defensive planning had deliberately left the area south of East Prussia devoid of roads and railways. But this was the way that the Russian 2nd Army now had to come as it aimed to envelop the German 8th Army and cut it off from its line of retreat across the lower Vistula. The Masurian lakes, which screened the central and south-eastern section of the frontier for over 100 km, separated the 2nd Army from its partner, the 1st Army, which was intended to fix the Germans frontally between the lakes and the fortified city of Königsberg (today's Kaliningrad). As the 2nd Army advanced, its front extended to left and right – the left reaching deep into Germany and towards the Vistula, egged on by the aspirations of Grand Duke Nikolay's third variant, and the right bidding to make contact with the 1st Army. The latter fought the Germans in defensive positions at Gumbinnen on the River Angerapp on 20 August, but Rennenkampf then paused to consolidate and resupply. The German 8th Army was free to break contact; by 23 August only a single cavalry division faced the Russian 1st Army.

As he was fighting the battle of Gumbinnen, the commander of the German 8th Army, Maximilian Prittwitz und Gaffron, received an aerial reconnaissance report saying that elements of the Russian 2nd Army were in Mława. Prittwitz's first reaction was panic. At 7 p.m. on the 20th he ordered the 8th Army to fall back on the Vistula. His response was ill calculated. The Russians were already closer to the Vistula than he was; he could not save the situation by retreat. Moreover, the territory that he proposed to give up was German; it ill behoved the much-vaunted German army to abandon its own citizens to Russian occupation. Prittwitz's superior, the chief of the general staff, Moltke, had told him: 'When the Russians come, not defence only, but offensive, offensive, offensive'.[6]

These instructions were not as absurd as the raw balance of forces suggested. The Germans had 158 battalions of infantry, 78 squadrons of cavalry and 774 guns to face a Russian force of 354 battalions, 331 squadrons and 1,428 guns. In addition, thanks to Manchuria, the Russian army had the advantage in recent combat experience: this was the first time the German army had been to war for over forty years. But East Prussia was where the German general staff had learnt its craft in staff rides and manoeuvres. It knew the ground, and Schlieffen had taught it that in a defensive battle the Masurian lakes provided the opportunity for operations on interior lines. In other words, the lakes would separate the Russians, while the railway network would allow the Germans to redeploy behind the lakes along the short chord from north-east to south-west. Max Hoffmann and Colonel Grunert, the 8th Army's quartermaster, set out to persuade Prittwitz that, 'it was necessary to stop the advance of the Warsaw [2nd] Army, and that the best way of doing this would be through an offensive thrust against the left wing of that army'.[7] I Corps on the left wing of the German front at Gumbinnen should move by train to the right wing of XX Corps, which faced the Russian 2nd Army's left; the other two corps at Gumbinnen should march directly westwards to the 2nd Army's right wing. Prittwitz was won over, but his conversion was too late to save his career. Moltke's headquarters at Koblenz had taken soundings with all Prittwitz's corps commanders, none of whom favoured the retreat to the Vistula. Moltke therefore dismissed Prittwitz and his chief of staff. In their stead he appointed a retired veteran of the 1866 war against Austria, Paul von Hindenburg, now aged sixty-seven, and, as Hindenburg's chief of staff, Erich Ludendorff. Ludendorff had been Moltke's chief of operations, but had lost his job when his outspoken advocacy of full conscription had upset conservative sensibilities. He was bourgeois and careerist, and his allegiance was less to the Kaiser than to his own ambition. In Hoffmann's estimation, 'He is the right man for this business – ruthless and hard'.[8]

Ludendorff's capacity for self-promotion had already secured him the credit for the fall of Liège. His own contribution had been the flamboyant seizure of the undefended citadel rather than of the forts that ringed it: the latter had ensured that Liège had held out five times longer than the forty-eight hours Ludendorff had predicted. Now luck favoured him once more. He inherited a manoeuvre which others had planned but which would bestow on Hindenburg and himself the victors' laurels.

Not the least of Hindenburg's functions – both now and through-out the war – was to settle the nerves of his anxious subordinate. Ludendorff was worried that Rennenkampf would resume his advance, and therefore delayed the departure of the two marching corps for a day. The effect was to lead the Russian 2nd Army on, broadening its front and deepening the sack into which it was plung-ing. General Aleksandr Samsonov, its commander, deprived of direct communication with Rennenkampf, and so unaware of his slowness, was buoyed by anticipation of success. On the evening of 26 August he invited the allies' military attachés to dinner 'and as we started sent back Postovski to get his sword, remarking that he was now in an enemy's country and must be armed. . . . There was a dramatic incident in the middle of the meal. An officer brought in a telegram . . . and said that the GOC 1st Corps wished to speak on the telephone with the Army Commander or the Chief of Staff. General Postovski put on his pince-nez, read the telegram, and he and General Samsonov buckled on their swords, said good-bye to the Commandant, and left at once.'[9]

Samsonov's supper had been disturbed by reports of the arrival of the German I Corps on his left flank. Its commander had refused to obey Ludendorff's order that he go into action on the morning of the 26th, so adding to the chief of staff's vexation but deepening the envelopment when he did at last advance on the morning of the 27th. On Samsonov's right flank the two German corps entered the battle at the same time as he was sitting down to dinner.

> As we at the head of the column came out of the dreadful wood, a shower of infantry fire suddenly hailed down on us. Lieutenant-Colonel Schulz stopped a bullet in the temple and fell like a board, but he soon came to, swore frightfully and asked for a cigarette. Meanwhile we had brought up artillery from the wood, and the

Russian rabble, leaving behind a number of rifles and packs, beat a hasty retreat, back into the darkness from which it had emerged. It was now fortunately midnight, pitch dark . . . The greater part of the marching column was still stretched along the narrow road through the wood. In a word, there was no alternative than to fall out where we were . . . So we dozed in half-sleep till first light. Finally it cleared and it became apparent that the enemy was in full flight towards Ortelsburg.[10]

Although the Russians acknowledged that the situation was changing rapidly on the 27th, Samsonov continued to underestimate the strength of the Germans facing him and to order movements calculated to worsen the predicament of the 2nd Army rather than extricate it. On 29 August, with his army losing cohesion in the woods and with his command collapsing through lack of intelligence and inadequate communications, Samsonov confronted the reality. He went off into the forest and shot himself. By 31 August the Germans had taken 92,000 prisoners and nearly 400 guns; 50,000 Russians were dead or wounded.

The Russian feeling of inferiority when confronted by German troops, as opposed to Austro-Hungarian, persisted for the rest of the war. The Germans vengefully named their victory after the village of Tannenberg, where the Teutonic Knights had been defeated by the Poles in 1410. The symbolism of the battle was more important than its strategic effect. Victory where the Germans had not expected it (in the east) was used to cover over its absence where it was actually most needed (in the west). Hindenburg and Ludendorff were elevated as national heroes. The long-term political effects in a constitution as ill-developed as that of Germany were enormous: these men became to the domestic politics of Wilhelmine Germany what Napoleon Bonaparte was to Revolutionary France. And their success convinced them that the war would be won on the eastern front. It was twice the length of that in the west, and its force-to-space ratio made for lower troop densities, so creating more opportunities for manoeuvre. Hindenburg and Ludendorff saw Tannenberg as confirmation that

Schlieffen's teaching was right. The answer to the tactical imponderables of the modern battlefield was envelopment. What had been achieved at Tannenberg through pragmatism and an awareness of contingencies became enshrined as dogma.

The reality was that the mass army, with all its supply needs and its artillery, relied on an effective network of roads and railways to sustain its advance. 'The Germans', a Russian guards officer recalled, 'had a line for every army corps and sometimes even for a division . . . Roughly, the Russian army had one line to supply an army of three or four army corps . . . The result was that the jamming of traffic affected the supply of the army, paralysed the evacuation of the wounded and interfered with the bringing up of the reserves.'[11] But once the German army operated beyond its own frontier, it was subject to the same constraints as the Russian. That was precisely the reason why Schlieffen had forsaken his predecessors' predilection for a war in the east and devoted greater attention to Germany's western front.

Tannenberg was a defensive victory. Following up speedily at the battle of the Masurian lakes, the 8th Army drove Rennenkampf back behind the Russian frontier. East Prussia was secure. But the Germans had not given the Austrians the aid they wanted: they had repulsed a Russian invasion but they had not drawn the bulk of the Russian forces away from the Austro-Hungarian front – nor, despite the scale of Samsonov's defeat, had they squashed Grand Duke Nikolay's plan to use Poland as the launching pad for an invasion of Silesia. At the beginning of September Conrad called for the implementation of the Siedlitz manoeuvre, the envelopment of Russian Poland from north and south. This held a double appeal for Hindenburg and Ludendorff: it would conform to their Schlieffenesque concept of operations and it would ward off the fresh threat to German territory. But the allies were now out of step. Conrad had summoned up a scheme to which his own army could not possibly contribute. It was retreating in disorder. By mid-September what he needed was direct assistance, not some ambitious plan hatched on the map and designed to wrap up the eastern front at a stroke.

Then the pressure on the Austro-Hungarian armies eased. Nobody stopped to ask what the Russians were doing. The two allies were able to effect a joint advance towards the Vistula. On 9 October Przemysl was relieved. But the success was deceptive. Grand Duke Nikolay was massing three armies behind the Vistula, ready for his own advance into Poland. He planned not only to provide direct aid to France, but also to consolidate and broaden the Russian victory in Galicia. He, too, hoped to achieve a massive envelopment, and the Germans were walking into the trap. 'On 11 October', wrote August von Mackensen, whose corps was closing in on Warsaw, 'the earlier appreciation of the overall operational situation changed utterly. A Russian order captured on the battlefield at Grojec . . . revealed the views of the supreme Russian command and the deployment of their forces on the entire Vistula front.'[12] The Germans fell back, blaming the Austrians rather than their own intelligence failures, and Przemysl was besieged once more. However, they had escaped the Russian envelopment, and transport difficulties again hampered the Russian pursuit.

Eastern Front v. Western Front

On 30 October Ludendorff travelled to Berlin to meet Erich von Falkenhayn. Nominally Falkenhayn was still minister of war, but since Moltke's disgrace on the Marne he had also been de facto chief of the general staff. Falkenhayn enjoyed the favour of the Kaiser, a factor of crucial importance in the months ahead. He was good-looking, young by the standards of German generals (he was fifty-three), and his career had followed a very different trajectory from those of the general staff officers over whom he now presided. While they were being schooled by Schlieffen, he was serving in China. His overseas service had left him with a strong impression of Britain's maritime and imperial power. Here for him was the hub of the Entente, and therefore the centre of gravity for German strategy. However, the fact that he was not fully part of that enclosed world of operational planning, of staff rides and map exercises, also meant that he had something to prove. His initial response in the aftermath of the Marne had been to seek envelopment through manoeuvre with all the zeal of a true pupil of Schlieffen. Each effort to do so had been thwarted by the French and British armies as they, too, cobbled together forces to extend their left flank northwards and so block German efforts to get into their rear. When Ludendorff and Falkenhayn met, the final stage of this process was being fought out in a vicious and protracted battle at Ypres, the ancient Flemish city whose fortifications guarded the Channel ports.

Six new corps were forming in Germany and Ludendorff appeared to accept Falkenhayn's wish to put them into the Ypres sector. But Falkenhayn, too, seemed to collude in Ludendorff's aspiration to fight envelopment battles in the east. The Schlieffen legacy created mutual misapprehension: at the strategic level it led Ludendorff to acknowledge the priority of the western front over the eastern; at the operational level it led Falkenhayn to realise that great victories were more likely in the east. The eastern front was twice the length of the western, and its armies were more thinly spread over terrain which was less urbanised. The opportunities for manoeuvre were therefore greater. Following the meeting, on 1 November Hindenburg was appointed commander-in-chief of all German troops on the eastern front, with Ludendorff as his chief of staff. The task of OberOst, as the new command was called, was twofold. It was to mount a local counterattack in Poland while Falkenhayn got on with fighting at Ypres, and it was to provide a counterweight to the Austrian high command. Conrad von Hötzendorff blamed the failure in Poland on Hindenburg and Ludendorff, and had made an absurd request for thirty German divisions for the eastern front. The gap between imagination and reality in Conrad's thought now meant that Falkenhayn was not alone in wanting to find a mechanism to curb him. Even Franz Josef wanted him to go.

The formation of OberOst empowered rather than appeased Falkenhayn's critics within Germany. Within two days, on 3 November, the mutual misapprehension between Falkenhayn and Ludendorff had flared into an open hostility which was to deepen over the next eighteen months and divide strategic counsels in Germany. Ludendorff elevated OberOst's limited mission into a massive envelopment battle. It culminated in desperate winter fighting round Łódź in Poland. He wanted more troops. But on 4 November Falkenhayn, now publicly appointed chief of the general staff, renewed the attack at Ypres. It failed, with a total German casualty bill of 80,000. Falkenhayn's response was not to redirect his strategic goals to where the Germans were able to achieve operational solutions. Instead he suggested that Germany abandon any hope of overall success. It was absurd for two conservative monarchies to be fighting each other in a war which could only benefit their real long-term rival, Britain. Germany should therefore seek a separate peace with Russia, so as to be able to concentrate its efforts in the west.

In the context of November 1914 such pragmatism was tantamount to betrayal. Arthur Zimmermann, the under-secretary at the Foreign Ministry, was aghast. He saw the Balkans and Turkey as the strategic crux of the central powers' war effort. This was their route to the wider world; their device to prevent the formation of a hostile Balkan league; and their means to outflank both Britain and Russia. In 1915 he was to be one of those in Berlin whose anxieties were focused on Gallipoli. The Austrians could hardly gainsay such arguments: this was what the July crisis had been all about. But Conrad was now of the view that the solution to the Dual Monarchy's Balkan problems lay on the eastern front proper, with the defeat of Russia: kill the viper, and the contents of the nest would also die. OberOst therefore had powerful allies. Not even the chancellor, Bethmann Hollweg, was on Falkenhayn's side. Although he recognised the force of Falkenhayn's logic, he believed that the Russians were more likely to be brought to the negotiating table if they had first been soundly beaten. Moreover, he – like many senior army officers – was appalled by Falkenhayn's pessimism. Thus Germany's best chance for the formulation of a sensible strategy – the formation of a pact between Falkenhayn and Bethmann Hollweg –

was forfeit. Bethmann Hollweg, whom many British observers at the time counted a closet liberal, delivered himself into the hands of Hindenburg and Ludendorff.

The debate between 'westerners' and 'easterners' in Germany was far more real than the one between soldiers and politicians in Britain that went under the same title. The latter was largely fought out after the war in the pages of their memoirs; this one resulted in the failure of any hopes for domestic political reform and ultimately committed the country to the pursuit of a total victory which it could not achieve. If Germany had possessed more robust allies than either the Ottoman Empire or, more particularly, Austria-Hungary proved to be, the arguments would never have gained such momentum. But their weakness meant that Germany had constantly to bail them out and could never concentrate on the western front to the exclusion of others.

On 25 November 1914 Falkenhayn recognised failure at Ypres and ordered the German armies in the west to abandon manoeuvre warfare and adopt deep, defensive positions for the foreseeable future. But his intention was not to elevate trench warfare into an end in itself; instead, it was a means to an end – the creation of disposable forces for use elsewhere. A systematic defence in the west would enable fewer men to hold the ground. In February 1915 the German army in the west was restructured: every division was reduced from four to three infantry regiments. This combination of tactical and organisational expedients created a strategic reserve for mobile and offensive operations elsewhere.

Falkenhayn had not yet accepted that these attacks would be in the east and when he did – in March 1915 – he did not adopt OberOst's agenda. Hindenburg and Ludendorff dreamt of massive envelopments in northern Russia and the seizure of the Baltic states. Falkenhayn's priority was different: to buttress Austria-Hungary and in particular to finish with Serbia. Success here might sway the neutral powers in the Balkans and could even persuade the Central Powers' nominal ally, Italy, to honour its obligations. But Conrad could not turn to the Balkans while he was under such pressure from the Russians in the Carpathians. Falkenhayn's political judgement was evident not only in his sensitivity to the possible diplomatic consequences of military success but also in his handling of the command issue. The idea for the offensive that followed was Austrian, but its execution was German. The sector chosen, in Galicia, between Gorlice and Tarnow, close to railway communications and free of river lines immediately to its front, lay in Conrad's area of responsibility. He said four German divisions would suffice for the attack, but Falkenhayn offered four corps, and so was able to create a joint Austro-German army group for the first time in the war. He then appointed a German, August von Mackensen, to its command, thus side-stepping not only Conrad but also Hindenburg and Ludendorff. Neither side forgave him. 'I can only love or hate', Ludendorff told Groener, 'and I hate General von Falkenhayn.'[13]

The Great Retreat

OberOst was left out in the cold in more ways than one. Mackensen's chief of staff was Hans von Seeckt. 'It is endlessly less important where Mackensen and the *Bug-Armee* break through,' Falkenhayn said of later operations, 'than that they should merely break through somewhere.'[14] In the conditions created by trench war breakthrough, not envelopment, was the crucial method. Seeckt had refined the technique at Soissons, on the western front, in December 1914. The key was the use of artillery – a short and sudden bombardment aimed to stun rather than destroy, and so less demanding of shell supply. At Gorlice–Tarnow the Central Powers collected 334 heavy guns to 4 Russian, 1,272 field guns to 675, and 96 trench mortars to none. It was the densest artillery concentration of the war so far: one heavy gun every 132 yards and one field gun every 45 yards. The Germans and Austrians could overlook the Russian positions to direct their fire. Their success was aided by the weakness of the Russian trenches compared with those in the west: they were devoid of overhead cover and the whole position – three lines of trenches forming a single defensive zone – lacked depth.

The artillery began its preliminary registration on 1 May. In the early hours of 2 May German patrols went forward to probe for soft spots and destroy the wire, and then at 6 a.m. an intense bombardment opened. At 7 a.m. Hauptmann von Loebell's Guards regiment pushed two of its battalions forward into an abandoned Russian position. At 10 a.m. the artillery lifted, seeking more distant targets and aiming to isolate the battlefield from Russian reinforcements. 'The defenders,' Loebell reported, 'who had suffered little under artillery fire, were ready for the storm, but they did not believe that the storming columns had already broken out from the position, since they had not observed our preparations. When we suddenly came up the slope, they were completely surprised and fired too high, and as a result our losses were amazingly light. My company only lost, in spite of heavy machine-gun fire, three men dead and four wounded . . . We captured six kilometres of ground.'[15] Within two days the Austro-German forces had broken through and within a week the Russians had lost 210,000 men, as many as 140,000 of whom were prisoners of war. Their entire position in the Carpathians was unhinged, and they had to fall back on a 160-km front. Przemysl was retaken on 3 June and Lemberg on 22 June. Mackensen and Seeckt, not Hindenburg and Ludendorff, were the most successful double-act in the German army in the First World War.

Falkenhayn's aims were limited and he had anticipated quickly turning against Serbia. But his stunning success reopened the hopes of a separate peace with Russia. In the north Hindenburg overran the Baltic states, providing cover for Gorlice–Tarnow but also reactivating his hopes for a massive envelopment. Falkenhayn accepted the case for a less ambitious operation with Poland as its focus. The offensive opened on 13 July and German troops entered Warsaw on 5 August. They crossed the Bug in the middle of the month, and captured the fortified cities of Grodno and Brest-Litovsk by its end. Vilna fell on 19 September. Russian losses since May totalled 1.4 million men.

More than half of them were prisoners of war. And that was true for the war as a whole, not just for the summer of 1915. In a major action on the western front casualties normally divided one-third dead, one-third wounded and one-third captured, and, averaged over the war as a whole, the proportion of prisoners of war in relation to total losses was much smaller. The greater fluidity of the eastern front gave greater opportunities for capture. But Russia's casualty profile is also revealing of the morale of the Russian army. Before the war the incidence of strikes – which had both soared in number and become increasingly politicised – peaked in July 1914, and conservatives had warned against war for its ability to stoke revolution. The actual experience of mobilisation suggested that such fears had been misplaced: 'As if by magic the revolutionary disorders had died down at the announcement of war'. In Petrograd (as St Petersburg had been renamed), 'patriotic military fervour had gripped the workmen ... They cheered us enthusiastically as we marched by their factories.'[16] Ninety-six per cent of reservists reported for duty, a rate not far behind that of France. But, as in France, public demonstrations of enthusiasm were urban phenomena, and of all the major armies of 1914 Russia's was overwhelmingly made up of peasants. Their loyalties were regional rather than national. They had crops to harvest and families to feed. Mobilisation prompted rioting in 49 out of 101 provinces [oblast] in European and Asiatic Russia. Russia's great resource in the eyes of its Western allies was its manpower. In 1914 Russia mobilised 6.5 million men, and it could still raise a further 5 million in 1915. But the loyalties of those men were brittle. 'What would be the feelings of these people for their Little Father [the Tsar],' Sir George Buchanan, the British ambassador, wondered, 'were the war to be unduly prolonged?'[17] As the army expanded, its cadres shrank. It had lost 60,000 officers by late summer 1915, and by September 'the number of officers of every kind in the normal division of sixteen battalions and six batteries had fallen to an average of 110'.[18] The surprise, as Britain's military attaché observed, was not that the retreat had been so great but that the army was intact at all.

This did not stop both Britain and France complaining that Russia had failed to maximise its potential. It raised 15 million men in the war, a massive number in absolute terms, but only 39 per cent of its population of military age. France, with a population one-quarter the size of Russia's, drafted 79 per cent of its male population of military age to create an army half as strong. Britain, which did not introduce conscription until 1916, and which argued that its contribution to the war was industrial and economic, still enlisted 49 per cent of its men aged fifteen to forty-nine for military service. Russia's response to its allies' criticisms focused less on its lack of officers and non-commissioned officers for such a massive army and more on its shortage of munitions.

All the belligerents faced a problem converting their industrial bases from peacetime to wartime production. In earlier wars armies had run out of shells because of difficulties with transport and supply. But in the winter of 1914–15 position warfare both eased that constraint on shell consumption and generated more targets for guns to engage. Given time to adapt plant and rejig machine-tools, industrialised societies could adapt to these demands. By late 1915 they mostly had. States struck compromises with capitalist enterprises which both presaged an intervention in the workings of the market and involved an acceptance of its freedom. But Russia had a further hurdle to surmount: it was an industrialising power rather than an industrialised one. Its comparative lack of railways, all too evident to its soldiers as they retreated across Poland and into Belorussia, was a case in point. It demanded help from its Western allies, whose production, particularly that of Britain, it seemed to regard as inexhaustible. But Britain, too, was having to convert its industry to war production and was simultaneously creating a mass army from scratch. Like Russia, it found that getting men was easier than giving them rifles with which to fight. It also wondered how far the aid it gave its ally was actually meeting the immediate demands of war rather than underpinning Russia's long-term infrastructural needs. It was doing both.

The great retreat compounded Russia's munitions difficulties in two ways. First, the army abandoned massive quantities of equipment. At Kovno, the Germans captured 1,300 guns, 53,000 rounds of heavy-artillery shell and 800,000 rounds of field-artillery shell. With the army falling back, the rifles of the dead and wounded could not be collected from the battlefield. 'The further we went', one Russian army commander recalled, 'the greater became the number of weaponless men, and now we no longer knew how to set about training them.'[19] As winter drew in, Prince A. Lobanov-Rostovsky 'saw infantry companies being formed of four platoons, of which two were armed and two were not. In case of battle the two unarmed platoons were to pick up rifles and ammunition from those who had fallen in front of them.'[20] Shortages of equipment in turn affected morale. Second, areas of production were themselves lost. Efforts were made to evacuate businesses, but they were frenzied and haphazard. In Riga firms had fourteen days to dismantle machinery. Once it was loaded on wagons and sent off to the interior, it stayed there, on sidings or even going in circles round the country, rusting in the Russian winter.

All the areas subject to invasion or confronting its threat came under military administration. The principal thought in the mind of the chief of the general staff, Nikolay Yanushkevich, was to scorch the earth, to leave the invaders nothing but wilderness. The effects were not only dire for industry; they were also dire for the civilian population. 'We were forced to burn our homes and crops, we weren't allowed to take our cattle with us, we weren't even allowed to return to our homes to get some money.'[21] By the end of 1915 there were about 3.3 million refugees in Russia. Propertied families had been impoverished; industrialised cities had been stripped of their workforce. In Warsaw the entire population was told to leave, on the grounds that the Poles were supportive of Austria-Hungary. In Vilna the same instruction was issued to all men of military age, and then the city was burnt. The refugees carried and spread disease, particularly cholera and typhus, and as they fled they resorted to looting and pillaging to survive, further jeopardising the authority of the state. The fact that as a result the army compounded the difficulties of its own retreat, clogging an already inadequate transport system, suggests that in some cases its response was more ideological than strategic. It took the opportunity to 'cleanse' certain areas of what it saw as unreliable elements, particularly German settlers, although many of them had relatives serving in the Russian army, and Jews. 'The complete hostility of the entire Jewish population toward the Russian army is well established', one army commander told Yanushkevich.[22]

That would not have been surprising. Several thousand Jews had been killed in pogroms in 1881 and 1905, and many more had been forced by state-supported persecution to emigrate. However, Yanushkevich's anti-Semitism was so extreme as to outrage even Russian opinion, particularly those circles anxious to woo the country's liberal allies, France and Britain. Moreover, the great exodus liberated the Jews from the Pale of the Settlement, the area to the west and south-west to which they had been restricted. The Pale was formally abolished in August 1915, and Jews were free not only to move further east but also to settle in the countryside as well as in the towns. For the Jews of Russia, the war opened doors rather than closed them. In Germany Jews were much more fully assimilated: most saw the war not as an opportunity for Zionism but as a means by which to consolidate their integration in the Reich. Although their alliance with Turkey prevented the Germans from publicly supporting the idea of a Jewish homeland, they did act as the protectors of Jews within the Ottoman Empire. The suspicions of the Russian army, therefore, were not totally without foundation: for Germany's army in the east, the Jews were indeed potential collaborators. The attractions to Germany of an alliance with Islam to undermine the British found its corollary in an alliance with the Jews of Poland and the Baltic states in order to defeat the Russians. A German committee for the liberation of Russian Jews was set up on 17 August 1914, and as the German armies advanced in the summer of 1915 they used Jews as interpreters and as middle-men in the procurement of supplies and transport.

Many German Jews were, however, repelled by the Jews of the east, who not only dressed and behaved very differently from themselves but also were more fervent in their beliefs. 'No, I did not belong to these people, even if one proved my blood relation to them a hundred times over,' wrote Victor Klemperer, who worked in OberOst's press section. 'I belonged to Europe, to Germany, and I thanked my creator that I was German.'[23] Klemperer's reactions were little different from those of most other Germans as they penetrated deeper into Russian territory. First, they realised that the western Russian empire was no monolith, but a hotch-potch of competing and overlapping nationalities and ethnic groupings – including Lithuanians, Latvians, Poles, and Ukrainians. Some of these might be potential allies. Second, the massive territories that they overran seemed backward and even primitive, under-cultivated and sparsely populated. As it assumed administrative and economic responsibility for the Baltic states it occupied, OberOst persuaded itself that 'this area could become a bread basket of wheat and cattle, wood and wool, of the very highest value'.[24] Ludendorff set out on a long-term project to civilise and cultivate Kurland, Latvia and Lithuania on the German model and through the instrumentality of the German army. The eastern front became more than an area for operational manoeuvre; now it was also a sphere for settlement and colonisation, a focus for political ambition as well as military.

The consequences for the population were disastrous. Enlisted in forced labour battalions, they were unable to till their land, and famine struck in the winter of 1916–17. Their resources were plundered to feed both their occupiers and the needs of Germany: Lithuania's wartime exports were valued at 338 million marks, but its imports at 77 million. To the south, Poland was placed under civilian control. However, that did not stop the army, including in due course Ludendorff, spelling out what they felt should happen to it. They wanted to tap its manpower by creating a Polish legion. A Polish army implied the promise of political independence, a solution which would carry the additional benefit after the war of creating a buffer state between Germany and Russia. But Poland had the potential to create a rift between Germany and Austria-Hungary. The latter regarded Poland, or at least its southern part, as an extension of its own lands in Galicia. Worries about exacerbating the nationality problem within the empire, fostered particularly by the Magyars, held it back from the idea of a full take-over, but equally powerful concerns about its overbearing ally prevented it from endorsing a German solution to the Polish question. On 13 August 1915 Bethmann Hollweg agreed to support an Austro-Polish solution, a self-governing state under the Habsburg crown. However, Germany's enthusiasm for the scheme became conditional on the understanding that the Dual Monarchy would itself be subordinated to Berlin. The mechanism for this control would be a central European customs union dominated by Germany, a scheme popularised by the liberal Friedrich Naumann in his book *Mitteleuropa*, published in 1915. These ideas, and their attendant appetites, became firmer as the chances of a compromise settlement with Russia receded: Russia would not negotiate on the basis of Poland's independence and the Baltic states' incorporation in a greater Germany.

The hope that Russia might seek terms had proved illusory. All three Entente powers had pledged themselves not to make a separate peace under the pact of London on 5 September 1914, and in March 1915 the Western allies had promised Russia the long-sought prize of Constantinople and control of the straits if the Entente won the war. By the end of September the German advance had reached its logistic limits. The sandy roads turned to mud as the autumn rains began. Russian railways, built on a broader gauge, had to be converted to German specifications. A total of 434 bridges were constructed in the Bialystok–Grodno area alone. The line stabilised as Falkenhayn expected. Yanushkevich was dismissed and his superior, Grand Duke Nikolay, shunted off to the Caucasus. Against the advice of his ministers, the Tsar took over the supreme command himself, as he had wanted to do from the outset. The survival of the regime now depended on its waging of the war. The difficulty for an autocrat was that many – including industrialists and Western allies – believed that Russia could best tap its potential by liberalisation. Russia certainly rallied in an extraordinary fashion in the winter of 1915–16. Shell production for field guns rose month on month despite the loss of territory and plant, doubling between May and July 1915 to reach 852,000 rounds in the latter month, and 1.5 million in November. Total output in 1915 was 11.2 million rounds, in 1916 28.3 million.[25] The strength of the field army, which had fallen to 3.9 million men in mid-September 1915, recovered to 6.2 million men by February 1916 and 6.8 million on 1 June. Three days later General Aleksey Brusilov launched an offensive in Galicia which showed that the Russian army, too, could master the techniques of the breakthrough battle, and which confirmed its continuing ability to defeat the Austro-Hungarians when they were not supported by their allies.

Italy Joins the Entente

The renewed stabilisation of the eastern front in the autumn of 1915 changed the complexion of Germany's debate on its war aims. Bethmann Hollweg had drawn up a programme of objectives on 9 September 1914. Its content – control of Belgium and north-eastern France, and the suggestion of comparable acquisitions in the east and in central Africa – was relatively constant over the rest of the war, but the context was not. In September 1914, the chancellor was confronted with two possibilities: a quick victory, in which case he would need to know the basis on which he was negotiating the peace, or a long war, in which case the coal and iron ore of north-western Europe would be fundamental to the maintenance of the German war effort. In any event, one idea scouted in the September programme – that German trade might be confined to a central European customs bloc, under German domination – made little sense in the long term. For the world's second largest manufacturer it was a considerable reduction on the pre-war opportunities for trade offered by the open market. However, it reflected two immediate requirements. The first was the expectation that after the war the Entente powers would do their best to close Germany off from world markets. The second was the need to accommodate the ambitions of their allies within an envelope shaped by Germany. As the war lengthened both these pressures increased, while the possibility of a negotiated settlement receded. Therefore war aims hardened and expanded. Given Germany's weak party structure and its under-developed parliamentary system, they became the vehicle for interest-group politics and divisive public debate. They were also less important for what they said about Germany's designs on the enemy than for their evidence of Germany's determination to woo or to appease its allies.

None of the original belligerents in 1914, including Germany, went to war in pursuance of so-called war aims. Most of the war's later entrants did. They exercised choice, and they sold their services to the highest bidder. Between 1914 and 1916 both sets of allies focused their recruiting efforts in the Balkans, broadly defined, wooing Italy, Bulgaria, Greece and Romania. Of these, the most blatant in its exploitation of the opportunities which the war presented was Italy. In October 1914, its prime minister, Antonio Salandra, characterised its policy as '*sacro egoismo*'. His aim was simple, to gain 'frontiers on land and sea no longer open to annexation, and [to raise] Italy, in reality, to the status of a great power'.[26]

The key question for Rome was which side was best placed to deliver what Italy wanted. When General Luigi Cadorna was appointed chief of the Italian general staff in July 1914, following the death of his predecessor, Alberto Pollio, he set about readying the army for war against France. This was entirely in accordance with Italy's membership of the Triple Alliance, but contrary both to the dictates of its geopolitical position and to the inclinations of its government. Geographically, Italy was a sea power, dependent on maritime trade and vulnerable to British naval pressure. Ideologically, the left favoured the Entente. The Italians had had to expel Austria from their peninsula in order to achieve unification in 1860: the relations of the two powers were more naturally characterised by enmity than by cooperation, and the navies they both built before 1914 were designed for use in the Adriatic, and therefore against each other. Salandra had little difficulty in interpreting the Austro-

Hungarian ultimatum to Serbia as an aggressive act, deeming Italy to be free of its alliance obligations and declaring it a neutral power on 31 July. The German defeat on the Marne confirmed for most Italians the wisdom of his move. But they did not necessarily conclude that this would be the last word. Cadorna began to ready his army for war against Austria-Hungary. Italy was now open to the highest bidder.

Germany was prepared to raise the ante, but at its ally's expense. About half the population of the Austrian provinces along the frontier with Italy, from Trieste to Tyrol, were Italian. Although they were both privileged and wealthy by comparison with the Slav population in the region, the latter was growing in numbers. The Austro-Italians turned to Rome. After effectively abrogating the Triple Alliance, Italy was free to respond to their call. Germany wanted Austria-Hungary to solve the problem by giving the Trentino to Italy. The Austrians responded that once they made that sort of concession to one national grouping they would be under pressure to do so to all the others, and the empire would collapse. They argued that they could hand over territory in the south-west of their empire only if the loss was offset by gains in the north-east: they demanded more of Poland in recompense. The internal wrangling between the Central Powers ensured that they lagged behind the Entente in the bidding for Italy. When the Austro-Hungarian common council eventually agreed to cede the Trentino on 8 March 1915, the fall of Przemysl two weeks later promptly led Rome to increase its wants. The Entente offered the Dalmatian coastline as well, a gambit Vienna could not match. Most Italian opinion was neutral, but not vehemently so. The neutralists latched on to the former liberal prime minister Giovanni Giolitti as their spokesman. Liberalism in a country that lacked the economic maturity to sustain its aspirations to great power status had shallow foundations. Giolitti was as ready as Salandra to use the war to promote Italy's expansion at Austria-Hungary's expense, but he reckoned that it could be done without Italy itself having to fight. Salandra was sufficiently aware of Giolitti's challenge to his hold on office to ensure that the jockeying for domestic power increased the stakes. Joining the war on the side of the Entente fused nationalism and liberalism, and even appealed to some revolutionaries. Benito Mussolini split with the Socialist Party to call for war: 'Revolution', he said, citing Napoleon, 'is an idea that has found bayonets.'[27]

Italy adhered to the pact of London on 26 April 1915 and declared war on Austria-Hungary (but not on Germany) on 23 May. The Italian army was not fully prepared for war in Europe, and indeed was still heavily committed in Libya. It was short of 13,500 officers. Although it mobilised 1.2 million men, it had equipment for only 732,000. The problems of its war economy were comparable with those of Russia: it was not a fully industrialised power. In 1912–13, the army had been allocated 47 per cent of state spending, and since 1862 it had received an average of 17.4 per cent. However, Italy's backwardness meant that the actual sums were small. Its re-equipment with quick-firing field artillery had just been completed, but it was short of heavier pieces and of mountain guns. The latter were particularly relevant, given the battlefield it now faced.

Of all the fronts of the First World War the Italian was the most ill suited for offensive operations, or indeed for any form of war at all. The frontier with Austria-Hungary was 600 km long, and four-fifths of it was made up of mountains. Several peaks rose above 3,000m; in the winter they were covered with ice and snow, and explosions could set off avalanches. In the summer the rock made entrenching impossible and sent off jagged splinters when hit by shellfire. Its northern sector was dominated by the Austro-Hungarian salient of Tyrol and the Trentino. Here Italy's task was to hold the passes to prevent the Austrians from debouching onto the Venetian plain. As the frontier moved east it formed a fresh, Italian salient, bounded to the north by the Dolomites and the Carinthian Alps. It then swung due south following the line of the River Isonzo as it made its way to the Adriatic. Even here the Italians were going uphill, in the face of good fields of fire, but this was the logical sector on which to attack. It was the shortest route to Trieste and Ljubljana. Cadorna deployed fourteen of his thirty-five divisions along its 100 km.

Italy's entry to the war caused less panic in Austria-Hungary than it ought to have done. The addition of a third front to an empire which a year before had embarked on a short war on one could only stretch its resources to breaking point. But in the pre-war years Conrad von Hötzendorff had suggested a pre-emptive strike against Italy almost as often as against Serbia. Its treachery in not honouring its alliance obligations confirmed that – in Conrad's words – it was 'a snake whose head has not been crushed in time'.[28] The prospect of war with Italy revitalised the Dual Monarchy. Slovenes, Croats and Serbs could rally against a common enemy, and the success at Gorlice–Tarnow was well timed in relieving the most obvious pressure on the empire. Under pressure from Falkenhayn to give priority to the east and not to divert forces to the Italian front, the Austrians fought defensively – and did so successfully and with determination. 'Will you tell me', Enzo Valentino, an eighteen-year-old volunteer from Perugia, asked his mother from the front on 3 September, 'why you persist in imagining and believing a lot of things which I do not write to you? . . . To be always going forward, and soon to be about to make a great advance? I have never heard anything of all this. As to advancing, it is now a month and a half that I have been up here and *always in the same place*.' In the same letter he reported the first fall of the snow. Seven weeks later he was killed by shrapnel fire, an edelweiss in his cap, as he ran forward, shouting 'Savoia, Savoia, Italia'.[29] Or at least that was what Captain Carlo Mayo told his mother. In four battles on the Isonzo in 1915 alone the Italians made no appreciable progress, suffering 235,000 casualties, of whom 54,000 were dead.

Serbia Defeated

Italy was no nearer achieving its objectives, but in the lapse of time between Enzo Valentino's mother receiving her son's report of the first snow and the news of his death, Bulgaria had gained all that it wanted from the war. Its heart's desire was Serbian Macedonia. The

Entente could not offer that, but the Central Powers could – and did. What held the Bulgarians back was the threats on their other frontiers – the possibility of Romania and Greece joining the Entente, and the dangers of a British and French victory at Gallipoli. By the autumn the success of the Turks and the defeat of the Russians not only removed these dangers but also made it unlikely that Romania or Greece would be persuaded to opt for the Entente. The lamentable Austro-Hungarian record against Serbia was still a consideration. So the Bulgarians made it a condition of their belligerence that the Central Powers attack Serbia from the north first, and that they do so under German, not Austrian, command; they would follow from the east within five days. A military convention to this effect was signed on 6 September.

Falkenhayn thus returned to his original strategy for the east. Neither Austria-Hungary nor Turkey wished to make Serbia a priority, arguing that victory against Russia would settle the Balkans. Falkenhayn reversed their logic: if Serbia was overrun, Russia's foothold in the Balkans would be removed. That would be reason enough for Russia to seek peace, but there would be another. The overland route from Berlin to Constantinople would be opened. Germany could then re-equip the Ottoman armies, enabling them not only to finish off the Gallipoli campaign but also to serve Arthur Zimmermann's schemes for taking the war to the British Empire. Russia's hopes that it might be resupplied through the warm-water ports of the Black Sea would be finished.

Falkenhayn's arguments were also operational. The approach of winter made continued progress in Russia impossible; further south there might just be time for a quick campaign. The rain was already heavy, and the Danube was in spate and in places a thousand yards wide. The Austro-Hungarian attacks of 1914 had been directed across the rivers Sava and Drina, from Bosnia and the west, with diversions from the north. Mackensen, who was given ten German divisions and the overall command, reversed the process, so shortening his lines of communications. Minor attacks along the Drina and a feint to the east at Orsova covered the main thrust from the north. Mackensen's men, supported by heavy artillery and Austro-Hungarian monitors on the river itself, and using the river's islands as staging posts, crossed the Danube between 7 and 9 October. On the 9th Belgrade fell to the Austrians once more, and to the east the German 11th Army began its advance up the valley of the River Morava. The Serbs planned to counterattack, but on 14 October were taken in their eastern flank by Bulgaria. The railway line from Niš to the south and Salonika was cut two days later.

To escape envelopment the Serb army had to retreat either south towards Greece or south-west to Albania. The Bulgarians were in the process of closing off the first route and mountains barred the second. Thomas Troubridge, who had been in command of the British navy's vessels on the Danube, met Radomir Putnik, the Serb commander-in-chief, on 30 October: 'I did not see any disposition to finally despair or any indication of immediately throwing up the sponge'. But the organisational skills of Putnik's staff did not match its chief's resolve. The roads were clogged not just with troops but also with their families and household goods. 'At the Headquarters Mess', a week later, 'at dejeuner there were 30 women & 20 children at least & wherever they move they have all the motors & take with them their servants & furniture & *batteries de cuisine* & everything.'[30] The worsening weather added to the problems of the retreat, but at least delayed Mackensen's forces, so giving the Serbs time to escape the jaws of the envelopment. By 25 November the Serb army was hemmed in on the plain of Kosovo. The path to the south was blocked by the Bulgarians, who were across the River Vardar. Putnik decided that Serbia's future lay not in a climactic battle on this emotive site but in the survival of its army. He ordered a retreat across the mountains to the Albanian coast. 'We slowly creep towards the sheer cliffs of Mount Čakor, step by step on the compacted snow', Josip Jeras wrote in his diary. 'On either side of the road refugees are resting. Immobilized by the snow their heads are glued to their breasts. The white snowflakes dance around them while the alpine winds whistle their songs of death. The heads of horses and oxen which have fallen off the path protrude from the snow.'[31] Following narrow tracks, rising to 3,000 feet, and with the temperature dropping to −20°, the Serbs struggled through snowdrifts and across ice to reach the Adriatic. A hundred and forty thousand got there and were taken off by Entente vessels to Corfu, and thence to Salonika. Of an original strength of 420,000 men in September, some 94,000 had been killed or wounded in action and a further 174,000 were captured or missing. Civilian deaths have not been calculated. The Serbs suffered the greatest losses in relation to population size of any participant in the war.

The Central Powers had now united the two halves of their alliance, creating a direct link from Berlin to Constantinople and enabling in particular the resupply of the troops in the Dardanelles. By contrast, the Entente's stock in the Balkans was at its nadir. In Britain David Lloyd George, now minister of munitions, had favoured sending forces to Salonika not Gallipoli at the start of the year. But Gallipoli shelved such ideas. Belatedly, on 5 October, the French and British agreed that they would each contribute 75,000 troops for an expedition to Salonika. The French were keen to find employment for the most obviously republican of their generals, Maurice Sarrail, and so saw the scheme as a means both to moderate the power of Joffre and the army within France and to help the Serbs. But the expedition had three obvious defects. First, its demands would conflict with the operations at Gallipoli, which were still ongoing even if bogged down. Second, such a large force could not reach Salonika until January, by which time the Serbs would probably be defeated. Third, Greece was still neutral. Lloyd George disingenuously argued that 'there was no comparison between going through Greece and the German passage through Belgium'.[32]

Kitchener, the British secretary of state for war, was inclined to agree: for him the purpose of the Salonika expedition was less to help the Serbs than to provoke the Greeks to do so. Those in Greece who favoured intervention, like the prime minister, Eleutherios Venizelos, could hardly mount a convincing case, given the dire position of the Entente at the end of 1915. Greece had refused to honour its obligation to support Serbia when it was attacked by

Bulgaria, and King Constantine's espousal of continued neutrality was entirely pragmatic and realistic. The British cabinet was told that 'His Majesty's decided opinion was that Germany was winning on all points, and that there were only two possible endings to European war, either that Germany would be entirely victorious or that the war would end in a stalemate largely in favour of Germany.'[33]

British and French forces landed at Salonika too late to aid the Serbs and too weak to advance against the Bulgarians. However, Falkenhayn did not attack them. Later he rationalised his actions by arguing that Salonika was an enormous internment camp, a front which tied down French, British and Serb troops, chipping away their strength through malaria, preventing their use in more promising theatres, and committing allied shipping to their supply. In reality his immediate decisions were dictated by the weather and the length of his supply lines. The longer-term considerations concerned Balkan politics. Serbia was crushed. Bulgaria had therefore achieved its principal objective in the war, and there was a danger that it would now seek a settlement. On the other hand, if Falkenhayn encouraged it to advance on Salonika, Greece would be compelled to throw in its lot with the Entente. A passive front in Macedonia allowed him to leave the Balkans to Bulgaria and Austria-Hungary. It seemed that at last he would be able to focus Germany's efforts on what for him was the principal front, that in the west.

Once again German calculations reckoned without Austria-Hungary. The defeat of Serbia had not resolved Vienna's Balkan problems. Conrad was furious that it had been achieved principally by German forces, not Austrian. Even when Falkenhayn pulled eight of eleven German divisions out of the Balkan theatre, a German, Mackensen, was left in command. Falkenhayn wanted a joint allied command, but Conrad knew that would mean Austria-Hungary's subordination to the 'secret enemy'. He feared that Serbia would become a German or Bulgar fiefdom, and he nicknamed Falkenhayn 'Ferdinand II' after the Bulgarian King. Relations between Conrad and Falkenhayn became so bad that for almost a full month, between 22 December 1915 and 19 January 1916, there was no direct communication. In that time strategies for 1916 were set. Conrad planned to mop up Montenegro during the winter and then turn against Italy. In 1915 the two allies had managed to coordinate their actions; in 1916 they diverged. Austria-Hungary's initial defeat in its war with Serbia had been offset by its share in the wider victory in the east; that wider victory was itself in turn forfeit to the even greater scale of the war as a whole. In shaping its strategy, Germany had identified its enemies' alliance as a source of weakness, not strength: it was to prove a fatal miscalculation but it was an accurate reflection of Germany's own experience of coalition warfare.

6

BREAKING THE DEADLOCK

Trench Warfare

'There are five families of rats in the roof of my dug-out,' Captain Bill Murray reported back to his family on 14 May 1915, 'which is two feet above my head in bed, and the little rats practise back somersaults continuously through the night, for they have discovered that my face is a soft landing when they fall.'[1] Rats did more than disturb sleep; they carried disease and they spoilt food. Trench warfare provided ideal conditions for their multiplication. They thrived on its detritus, including the bodies of the unburied dead. For those who yet lived, even more irksome was the blood-sucking louse. Ninety-five per cent of British soldiers coming out of the line were infested. Lice spread from man to man, living in the seams of his clothing and irritating his skin. They were known to cause typhus, but by 1918 it was established that they were also responsible for trench fever, one of a host of new conditions which the positional warfare of the western front generated. The intensely cultivated soil of Belgium and northern France, well tilled and manured, meant that wounds were rapidly infected with gas gangrene: 21 per cent of French soldiers wounded in the legs or thighs died as a result. And standing in the cold, wet mud of the trenches promoted trench foot and frostbite. But these were the first armies to benefit from the use of antiseptics, from mass inoculation programmes, and from an understanding of bacteriology. In wars before that of 1914–18 disease, not battle, was the major killer. On the western front it was not – a product of major advances in preventive military medicine as well as of the fact that it was wounds which introduced many of the more life-threatening infections. Disease was still a principal cause of death in every other theatre of war.

Trenches created health problems but they saved lives. To speak of the horror of the trenches is to substitute hyperbole for common sense: the war would have been far more horrific if there had been no trenches. They protected flesh and blood from the worst effects of the firepower revolution of the late nineteenth century. 'They bent their heads and went on,' Jean Bernier wrote of his and his comrades' experience of entering the trenches, 'curiously calmed and strengthened by this regained contact with the earth, their habitation and their element.'[2] The dangers rose when men left the embrace of the trenches to go over the top, and when war was fluid and mobile. German deaths per month were highest in 1914 on the western front, in 1915 on the eastern front, and in 1918 again in the west – in other words when and where they were on the attack. French monthly losses peaked at 238,000 in September 1914, the month of the Marne. Their next worst month was October 1915, when an offensive in Champagne (which formed the centrepiece of Bernier's autobiographical novel) pushed the tally up to 180,000. Thereafter they rose above 100,000 on only three occasions in the war, never in 1916 – despite the battle of Verdun – and twice in 1918, when the war became mobile again. The big 'pushes' of positional war caused death rates to rise, but, provided those offensives were carefully prepared and well supported with artillery, the attackers' casualties were frequently comparable with the defenders'. Broadly speaking this was true for both the major battles of 1916, Verdun and the Somme, and the Germans lost more men defending on the Somme than they had attacking at Verdun earlier in the year. In August 1917, at the height of the third battle of Ypres, the epitome of trench warfare's waste and futility for many commentators, British casualties on the western front totalled 81,080. Exactly a year later, when the British army inflicted a major defeat on the Germans at Amiens and began its advance to victory, they soared to 122,272.

Trench warfare redefined what a battle was. 'Of course I've been in all the usual shows,' wrote Alexandre Arnoux, who served at the front from May 1915 until the war's end, 'night assaults, reconnoitrings, raiding parties, and all that. I copped a machine-gun bullet in the thigh and a splinter of shell in the head and I've had mustard gas, but I've never been in what I call a real battle. A pukka show with the whole line moving forward and the reserves coming up all the time, I've never been in that.'[3] In the past battles had been affairs of single days, and losses of perhaps 30 per cent had rendered armies unable to fight again until the following campaigning season. Few, if any, individual days of the First World War were as bloody, relatively speaking, as the battles of Frederick the Great or Napoleon. In 1914–18 casualties mounted because the fighting was continuous. What were called battles sometimes lasted months, and previous generations would have described them as campaigns. Longer hours of daylight in the summer gave more opportunity to kill, although even these major offensives had to close down by November. But the soldiers of the First World War did not then go into winter quarters. War was stopped neither by the seasons nor by the divisions of night and day. The advent of the aircraft meant that, weather permitting, all activity outside the hours of darkness could be observed from the air. Reliefs and resupply became nocturnal activities. So, too, was the endless business of trench repair, making good the depredations of shellfire or the erosion of continuous rain. 'When dusk fell,' Charles Carrington recalled, '. . . troglodytes emerged from their burrows in the sunken road to relieve platoons in the posts, to bring up rations from the village, to dig and wire in pitchy darkness. Heavy labour at a score of trades in awkward places must be relentlessly performed without showing a light or making a sound.'[4] Men were continuously exhausted: they dozed by day, and, paradoxically, as the nights became shorter the opportunities for sleep became greater.

When Falkenhayn ordered the adoption of defensive positions on the western front at the end of November 1914 he saw them as a means to an end: tactically to confer on his troops the benefits of the defensive, and strategically to enable him to manoeuvre elsewhere. For the German supreme command, with its possibilities in the east, that relationship was always explicit. But for those who served only on the western front trench warfare became institutionalised, a self-fulfilling routine, and ultimately an end in itself. British and French troops were taken out of the line less to be deployed to other theatres, and more to go into reserve. Charles Carrington reckoned that he spent 101 days of 1916 under fire, in the front-line or support trenches. He passed more than two-thirds of the year in the hinterland of reserve positions, training areas, billets and munition dumps. The longer positions were held, the stronger the labour of their occupants made them. In the chalk-lands of Picardy deep dug-outs almost domesticated the line. Further north the land was lower lying and boggy, but the result was that the front came to consist of breastworks and pillboxes, structures which not only took the defenders clear of the water-table but also conferred an air of permanence. At its most extreme, this pattern prompted the phenomenon of 'live and let live'. 'The military situation at le Touquet was curious,' George Coppard remembered of his service in 1915, 'for it seemed almost as if both sides, the Germans and ourselves, had tacitly agreed that this part of the line should be labelled "Quiet", it being understood that if one side started up any bloody nonsense, then the other would follow suit.'[5]

Raids, another night-time activity, were designed to disrupt these patterns. They prevented the loss of the skills of mobile warfare; they asserted the dominance of one side over no man's land; and they might bring back valuable intelligence. This was a form of fighting which relied on stealth and surprise, which bypassed long-range fire, and instead required the weapons of an older generation, not only grenades and bombs but also picks and shovels. However, as raids, too, became institutionalised, so they grew in scale and elaboration, 'a battle in miniature with all the preliminaries and accompaniments magnified'. Watching a raid from the fire-step of a trench held by the Royal Welch Fusiliers on 25 April 1916 was 'a hair-raising affair at the start, for our field-guns had so little clearance that the draught of their shells could be felt on the back of one's neck. What was to be seen was like nothing else. Against the night there was a wild dance of red fan-shaped spurts of fire seen through a thickening haze.'[6]

Artillery was the key weapon of trench warfare. Envelopment, the leading operational idea of staffs before the war, still found its proponents in the east, but in the west there were no exposed flanks. The task that confronted the French and British armies, committed to the recovery of the lost territory of northern France and to the liberation of Belgium, was that of breaking into and through the German positions. Only then could they break out and manoeuvre. In the winter of 1914–15 this seemed to be a matter of guns and high-explosive shell. 'Breaking through the enemy's lines', the British commander-in-chief, Sir John French, minuted in January 1915, 'is largely a question of expenditure of high explosive ammunition. If sufficient ammunition is forthcoming, a way can be blasted through the line. If the attempt fails, it shows, provided that the work of the infantry and artillery has been properly coordinated, that insufficient ammunition has been expended, i.e. either more guns must be brought up, or the allowance of ammunition per gun increased.'[7]

In mobile war the constraint on the use of artillery was the supply problems of batteries in the field – not only in terms of shells for the guns but also of fodder for the horses. The quick-firing 75mm field gun, the agent of the French victory on the Marne, could loose fifteen – and some claimed twenty – rounds a minute, and a battery of four guns could fire off its total stock in a couple of hours. Static war minimised the logistical constraints, especially as light railways replaced horse-drawn transport, but increased the numbers of targets. The first consequence of the generals' responses to trench war was pressure not on their supply services but on home production.

Munitions Production

The conversion of factories to the output of munitions proved as contentious for the industrialised economies of Western Europe as it was problematic for Russia. When Douglas Haig's attack at Aubers Ridge failed on 9 May 1915, Sir John French deflected blame from the army to the government by attributing the defeat to the lack of high-explosive shell for the British 18-pounder field gun, a misleading refrain which *The Times* picked up and which was in flat contradiction to statements which the prime minister, Asquith, had given in a speech to munitions workers in Newcastle. When the shells crisis broke, Britain's last Liberal government was already under challenge. It coincided with the resignation of the First Sea Lord, Jackie Fisher, who opposed 'further depletion of our Home resources for the Dardanelles' and now regarded his political superior, Winston Churchill, as 'a bigger danger than the Germans'.[8] The upshot was the formation of a coalition government, albeit still headed by Asquith, and of a Ministry of Munitions under Lloyd George.

Britain was not the only country where shell shortage generated civil–military conflict. In France the invasion and the evacuation of the government to Bordeaux in September 1914 vastly increased the powers of Joffre and his headquarters. However, here, too, the failures of spring 1915 prompted the generals to seek scapegoats outside the army. Abel Ferry, a reserve officer and junior minister, attended the Council of Ministers on 4 July 1915: 'One feels that the military, becoming less optimistic, are preparing themselves to point the finger at the civilians and say: "It is your fault."'[9] Albert Thomas, 'a killing, fat little man, all round with shaggy hair, spectacles an impossible tan-colored beard ending in two impossible curls',[10] had been appointed under-secretary of state for war with particular responsibility for artillery and munitions on 18 May 1915. Just as Lloyd George did in Britain, the government responded to the generals' accusations by pinning the failures in munitions procurement on the army itself. These debates were predicated on national circumstances, and their resolutions were administrative and ministerial. However, the fact that shell production rose in 1915, and did so for all the belligerents regardless of political complexion, confirms that the phenomenon of shell shortage had some common characteristics.

First was the issue of raw materials. It was particularly acute for Germany, whose imports from overseas were cut off by the allied blockade. On 9 August 1914 Walther Rathenau, who as a Jew could not be sure of his reception by the army, persuaded Falkenhayn, in his capacity as minister of war, to establish a raw materials agency. Its initial task was to take stock of the raw materials within not only the Reich but also the occupied territories, particularly Belgium, so as to allocate them centrally to the firms that could make best use of them. Each commodity was the subject of its own raw materials company, with a board drawn principally from the very firms that used the materials in question. Rathenau himself ran the electronics giant AEG, which was anxious about copper supplies. The accusation that the free market had been enlisted to serve the state, but on its own terms and with guaranteed profits, was repeated elsewhere. In France Thomas, a socialist, was criticised for being too close to the industrialists of the Comité des Forges, and in Britain Lloyd George turned his new ministry over to those he called 'men of push and go', in other words businessmen and entrepreneurs.

More pressing for the French and British than the issue of raw materials was that of labour. Conscription had mobilised skilled workers in the munitions industries but also enabled their return. The state which ordered men into uniform could also, if it suited the national interest, order them out of it. By June 1916 the French army had released 287,000 men back to the arms industries. They remained liable to military law and so were not free to strike. With industry an arm of the war effort, the need to get a sensible division of labour between the armed forces and domestic production was as important a pressure as the manpower demands of the army. When Britain at last introduced conscription in January 1916, this was the essence of the debate within the cabinet, not any principled objections to compulsion. In 1914 employees of the major arms firms had responded with disproportionate enthusiasm to the call for volunteers for the army. By June 1915 even those firms already engaged in arms production before the war were short of 14,000 skilled workers, and plant was lying idle for lack of hands to use it.

One solution to the manpower needs of the munitions factories was to 'dilute' labour, to replace skilled workers with unskilled. The greater use of automated processes and the division of production into a large number of distinct, but repetitive, operations permitted such a switch. The principal job of the skilled worker was to maintain the plant that made the arms, not to produce the arms themselves. In Britain the trade unions feared that working methods brought in under the umbrella of wartime necessity would be perpetuated in peacetime and so undermine both their status and their restrictive practices. On 5 March 1915 Lloyd George persuaded both employers and trade unions to accept dilution, but only for the duration of the war and only in the production of munitions.

The result was that in Britain, as in France, women were engaged in the manufacture of armaments in disproportionate numbers. Before the war French peasant women, like their equivalents in Germany, worked on the land: the war did not alter that. In 1916 the French censors reported that 'moving letters written from the countryside show us women killing themselves with work without being able to replace the men who fight or who are dead'.[11] Across Europe, large numbers of women were already in employment before the war, and the numbers entering work for the first time during the war should not be exaggerated. In 1914 7.7 million French women already had jobs, and they made up 32 per cent of the total workforce; by the war's end they accounted for 40 per cent of the workforce. In Britain women workers rose from just under 6 million, or 26 per cent of the workforce, to just over 7.3 million, or 36 per cent, in the same period. In Germany the number of females in insured employment expanded so quickly in the two decades before the war that the increase during the war, from about 3.5 million to just over 4 million, represented a decline in the rate of growth. Germany makes very evident the pattern that prevailed elsewhere, too: that those who entered munitions production did so from other occupations; the war caused working-class women to change jobs more than it brought women into the workplace. In Bavaria, by December 1916 three times as many women were involved in gun-

Armenian victims: many photographs of the Armenian massacres were taken by Armin Wegner, a German medical officer, who took up Armenia's cause after the war. Unfortunately he was not precise as to places or dates.

Unable to penetrate inland at Gallipoli, British troops perched on the cliffs close to the sea. The scene at Gully Ravine, on the Aegean side of the peninsula in September 1915, is of a military shanty-town.

Charles Townshend goes into captivity at Kut. Unlike his men, few of whom survived prison, he spent the rest of the war in what he described as 'a sort of country vicarage' on an island in the sea of Marmara.

Call-up was more widely opposed in Russia than in any other country whose army was mobilised in 1914. Peasants worried about what would happen to their families and the land in their absence. None the less, 96 per cent reported for duty.

Falkenhayn, fourth from right, directs the German 9th Army in its invasion of Romania, autumn 1916. The scale and speed of his victory gave the lie to those who questioned his grasp of operations.

The Germans first entered Szawle, in the centre of Lithuania, on 30 April 1915, but they had to withdraw again on 11 May, and did not finally take it until 21 July. Realising that the Baltic states were not Russian, they determined to make them culturally German.

The Russian army destroyed what it could not take with it when retreating in May 1915. In this photograph the Austro-Hungarian oil installations at Boryslaw in Galicia are still smouldering.

Although the German army was not free from anti-Semitism, Jews were sufficiently integrated to be able to observe their own traditions, including Hanukkah, the 'Festival of the Lights', in Poland in December 1916.

Serb field artillery battles through the snow to the Albanian frontier, November 1915. The French had sold Serbia 75mm quick-firing guns before the war.

A British fatigue party carrying duckboards over a support trench line at night, Cambrai, 12 January 1917. A million helmets, made of hardened manganese steel, were issued to the British army in the first half of 1916, with the result that head wounds fell by over 75 per cent.

27

The French were experimenting with helmets when the war broke out, and issued the Adrian helmet in mid-1915. It was also adopted by Belgium, Italy, Serbia and Romania. But the best protection against shellfire for these soldiers was the dug-out itself.

28

29

Salvage and recycling, especially of metals, were essential features of industrialised war. French women unload spent shell-cases at Toulon.

30

One reason why activity on the ground became nocturnal: German soldiers mount a camera on to an observation balloon. Although the balloon would float behind German lines, it was still vulnerable to attack by enemy aircraft.

The 120mm and 155mm guns were vital to French success on the Somme in July 1916, although French heavy artillery was not fully modernised until 1917. The gunners take a rest to eat.

31

32

The 3rd Battle Squadron of the German High Seas Fleet at sea, 31 May 1916, from aboard Scheer's flagship, *Friedrich der Grosse*. Her main armament, of 12-inch guns, was inferior to the 13.5-inch guns on Jellicoe's flagship, *The Iron Duke*.

The German navy attacked the British mainland from the air as well as by sea. On 8 September 1915 a Zeppelin commanded by Heinrich Mathy, the greatest airship commander of the war, killed twenty-two people and caused £500,000 worth of damage to Aldersgate in London.

33

Communal feeding was one German response to the British blockade. The *Mittelstand*, white-collar workers often on fixed incomes, were particularly affected by rising food prices, and their corollary – falling real wages. For them the war meant loss of status.

In the early hours of 30 June 1916 dynamite and munitions, loaded in rail cars and barges on Black Tom, a promontory in New Jersey, caught fire. The explosions shook the Brooklyn Bridge and blew out windows in Manhattan. Believed at the time to be an accident, this was in fact the work of German saboteurs.

powder production as before the war, but half of them had previously worked in factories and only a quarter had not had a job.[12] British women in 1914 were employed overwhelmingly in domestic service or in the textile industry. Munitions production, freed from the constraints of trade-union dominance and expanding under the demands for shell from the front, provided newly created and better-paid jobs. Much of the work involved the use of toxic chemicals, and TNT caused bilious attacks, blurred vision, depression and, in particular, jaundice: Lilian Miles saw her black hair turn green, and remembered that 'you'd wash and wash and it didn't make no difference . . . Your whole body was yellow'.[13] The British metal and chemical industries and the government factories employed a total of 212,000 women in July 1914, and 923,000 by July 1918. Before the war 17,731 French women worked in the metal industries, but 425,000 at its end.

The rapid expansion of munitions output and the equally dramatic shift in how that production was carried out had long-term benefits for battlefield performance, but could only be achieved quickly by the lowering of standards over the short term. In August 1914 Louis Renault said that his car factories could manufacture shells using turning lathes rather than hydraulic presses. The resulting shell had to be made in two parts because the lathes could not shape the shell's nose cone. The so-called 'bi-blocs' helped overcome France's shell shortage, but their weaknesses generated shortages in other areas: over 600 French guns were destroyed – and their crews killed or injured – by premature explosions in 1915. Germany likewise used turning lathes to produce what it called 'auxiliary ammunition' from cast iron: in 1915 it lost 2,300 field guns and 900 light howitzers to premature explosions, as many as were disabled by enemy action. The difficulties were not just those of materials and plant. Expansion had overtaken the procedures for quality control. In January 1915 one German observer reckoned that half the shells fired by the French were duds. Some failures were the result of incompetence and haste, but others were the fruit of profiteering and fraud. At the battle of the Somme in July 1916, 25 per cent of British guns were put out of action as a result of design faults and inferior materials, and 30 per cent of shells failed to explode.

Much of the manufacturing effort in the first half of the war therefore failed to reap any reward on the battlefield until the second half. French and German holdings of field guns were essentially static, as new guns replaced those that had been lost, and plant was devoted to the repair of those that were damaged. Germany had 5,096 field guns on mobilisation and 5,300 at the end of 1915. Increased output only met increased wear and tear. Factories which had not been in the arms business before the war could not acquire either the expertise or the machine-tools for weapons production in a matter of months. One short-term solution to the problems of conversion was the production of weapons with less demanding specifications and lower performances. Here the reintroduction of the mortar stands as the supreme example. A portable tube which fired bombs and mines at high angles over short ranges, it was ideally suited to the tactical conditions of trench warfare. But, just as importantly, it and its projectiles were sufficiently simple to enable firms without weapons expertise to make them. In August 1914 the German army possessed 180 *Minenwerfern* of all calibres; by January 1918 it had taken receipt of 16,127. The British adopted the Stokes mortar in 1915, and 11,421 were manufactured in the war.

The links between the conversion to war production at home and tactical application on the battlefield were not completed until 1917. Douglas Haig, reflecting on the lessons of Aubers Ridge two days after, on 11 May 1915, made clear why:

1. The defences in our front are so carefully and so strongly made, and mutual support with machine-guns is so complete, that in order to demolish them a *long methodical bombardment* will be necessary by heavy artillery (guns and howitzers) before Infantry are sent forward to attack.
2. To destroy the enemy's 'material' 60 p[ounde]r. *guns* will be tried, as well as the 15-in[ch], 9.2 and 6-in[ch] siege how[itzer]s.

> Accurate observations of *each shot* will be arranged so as to make sure of flattening out the enemy's 'strong points' of support, before the Infantry is launched.[14]

In 1915 the British did not have enough heavy artillery to do what he wanted. During the course of the entire year they took delivery of just 134 60-pounders. In August they adopted a programme which aimed to produce 2,825 heavy guns by December 1916. Only the existing arms manufacturers, like Vickers and Armstrong, had the capability to undertake this work. Consequently the pressure on them to produce other armaments was reduced. While Germany and France grappled with maintaining their existing numbers of field guns, the British Ministry of Munitions cut back on the output of lighter guns by 28 per cent, while increasing that of medium calibres by 380 per cent and of heavy artillery by 1,200 per cent. From the very outset, British generals, even cavalrymen like Haig and French, were dedicated to using weight of material and sophisticated technology in the pursuit of breakthrough. It was an approach to war which suited Britain for two reasons. It was the first industrialised nation in the world, and before 1914 it alone of the major powers had spurned the mass army. Its ability to hold a sprawling empire had relied not on manpower but on the use of technology as a force multiplier.

Tactical Adaptation

The year 1915 was a formative experience, one in which the lines of development which would be followed through into the battles of 1918 were put in place. Although the front was static, the thinking of the armies was not. The western front was an intensely competitive environment, where the innovation of one side was emulated, improved upon or negated by the other. Ironically, it was this very cycle of action and reaction, designed to break the deadlock, which confirmed it. But at its conclusion the armies of both sides were equipped, organised and fought in very different ways from those of 1914.

Immediately Haig's prescription created fresh problems more than it resolved old ones. 'In this siege war in the open field, it is not enough to open a breach', General Marie-Emile Fayolle confided to his diary on 1 June 1915, 'it is necessary that it is about 20 km wide, at the least, or one cannot fan out to right and left. To do that needs a whole army and there has to be another one ready to carry on.'[15] But in 1915 neither the British nor the French had enough guns or shells, let alone heavy artillery, to be able to attack on a broad front. By concentrating on a narrow front, the available guns might reach into the depth of the enemy positions, but the attackers were then liable to enfilade from the flanks. Furthermore, the concentration of artillery and its preliminary, and increasingly extended, bombardment forfeited the element of surprise. Most attacks succeeded in breaking into the enemy's position. The problem was that of reinforcing and exploiting success, and that in turn depended on immediate support from troops to the rear.

Haig's belief that offensives should be fought on broad, not narrow, fronts, and be preceded by long, not short, bombardments was born at the battle of Neuve Chapelle, the first of the British spring offensives in 1915. But Neuve Chapelle also highlighted the intractabilities of communication, and the consequent difficulty of knowing when and where to commit reserves. On 10 March 1915, at 8.05 a.m., after a short (thirty-five-minute) bombardment, the infantry launched a surprise attack. In the centre the German front line was taken in ten minutes and the village of Neuve Chapelle itself was in British hands before 9 a.m. Reports of these initial gains reached Lieutenant-General Sir Henry Rawlinson, the corps commander, within an hour. Douglas Haig, by now commanding one of the two armies into which the expanding British Expeditionary Force had been divided, ordered a cavalry brigade to ready itself and harboured hopes of his whole army beginning a general advance. But the artillery had been less effective on the left, and there the attack came under fire from its flank. The British did not take the German front line until 11.20, and therefore the lead units on the right were in danger of being isolated, and were told to wait for further instructions. Communications went up the command chain from battalion to brigade, from brigade to division, and at last reached corps headquarters five miles back. At 1.30 p.m. Rawlinson issued instructions for a fresh advance at 2.30 p.m., but the supporting units were not ready, and at 3 p.m. he set the attack for 3.30. Orders had to be transmitted back down the line of command, acquiring more detail as they went. Those passing between division and battalion had taken between one and two hours throughout the day. At 3.30 the artillery opened fire; and hit its own infantry. By 4 p.m. both the forward brigades were attacking but without artillery support or effective lateral communications between themselves. The light was failing, surprise had been lost and enemy defence was hardening.

Neuve Chapelle confirmed that the biggest constraint on the conduct of land war was the lack of real-time communications. Infantry in fixed positions could bury telephone wire from the front line back to their supporting artillery and higher commands. However, as they went forward to attack they lost contact. They could unroll wire as they advanced but it was frequently cut by shellfire. Wirelesses were still too heavy to be man-portable; they were the preserve of higher commands and navies. Pigeons could do the job if the wind and weather conditions were right, but they were reluctant to fly on the damp, still days which tended to prevail on the western front. Drizzle or mist prevented other forms of observation – the firing of rockets or flares, or the waving of flags in order to indicate progress. The Germans used dogs to carry messages, but the usual method of communicating progress or of calling for support was human. Runners had to renegotiate the open ground they had just crossed in the attack. Even if they survived, their information was old by the time it was in the hands of those for whom it was destined.

Accordingly, generals could do little to intervene in the immediate decision-making of a battle. The creation of mass armies and the necessity of dispersion in the face of modern firepower meant that the battlefield had extended, while at the same time apparently emptying. The supreme commander could not take in the situation with a sweep of his field glasses from some vantage point. Now his tasks were more managerial than inspirational. He found 'himself further back in a house with a spacious office, where telegraphs, telephones and signals apparatus are to hand', Schlieffen had written before the war. 'There, in a comfortable chair before a wide table, the modern Alexander has before him the entire battlefield on a map.'[16] Linear, positional warfare exacerbated this trend, forcing the commander to place himself behind his troops. The German response to the problem was to delegate command forward, confining instructions to general directives and avoiding detailed orders. British officers were used to smaller forces and more hands-on command in colonial campaigns. Moreover, mobile warfare in 1914 had briefly kept alive the notions of a more heroic age. In the course of the entire war seventy-one German and fifty-five French generals lost their lives, and it is reasonable to assume that most of those who did so in battle were killed in the opening months. British generals proved almost foolhardy by comparison: between 1914 and 1918 seventy-eight were killed in action, an enormous total given that the army did not really expand until the front had stabilised and startling confirmation of the assertion of Cyril Falls, himself a staff officer, that British generals were in fact 'too eager to get away from their desks'.[17] What they found hard to accept was that vital decisions were being taken at lower levels of authority. At the beginning of the war the corps of, say, 30,000 men was the key operational command. But the corps was squeezed from the top by the creation of army and army group commands, and from the bottom by the division of about 12,000 men. The latter took the corps' place as the lowest all-arms operational formation, and acquired an identity which was more lasting and cohesive than that of the corps. The task of heroic and inspiring leadership passed even lower down the command chain to junior officers, the commanders of companies, platoons and even sections.

In 1915 Entente strategy had an ad hoc quality. The western front represented an irreducible minimum. That was particularly the case for France, although it did not prevent the French from pursuing other options in the eastern Mediterranean, at Gallipoli and Salonika. The British seemed still to have a measure of choice. Some Liberals, particularly Reginald McKenna, Lloyd George's successor as chancellor of the exchequer, cleaved to the notion that Britain's primary contribution should be naval and economic: it should be the arsenal and financier of the Entente. McKenna argued that British manpower would be best used if it sustained home production and thus ensured the flow of exports that would fund Britain's international credit and its ability to buy arms overseas and supply them to its allies. But McKenna's hopes were ill founded. When Kitchener was appointed secretary of state for war in August 1914, he set about the creation of a mass army for deployment on the continent of Europe. By July 1915 the War Office was talking of seventy divisions, a tenfold increase on the army's size a year before. Although originally raised through voluntary enlistment, such an army could be kept up to strength only by conscription. Many of the men McKenna wanted on the factory floor were needed by the army, and the produce of those that remained went to equip that army, not to support Britain's overseas balance of trade.

Kitchener himself suggested Britain should delay its major effort until 1917, by which time the Continental armies would have fought each other to a standstill and the British could take the credit for ending the war. The New Armies' training and equipment was a lengthy process, but they could not realistically be held back for that long. In the short term the obvious reserves of manpower lay in Russia, but if the Russians were to do the hard fighting in 1915–16 they – not Kitchener's New Armies – should get the fruits of Britain's war industries. The retreat of the Russian armies in the summer of 1915 and the defeat at Gallipoli confirmed that Kitchener's notion of choice was as illusory as McKenna's. The Russians had now even greater need of British munitions, but they were also desperate for direct military support from the west to draw off the Germans. Furthermore, in France Joffre faced hardening political opposition. By sacking the most republican of his army commanders, General

Maurice Sarrail, for perfectly proper military reasons, he provided a focus for the left's criticisms of the army's independence of political control. The government of René Viviani came under threat, and with it the national cohesion embodied in the *union sacrée*. Britain feared the upshot of a domestic political crisis in France. Their worst nightmares embraced a government under Joseph Caillaux and the possibility that he might seek an accommodation with Germany. Kitchener reversed his views of Britain's role on the western front: on 19 August 1915 he told Haig that 'we must act with all our energy, and do our utmost to help the French, even though by so doing, we suffer very heavy losses indeed'.[18] British strategy was tied to that of its allies, and of France especially.

Thus, as the Central Powers began to pull apart, those of the Entente converged. On 29 June 1915 Joffre warned of the dangers of allowing the Germans to pick off one power at a time: 'An energetic combined offensive, involving all the allied armies other than the Russian, is the only means of warding off this danger and of beating the enemy'.[19] Attacking on the western front was vital not just for strategic reasons: if on the defensive, he argued, 'our troops will little by little lose their physical and moral qualities'.[20] He had been planning an attack in Champagne since late June. The president of the republic, Poincaré, was among those opposed to further offensives, but British support gave Joffre the leverage over his political masters that he needed in order to go ahead. Operations in Artois in May had convinced the French, like the British, that if they had enough artillery and attacked on a sufficiently broad front they could break through; the key was to have supporting formations ready to carry the attack beyond the first line and so to enable the breakthrough to be achieved in one bound. On a front of 35 km, the French had 900 heavy guns, over 1,000 field guns, and thirty-seven divisions: at the point of attack the Germans could match nineteen divisions with five. On 24 September, after five days of French artillery preparation, Karl von Einem, commanding the German 3rd Army, got Falkenhayn to come to the telephone: 'I spoke to him for a moment, and so was able to tell him that personally everything was going very well. One must always show these people a serene countenance and a confident spirit, otherwise one would be deemed nervous – whether with good reason or not would not matter.' At 11 a.m. on the following morning, von Einem spoke to Falkenhayn again. Von Einem had just been told that the French had broken in at Souain, and asked for at least four divisions as reinforcements. 'He answers me that the British are attacking in the north, and that His Majesty therefore relies on every man to do his duty.'[21]

The British attack was part of a second and simultaneous allied offensive, in Artois, and running from the slag-heaps of Loos in the north to the dominating ground of Vimy Ridge in the south. Joffre later calculated that fifty-four French divisions and thirteen British were engaged on a total front of 90 km. But Falkenhayn's and von Einem's *sang froid* was justified: the Germans had constructed a second position, five to six miles behind the front line, beyond the range of the French artillery, and on a reverse slope so that it was out of direct observation. Total Entente losses reached a quarter of a million for minimal gain. Foiled in his attempt at breakthrough, Joffre fell back on another rationale for his attack: 'We shall kill more of the enemy than he can kill of us'.[22] It was to become a familiar justification for the failure to break through. But in this case German losses were only 60,000.

Joffre did not fall; Viviani did, albeit over developments in the Balkans rather than on the western front. A new government under Aristide Briand fended off the threat from the left, which was appeased by Sarrail's appointment to the Salonika command. In the event Loos affected the British running of the war more profoundly than did the failures in Champagne that of the French.

Both British and French generals were agreed that the breakthrough would be achieved not by the first wave of troops, who would break into the enemy front line, but by the second, who would pass through the first wave once it was on its objectives and carry the attack forward. Traditional notions of generalship dictated that the reserve should be in the hands of the supreme commander, who would decide when to commit it in the light of the overall situation.

But the delays in communication and in getting forward over a shelled and fractured battlefield in muddy weather argued that control of the reserves – and therefore command authority – should be delegated. Charles Mangin, commanding a French division at Vimy on 25 September, waited thirty-five hours for two battalions to get forward: 'For fifteen days I have said that it is necessary', he fulminated three days later, 'not only to place the reserves near the front, but to put them in the hands of those who have to employ them, the divisional commanders.'[23] In the British case, Douglas Haig, commanding the 1st Army at Loos, had asked his commander-in-chief, Sir John French, to release two reserve divisions before the battle. French had refused, perhaps in part because unlike Haig he could not persuade himself that the attack was going to succeed. He did commit the two divisions by 9.30 a.m. on the 25th, within forty-five minutes of Haig requesting them, but the disorganisation and the distance of their march meant that they did not enter the battle until the following day. Haig used the episode and his influence with King George V to have French recalled and himself installed as commander-in-chief.

Haig brought to the responsibility he now exercised more than royal favour and a capacity for intrigue. He possessed an inner certainty, buttressed by his Presbyterian faith, which gave him resolve and direction. His biggest difficulty was that which con-fronted all his colleagues in an army which had expanded so quickly: used to exercising personal command in small formations, he did not know how best to lead a mass army or how to get the best from his staff. He none the less created a team at General Headquarters in France to whom he proved exceptionally – and even excessively – loyal. He also used his position to lobby in London for a change in the strategic direction of the war. The army in France, like the cabinet at home, had lost faith in Kitchener. His insights were not matched by organisational ability, and his enthusiasms could be at variance with the consistent support that French had needed but had not necessarily received. Under Kitchener, the army's general staff, newly formed just before the war, had been allowed to wither. Haig wanted Sir William Robertson, whose career had blossomed thanks to the opportunities staff-work afforded, appointed as its chief. Robertson had served in France as quartermaster-general and then chief of staff, and 'contained in his cylindrical person a quite unusual proportion of character and common sense to the cubic inch'. The King not only backed Robertson's appointment but also agreed that he should be responsible not to the secretary of state for war but to the War Council, the committee of the cabinet responsible for the formulation of strategy. Thus in early December 1915, six months before he was drowned when en route to visit Russia on board HMS *Hampshire*, Kitchener was being bypassed in the formulation of policy.

Robertson is too often remembered simply as the doughty defender of Haig and the supporter of the western front. He was both those things, in that he saw it as his job to enable the commander-in-chief of the principal British army in the field to get on with the conduct of operations in Britain's major theatre of land war. But he was far from being simply Haig's puppet. Robertson had joined the army as a private soldier and lacked the obvious social graces of those with whom he now had to deal: 'Arrogant, aitchless when excited, and flat-footed (figuratively and physically), he lurched down Whitehall, an ambulating refrigerator'.[24] His difficulties were compounded by the fact that he said not what the politicians wanted to hear but what his professional judgement indicated was right. He could not promise a quick victory. His message on 8 November 1915 was one of realism: the defeat of the Central Powers 'can only be attained by the defeat or exhaustion of the predominant partner in the Central Alliance – Germany'.[25]

By 1917 the key word here was to be exhaustion, but in December 1915 Robertson, like other Entente commanders, was less sure. Writing to Kitchener on the 27th of that month, he said that 'we can only end the war in our favour by attrition or by breaking through the German line'.[26] In having it both ways Robertson reflected Joffre's response to the Champagne battle: designed to achieve breakthrough, it was explained as '*grignotage*', or nibbling, when it failed. But ambiguity vitiated clear planning. At Neuve Chapelle, Haig had scented the opportunity for breakthrough and had readied his cavalry accordingly, but General Rawlinson had set more limited objectives from the outset. Rawlinson argued that, as a well-prepared and well-supported attack could break into an enemy position but not could not break clean through, this reality should be reflected in planning. Attacks should aim to take a 'bite' out of the enemy line, and then hold it; that would force the enemy to counterattack and so confer the tactical advantages of the defender on the attacker.

Rawlinson's method promised to exhaust the enemy, but it faced two significant imponderables. First, it passed the initiative to the enemy: he might decide he did not need to regain the lost ground, and so call the attacker's bluff. Rawlinson could guarantee only that this would not occur where it was important for the enemy to regain the ground he had lost. Vimy Ridge, with its commanding height, was an example, as was the ring of hills to the east of Ypres: the town screened the Channel ports and the pivot of the British Expeditionary Force's supply system, and the high ground guarded the Roulers railway junction and the hub of Germany's transport network behind the western front. A breakthrough at either Vimy or Ypres might have major operational consequences. As a result attritional battles tended to occur at locations where breakthrough battles also were likely to occur. And that was the second imponderable implicit in 'bite and hold'. It was only a method, a means to exhaust the enemy; the point would come when that had been accomplished and an allied attack would be able to break through. Haig, both at Neuve Chapelle and at Loos, had persuaded himself that the exhaustion of the enemy and the breakthrough could be part of the same battle. Neither Rawlinson nor Robertson shared that assumption.

Central to Robertson's thinking about the exhaustion of the German army was the nature of the intelligence that the War Office in London received. Most of it concerned train movements across Europe, showing the deployment of German divisions between east and west, and enabling him to build up a clear order of battle for the German army and its reserves. For Robertson, as a classically trained staff officer, the Germans were operating on 'interior lines', able to shift their troops across short chords to meet different threats with rapidity. The allies, by contrast, were ranged round the Central Powers and had to move greater distances and on 'exterior lines', often by sea and certainly slowly. His belief that Britain's principal contribution should be on the western front did not prevent him realising that each of the allied fronts had the potential to support the others if only their efforts could be concentrated in time. If the Central Powers were attacked simultaneously in the west and in the east, and also in Italy, the Germans would not be able to shuttle their reserves along the chords to the circumference.

Verdun and the Somme

That was exactly the point Joffre had made in the summer, and it formed the broad outlines of an allied strategy agreed at a conference at Chantilly on 6–8 December 1915. The British representatives were the commander-in-chief, then still Sir John French, and Robertson's predecessor, Sir Archibald Murray. They and their allied colleagues agreed that 'Decisive results will only be obtained if the offensives of the allied armies are delivered simultaneously or at least on dates that are close enough to prevent the enemy from transporting his reserves from one front to another'.[27] That, they reckoned, meant attacks within one month of each other. Combined attacks should be launched as soon as possible, and in the interval local attacks should continue in order to wear out the enemy. The Chantilly conference specified neither a time nor a place for the Anglo-French offensive on the western front in 1916. From the British perspective the Ypres salient was the more obvious sector from which to attack, not least because it was closest to the Channel ports and the British Expeditionary Force's supply lines. But militarily Britain was the junior partner of the coalition. French's replacement by Haig promised an improvement in Anglo-French relations, and when Haig met Joffre on 14 February 1916 he readily agreed that the attack should be in Picardy, astride the River Somme, where the two armies met. The sector lacked the roads and railways of Flanders but its chalky, undulating terrain was less likely to become waterlogged, particularly given the preferred start date of around 1 July. Rawlinson, now commanding the 4th Army, which was to take the brunt of the British effort, declared it was 'capital country in which to undertake an offensive'.[28] The crucial point, however, was that the British role would be a supporting one; the main attack would be in the hands of the thirty-nine divisions and 1,700 heavy guns that Joffre promised Ferdinand Foch, commanding the French on their right.

On 21 February, one week after Haig's meeting with Joffre, at 7.12 a.m., a German 38cm long-barrelled gun signalled the opening of a bombardment by 1,220 guns on a 20-km front straddling the two sides of the River Meuse north of Verdun. In the Bois de Ville, at the apex of the French front line, forty heavy shells fell every minute. Within an hour almost all telephone links between the forward positions and brigade headquarters were cut, and the long-range German guns raised their elevation to seek out the network of fortifications that protected the city of Verdun itself, symbol of France's resistance since 1914. The German field guns and trench mortars continued firing on the French forward positions. 'The trees are mown like straw; individual shells disengage themselves from the smoke; the dust produced by the earth that is thrown up forms a fog which prevents us seeing very far', reported G. Champeaux, an artillery liaison officer with the 164th Regiment of Infantry at Herbebois, on the right of the Bois de Ville. 'All day, we hunch our backs . . . We have to abandon our shelter and go to ground in a large crater; we are surrounded by wounded and dying whom we cannot even help.'[29] At 4 p.m., as the light was fading, the German infantry patrols left their trenches, probing for the soft spots in the French defences, and identifying where there was still resistance. That night and into the following morning, amid falling snow, the German artillery renewed its bombardment. On the afternoon of 22 February six divisions attacked on the east bank of the Meuse only, on a front almost half that on which the artillery had opened up. Again patrols preceded the main assault formations, establishing where the artillery had not done its work and where it had. The latter points were hit by groups of storm-troopers, selected infantrymen, equipped with grenades and flamethrowers, and trained to re-establish the links between fire and movement which trench warfare had sundered. The principles had been developed in the front line by Captain Willy Rohr in 1915 and were disseminated throughout the army on Falkenhayn's instructions: a clear case of tactics being developed from the bottom up. Behind the storm-troopers came reserve sections carrying the equipment to consolidate the ground won. By 25 February, the French 51st and 72nd Divisions, holding the line from Herbebois west to the banks of the Meuse, had suffered over 60 per cent casualties. Lack of artillery support was undermining the morale of the infantry: 150 km of wire were needed for telephone repairs on 21 February alone, and communication failures prevented both the infantry from calling up fire support and the gunners from demanding more shells. At 3.30 pm on the 25th, Fort Douaumont, the heart of the Verdun defensive system, fell without a shot being fired. A German breakthrough seemed imminent.

On the evening of 21 February, Konstantin Schmidt von Knobelsdorff, chief of staff to the German 5th Army, had ordered the two attacking corps 'to advance as far as possible'.[30] When Falkenhayn issued his orders for the attack he had spoken of 'an offensive in the Meuse area in the direction of Verdun', and Crown Prince Wilhelm, the 5th Army's commander and the Kaiser's son, had declared that the objective was 'to capture the fortress of Verdun by precipitate methods'.[31] The sector was the best suited of any on the western front for an attempted breakthrough by the German army. Because of their commitments on the eastern front, the Germans lacked the reserves to be able to mount an attack on a broad front. The Verdun salient, forming a bulge in the line and executing a right-angle turn close to German territory, could be deemed a narrow one. During 1915 the French had begun to treat it as a quiet area, stripping the fortresses of their artillery, and ignoring intelligence of an impending German attack. The main railway line from Paris to the town lay behind German lines, so that the Germans could feed the battle more effectively than the French. Troops and shells were brought up by night and hidden in underground galleries. Overhead the Germans concentrated 168 aeroplanes to establish aerial supremacy, and French reconnaissance was further impeded by the bad weather and short days of January, so enhancing the Germans' chances of maintaining secrecy and achieving surprise. If the 5th Army could gain the heights of the Meuse, the town of Verdun would lie at the mercy of its heavy artillery.

The strategic context into which the battle fell was clear enough. Throughout 1915 Falkenhayn had seen the western front as the decisive theatre of the war. He now assumed that the Austrians would guard his back against a severely weakened Russia, while he concentrated Germany's efforts against France. The fact that he did so in the very month when his relationship with Conrad von Hötzendorff reached its nadir meant that his decision was not coordinated with his principal ally. Conrad overran Montenegro and then readied his army for an operation much more to Austrian liking, an attack on Italy in the Trentino. The pressure on Russia eased. Falkenhayn also miscalculated with regard to Britain. He saw it as the hub of the Entente, but hoped that, while the German army defeated its principal European ally, the navy would engage its economic might with submarine warfare. It did not.

The fact that Falkenhayn's strategy did not join up was largely outside his control, but its assumptions were logical enough. Much more perplexing are Falkenhayn's proposals for turning these ideas into operational practice. After the war, in his memoirs, he claimed to have written a memorandum at Christmas 1915, in which he said that he intended not to take Verdun but to suck the French army into the defence of the city and so bleed it to death. This was a different conception of attrition from that advanced by Rawlinson. It elevated the exhaustion of the enemy from a means to an end. But as the orders emanating from the 5th Army make clear, there is little evidence of the logic of 'bite and hold' in what it proposed to do at the time. It was not seeking limited objectives and aiming to max-imise French losses while minimising German. Instead, it advanced as far and as fast as it could, and as a result by 25 February it had suf-fered almost as many casualties as the French. That remained true for the battle as a whole. By the time it closed down in December German losses had mounted to 337,000, of whom 143,000 died, to France's 377,231, including 162,440 dead. Not until mid-March did Falkenhayn regularly use the vocabulary of attrition to explain the purposes of the Verdun battle. It was a way for Falkenhayn to ration-alise the failure to achieve a breakthrough, but it was a thin one. France had allies in the west, Germany did not; and Germany, unlike France, was heavily committed elsewhere. The absolute numbers may have been in Germany's favour, but the relative loss was not. Moreover, the battle of Verdun redefined both France's commit-ment to the war, and the symbiosis between France and the Third Republic. 'They know that they are saving France', a censor reported of the soldiers in July, 'but also that they are going to die on the spot.'[32]

What turned Verdun from a breakthrough battle to an attritional one was France's resolve not to abandon the town. At midnight on 25–26 February 1916, Philippe Pétain, commanding the French 2nd Army, took over the Verdun sector. As a brigadier about to go on the retired list in 1914, Pétain had seen the evolution of trench warfare from the perspective of a front-line commander rather than from the rear. In 1915 he had concluded, as Rawlinson had done, that it was impossible 'to carry in one bound the successive positions of the enemy'.[33] In a memorandum written after the autumn battle in Champagne, he had recommended limited offensives, to go no further than artillery support could reach: material should substitute for manpower. Only after the enemy had been exhausted could a series of breakthrough operations be launched and manoeuvre warfare restored. His defence of Verdun was the corollary of such conclusions. Permanent fortifications built of reinforced concrete had been down-graded in the minds of field commanders by the fall of the Belgian forts in 1914, but Pétain made the inner ring of forts at Verdun the spine of his tactical scheme. He called it a 'barrage position', with its artillery being used to counter German preparations for the attack. By 27 February thirteen heavy batteries were assembled on the west bank to deliver 'bursts of concentrated fire which really constituted independent operations',[34] striking the Germans in the flank as they advanced along the east bank. On 6 March Falkenhayn was forced to attack on the west bank of the Meuse as well, so confirming the effectiveness of the French guns. 'All [the infantry] are doing', Lieutenant Raymond Jubert wrote in May, 'is to act as a standard-bearer marking the zone of superiority established by the artillery.'[35] With the infantry holding shell holes and craters rather than trench lines, the guns frequently hit their own men. To improve observation, the French regained the initiative in the air by grouping fighter aircraft in squadrons and so overwhelming German reconnaissance efforts. On the ground shell supply was maintained by a light railway, constructed during the battle, and by lorry. By June 12,000 vehicles, one every fourteen seconds, were passing up the road from Bar-le-Duc, 'la voie sacrée', as it was dubbed by Maurice Barrès in April.

What made the way sacred was not its cargo of shells and supplies but its human burden and its connotations of Christ-like sacrifice. By 1 May forty French divisions had been through the 'mill on the Meuse'. Pétain's policy was to rotate units in and out of the battle fast enough to prevent its physical and psychological toll destroying their fighting effectiveness. Joffre, on the other hand, was determined to contain the fighting at Verdun in order to minimise the consequences of Falkenhayn's action for his own plans. As the battle lengthened and its demands on French manpower multiplied, Joffre came to regret his selection of commander, but he could not avoid scaling back the French contribution to the Somme offensive. By 26 April the French planned to attack on a 25-km, not 40-km, front with thirty divisions, not thirty-nine, and 312 heavy guns, not 1,700. In the event, on 1 July the French attacked on a 15-km front with twelve divisions but with 688 heavy guns.

Britain therefore found itself moving from a limited liability on the Continent to taking the principal burden in the major Entente offensive in the west in 1916. It did not do so primarily to relieve the French at Verdun. That particular task was accomplished by the Russians. Their principal contribution to the allied joint plan was to have been an attack in the north, near Vilna, but it was usurped by the diversion that preceded it. Mounted by Brusilov in Galicia, it employed principles for the achievement of breakthrough similar to those in the west: careful preparations, a broad front but one within the compass of the artillery, and reserves well up to exploit the initial success. In two days, by 6 June, the Russians had broken the Austro-Hungarian 4th Army, and advanced 75 km on a front of 20. They took 200,000 prisoners within a week, and captured so few guns only because the bulk of the Austro-Hungarian heavy artillery had been redeployed to Italy. Conrad's offensive in the Trentino, which had overrun the Asiago plateau in the second half of May, was already losing its impetus. Now he had to close it down as he shuttled divisions back to the north-east.

On 15 June Conrad told Falkenhayn that they faced the biggest crisis of the war. Falkenhayn was taken completely by surprise. Although by May he recognised full well that the 5th Army was unlikely to achieve a breakthrough, he believed German intelligence estimates which suggested that French casualties at Verdun had now reached 800,000, and was encouraged by the pacifism of French radical socialists to believe that France might seek a separate peace. Signs of British preparations on the Somme were also used to reinforce the logic of the Verdun battle: it was forcing Britain to react elsewhere on the western front and so might trigger the opportunity for a German counter-stroke. He therefore played for time, urging Conrad to recover the situation by withdrawing troops from Italy and looking to Hindenburg to provide Germans from the northern section of the eastern front. None the less he had to release four divisions from the west. Although he was able to attack at Verdun on 23 June, the advance was on too narrow a front and the French were able to counterattack. On 24 June the allied artillery bombardment opened on the Somme.

If it had followed the logic embraced by Rawlinson and reflected in the British heavy-artillery programme, the battle of the Somme would have pursued limited objectives and eschewed any hope of rapid breakthrough. That indeed was what Rawlinson favoured: the frontage and the depth to be tackled would reflect what the artillery could do, and its long, methodical bombardment would be designed to kill Germans, not to enable the infantry to gain ground. Haig, however, decided that Verdun had fulfilled the function of the wearing-out battle and that he now had the opportunity to break through. He wanted a hurricane bombardment and a deeper and faster advance: 'D. H. is for breaking the line and gambling on rushing the third line on top of a panic,' Rawlinson wrote in his diary on 1 April.[36] To this end he created a Reserve Army behind Rawlinson's 4th Army and commanded by a cavalryman, Hubert Gough.

The first cause of the British failure on the first day of the Somme, therefore, was that its planning was the result of compromise. Rawlinson went along with his chief's desires but retained features reflecting his own. The accusation to be levelled against Haig was not so much that he was wrong to seek a breakthrough, for there were moments in the course of the battle when such opportunities beckoned, but that he failed to impose his vision on his subordinate commanders.

The second cause was that the battle was one for which the British artillery was not ready. The 4th Army had over 1,437 guns available to it, more even than the Germans had had at Verdun; it had a gun for every 17 yards of front, and they fired over 1.5 million shells in the preliminary bombardment. However, the Somme front was twice as long as that of Verdun, reflecting Haig's determination to avoid flanking fire. The effect was scattered, especially as only 182 of the 4th Army's guns were heavy. Bad weather spread what had been designed as a five-day bombardment over seven days, further diluting its effect. The principal targets were the enemy wire and dug-outs, but that left the German artillery free of counter-battery fire, and so able to concentrate on the attacking infantry as it formed up to go over the top. Some of the gunnery problems were technical, others were issues of command and training. Britain was improvising a mass army in the middle of a war, and the preparation and equipment of a scientific arm like the artillery took longer than those of the infantry. For the gunners, the Somme had come a year too soon.

It was the infantry who paid the penalty. 'At 7.30 we went up the ladders, doubled through the gaps in the wire, and lay down, waiting for the line to form up on each side of us. When it was ready, we went forward, not doubling, but at a walk. For we had 900 yards of rough ground to the trench which was our first objective.' R. H. Tawney was in the 7th Division, near Fricourt. Most divisions did not have so far to go. Some went out into no man's land before zero hour, and were on the enemy trenches before the German infantry could emerge from their dug-outs and man their machine-guns. Like Rawlinson himself, corps and divisional commanders were left to develop their own ideas. One or two adopted creeping barrages, allowing the infantry to follow up close behind the fall of their own gunfire, but this was a new, experimental idea. Progress was greatest in the south, nearest the river. But Tawney found that his unit's advance could not keep up with the artillery as it lifted onto more distant targets. He was wounded. 'What I felt was that I had been hit by a tremendous iron hammer and then twisted with a sickening sort of wrench so that my back banged on the ground, and my feet struggled as though they did not belong to me.'[37] Tawney survived to become a famous historian, but of the 57,470 British casualties that day 19,240 did not. Nowhere had the advance reached its objectives.

The pattern continued over the next ten days, when Rawlinson abandoned the logic of his own approach, which required progress in the centre and north, for that of Haig, which required the exploitation of the gains in the south. A total of forty-six separate attacks were launched by individual corps but without coordination and with a further 25,000 casualties. A night attack at Longueval on 14 July, orchestrated according to Rawlinson's principles, succeeded but left its author pondering the missed opportunity for a breakthrough.

The Somme battle continued until mid-November, with its purpose oscillating between attrition and breakthrough according to the nature of the latest success or the audience to whom reports were directed. Between mid-July and mid-September Haig convinced himself that the Germans were 'off balance' and about to collapse. Many of the ninety attacks launched in this period were small affairs: ill-coordinated, hurried and launched on narrow fronts, they gained under three square miles of ground for 82,000 casualties. Haig rationalised his failure to achieve breakthrough by saying that his purpose was now attrition. Having dissipated his own strength, he planned a major offensive for mid-September, declaring that it was 'to be planned and carried out in such a way that it may be possible for our troops to achieve a decision if such a result is at all realizable'.[38] The attack at Flers on 15 September, when tanks were used for the first time, like the Longueval night attack, fleetingly raised hopes of breakthrough. But thereafter, as the weather worsened and the mud hampered operations, the battle was again explained in terms of attrition. In truth it should have been closed down. The learning process which the British army's high command was passing through did pay dividends in 1918, but its route there need not have been so sanguinary.

South of the river the French had much greater initial success. They did so because they had 688 heavy guns on a much smaller front. But the momentum was not sustained. Foch was as divided as Falkenhayn and Haig as to whether his objective was breakthrough or attrition, and like them tried both. As early as 12 July General Fayolle, commanding the French 6th Army astride the Somme itself, concluded: 'This battle has . . . always been a battle without an objective. There is no question of breaking through. And if a battle is not for breaking through, what is its purpose?'[39] Almost as many divisions, thirty-nine, were rotated through the Somme battle in seven weeks as through the Verdun battle in six months, and by September the censors' reports suggested that French soldiers regarded the former with greater foreboding than the latter.

That response was not irrational. On 19 April 1916, Joffre had resolved his frustration with Pétain by promoting him to the command of an army group, and introducing Robert Nivelle as his replacement at Verdun. Nivelle orchestrated a series of counter-attacks in the autumn which resulted in the recapture of Forts Douaumont and Vaux. He found that the emphasis on method could be counter-productive when the enemy held improvised positions which he had just captured. Nivelle therefore stressed speed in the attack. On the Somme Fayolle, too, reacted against the influence of Pétain, when he reminded the soldiers of the 6th Army that they could not expect the artillery to do everything for them: the role of the infantry was not just to occupy ground neutralised by shellfire but to fight. On 16 December the French army was told to aim its attacks as deep as possible, up to and including the German gun line; it was warned not to be 'surprised by a success that one had not believed would be so easy'.[40]

Local and particular experiences on the Somme and at Verdun had been hardened into a general doctrine. A month previously the allied generals had once again met at Chantilly to coordinate their plans for 1917. The broad strategy was to be unchanged from 1916: simultaneous attacks on all fronts to prevent the Germans switching resources from one to another. The offensive should begin in February to prevent a repeat performance of 1916, and no operation was to be delayed for more than three weeks beyond the start date. The Anglo-French plan for the western front was to take out the salient bounded by the River Aisne to the south and the Somme battlefield to the north.

The assumption that underpinned these calculations was that the German army was beginning to crack. By the battle's end two-thirds of the German divisions serving on the front had passed through it. Total German losses on the Somme are the subject of dispute, and range from 465,000 to 650,000, depending on whether the lightly wounded are included. The latter figure is significant because of the profit-and-loss accounting generated by attrition: allied casualties reached 614,000, 420,000 of them British. But throughout October Haig and his director of military intelligence, John Charteris, had stressed how close to breaking point was German, not British, morale. Robertson, receiving information from different sources, was not convinced: in the same month he told the cabinet that Germany 'was fighting with undiminished vigour'.[41]

Plenty of evidence suggested that he was right. At the end of August the Brusilov offensive had at last persuaded Romania to throw in its lot with the Entente, the price being Hungarian-held Transylvania and Bukovina. The blow to German expectations toppled Falkenhayn, who ironically went off to the Romanian front and – together with Mackensen – had overrun most of it by Christmas. Hindenburg and Ludendorff became chief of the general staff and first quartermaster-general respectively. On 6 September Ludendorff made his first visit to the western front for two years. The comparison between the eastern front and what he saw on the battlefields of Verdun and, especially, the Somme appalled him. But neither he nor Hindenburg considered giving up the struggle. Instead, they responded in kind. Hindenburg declared, with more rhetorical flourish than economic sophistication, that Germany should double its output of shells and triple its production of machine-guns and artillery by May 1917. In October, although the effect was often to duplicate the functions of the existing Prussian War Ministry, the two created a new office to supervise the war economy. And in December the War Office steered through the Reichstag a law conscripting all males aged seventeen to sixty for the purposes of war production.

At the front itself, Hindenburg and Ludendorff put in hand the construction of a series of defensive positions in the west, of which the most important was the Siegfried position (known to the British as the Hindenburg line). By cutting the very salient that the Entente had decided to make the focus of its 1917 offensive, the Germans released thirteen infantry divisions, fifty batteries of heavy artillery and a comparable number of field guns. In February 1917 the Germans fell back, leaving a wasteland of poisoned wells, razed villages and felled orchards. They reckoned that they had gained an eight-week respite before the British and French could resume their attacks. They were right. But they had done more: by retreating without a fight they had created uncertainty in allied counsels, and left the planned allied blow aiming at thin air. Those who wished for evidence to vindicate the attrition of the Somme found it – with some reason – in the German decision to fall back. However, the German response revealed a deeper difficulty. Attritional battles fought over terrain without significant objectives could simply be negated by the refusal to fight. Attrition and breakthrough were not alternatives but two sides of the same coin, and it was for precisely this reason that so much of the thinking on the topic had proved either confused or vague. Battles on the western front did and would wear out the enemy, but only where he could not afford to give ground.

7

BLOCKADE

The North Sea

Britain was the financier and armourer of the Entente; Germany was the military mainstay of the Central Powers. By 1916 both were, to varying degrees, the principal props of their allies. If it was a principle of strategy that mass should be concentrated on the decisive point, one needed to knock out the other in order to win the war. Thus the Anglo-German antagonism became the pivot of the conflict. The polarity was best expressed in competing ideologies: liberalism and individualism against militarism and collectivism, the pursuit of mammon against the spirit of heroism. However, the bitterness of the rhetoric could not be easily converted into strategy. When the war broke out, neither had a coherent plan for dealing with the other.

Britain was principally a sea power, Germany a land power. At one level, therefore, this lack of preparedness was not surprising. At another it was: for a decade before the war, the building programmes of the two navies had been shaped principally by the arms race between the two sides. But that rivalry had not precipitated the conflict. Furthermore, once the war was declared, the Royal Navy had no strategic interest in fighting a major action against the German navy. As the world's greatest sea power, Britain already enjoyed maritime supremacy. Its task was to defend what it had. 'Tomorrow is Trafalgar Day', Vice-Admiral Sir David Beatty wrote to his wife on 20 October 1914. 'The powers that be have forgotten it. Ye shades of Nelson that we should be in the hands of such is past enduring but one is powerless to do anything but wait day after day.'[1]

Beatty was the embodiment of the fighting sailor. In 1898 he had won a DSO commanding gunboats on the River Nile in Kitchener's reconquest of the Sudan, and in 1900 he had been seriously wounded in the Boxer Rising. Still only forty-three, he now led the Battle Cruiser Squadron based at Rosyth. He owed his rapid promotion in part to another combative veteran of the Sudan campaign, the First Lord of the Admiralty, Winston Churchill. Beatty had been Churchill's naval secretary before the war, and in 1912 had spelt out for his political master the geographical realities that were to shape Britain's conduct of the war at sea: 'The British Isles form a great breakwater across German waters thereby limiting the passage of vessels to the outer seas to two exits, the one on the South, narrow, easily blocked and contained, and the other on the North of such a width (155 miles) that with the forces at our disposal it could be easily commanded so as to preclude the possibility of the passing of any hostile force without our knowledge and without being brought to action by a superior force.'[2]

Britain would bottle up the German navy in the North Sea. The legacy of Trafalgar encouraged British naval officers to hope that the Germans would seek a battle to break the blockade – that the latter would be the means to an end, not an end in itself. Their expectations were reasonable in so far as Germany had to attack if it was to change the balance of power at sea. But that was not the Kaiser's intention at the war's outset. Tirpitz had created the fleet to be a deterrent – to support the idea of *Weltpolitik*, and to persuade the British that Germany was to be taken seriously, either as an ally or as a potential enemy. The logic that underpinned that view did not change during the war itself. For the Kaiser, the ultimate purpose of the fleet's capital ships was to give Germany leverage at the peace negotiations. In August 1914 Germany had eighteen battleships and battle cruisers to Britain's twenty-nine. If its High Seas Fleet responded to the challenge to break the blockade by taking on Britain's Grand Fleet in a major battle, it would lose.

But doing nothing was as frustrating for German naval officers as it was for Beatty. Indeed, it might prove as prejudicial to the long-term survival of the fleet as sailing into the teeth of the British guns. As the junior service, the German navy still had to prove its value to the new nation in a way that the army did not. Tirpitz had spent the best part of two decades battling in the Reichstag for funds to ensure the fleet's steady expansion. If those ships spent the war safely in the harbours of Wilhelmshaven and Kiel, apparently doing nothing, while the army overran much of Continental Europe, continued high spending on the fleet after the war would be hard to justify. The answer was *Kleinkrieg*, small operations to erode the Royal Navy's superiority through the use of mines, coastal batteries and sub-marines. When the Grand Fleet had lost a few battleships, the strengths of the two sides would be more equal and the High Seas Fleet would be able to risk a battle.

The trouble with this strategy was that its weapons were those of coastal waters. It depended on the British positioning their ships off the German mainland, mounting what was called a 'close' blockade. As Beatty's memorandum for Churchill made clear, the Royal Navy did not need to do this to achieve its objectives. Closing the exits from the North Sea, a 'distant' blockade, was just as effective in denying Germany access to the world's oceans and trading routes, and obviated the risk of losses caused by Germany's maritime defences. Distant blockade, which Britain adopted at the outbreak of the war, closed down one German option; however, it opened up another. The Grand Fleet itself was based at Scapa Flow in the Orkney islands, so shutting the northern exit from the North Sea to the Atlantic. Although smaller units were stationed elsewhere, much of the east coast of England was comparatively undefended. German attacks on the British coast, as opposed to British attacks on the German coast, might sting the British into a response and so enable the German navy to take on fractions of the Royal Navy and grad-ually whittle away its strength.

At 8 a.m. on 16 December German battle cruisers of Franz von Hipper's Scouting Squadron bombarded Hartlepool and Scarborough, killing over a hundred civilians. The British press made much of another instance of the Huns' brutality, but the sufferings of non-combatants were not the prime purpose of the raid. The Germans hoped to tempt British forces into pursuing them over freshly laid minefields. Moreover, the battleships of the High Seas Fleet lay offshore to give support to the Scouting Squadron. Beatty's own battle cruisers had been reduced in number by the despatch of *Invincible* and *Inflexible* to the South Atlantic to deal with Spee, and the decision was taken to keep the bulk of the Grand Fleet in harbour. As a result ten British capital ships set out in search of twenty-four German. The latter had succeeded better than the fleet commander, Admiral Friedrich von Ingenohl, realised: he had in his grasp what proved to be the only opportunity for a major naval victory vouchsafed the Germans in the entire war. But he did not know that the Grand Fleet was confined to Scapa Flow. Alarmed by the volume of British wireless traffic, he turned for home.

In this there was a double irony. First, the British were as a general rule far more observant of radio silence than the Germans, preferring to use flags for tactical communications, even when the weather or smoke obscured visibility and made the flags hard to read. Second, the fact that the encounter had taken place at all was the product of German wireless transmissions, intercepted by British signals intelligence.

Within four months of the war's outbreak the British were in possession of all three German naval codes. The Australians laid their hands on the code book for merchant shipping; the imperial naval code book was taken by the Russians from a cruiser which went aground in the Baltic; and the traffic signals book from a sunk destroyer was picked up in the nets of a British trawler. Listening stations were set up along the east coast, so that cross-bearings could enable the position of the vessel sending the message to be fixed, and the intercepted signals were analysed in a newly created department within the Admiralty Old Building, Room 40. Staffed by academics, not professional sailors, its operational effectiveness was principally the achievement of the director of naval intelligence, Reginald 'Blinker' Hall, so called from his constant blinking, a habit his daughter somewhat improbably attributed to the terrible food at his preparatory school. But there was much that was unlikely about Hall, a fearsome interrogator of prisoners and a devious runner of agents and spies: 'all other secret service men are amateurs by comparison', the American ambassador in London told President Wilson.[3] Room 40's work was aided by the Germans' belief that wireless might offset their numerical inferiority: it enabled real-time communication and so facilitated the concentration of forces in space and time. The effect was that their chatter, which continued between ships even when in harbour, conferred exactly those advantages on their enemy.

Not that the British got it right all the time, as the missed opportunity of 16 December 1914 showed. British naval intelligence's ongoing achievements were negative. It prevented the German navy from appreciating that its codes were compromised, although the captain of the *Königsberg* in East Africa in 1915 did realise as much, and its ability to give the fleet warning of a German sally enabled the British east coast to be defended despite the Royal Navy's abandonment of the North Sea. What the Royal Navy found much more difficult was the integration of intelligence with operations, and doing so without compromising long-term security. Commanders at sea were told no more than the naval intelligence directorate felt they needed to know. In particular, they were refused permission to decode intercepts at sea. The evidence of their own eyes might be at odds with the incomplete and progressively obsolescent information fed them from the Admiralty. Intelligence created opportunities for the budding Nelsons of the Great War but then curbed their initiative.

On 23 January 1915 Room 40 warned Beatty and his battle cruisers that Hipper's Scouting Squadron was once again putting to sea. But the Admiralty assumed that the Germans planned to raid the east coast as before, and therefore put the weight on the defence of the British mainland and not on cutting Hipper off from his base. In fact, Hipper was instructed to reconnoitre the Dogger Bank, with a view to attacking fishing boats and to laying mines off the Firth of Forth. Consequently the battle which ensued took the form of a pursuit rather than an envelopment. At 7.05 a.m. one of Beatty's destroyers reported contact with the enemy. At 8.34 Beatty ordered his battle cruisers to raise their speed to 27 knots, four knots faster than the maximum speed Hipper could maintain. Twenty-six minutes later his flagship, HMS *Lion*, opened fire at a range in excess of 20,000 yards. The wind was north-easterly, with the result, according to her captain, that 'the smoke of the enemy coming almost straight towards us, combined with the gloom, made spotting very difficult. Flashes of the enemy's guns were extraordinarily vivid, so that it could not be seen whether we were hitting the enemy or not.'[4] They were: the leading German ship, *Seydlitz*, caught fire. However, she was saved by the deliberate flooding of her magazines. Ultimately, of four German ships, only the weakest and oldest, the *Blücher*, a so-called 'five-minute' ship in reference to her likely survival time in battle, was sunk. The restrictions of flag signals created ambiguity in Beatty's orders. Greater use of wireless would not only have ensured the more effective distribution of his ships' firepower, but also have prevented him breaking off the action prematurely. At 10.54, Beatty persuaded himself that he saw the wash of a periscope. Fearing that Hipper might be luring his battle cruisers over a submarine screen, he turned away rather than risk being torpedoed. There were no submarines in the vicinity, a fact known to Room 40 but not relayed to Beatty.

Beatty blamed his disappointment on the problems of communication. But by focusing attention here he prevented a more thorough discussion of the design problems of the battle cruiser itself. The First Sea Lord, Jackie Fisher, is most often remembered as the mastermind behind the Dreadnought, the all-big-gun battleship, adopted in 1905. However, Fisher's favourite project was not the battleship but the battle cruiser. He recognised as clearly as did the Germans that Dreadnoughts were vulnerable to torpedoes, launched from destroyers or more particularly submarines, weapons which might prove especially effective in confined waters like those between Britain and mainland Europe. His belief that lighter – and cheaper – vessels might be sufficient to protect Britain from invasion did not mean that he saw the capital ship as redundant. Its role, like

Britain's, was global, and its task to dominate the world's oceans. The Dreadnought was an evolutionary design, a staging post to the battle cruiser, a vessel which would have the speed of the cruiser but the punch of the battleship. The first Dreadnought mounted 12-inch guns and could maintain a speed of 21 knots; in December 1914 Fisher secured approval for battle cruisers with 15-inch guns and a speed of 30 knots. The victory at the Falklands seemed to vindicate Fisher's designs. But in the pursuit of speed he had shed armour, particularly on the deck, which was rendered vulnerable to the plunging fire that long-range gunnery encouraged. The ship's survivability depended on her speed and on the range at which she fought, but the pursuit of both these attributes militated in turn against effective gunnery. Gunnery was the most venerated specialisation of the Royal Navy, but it was not very good at it. At the Falklands *Invincible* and *Inflexible* achieved one hit per gun every seventy-five minutes, and took five hours and 1,174 shells to sink two inferior vessels. At the Dogger Bank, when confronted with more equal opposition (if the *Blücher* is discounted) only six heavy shells out of 1,150 had found their targets.[5] The response was to stress the rate of fire over its accuracy, and therefore cordite charges, ready for use, were stored in the gun turrets themselves, and doors to magazines were left open. The safety of a ship was deemed to rest more on quick firing than on her formal protection.

The Germans concluded from the battle of Dogger Bank that relative technological advantage was more important than numbers. They did not come out again for over a year, but when they did – on 31 May 1916 – they deployed ships whose key characteristic was survivability. Armour was thickened, anti-flash precautions improved, and the quantity of ammunition ready for use in each gun turret was restricted. But in another sense the gap between the German navy and the Royal Navy only widened. The numerical difference in capital ships, having closed in the winter of 1914–15, increased again. The Grand Fleet contained thirty-seven capital ships to the High Seas Fleet's twenty-seven, and its guns mounted a broadside that was twice as great. The German army's needs for men and material eroded the navy's ability to command resources, and the debate about the best use of the latter became even more heated. Those committed to the offensive were encouraged by the army's success in the east to call for operations in the Baltic against the Russians, and others said that the submarine, not the capital ship, should be the principal weapon against the British.

Reinhard Scheer, who succeeded to the command of the High Seas Fleet in February 1916, was a decisive, even impetuous, man, in stark contrast to his predecessors. He won the Kaiser over to a more aggressive use of the fleet, its guiding principle being that, as before, Hipper's Scouting Squadron should lure Beatty's battle cruisers out to sea. This time, however, both submarines and the battleships of the High Seas Fleet would be waiting. The Germans were the last of the major powers to develop submarines and in 1914 had only twenty-eight, compared with fifty-five in the Royal Navy and seventy-seven in the French navy. But their late entry to underwater warfare meant that they profited from the trials and errors of the pioneers, and they were therefore building better vessels at a faster rate. In September 1914 German U-boats sank four British cruisers, including three in a single action. The shock effect was considerable, but the long-term lesson misleading. If warships exercised basic precautions, above all those of steering a zig-zag course and of maintaining a reasonable speed, they were safe. The submarine had to submerge to attack but in doing so she restricted her speed to about 10 knots, half that of a warship. She therefore could not act in conjunction with surface warships unless she was already in position. Moreover, she had to reckon on engaging an enemy warship head on, and therefore from the angle at which the latter presented the smallest target. By the end of the war not a single Dreadnought had been sunk by a submarine. But Scheer did not know that in 1916, of course, and nor did his counterpart, Sir John Jellicoe, commanding the Grand Fleet. The latter was a worrier, a centraliser and a hypochondriac, only too well aware of the awesome responsibility he carried as the protector of British maritime supremacy. For him, the German U-boat was a potent threat: 'It is quite within the bounds of possibility', he told the Admiralty on 30 October 1914, 'that half our battle-fleet might be disabled by under-water attack before the guns opened fire at all, if a false move is made'.[6]

To avoid that danger Jellicoe proposed to refuse action in waters of the Germans' own choosing, however 'repugnant to the feelings of all British Naval Officers and men'. On 17 May 1916 Scheer ordered nineteen U-boats to positions off the Firth of Forth. He planned to raid Sunderland, hoping that the Battle Cruiser Fleet would put to sea from Rosyth and using airships to warn him if the Grand Fleet left Scapa Flow. But bad weather prevented the airships from taking any part in the action, and he therefore concluded it would be too risky to approach the British coast. Instead, he ordered a sortie to the north, to the Skagerrak, the waters between Norway and northern Denmark, off the Jutland peninsula. Here his line of retreat would be more secure, but now the principal submarine danger, in contradistinction to Jellicoe's fears, would be mines, not U-boats.

Room 40 gave Jellicoe warning of Scheer's intentions from 28 May, and late on the night of 30 May, over two hours before the Germans left their base in the Jade, the Grand Fleet and the Battle Cruiser Fleet both got up steam with a view to reaching positions off the Skagerrak. But on the following morning, at 11.10 Greenwich Mean Time, misreading of the German call-signs, and poor liaison between Room 40 and the operations division of the Admiralty, placed Scheer, and therefore the High Seas Fleet itself, still in Wilhelmshaven. The result was that the Grand Fleet advanced slowly, so conserving fuel but losing daylight. At 2.20 Beatty signalled that Hipper's Scouting Squadron was in sight. He manoeuvred on a south-south-easterly course in order to cut the Germans off from their base, while Hipper also turned south, aiming to draw Beatty on to the approaching guns of the High Seas Fleet. In this 'run to the south', German gunnery proved more accurate than British. Beatty's principal armament was the 15-inch guns of the latest Dreadnoughts of the 5th Battle Squadron, which had been detached from the Grand Fleet to support the Battle

Cruiser Fleet in February. However, the yeoman on the battleship *Barham* could not read the flags signalling Beatty's decision to turn south-south-east, and initially the 5th Battle Squadron drew away from the Battle Cruiser Fleet, assuming that the intention was to sail north-west to rendezvous with the Grand Fleet. The battleships were marginally slower than the battle cruisers, and fell behind. At about 4.00 they still had not opened fire, when a midshipman on one them, *Malaya*, suddenly said to Sub-Lieutenant Caslon, "'Look at that!'" Caslon 'thought for an instant that the last ship in the line had fired all her guns at once, as there was a much bigger flame, but the flame grew and grew till it was about three hundred feet high, and the whole ship was hidden in a dense cloud of yellow brown smoke. This cloud hung in the air for some minutes, and when it finally dispersed there was no sign of the ship.'[7]

The battle cruiser *Indefatigable* had blown up within thirty seconds of being hit. All but two of her complement of 1,019 were killed. *Lion*, Beatty's flagship, had dropped out of the line: she had already received a direct hit on one of her turrets, which set the cordite charges ablaze, and the ship herself had been saved only by the timely closing of the magazine doors. Now two German battle cruisers, *Seydlitz* and *Derfflinger*, were able to concentrate their fire on a third British battle cruiser, *Queen Mary*. Following a hit on her centre turret, the explosives throughout the ship were detonated, and she sank in two minutes. 'There seems to be something wrong with our bloody ships today', Beatty famously remarked.

It was 4.24. Six minutes later light cruisers began reporting that they could see the High Seas Fleet. At 4.40, when within 20,000 yards of the German battleships, Beatty ordered the Battle Cruiser Fleet to turn about. His task was no longer to defeat Hipper but to draw the High Seas Fleet northwards, towards the Grand Fleet. The 5th Battle Squadron now brought up the rear, and for over half an hour bore the brunt of the German battleships' attack. Its tactics were, according to Georg von Hase, the gunnery officer on *Derfflinger*, to keep 'as much as possible out of our range, but . . . within reach of their own long-range guns'. Declining visibility also militated against accuracy, but 'when a heavy shell hit the armour of our ship, the terrific crash of the explosion was followed by a vibration of the whole ship, affecting even the conning tower'.[8] Aboard his flagship, *Friedrich der Grosse*, Scheer could see even less. He had begun to consider breaking off the pursuit for fear of a night action, in which his battleships would be vulnerable to British light forces, when at 6.26 (7.26 German time) he received a signal that captured survivors from an enemy destroyer reported that there were over sixty large enemy warships in the area, and that twenty of them were new battleships. Minutes later the horizon over a six-mile arc erupted in a line of gun flashes.

Beatty's reporting to Jellicoe had been inadequate and misleading. As their two forces converged on but could not see each other, the commander-in-chief had to decide when to deploy the Grand Fleet into line, so that it could 'cross the T'. This manoeuvre would set the British battleships at right angles to the High Seas Fleet, still in line ahead, and enable them to bring all their guns to bear. If he mistimed it, Scheer would be able to cross the T of the Grand Fleet. Jellicoe's responsibilities at sea were very different from those of a commander on land. Here there was no arbitrary division between tactics and strategy: Jellicoe could see as much or as little of the battle as any other participant, and yet knew only too well that one moment of tactical miscalculation might result in the loss of British maritime supremacy for the remainder of the war.

At 6.15 he began the deployment of the fleet to port, so putting the Germans to his south-west, and silhouetting them against the evening light. Each Dreadnought opened fire as she was free to do so, but because of the poor visibility could see only three or four enemy capital ships at a time. At 6.35 a third battle cruiser, *Invincible*, also struck in the turret, blew up and split in two. But the position of the High Seas Fleet was desperate: ranges were down to 12,000 yards, and the British could concentrate all their fire against portions of the German line. Scheer turned away to the south-west. But in so doing he was moving further from his base. Jellicoe could see less and less in the fading light, but he had the consolation of knowing that he lay between the Germans and their line of escape. This consideration was presumably what prompted Scheer to turn about and strike Jellicoe's line once more. For twenty minutes, from 7.15, the whole of the Grand Fleet was engaged. Then again Scheer withdrew, and to cover his retreat ordered his destroyers to unleash their torpedoes. Fearful of further loss, Jellicoe turned the Grand Fleet away to port, and therefore to the east. In so doing he broke contact with the German fleet. His aim now was to avoid the dangers of night fighting, but to keep the High Seas Fleet to the west, so that it would have to seek a fleet action on the following day.

At 11.30 Jellicoe received a signal from the Admiralty relaying an intercepted German signal, giving the course and speed of the High Seas Fleet two hours previously, at 9.14, when it was ordered home. But Jellicoe's faith in the Operations Department of the Admiralty had been undermined: twice already that day, in the morning and again at 9.58 p.m., it had managed to place Speer in the wrong place. Only three of the sixteen decrypts passed over by Room 40 between 9.55 p.m. on 31 May and 3.00 a.m. on 1 June were relayed to Jellicoe, and therefore he had no context into which to set the intelligence he did receive. But it was not only the Operations Division which was guilty of inadequate communication. Jellicoe knew that his greater speed would prevent Scheer cutting across his bow. Therefore the Germans' most obvious escape route lay astern, via the Horns Reef. This was screened by destroyers. They duly found themselves in confused and sustained fighting throughout the night, but they failed to report to Jellicoe. By the morning Scheer was safely through.

The High Seas Fleet claimed that the battle of the Skagerrak was a German victory. At first the British press tended to agree. At Scapa Flow the mood was despondent, a mixture of combat exhaustion and disappointed expectation. The battle of Jutland (as the British called it) engaged 100,000 men in 250 ships over 72 hours. It dwarfed Trafalgar in scale but not – it seemed – in outcome. The Royal Navy had lost fourteen ships, including three battle cruisers, and had sustained 6,784 casualties. The Germans had lost eleven ships, including one battleship and one battle cruiser, and had suffered 3,058 casualties.

But ten of Scheer's ships had suffered heavy damage, and only ten were ready for sea on 2 June. Jellicoe, with eight ships undergoing repairs, could have put twenty-four capital ships to sea. On 4 July 1916 Scheer renounced fleet action as an option. Jutland left the Royal Navy's supremacy unimpaired and Britain's strategy intact. 'It is absolutely necessary', Captain Herbert Richmond reminded himself, 'to look at the war as a whole; to avoid keeping our eyes only on the German Fleet. What we have to do is to starve and cripple *Germany*.'[9]

Economic Warfare

The blockade remained intact. Economic warfare rather than battle was the means of exercising maritime supremacy, particularly against a Continental coalition. But in the years immediately preceding the outbreak of war even its strongest advocates had been forced to doubt its efficacy. Three obstacles presented themselves. The first was the fear that Britain was more vulnerable to economic pressure than Germany. By 1914 almost 60 per cent of the food consumed in Britain was imported from overseas. Germany, its agriculture (unlike Britain's) protected from foreign competition by tariffs, claimed to be self-sufficient in foodstuffs, although in fact about 25 per cent was imported. The second was legal. In 1909 the Declaration of London had defended the rights of neutrals by defining contraband, the goods that a blockading power in time of war might legitimately sequester, in narrow terms. Foodstuffs for the civilian population most certainly were not contraband. If Britain were neutral, the Declaration of London served the country's interests as a trading nation. If it were a belligerent, it did not. Britain refused to ratify the Declaration of London, but the divisions in its counsels revealed the practical – and third – objection to blockade. Germany would be able to circumvent it by importing through the neutral powers on its borders.

The most forceful spokesman of economic warfare in government was the secretary of the Committee of Imperial Defence, Maurice

Hankey. He bolstered Britain's pre-war policy, in 1911 establishing the general principle that trading with the enemy would cease when war broke out, and in 1912 preparing the 'war book', which spelt out the legal steps and the financial initiatives to put economic warfare in place. He sustained that commitment once the war had begun. In June 1915, now secretary to the war committee, Hankey told the prime minister that the effects of blockade were cumulative 'and the process inevitably slow. It may be that years must elapse before its effect is decisive. But when the psychological moment arrives and the cumulative effects reach their maximum and are perhaps combined with crushing defeats of the enemy, the results may be not merely material but decisive.'[10]

The long-term nature of the blockade frustrated Britain's soldiers and their allies, confronted with desperate fighting in the present, and sometimes uncertain whether they had a future. And the slowness also created a difficulty in assessing the blockade's effectiveness after the war. The economic pressure on Germany did not reach its maximum effect until 1917–18, and by then other factors, including the sustained nature of land warfare and the demands it made on German resources, also contributed to shortages in German production and to the deprivations suffered by the populations of the Central Powers.

The problems of assessment were compounded because, of all the enemy's assets, his armed forces suffered least from the blockade's effects. The focus of economic warfare lay not simply where pre-war German calculations had located it – in the denial of raw materials vital for munitions production – but also in food supplies. Because in time of war the state gave priority to feeding its direct defenders, the soldier and the factory worker, those most likely to suffer from shortages were the militarily useless, the old and the weak. Death rates among epileptics in Bethel, near Bielefeld, rose from 3.9 per cent in 1914 to 16.3 per cent in 1917, and in all Prussian sanatoriums from 9.9 per cent to 28.1 per cent.[11] The British official history attributed 772,736 deaths in Germany during the war to the blockade, a figure comparable with the death rate for the British armed forces, and by

1918 the civilian death rate was running 37 per cent higher than it had been in 1913.[12] Indirectly, at least, the blockade breached the principle of non-combatant immunity. Its naval aspects were the simplest and most immediate part of the undertaking. The deliberation of diplomacy was crucial to its international acceptance and to the cooperation of neutrals in its implementation.

The United States, in particular, with its large German population in the Midwest and a vociferous Irish immigrant community, had good reasons to take exception to a British policy designed to close off overseas markets. Britain did of course also have immense advantages in its courting of American opinion, the English language and a common constitutional inheritance among them. The News Department of the Foreign Office distributed the publications of the War Propaganda Bureau through its embassies and consulates to opinion-formers – newspaper editors and politicians. Books and pamphlets, written by famous authors like John Buchan and Sir Arthur Conan Doyle and produced by private publishing houses, eschewed bombast for subtlety. Moreover, the British navy had taken control of the world's underwater cable networks at the outbreak of the war, so all German communications to destinations outside Europe had to be transmitted by wireless and were therefore vulnerable to interception. Room 40 acquired the German diplomatic code in 1915, and also began reading neutral mail. In due course 'Blinker' Hall was enmeshed in counter-intelligence in the United States, exposing German sabotage and pre-empting Germany's own propaganda.

In this battle for the ideological high ground, Britain had a clinching if less idealistic argument. America's protests about the obstacles created to free trade were silenced by the profits that allied orders generated. In January 1914 US exports by value totalled $204 million. In July the economy was in depression and exports had fallen to $154 million. By December they had climbed back to $245 million. A year later, in December 1915, they reached $359 million, and in December 1916 $523 million. American shares soared: the Dow Jones index showed an 80 per cent gain between December 1914 and December 1915.[13]

The Central Powers were just as ready as the Entente to pay high prices for goods, and could – as the pre-war British pessimists had recognised – channel imports, especially those which were not contraband, via private businesses in neutral states. The opportunity for profit not just in the United States but also in Holland, Switzerland and Scandinavia was immense. Therefore, in addition to propaganda, the Foreign Office had a second task, that of industrial espionage. Britain took on responsibility for the blockade at sea and France that for the control of land routes. Each had to establish from scratch an enormous database on European trade. Bills of lading and ships' manifests were scrutinised. Consuls paced quaysides checking the transhipment of goods. Captain M. Consett, the British naval attaché in Scandinavia throughout the war, reported from Copenhagen that 'consignments of oil from New York consigned to —— are reaching Germany though the intermediation of Mr. —— residing in this town. The oil, which is in barrels, is marked "in transit at the buyer's expense," and addressed Nykjebing, Gottenberg and other ports. The barrels are brought down to the wharf ostensibly for shipment on vessels sailing for neutral ports, but on the other side of these are moored vessels bound for Lubeck and other German ports. The barrels are merely passed across the decks of the vessels which are supposed to receive them, and placed on board the vessels bound for Germany.'[14]

With information like this, the British were able to use commercial pressures to persuade businesses to collude in the blockade, regardless of the political sympathies of their parent governments. Naval control meant they could disrupt normal maritime trade by stopping ships, checking their cargoes and directing vessels to port, where they might be detained for three to four weeks. Neutral firms therefore had an incentive to form cartels to which goods could be consigned. The cartels guaranteed that the imports for their member firms were destined for domestic consumption and not for re-export to the Central Powers. The Netherlands Overseas Trust, set up in December 1914, was the first. In July 1915, 135 out of 186 vessels arriving in Holland were not detained; about three-quarters of those bound for Denmark,

Norway and Sweden were.[15] The Netherlands Overseas Trust therefore became a model for other trades. During the course of 1915
coercion gave teeth to the pressures for cooperation. Britain followed
France in restricting the imports of the neutral states bordering
Germany to their pre-war levels. Sweden found its rubber imports
curtailed and the King complained that he could not play tennis. But
such a policy only checked the escalation in transhipments; it did
nothing to prevent the neutrals selling their own domestic produce.
By 1915 Dutch cheese exports to Germany had tripled since 1913,
and those of pork had risen five times. Sweden shipped four times
the quantity of herring. In 1916, therefore, the Entente began the
practice of pre-emptively purchasing the neutrals' produce: this was
particularly important in the one sea it did not control, the Baltic.

The growth of the blockade's bureaucracy resulted in the creation in Britain in 1916 of a Ministry of Blockade, an offshoot of
the Foreign Office. Both Britain and more especially France now
saw the blockade as a means by which not only to defeat Germany
but also to exclude it from markets after the war. In June 1916 an
allied economic conference in Paris, following an agenda set
largely by Etienne Clementel, the French minister of commerce,
responded to the hot blast of pre-war German competition by proposing to protect key national industries after the war and to reserve
allied raw materials for the use of the Entente partners. Thus far
Britain had maintained the fiction of free trade by doing deals with
business interests in neutral states. But its commitment to the principle of the open market had never been doctrinaire. At home, the
slogan of 'business as usual' exemplified the idea not that the political economy of the state was unchanged by the outbreak of war,
but that business must carry on because it was a key component
in Britain's war effort. Abroad, obeisance to the idea of free trade
reflected that same principle: trade with the United States was
crucial not simply to Britain's own war effort but even more to
those of its allies. While Washington remained neutral, market
forces, not government policy, had to determine the pattern both of
allied purchasing and of the allied blockade.

German imports during the war fell by 60 per cent. But exports also fell – rather more, and for reasons which were not exclusively the consequence of the blockade.[16] The war demanded that resources be channelled to sustain the military effort rather than the balance of trade. The blockade therefore made a virtue of autarchy, and nowhere was this principle more deeply etched than among German farmers and food-processors. Germany produced enough food to feed itself in the war. On the basis that an average daily intake of 2,240 calories was the norm, the German population experienced real hardship only in the months immediately after the failed harvest of 1916. In February 1917 daily rations dropped to 1,000 calories per person. This so-called 'turnip winter' – when turnips replaced potatoes – makes the point. Germans saw the turnip as animal feed. Their hunger, genuinely felt, arose from expectations derived from pre-war diets – varied, rich in fats and meat, and at least 15 per cent greater than the population's physiological needs. Those were the norms to which they aspired. The fact that after the winter of 1916–17 the average calorie intake did not again fall below 95 per cent of the norm did not offset the monotony of what was available.[17] Coffee was a case in point. It served a psychological function more than a physical one. The War Food Office, created in 1916 under the auspices of the Prussian Ministry of War, recognised 'the meaningful influence that coffee and quasi-coffee drinks had on the general morale of the population', and deemed it a 'most important food'.[18] Wartime coffee, however, was no longer made even of chicory or beet, but of bark. Bread was another example. In January 1915 K-Brot was introduced: the 'K' stood for Kartoffeln, or potatoes, whose flour was used in its baking, but for propaganda reasons it was dubbed Kriegsbrot or 'war bread'. Nutritionally K-Brot was perfectly adequate, but it did not taste as Germans felt bread should taste. Sausages inspired particular inventiveness and comparable contempt. They contained 5 per cent fat, most of the rest being water, although cooking salt and vegetable leaf provided some flavour. Over 800 types of substitute sausage were recognised by the war's end, and over 10,000 other Ersatz foods.[19] Indeed Ersatz itself ceased to mean substitute and came to mean fake. Nor was it much compensation to be told that, as the body shed weight, it needed less food to sustain itself. In October 1916 Ethel Cooper, an Australian living in Leipzig, noticing that three of her German friends had each lost 2 stone, realised that she too was 'down to 6 stone 10 . . . There is so little nourishment in the present food, that one always has an empty feeling an hour after a meal.'[20]

Averages were not the same as each individual's daily food consumption. This varied according to age, sex, occupation, class and region of residence; it depended on the time of year and the year of the war. Many Germans did not have enough food and what there was was unfairly distributed. Food shortages were not exclusively the product of the blockade; the allies' efforts interacted with difficulties of the Germans' own making. Between 1890 and 1913 imports of fertiliser to Germany had risen fourfold and as a result yields of cereals had increased by between 50 and 60 per cent per hectare. The blockade cut off imports of saltpetre from Chile, and the quantity of nitrates used in agriculture halved. Fritz Haber had developed the synthetic production of nitrogen, but in 1914 the process's value to Germany lay particularly in the production of explosives. Mobilisation took horses, as well as over 3 million agricultural workers, from farming, and therefore reduced the supply of both manure and labour. Between 1913 and 1918 the area of Germany under cultivation fell by 15 per cent and yields of cereals by a minimum of 30 per cent.[21]

The German government realised very early in the war that food would be a problem: it introduced its first food controls in 1914, four years before Britain. But it responded to rising food prices and their consequent pressure on real wages by fixing prices at the point of production, not at the point of sale. The result was that producers withdrew from the market. Milk was deemed a staple, vital to children, to nursing mothers and the weak, but in 1915 the price of milk rose from 12 pfennigs per litre to as much as 33 pfennigs, an increase which in percentage terms workers' wages had still not matched by the war's end in 1918. In Berlin in November 1915 the price was set at 30 pfennigs, but that did nothing to promote city deliveries, which continued to decline.[22] Price control prompted farmers to switch to the production of butter and cheese, which were not regulated. The most notorious consequence of this fragmented approach was the so-called 'pig massacre'. By early 1915 potato shortages were attributed to the fodder requirements of pigs, which were consequently deemed to be getting priority over people. Pigs were slaughtered, resulting first in a glut of pork and then in a shortage. Thereafter it was not only the price of pork which rose, but also that of other livestock, to which both farmers and consumers now turned. At the same time the government held down the prices of bread and potatoes, and therefore paid relatively more to farmers to bring what the latter judged to be animal fodder to the human market 'at a loss'.[23]

Price controls were largely fictional, in any case. Inflation fed by an increase of the note issue meant that an excessive supply of money was chasing too few goods. In the autumn of 1917 rye was being sold for 380 per cent more than the official price, beans for 200 per cent and butter 90 per cent. The black market was so pervasive that for most of those directly involved in Germany's war effort rations were no more than notional. Even the army colluded in the black market to feed its soldiers, and perhaps one-third of Germany's food was sold this way by 1918. Money not need therefore determined who got food, so it became a source of class division. All were encouraged to buck the authority of the state and descend into petty criminality. 'Everybody who can afford it bribes his trades people,' Ethel Cooper reported in December 1917. 'Those who will not, or cannot bribe, are told that the meat is sold out, and the others get four times the proper amount.'[24] The farmers became convinced that the city-dwellers were profiteers, and the latter were persuaded that the farmers were well-fed hoarders. Townspeople went into the country, evading inspectors at the stations, on so-called hamster trips, 'to see if the farmers and peasants can be persuaded to sell us something to eat'.[25] Failing that, they simply stole. Thus the town was set against the country. Regional imbalances were also the product of local administration, and so deepened the political divisions within the federation of Germany. The blockade worked not in isolation but through its interaction with the fault lines in German society and in the structure of the German polity.

U-boat War

It was of course easier to blame food shortages on the allied blockade than on maladministration. As a result the demand for retaliation in kind was genuinely popular. With the elimination of the German cruiser threat by the end of 1914, these hopes came to be pinned on the U-boat. Before the war Jackie Fisher had scandalised his associates in the British Admiralty with the suggestion that the submarine might be used for commerce raiding, but in October 1914 Hermann Bauer, the leader of the German submarine service, made exactly that proposal to Admiral Ingenohl. The constraints were technical, numerical and legal. The submarine was designed above all for use in coastal waters, not for long voyages. Moreover, the Germans possessed so few that there were unlikely to be sufficient to overwhelm the volume of incoming British trade. Their effects would be achieved less through damage than through terror, and through scaring off neutral tonnage in particular. But this was where the legal requirements of cruiser warfare impinged. The laws of war at sea expected the submarine to behave in the same way as a conventional warship. In other words, she had to surface, give notice of her intention to sink a vessel and allow time for the crew to abandon ship. In the process the safety of the submarine herself was compromised.

None the less, support for Bauer's idea gathered after 2 November 1914, when as part of the blockade the British declared the North Sea a military area. From the outset Bethmann Hollweg and the Foreign Ministry were concerned about the possible reactions of neutrals, but the combination of press agitation and naval frustration overbore both of them, and on 4 February 1915 the Kaiser announced that the North Sea was a war zone and that all merchantmen, including neutral vessels, were liable to be sunk without warning. The US government immediately protested in the strongest terms, and in so doing opened a fault line between Germany's politicians, anxious to avoid incurring American wrath, and its sailors, determined to prosecute the U-boat campaign as vigorously as possible. Orders regarding the treatment of neutral vessels became ambiguous and the accusations directed by one belligerent against the other increasingly heated – and on the whole justified. The British flew neutral flags, and they armed merchant ships. If the U-boat captain obeyed international law he was liable to have his submarine attacked, particularly if he had fallen for one of the British decoys, the heavily armed but equally heavily disguised Q ships. In July 1916 the Germans court-martialled Charles Fryatt, master of the *Brussels*, a British merchant vessel, on the grounds that on 28 March 1915 he had attempted to ram a U-boat although not himself a member of a combatant service. Fryatt was executed.

In terms of propaganda and diplomatic effect, Fryatt's 'deliberate murder', as the *New York Times* called it, worked in Britain's favour.[26] But even more powerful ammunition was the sinking of the *Lusitania* off the Irish coast on 7 May 1915. She was indubitably a British-owned vessel, and as it happened she was carrying munitions. But she was principally a passenger ship, and among the 1,201 who died were many women and children, including 128 American citizens. Colonel Edward House, plenipotentiary of Woodrow Wilson, the American president, had crossed the Atlantic in the Cunard liner only weeks before and was about to sit down to a dinner in London organised by the American ambassador when the news came. House telegrammed the president to say that 'America has come to the parting of the ways, when she must determine whether she stands for civilized or uncivilized warfare. We can no longer remain neutral spectators. Our action in this crisis will determine the part we will play when peace is made, and how far we may influence a settlement for the lasting good of humanity. We are being weighed in the balance, and our position among nations is being assessed by mankind.'[27]

Such sentiments were calculated to appeal to Wilson's idealism, but so, too, did his own argument that 'there is such a thing as a nation being so right that it does not need to convince others by force that it is right'.[28] Wilson, an academic and a Democrat, whose high principles reflected his Presbyterian upbringing, had been president since 1913. For the moment he held back from war. In doing so he reflected the views of most of his fellow citizens, but he still went further than his pacifist secretary of state, William Jennings Bryan, was prepared to accept. Bryan resigned when Wilson sent Germany a strong note demanding that it cease submarine warfare against unarmed merchantmen. It was a significant step: the sinking of the *Lusitania* had convinced his successor, Robert Lansing, that ultimately the United States would have to enter the war against Germany.

In Germany itself, the incident inclined both Bethmann Hollweg and the Kaiser's circle in favour of operating under cruiser rules once more. In the short term the quantity of tonnage sunk actually rose rather than fell, as surfacing enabled the U-boats to use their guns and so economise on torpedoes. But on 19 August 1915 the crew of the British Q ship, *Baralong*, sailing under the American flag until she opened fire, sank the U 27 and then killed out of hand the boarding party the Germans had put on a captured merchant vessel. British attempts to justify the *Baralong*'s action by reference to the fate of the *Arabic*, a passenger liner sunk without warning the same day, were somewhat specious but worked in the United States, because three Americans had been aboard her. By September the constraints on the U-boat commanders imposed by the Kaiser, as well as the internal friction they were generating within the navy itself, were sufficient to persuade the naval staff to suspend U-boat warfare.

Scheer was not prepared to accept such passivity, and after Jutland his assertion that the submarine was the most obvious weapon with which to strike Britain gained in stridency. He now had powerful support from the army. Falkenhayn had proposed a U-boat campaign against Britain to accompany his attack on France at Verdun, and when Hindenburg and Ludendorff replaced him they, too, accepted that economic warfare, not direct confrontation on the battlefields of France and Flanders, was the way to tackle Britain. However, they wanted to wait until they had sufficient forces available to deal with Holland and Denmark, should an unrestricted campaign drive the neutral states into the arms of the Entente. At the end of August 1916 Romania had finally been persuaded by the success of Brusilov's offensive in Galicia to declare war on the Central Powers, and therefore a new front had just opened for Germany. By December Mackensen and the recently demoted Falkenhayn had overrun most of Romania. The army supreme command planned to remain on the defensive in the west in 1917, and endorsed a memorandum written on 22 December by the chief of the naval staff, Henning von Holtzendorff, arguing that unrestricted U-boat warfare could win the war by autumn 1917. Once again German strategy was out of step. At the beginning of 1916, military action had not been accompanied by naval; at the beginning of 1917, naval action was seen as partial compensation for the renunciation of military.

Bethmann Hollweg remained very worried about the likely American response. At one level this seemed irrational. In the autumn of 1916 Wilson fought his campaign for re-election as president with the slogan 'He kept us out of the war'. But his success reflected other factors – his record in domestic policy, above all. Moreover, although he had not done as much to prepare the United States for intervention in Europe as Theodore Roosevelt and other Republicans demanded, he had secured the passage of the National Defense Act in May 1916, doubling the regular army and expanding the National Guard, and of the Naval Appropriations Act in June, setting out to create a US navy equal to the most powerful in the world by 1925. Wilson's policy was one of internationalism, but he recognised that its fulfilment might require the United States to take up arms. A German move to unrestricted submarine warfare was likely to be the precipitant to such a step. The chancellor resolved to appease potential American wrath by himself proposing peace.

For Hindenburg and Ludendorff peace could only be a 'German peace', the product of an overwhelming German victory. The conquest of Romania enabled Bethmann Hollweg to persuade the army that, if Germany took the initiative in suggesting peace negotiations, it could not be interpreted as doing so out of weakness. But the chancellor was so constrained by the army's shopping list of war aims that his offer, when it was published on 12 December, was meaningless. It failed to specify terms, and it was accompanied by an order to the armed forces stating that the peace offer rested on a German victory. Realising that the Entente was likely to reject the German initiative, Wilson stepped in with one of his own. On 18 December he invited the belligerents to state their terms. But the Entente did not want a peace set by America, and the Germans did not want a public debate on war aims, which was likely to divide the country internally. The failure of the December 1916 peace initiatives was not simply the consequence of diplomatic manoeuvres and the great powers' *amours propres*. There were irreconcilable issues here, which, if exposed in negotiation, would have deepened and explained the war's continuation, not ended it. France could not agree terms without securing the return of Alsace-Lorraine, and Germany could not accept that the provinces were not German. Britain had gone to war to restore Belgian sovereignty, but the German navy was now clear that access to the Channel ports would be vital for Germany's future security, especially in the event of what many in Germany were already billing as the 'Second Punic War'. December 1916 was a caesura in the war's course, but not one which opened up a real possibility of ending it. Instead it confirmed its rationale.

The Entente side-stepped Wilson by declaring that it could not agree to talks on the basis of the German initiative. At 7 p.m. on 8 January 1917 the navy and army presented a united front in an audience with the Kaiser, 'who has suddenly come round to the idea that unrestricted U-boat warfare is now called for, and is definitely in favour of it even if the Chancellor is opposed to it. He voiced the very curious viewpoint', Georg von Müller, head of the naval cabinet, noted in his diary, 'that the U-boat war was a purely naval affair which did not concern the Chancellor in any way.'[29] Bethmann Hollweg was not even at the meeting, and when he was informed of the Kaiser's decision he simply accepted it. He had run out of options, hemmed in between the armed forces on the one hand and public opinion on the other. When at the end of the month he rose in the Reichstag to announce the decision to begin unrestricted U-boat warfare on 1 February 1917, 'his voice was hoarse and rough. It was evidently very painful for him to plead for a policy which formerly he had passionately opposed.'[30]

The United States Enters the War

Wilson too had failed. It was now clear that the United States could not participate in the creation of a liberal international world order by staying out of the conflict. On 3 February America broke off diplomatic relations with Germany. Its reason for doing so was the danger to American shipping, but within sixteen days its ambassador in London knew of a possible German threat to the United States itself. In 1916 John J. Pershing had led an American military expedition into Mexico to capture Pancho Villa, a bandit backed by the Germans. Mexico's resentment at this intervention encouraged Arthur Zimmermann, the German foreign minister, to think that the Mexicans might relish the opportunity to invade Texas. He therefore signalled Germany's ambassador in Washington, telling him to broach the idea of an alliance with Mexico in the event of war between Germany and the United States. He used three different routes to send the message and Room 40 intercepted all three. By 17 January 'Blinker' Hall had an incomplete version and on 19 February he was able to brief the US ambassador in London. Wilson published the Zimmermann telegram as though the Americans had deciphered it themselves, so protecting Room 40's secrecy.

The revelation, and Zimmermann's own acceptance of its truth, persuaded those of the American people who remained to be convinced that America should intervene in the war. However, despite the appearances that it and the German declaration of unrestricted submarine warfare created, Wilson's decision for war was neither reactive nor defensive. On 2 April 1917 he addressed the American nation, telling it of the cabinet's unanimous resolve: 'the right is more precious than peace, and we shall fight for the things which we have always carried nearest our hearts – for democracy, for the right of those who submit to authority to have a voice in their own governments, for the rights and liberties of small nations, for a universal dominion of right by such a concert of free peoples as shall bring peace and safety to all nations and make the world itself at last free.'[31]

He meant what he said, and in saying it he revalidated and reformulated the big ideas which Britain and France had espoused in 1914, but which had lost their lustre in the mud and blood of the intervening years. But he had little to offer in terms of immediate contribution, despite his measures to improve America's military preparedness in 1916. The army mustered 100,000 men, a third of whom were in the cavalry or coastal artillery. Pershing's expedition against Pancho Villa marked the limits of its capability. Wilson immediately adopted conscription, on the grounds that it was the most democratic form of military enlistment, but the creation of a mass army had two short-term consequences likely to work against the rapid despatch of the American Expeditionary Force overseas: first, it required the existing army to become the cadre for the new, and second, the latter was likely to commandeer the war production of American factories carefully nurtured by Britain and France. When Ludendorff dismissed the military implications of America's entry, he was not just resorting to bravado. He reckoned that the United States could not put a major army on the continent of Europe until 1919, an assessment which exactly reflected America's own assumptions, and he knew that Germany would have to have won the war by then.

What Ludendorff's calculations failed to take into account was the consequences of America's entry for the conduct of economic warfare. They were much more immediate, and paradoxically it was they which were in large part responsible for his conclusion that the war would have to be over by 1919.

On 28 November 1916 the Federal Reserve Board, the nearest agency the United States had to a central bank, had published a warning to its member banks, advising against the purchase of foreign treasury bills. By this stage of the war Britain was spending about $250 million per month in the United States, both on its own behalf and on that of its allies. Much of it was devoted to supporting the sterling–dollar exchange rate, in order to control the price of American goods. It reflected a dependence on American industry and on the American stock market which in German minds both justified the submarine campaign and undermined the United States's claim to be neutral. Britain and France had calculated on spending $1,500 million in the United States in the six-month period between October 1916 and April 1917, and they anticipated funding five-sixths of it by borrowing in New York – in other words, by selling treasury bills. On 28 November the Federal Reserve Board had been swayed by the views of one of its members in particular, Paul Warburg, a German by birth, who argued that the average American investor was too deeply dependent on an Entente victory. He believed that this over-exposure should be wound down. What followed was better described as a crash: $1,000 million was wiped off the stock market in a week. By 1 April 1917 Britain had an overdraft in the United States of $358 million and was spending $75 million a week.[32] The American entry to the war saved the Entente – and possibly some American speculators – from bankruptcy.

Allied borrowing in the war after the United States's entry became the goad with which the United States could drive forward allied economic cooperation. The US Treasury refused to see the Entente's funding needs in isolation. It aimed to reduce wastefulness in their orders and above all to eliminate price inflation caused by the rivalries of competitive tendering. A joint committee on war purchases and finance was established in August 1917. The committee's remit extended to purchases from neutrals. The Entente had created a wheat executive in 1916; after America's entry, the model spread to other commodities. By 1917–18 the alliance was the most powerful economic bloc in the world's commodity markets, and its ordering created what were virtually global monopolies in the purchasing of major foodstuffs.

What underpinned this was the blockade, which gave the allies the power of coercion. Moreover, the entry of the most powerful remaining neutral to the war removed any final constraint on the enforcement of blockade. America showed few of the reservations in dealing with the neutrals bordering on Germany displayed by Britain. Holtzendorff had hoped that the submarine would scare neutral shipping away; in reality, it had the effect of cutting the flow of imports to Germany's border neutrals and so reduced the quantities available for onward transhipment. Shipping losses, as much as shortage of foreign exchange, forced the allies to coordinate their controls on purchasing, thus squeezing the Central Powers even more out of world markets. Both indirectly and directly, the German decision to adopt unrestricted U-boat war tightened the economic stranglehold in which it was gripped.

And that was where the United States's military contribution was first felt. Pershing, appointed to command the American army in Europe, did not arrive in France until 14 June. Rear-Admiral W. S. Sims, commanding the American naval forces in European waters, reached Britain on 9 April, three days after the formal declaration of war. In London, the US ambassador and he drafted a cable to the president: 'Whatever help the United States may render at any time in the future, or in any theatre of the war, our help is now more seriously needed in this submarine area for the sake of all the Allies than it can ever be needed again, or anywhere else.'[33]

8

REVOLUTION

Liberalism under Challenge

'No one for a moment believes that we are going to lose this war,' Lord Lansdowne wrote in a memorandum for the British cabinet on 13 November 1916, 'but what is our chance of winning it in such a manner, and within such limits of time, as will enable us to beat our enemy to the ground and impose upon him the kind of terms which we so freely discuss?'[1] Lansdowne's colleagues were quick to condemn him as a tired old man. Sir William Robertson lumped him together with 'cranks, cowards and philosophers, some of whom are afraid of their own skins being hurt'.[2]

Lansdowne was none of those things: he had been secretary of state for war during the Boer War and had then moved to the Foreign Office. To speak as he did showed that he did not lack moral courage. Nor was he as isolated as his critics subsequently maintained. 'I am very depressed about the war', Lloyd George, himself now secretary of war, confided to Lord Riddell over dinner six days later. 'Perhaps it is because I am tired. I have not felt so depressed before. I want to go away for a week alone, so that I may think quietly by myself. Things look bad.'[3]

Ironically, Lloyd George was, in one sense, Lansdowne's target. On 27 September, in an interview with an American journalist, he had pre-empted any suggestion that the United States might mediate in the conflict: 'there can be no outside interference at this stage. Britain asked no intervention when she was unprepared to fight. She will tolerate none now that she is prepared, until the Prussian military despotism is broken beyond repair.'[4]

Lansdowne rejected Lloyd George's commitment to the 'knock-out blow'. 'Surely it cannot be our intention,' his memorandum stated rather than asked, 'no matter how long the War lasts, no matter what the strain on our resources, to maintain this attitude, or to declare as M. Briand declared about the same time, that for us too "the word peace is sacrilege".'[5] A Conservative, he saw the society and values with which he identified being destroyed by the very process designed to defend them. Across the Channel, on 27 December, Daniel Halévy, a middle-aged French intellectual who had dabbled in socialism and anarchism before the war, summarised his reactions to the subsequent failure of Wilson's peace initiative: 'Europe is at its last gasp; and that can only last a few months more'.

Halévy's professional contacts had fed his unease. 'Guy-Grand knows the socialist world. He is worried about the ascendancy of Alphonse Merrheim, antipatriotic radical, who has again taken hold of the metal-workers' union, that is to say the labour force which works for the war. . . . Gregh, who knows the political world, has doubts about even it: it is giving up, it is discouraged.' As an official in the French Foreign Ministry's propaganda department, the Maison de la Presse, Halévy appreciated as well as anybody the role of ideas in legitimating and explaining the sufferings of the previous two and half years. And by 6 February 1917 that realisation fortified him: 'I think that the discouragement and lassitude of individuals are not of great importance when the cause from which they derive is not individual, when it is a cause which is either national or idealis-tic, a cause ultimately which dominates the individual and employs him for its own ends without any consideration of what he suffers or what he wants.'

For Halévy, and for the Entente as a whole, the entry of the United States to the war in April 1917 had two direct benefits. The first was economic: 'America's intervention brings the certainty of permanent material aid; of useful maritime aid; it reassures us against exhaustion, it distances it, it lengthens our time, and the lengthen-ing can be the victory'. Halévy appreciated that, for those who had begun to doubt the rationale for the war itself, the certainty that the allies would prevail in a war of exhaustion was not so reassuring. For them America could be seen in negative terms, as prolonging the ordeal rather than terminating it. Thus in many ways the second American contribution was even more important than the first, and at the very least made sense of it: 'The intervention of America brings an immense boost, not only moral but also ideological. It is wholly liberal. It wants disarmament by cooperation and negotiation. . . . Our war was in the process of becoming a struggle of nationalisms, and the most robust, the most genuine, was European nationalism. It has become, thanks to Wilson, a struggle of humanitarian cooperation against nationalist absolutism.'[6]

By the beginning of 1917, as both Lansdowne and Halévy recognised, the business of making war threatened the liberal values that France and Britain had espoused with such fervour in 1914. The power of the state trumped the rights of the individual. Although this was a matter of natural law, its most immediate and real effect was financial. The normal system of budgetary controls was forfeit as the belligerent governments became the principal purchasers of goods, which they paid for with money they had raised largely through borrowing and taxation, devices they regulated. The moral consequence was a denial of personal responsibility. 'He signed cheques', Georges Clemenceau said of Lucien Klotz, France's last wartime finance minister, 'as though he was signing autographs.'[7]

In France the Law of Siege, invoked on 2 August 1914, gave the army the power to requisition goods, to control the press, and to apply military law to civilians; it even subordinated the police to military control. Not until 1 September 1915 did the civilian administration in the interior regain control of policing, and not until April 1916 were strict limits set to the courts martial of civilians. In the military zone, close to the front, the army jealously guarded its prerogatives. Throughout 1915 efforts to inspect it by the Army Committee of the Chamber of Deputies were rebuffed. In October the appointment as minister of war of General Joseph-Simon Gallieni, seen as the saviour of Paris in September 1914 by many – and of all France by some – made approval for such visits easier, but only on a case-by-case basis. Gallieni, while anxious to curb the power of Joffre and his headquarters, was still a soldier: 'As for the ministry', he noted on 21 October, 'I am more and more resolved to accept it only if I have complete freedom and am independent of parliament'.[8] When Gallieni resigned as a result of ill health in March 1916, his successor, another general, Pierre-Auguste Roques, tried to claim a greater independence of general headquarters than was the case: 'I do not want to be a sub-Joffre, but rather a ministerial friend of Joffre's'.[9] Verdun discredited the French commander-in-chief and so aided the efforts to re-impose civilian control over the military. But the chronic instability of the governments of the Third Republic meant that for the time being their fortunes were still tied to the success or failure of their armies.

In Britain, the army never achieved that degree of autonomy, but the executive arrogated to itself powers which were contrary to any idea of parliamentary accountability and which affected the independence of the judiciary. The Defence of the Realm Act, passed on 8 August 1914, although primarily designed to safeguard Britain's ports and railways from sabotage or espionage, permitted the trial of civilians by court martial. Its provisions were progressively extended to cover press censorship, requisitioning, control of the sale of alcohol (Britain's licensing laws date from 1915), and food regulations. After March 1918 a woman with venereal disease could be arrested for having sex with her husband if he were a serviceman, even if he had first infected her. Piecemeal, the state acquired the right to intervene in the workings of the economy. Traditional Liberals complained that the import duties introduced in 1915 breached the party's axiomatic commitment to free trade; capitalists saw the excess-profits duty introduced in the same budget as an affront to the principles of Adam Smith. Nor were the mechanisms designed to soak up the liquidity generated by wartime business confined to the obviously wealthy. In 1914 income tax was a burden on the rich minority; during the war 2.4 million workers became liable to pay income tax for the first time, and by 1918–19 they made up two-thirds of all taxpayers. As significantly, those who did not pay tax avoided it because they were exempted on the grounds of family circumstance: in other words, they were no worse off financially (and probably the reverse) but they had now come under the purview of the state. The most significant step in the extension of state authority in Britain was compulsory military service, adopted by the Asquith coalition in the first half of 1916. 'The basis of our British Liberty', Richard Lambert, a Liberal member of parliament opposed to conscription, averred, 'lies in the free service of a free people ... Voluntary service lies at the root of Liberalism just as Conscription is the true weapon of Tyranny'.[10]

By the mid-point in the war Lambert was a comparatively isolated figure. This is the essential point with regard to the accretion of state power. The press and public grew angry more because not enough was done, than because the state had become the enemy of civil liberties. Asquith's government followed public opinion rather than driving it. When it acted it did so with consent. 'For the time, but it is to be hoped only for the time,' William Scott, Adam Smith Professor of Political Economy at Glasgow University, declared in a series of lectures given in London in early 1917, 'the freedom of the individual must be absorbed in that of the national effort. His true and permanent interest is interwoven with that of his country.'[11] The erosion of the principles of liberalism and of constitutional government was never really interpreted in Lambert's terms: in the short term people were prepared to become more like Prussia to defeat Prussianism. In France the debate on the extension of the state's power was even less emotive: the legacy of the French Revolution meant that the use of totalitarianism in the name of national defence had a powerful pedigree. In both countries, the popular cry was for more government direction, not less.

It was on the back of this sentiment – the demand for a small war cabinet to direct the nation's strategy – that Asquith fell from power at the beginning of December 1916. An election should have been held in 1915, and was therefore overdue; the principle of universal military service had been introduced without the adoption of universal adult male suffrage (indeed, Britain had the most restrictive franchise of any European state except Hungary); and the formation of the coalition in May 1915 meant that opposition within parliament was effectively silenced. Lloyd George's arrival as prime minister in Asquith's stead might have presaged a return to democratic norms. He came from the radical wing of the party, so popular consent validated his actions, as well as keeping the illusion of liberalism alive. But he made clear to the Liberal members of parliament that 'the predominant task before the Government is the vigorous prosecution of the War to a triumphant conclusion'. As the Conservative and courtier Lord Esher wrote to Haig, 'To achieve that, his only chance of success is to govern for a time as Cromwell governed. Otherwise Parliamentarianism (what a word!) will be the net in which his every effort will become entangled. It is of no use to make a *coup d'état* unless you are ready with the whiff of grapeshot.'[12]

Esher and Haig were the sorts of men on whom the new prime minister relied. His was a ministry dominated by Conservatives. The constraints on his actions came less from the left than the right. Both the King and the Tory press supported the generals, despite the outcome of the Somme battle, and at the end of 1916 Haig's position – although the British government had never delegated as much authority to one soldier as the French had done to Joffre – looked secure. Of the crown, the army and the Conservative party, none was temperamentally drawn to the garrulous, philandering Welshman, a Nonconformist and a supporter of the Boers in the South African war, but they recognised that the combination of energy, self-promotion and rhetorical skill made him a more convincing war minister than the consensual Asquith. Liberalism, however compromised, had honed a remarkably flexible ideological and economic base for the conduct of war.

Revolution in Russia

Some British and French observers therefore convinced themselves that liberalism in Russia would tap the energies of the middle classes, promote the talented and permit the full flowering of that country's latent potential. After the 1905 revolution, the Tsar agreed to the establishment of the Duma, an assembly elected on a broad suffrage and initially dominated by liberals. At the local level, the Zemstvo, a form of county council, became a vehicle for welfare activity and for the involvement of professionals in public service. In 1914 a Union of Zemstvos was created, with the backing of the Council of Ministers, to support the war effort, through helping wounded soldiers and displaced persons. At the economic level, too, the years before the First World War suggested that liberalisation would strengthen Russia. Between 1908 and 1914 the economy grew at an average of 8.8 per cent, soaring to 14 per cent in 1914 itself. The Association of Trade and Industry hoped to establish a wartime part-nership between the private sector and the government comparable with those in Britain and France. In June 1915 it proposed the for-mation of the War Industries Committee to oversee full industrial mobilisation by liaising with the regions and with bodies like the Duma and the Union of Zemstvos. But by 1916 the committee had secured only 7.6 per cent of the orders placed within Russia by the government since its inception. Dominated by the heavy industries of Petrograd and Moscow, it was a casualty in part of industry's own internal divisions, but also of rivalries with the Duma and the Union.

However, just as important as the opportunities the war gave Russian liberals were those it accorded for the revival of political conservatism. The Tsar had accepted the Duma with a bad grace, and his ministers resented the erosion of their competence that bodies like the Union of Zemstvos and the War Industries Committee represented. Neither war nor foreign policy lay within the competence of the Duma, and it rapidly became clear that if it had any purpose after July 1914 it was to discuss and not to legislate. In the summer of 1915, as the Russian armies fell back, the Tsar agreed to reconvene the Duma, which had so far been restricted to the briefest of wartime sessions. The moderate intellectuals, busi-nessmen and professionals coalesced in a Progressive Bloc, and, under the umbrella of foreign policy and liberalism, demanded 'the formation of a united government' and 'decisive changes in the methods of administration'.[13] Pavel Milyukov of the Kadet Party said, 'we don't seek power now . . . the time will come when it will simply fall into our hands, it's only necessary at present to have a clever bureaucrat as head of the government'.[14]

That was not the Tsar's vision. He saw both the bloc and the Duma not as vehicles for national unity but as threats to his power. Dynastic duty impelled him to prorogue the Duma in September, just as it had already prompted to him to transfer his uncle, Grand Duke Nikolay, to the Caucasus command and to take over the supreme command of the army himself. 'God's will be fulfilled', he wrote to his wife as he arrived at headquarters. 'I feel so calm. A sort of feeling after the Holy Communion!'[15] His sense of responsibility made him deaf to contrary advice. The British ambassador, Sir George Buchanan, was only too conscious of criticisms of Russia's autocracy both in his own country and in France: they dented the Entente's claim to be fighting for liberalism. In September 1915 he suggested to the Tsar that the Asquith coalition might be a model for united government, and in February 1916 urged him to concede to liberal pressures 'as an act of grace for services rendered'. But the Tsar dismissed those of his ministers who took a similar tack and distanced himself from those he appointed in their stead by removing himself to the army's headquarters at Mogilev. Here he retreated into a fantasy world where there was no war and no threat of revolution. He was not far enough forward to create a bond with the soldiers of his army, but too far from Petrograd and Moscow to be sensitive to the currents of political opinion. The second gap was mediated for him by his wife, who, despite being the granddaughter of a British queen, believed, Buchanan said, that 'autocracy was the only regime that could hold the Empire together'.[16]

Writing after the war, Buchanan confessed that she might have been right. It was one thing for well-established liberal states to move in the direction of authoritarianism for the duration of the war; it was quite another for an authoritarian government to move towards liberalism which many hoped would last beyond the return to peace.

Moreover, the strains the war had imposed on Russian society, and the expectations that those strains had generated, looked increasingly unlikely to be controlled by constitutional reform. Most members of the Duma were monarchists; they were fearful of the urban masses and their republicanism.

In Petrograd what loomed was not liberalisation for the better conduct of the war, but socialism to end the war. The population of the city had increased by one-third between 1914 and 1917 as the war industries expanded. Those employed in the metal-working industries rose by 136 per cent and in the chemical industry by 85 per cent. But output per worker fell, despite longer working hours. Skilled males were replaced by unskilled females, children and prisoners of war. Many under-performed because of weakness and hunger. Significantly, the workforce in food-processing fell by 30 per cent. Food was simply not getting into the capital in sufficient quantities. Peasants withdrew from the market in response to inflation, either hoarding or speculating, and what they sold went in the first instance to the army. Russia's fragile railway network was creaking under the demands of supplying the troops at the front. Petrograd's special council on food supply, set up at the beginning of September 1915 to get food into the urban areas of the province, calculated it needed 12,150 wagonloads per month; in 1916 that figure was exceeded only in September and October. In December 8,654 wagonloads arrived in Petrograd, and in January 1917 6,556. By then the average unskilled worker had to spend over 52 kopecks a day to feed himself, exactly twice the amount he had required in July 1914. Over the same period the average wages of a textile worker rose from 17.6 roubles to 28.3, which represented a fall of 22 per cent in real terms. Only those in war-related industries had experienced a rise in real wages, and even for those in the metal industries it was 21 per cent at best.[17]

One of the causes of the transport problem was insufficient fuel. Some locomotives were fired by wood or peat, reducing their carrying capacity. Because of labour shortages and falling output per worker, Russia's coal output did not increase to meet rising demand.

Moving coal by rail from the Donets basin and the Urals to factories in the north-west further depleted what was available to the end user. Blast furnaces fell idle for lack of fuel. By December 1916 many war industries had to cease production for a week or longer, and the workers, with nothing to do, returned along icy, unlit streets to slums they could not heat.

In January 1917, an agent of the secret police reported that 'Children are starving in the most literal sense of the word. A revolution', he concluded, 'if it takes place will be spontaneous, quite likely a hunger riot.' So far strikes had been driven largely by falling real wages, but on 22 January 150,000 workers marched through Petrograd, and tens of thousands did so in other Russian cities. Although most were doing so to protest their hunger, a significant minority bore banners which linked social distress to political calls: 'Down with the war', or 'Down with the autocracy'.[18] Revolutionary socialists wanted delay in order to coordinate these protests. But on 8 March women textile workers took to the streets to demand bread. By the afternoon they had been joined by metal-workers from the war industries, and now the targets were the government and the war. Within two days 200,000 workers were on strike. Maurice Paléologue, the French ambassador, must have felt some ambivalence on hearing the strains of the *Marseillaise*. At Tsarskoye Seloye the Tsarina wrote one of her tender, loving letters to her 'own priceless, beloved treasure', fortifying him and blaming the Duma: 'It's a hooligan movement . . . But this will all pass & quieten down.'[19]

Her husband was relying on the Petrograd garrison to restore order. That, after all, was what it was there for. However, its Cossacks were already fraternising with the strikers. There were five regular regiments in the city, but compared with the rest of the Russian army they were disproportionately urban, and their off-duty socialising had alerted them to the grievances of the working-class population. On Sunday, 11 March soldiers in the Pavlovskiy barracks mutinied. By the following morning 20,000 of them were on the streets. The instrument of the Tsar's authority had not exactly broken in his hand, as Nicholas himself was unable to get to Petrograd. Let down by the railways, he was stranded at the headquarters of General Nikolay Ruszkiy, commander of the northern front. Ruszkiy urged the Tsar to establish parliamentary government. General Mikhail Alekseyev, the chief of staff, on whose advice the Tsar had depended but who had been sick in the period immediately preceding the revolution, endorsed Ruszkiy's view. But by now the situation was irrecoverable. The Duma had established a provisional committee, which called on the monarch to abdicate, advice which Ruszkiy seconded. Faced with the choice between loyalty to the crown and loyalty to the nation, the Russian army opted for the second. 'Your Majesty must remember', Buchanan had sagely advised the Tsar in their last interview two months earlier, 'that the people and the army are but one.'[20] Not much had united the Tsar and the Duma in the past, and the former still misinterpreted the situation sufficiently to blame the latter for the revolution. However, both now rallied to the idea that by going the Tsar would enable Russia the better to wage the war. The Tsar, as ever, did his duty.

Russia's Western allies may not have welcomed the revolution but they were hardly surprised by it. Representatives of all three powers, Britain, France and Italy, had conferred with the Russians in Petrograd at the end of January. At one level this was a high point of Entente collaboration: the meeting ranged over strategy, finance and production, and it gave coherence to the idea that simultaneous attacks on all fronts was the best policy. But both the British and French military representatives came away convinced that the Russian army would not be able to mount a major offensive in 1917. The hope that it would come good in 1918 was one which optimists clung to after the revolution: if, as a result, 'efficient people' took charge, Christopher Addison, the British minister of munitions, wrote in his diary on 16 March, 'it is the biggest blow to the Germans since the beginning of the War.'[21] Others who knew Russia better, and recognised the challenges faced by its Provisional Government, appointed by the Provisional Committee of the Duma pending the election of a Constituent Assembly, found their faith that the war could be won through liberalism wavering.

The Nivelle Offensive

'Don't forget', Paléologue had communicated in a message to the Provisional Government on 13 March, 'that the French army is making preparations for a great offensive and that the Russian army is bound in honour to do its share.'[22] But even before the revolution, at the Petrograd conference, the Russians had made it clear that they could not support the offensive in the west. The Anglo-French plan for the spring of 1917 was therefore unravelling at two levels. First, the German withdrawal to the Hindenburg line had upset its operational assumptions: the left wing of the French offensive on the Aisne now had no opponent. Second, it would not be part of a coordinated assault on Germany's central position.

The logical conclusion was to call the whole thing off. But the Tsar's abdication in Russia coincided with a succession of governmental crises in France, the result in part of the reassertion of civilian controls over the army. Meeting in secret session, the Chamber of Deputies had blamed Joffre not only for France's military ills at Verdun but also for the overrunning of Romania and the neglect of the Salonika front. In December he was replaced by the bumptious Nivelle, who was convinced that he could scale up the tactics he had used in the Verdun counterattacks to achieve a breakthrough on the western front in forty-eight hours. After that, he asserted, 'the ground will be open to go where one wants, to the Belgian coast or to the capital, on the Meuse or on the Rhine'.[23] But with Joffre's departure power had flowed from general headquarters to a ministerial war committee, and its principal strategic adviser was not the commander-in-chief but the minister of war. The conqueror of Morocco, the royalist Louis Lyautey, whom Briand appointed to the post in the December reshuffle, loved neither Nivelle nor parliamentary accountability. His distaste for democracy, expressed publicly once too often, brought Briand down.

On 18 March a former finance minister, seventy-five-year-old Alexandre Ribot, reshuffled the ministerial pack and appointed a civilian and a socialist, Paul Painlevé, minister of war. Painlevé's military thinking was shaped by the defensively minded Pétain, who in turn was unconvinced by Nivelle. In a series of meetings in late March, Nivelle argued that his principal worry after the Germans' withdrawal to the Hindenburg line was that they would do the same again before he had a chance to attack. By carrying on, he would save Russia. The strategic logic was now the reverse of that adopted in December: the Italians were also not ready to attack, so that now the western front offensive was justified precisely because there were not going to be attacks on the other fronts. So fraught had the situation become, with Painlevé caught in a crossfire of competing professional advice, that a meeting was convened at Compiègne under the chairmanship of the president of the republic, Poincaré. Nivelle threatened to resign if the offensive did not go ahead. The Ribot government was caught. It felt that it had to attack somewhere, if only in response to the German declaration of unrestricted U-boat warfare. It was too weak to survive Nivelle's departure, especially when he had not yet lost a battle: the military still had that much leverage over the civilians. And it was boxed in by its alliance obligations. Lloyd George, himself only just in office and not yet fully established, had taken to the English-speaking Nivelle with so much enthusiasm that he had attempted to have the British army subordinated to French command. He had been stopped, but for this operation Haig was answerable to Nivelle and was loyally cooperating with his plan.

Three days after the meeting at Compiègne, on 9 April the British launched their attack round Arras, at the northern extremity of what would have been the German salient. Its role was strictly limited: to pull German reserves away from the River Aisne. Well planned and well executed, it revealed that the learning curve on which the army had embarked in 1915 was now bearing fruit. Restricted to a front of 24 km, the battle was fought as a series of limited and staged attacks, leap-frogging each other, and with pauses to consolidate after each. The artillery now had both the equipment and the expertise to fight the sort of battle to which it had aspired on the Somme and which was to shape the nature of allied successes for the rest of the war.

Nearly 2.7 million shells were fired, over a million more than on the Somme, and 99 per cent of them detonated. Fast-acting graze fuses meant that shells did not bury themselves in the ground, breaking it up and losing their force, but exploded on impact, and in particular cut barbed wire. This firepower was used more discriminatingly: bombardments elsewhere along the line deceived the enemy as to the true point of attack, and intelligence focused the guns on the key sectors. Of nearly 1,000 heavy guns, 377 were concentrated on a 6-km front facing Vimy Ridge, a high point commanding the plain to Douai and the east. Its capture was the task of the Canadian corps, which spent the winter training at platoon and section level for the assault, familiarising itself with models of the ground, and learning to advance in close conjunction with the creeping barrage of the artillery. 'All you have to do', one sergeant instructor explained, 'is to hang on to the back wheel of the barrage, just as if you were biking down the Strand behind a motor 'bus; carefully like, and not in too much of a hurry.'[24] Above the ground, aerial reconnaissance provided the photographic images on which the planning could be based, and later reported progress as the attack went in; beneath it engineers tunnelled into the chalk to lay charges beneath the German front line.

The Canadians breasted the crest at 1.18 p.m., having penetrated 4,000 yards of German defences. The capture of Vimy Ridge was a national triumph for Canada, a more auspicious coming of age than the mismanaged landings at Gallipoli had been for Australia. It was also proof that combined arms tactics and careful preparation could successfully link fire and movement to break into the enemy's position. As well as the integration of artillery support, each Canadian brigade had eighty machine-guns, including a Lewis-gun section for every platoon. Donald Fraser was in the last phase of the attack but still found that as a result of the rehearsal 'I had absolutely no difficulty in making for my objective without the least deviation'. As the day developed, 'sleety snow driven by gusts and squalls soon melted making the ground extremely muddy and slippery'.[25] The deterioration in the weather slowed the attack in subsequent days, but so did the impossibility of progressing beyond the range of effective artillery support: in the case of field artillery cutting wire, this was about 2,000 yards. However, the battle of Arras achieved its principal strategic objective: the Germans doubled their strength in the sector within a week.

It proved of no assistance to Nivelle on 16 April. As a result of the German evacuation of Artois, his front had moved to his right, and he was now attacking out of a cul-de-sac, going from south to north, towards the River Oise. Few roads and railways ran in that direction. The towns on the south bank of the Aisne were small for the infrastructure now required of them. On the north bank the intersected slopes rose steeply to the ridge, along which ran the Chemin des Dames. The Germans had been here since September 1914, and their positions were both strong and deep, the main line hidden on the reverse slope, and behind that and out of artillery range a fourth line was under construction. Nivelle had collected enough guns on his 40-km front to allocate one field gun and one trench mortar for every 23 metres and one heavy gun for every 21 metres. But the depth of the German positions meant that the number of guns per metre of enemy trench was half that. The Germans had ample intelligence of French intentions, and they had 100 machine-guns for every 1,000 yards of front.

Despite the enemy fire, the gradient and the atrocious weather, the infantry had been set a rate of advance of up to 2 kph, with only the briefest of pauses. Nivelle intended to be on positions 8–9 km deep by the end of the first day. In anticipation of a major breakthrough, the infantry carried rations for three days, and were so encumbered that those with light machine-guns frequently ended up dumping their weapons. At Berry-au-Bac and Juvincourt, tanks, used in numbers for the first time by the French, carried so much petrol that some caught fire, and the remainder outstripped the exhausted infantry meant to accompany them. By the end of the first day, of 132 tanks 57 had been destroyed and 64 had become bogged. None the less, the Nivelle offensive was not as big a disaster as its aftermath suggested. By 20 April, the French had advanced up to 7 km on the west of the front; they had taken 20,000 prisoners and only sixteen of the fifty-two German divisions available had not been through the battle. But in relation to Nivelle's own declared objectives, trumpeted throughout the army as well as in allied councils, the effects were disastrous. On the rest of the front the gains were negligible, and within a week the hospitals, told to expect 10,000 wounded, were coping with 96,000. Across the army as a whole casualties by 10 May had reached 20 per cent, and in those units directly engaged they were at least double that: one Senegalese division, its soldiers already suffering from frostbite, lost 60 per cent of its strength.

'We decided not to make another attack. We expressed our extreme exhaustion, our miseries, our suffering. The high command will doubtless conclude something else.'[26] Mutinies began in late April, grew in May, and peaked in June. In all, sixty-eight divisions were affected, and about 40,000 troops. Concentrated in the sector from Soissons to Reims, many of them involved units which refused to return to the line, having had too little opportunity to recover and rebuild. They can be characterised as soldiers' strikes, reactions to bad command, inadequate officers and poor conditions of service. The French army, it seemed, was still ready to defend France, but on its own terms.

The mutinies seemed to be a very precise episode, linked to the fiasco on the Chemin des Dames. However, they need to be set in a context which is both chronologically longer and socially broader. Verdun had taken its toll. Desertion rates were already rising in the first three months of 1917. And the after-shocks continued into 1918. On the military side of the equation, therefore, the consequences of Nivelle's offensive represented the culmination of a process begun in 1914. Moreover, France's generals, while ready to address the problems with military palliatives, were quick to blame them on the mood of pacifism and political uncertainty at home. In doing so, they were of course side-stepping their own responsibilities, but they were also reflecting the fundamental social truth of a mass army in a major war – the truth that the Tsar had been slow to grasp. Citizens who had become soldiers for the duration of the war had not thereby lost their civilian identities. They would become conscious of the degree to which that had happened only when they got home (if they got home) after it was over.

French civilian morale also drooped in the first half of 1917. Strikes in January and May 1917 spread from textile workers to munitions factories. For all Halévy's concerns about the influence of the radical socialist, Alphonse Merrheim, most of the protests were reflections of the cost of living rather than of revolutionary sentiment. By January 1917 food prices in Paris had risen 40 per cent since July 1914, and by July 92 per cent: real wages had fallen 10 per cent. A survey conducted in June 1917 on the orders of the ministry of the interior found morale good in three departments, fairly good in thirty, indifferent in twenty-nine, and bad in eight.[27] Significantly in those regions with low morale, the behaviour of soldiers on leave was cited as a factor. The Gares du Nord and de l'Est, the railway stations in Paris through which most troops going to and from the front passed, became a focus for pacifist agitators, and symbolised this link between feeling at the front and in the civilian population. The general mood may not have been pacifist, but it was certainly defensive rather than aggressive. Joseph Caillaux, prime minister in the 1911 Moroccan crisis, who had condemned the war in 1914 and was rumoured to have German contacts, was canvassed as a possible prime minister. Caught between socialist demands for a negotiated settlement and the publication of an extensive war aims package agreed with tsarist Russia, Ribot's government collapsed at the end of August. He was replaced by Painlevé, a compromise candidate, but a compromise to which the socialists refused to subscribe; the *union sacrée* of 1914 was broken.

On 31 May 1917 Bandsman Poitou wrote home to his wife that he had seen a train bringing soldiers back from leave in Paris to Château Thierry: 'the *poilus* were singing the Internationale, crying down with the war, long live the revolution[.] I believe it is the portent of an imminent revolt.'[28] It was not, but that was not evident at the time, and it worried more significant players than Poitou. On 8 May Pétain was appointed to succeed Nivelle as commander-in-chief. He responded to the complaints about leave and rest. He handled the mutinies with restraint: of 629 soldiers condemned to death between May and October 1917, only 43 were executed.[29] But he also embarked on a programme of political education for the troops, emphasising the wider strategy of the war and the contribution to its purpose that the United States's entry would make. His solutions, in other words, were both military and political. His closeness to Painlevé reunited the strategic outlooks of general headquarters and the government, and confirmed that France would adopt the defensive for the time being.

The Entente under Strain

Pétain planned to wait for the Americans. He put no pressure on the British to take up the gauntlet, and the fact that the British did so was not due to the travails of the French troops: indeed, until very late in their planning the British assumed that they would have more support from the French than they received. Douglas Haig, Pétain's British counterpart, was not prepared to forgo the offensive. And he was right, both politically and strategically. In May 1917 the French policy of inactivity on the western front implied that the Central Powers would have an unimpeded run against Russia and Italy until at least 1918 and possibly 1919. Lloyd George had wanted to lend artillery to the Italians so that they could take the initiative, but Cadorna feared that an offensive launched in isolation from efforts on other fronts would bring the German army as well as the Austro-Hungarian down on Italy. By then supporting Nivelle, the prime minister had revealed his hand: he was ready to accept an offensive on the western front, provided it was not under Haig's command. The fact that he had backed the wrong horse undermined his authority in British strategic counsels. Here an unlikely alliance had grown up between Robertson and Admiral Jellicoe, who had moved from the Grand Fleet to be First Sea Lord in December. Jellicoe was anxious to take out the German naval bases at Ostend and Zeebrugge.

His caution at sea had turned to pessimism in Whitehall. His worries were not simply focused on the threat of the U-boat; they also concerned torpedo boat activity in the Channel and even a cross-Channel attack. On 27 April he wrote a memorandum which was placed before the war cabinet: 'We are carrying on this war . . . as if we had the absolute command of the sea. We have not . . . Disaster is certain to follow, and *our present policy is heading straight for disaster*.'[30]

Robertson was suitably impressed, and he told Haig. For Haig, it confirmed the need for an offensive in Flanders, the British Expeditionary Force's most logical area of independent operations given its lines of communication. He had twice – at the beginning of 1916 and of 1917 – been compelled to subordinate his own preference for operations here to the need to cooperate with the French, and the sensitivity of the sector had been exploited by the Germans in a deception operation mounted to cover their withdrawal to the Hindenburg line. The battle that followed, the third battle of Ypres, which culminated in a muddy morass at the village of Passchendaele in November, has become for the British the embodiment of the First World War's waste and futility. But it had a clear strategic purpose. If the army could advance to Roulers, it would command the key German railway junction in the northern half of the western front. At that stage a daring amphibious operation would outflank the German positions from the sea and secure Ostend and Zeebrugge.

Its very ambition appealed to Haig: it might win the war in 1917. It also worked on the imagination of the prime minister, his most obvious protagonist. A victory on that scale would work political wonders, both domestically and internationally. Lloyd George's position, as a Liberal prime minister dependent on Conservative backing, would be secured; in alliance terms, Britain would not have to defer to American wishes at the peace talks. But after 1916 Lloyd George's cabinet colleagues were wary of Haig's ambition: they did not want another Somme, and when they finally gave the battle their blessing (on 20 July, long after they were committed to it) they specified that it was to be a step-by-step battle, which could therefore be broken off as and when it ceased to deliver results commensurate with its losses.

That was an endorsement not for breakthrough but for attrition. 'The best plan', Robertson wrote to Haig on 20 April, when Nivelle's failure to achieve a breakthrough was evident, 'is to go back to one of the old principles, that of defeating the enemy's army. In other words instead of aiming at breaking through the enemy's front, aim at breaking down the enemy's army, and that means inflicting heavier losses upon him than one suffers oneself.'[31] That indeed was how Robertson packaged and sold the offensive in May, both in London and to his allied colleagues. They met in Paris on 4–5 May. The rate at which the Germans were relieving divisions, when compared with 1916, led to the conclusion that the enemy had lost 350,000 men between 9 April and 27 May 1917, and that by 9 July the figure would have risen to over 450,000.[32] Allied calculations about a crisis in German morale, even if not on the scale of that of the French army, were not without foundation. Robertson reported that it was agreed that: 'It is no longer a question of aiming at breaking through the enemy's front and aiming at distant objectives. It is now a question of wearing down and exhausting the enemy's resistance, and if and when this is achieved to exploit it to the fullest extent possible. . . . We are all of opinion that our object can be obtained by relentlessly attacking with limited objectives, while making the fullest use of our artillery. By this means we hope to gain our ends with the minimum loss possible.'[33]

Pétain was at the meeting and endorsed what Robertson had said. The operational conception of attrition, towards which both had been working since late 1915, was now fully developed. Haig was also present, and both in Paris and London was ready to pay lip-service to the ideas Robertson had articulated. But he did so for the sake of professional unity in the face of political inquisition. He did not believe in them. A rift now opened between the commander-in-chief and the Chief of the Imperial General Staff. Robertson, like Pétain, thought the war was not winnable in 1917. His intelligence picture, built up from a wider range of sources than that of Haig's headquarters, offset any positives derived solely from the western front. Haig saw what was in front of him, and interpreted that in the best possible light: his devout Presbyterianism gave him an inner certainty which interpreted setbacks as challenges, a not undesirable quality in a commander. He believed he could achieve a breakthrough in 1917, and would rationalise his battle as attrition only if he failed. By attacking in a sector as vital to both sides as Ypres, where neither could afford to let the other break through, he seemed likely to win either way.

The offensive began well enough. On 7 June the British 2nd Army under Herbert Plumer, whose red face, rotund frame and white moustache were suggestive of David Low's cartoon character Colonel Blimp, won a crushing victory at Messines. Like the attack at Vimy, it benefited from careful preparation, particularly by the artillery, which by dint of excellent intelligence was able to focus on counter-battery work. Nearly a million pounds of explosive had been placed in tunnels under the German positions, and at 3.10 a.m. 'nineteen gigantic roses with carmine petals, or . . . enormous mushrooms, . . . rose up slowly and majestically out of the ground and then split into pieces with a mighty roar, sending up multi-coloured columns of flame mixed with a mass of earth and splinters high in the sky'.[34] Thus a German observer caught an irony of industrialised war: the beauty in its destructive effects. His own side's losses included 6,400 prisoners, too dazed to respond to the infantry assault.

The attack also succeeded because it was limited and staged. It gave the British a foothold on the end of the ridge that swept round to the east of Ypres, and it secured the right flank of the main thrust onto the Gheluvelt plateau, launched on 31 July. Here the commander was Hubert Gough, a cavalryman, attractive to Haig because he would aim for more distant objectives. In reality, there was little to choose between him and Plumer. When by the end of August Gough had made only minor gains, Plumer's army was given the task of getting onto the plateau. Neither commander opposed Haig's determination not to break off the battle, despite mounting casualties for minimal advantage. The ideal of the staged, leap-frogging battle, set by the artillery timetable, had fallen foul of appalling weather. The rain in August was almost continuous. Mist prevented aerial reconnaissance. The drainage system of the flat, well-tilled land was broken up by shellfire, and the mud meant shell supply had to be performed by mules. 'If animals slipped off the planks into the quagmires alongside,' E. C. Anstey recalled, 'they often sank out of sight. On arrival, shells had to be cleaned of the slime coating before they could be used.'[35] Every time a gun was fired, its trail sank into the soft ground, thus wrecking its bearing and elevation: rapid, predicted fire was impossible.

By the time the battle petered out in mid-November, the British had suffered 275,000 casualties, of whom 70,000 were dead. 'Reinforcements of the new armies', Aubrey Wade reported, 'shambled up past the guns with dragging steps and the expressions of men who knew they were going to certain death. No words of greeting passed as they slouched along; in sullen silence they filed past one by one to the sacrifice.'[36] In December instances of drunkenness, desertion and psychological disorders among British troops were reported to be on the increase. In fact, the number of shell-shock cases was smaller than on the Somme, a rate of 1 per cent, partly owing to different diagnostic procedures. Nor did the total number of courts martial rise exponentially, particularly when set against the increasing size of the army. An end-of-year report based on 17,000 letters concluded that morale was sound. The traditional paternalism of a long-service army – rest and recreation, food and drink, good officer–men relations – acted as an effective disciplinary tool even for conscripts. The British army did not mutiny – at least, not on a scale which bears comparison with the French.

The grouses the censors picked up were not those of professional servicemen but the anxieties of citizen soldiers: war-weariness, talk of peace, a desire for leave. More united than divided those at the front and at home. In 1917 5.5 million working days were lost in Britain, and as in France they peaked in May, with 200,000 workers out. Real wages were the prime complaint, but the possibility that the complaints might become politicised was reinforced in June, when the Independent Labour Party and the British Socialist Party met in Leeds and resolved to establish a Workers' and Soldiers' Council. It did not happen, but it fed government anxieties. Indicative was John Buchan's 'shocker' for the year. In 1916 *Greenmantle* had concerned a German plot to spread holy war in the empire; in 1917 *Mr Standfast* pivoted on German attempts to exploit pacifism and labour discontent to provoke revolution at home. Buchan himself was chosen to head the Department of Information, created in February 1917 under the aegis of the Foreign Office, a recognition of how important to Lloyd George was the battle for ideas. In June 1917 the National War Aims Committee embarked on a programme of political education in factories and workplaces, and in January 1918 the Canadian Lord Beaverbrook was appointed to lead a fully fledged Ministry of Information.

At the end of 1917, therefore, the British army and the British people were desperately tired. On 29 November Lansdowne voiced the reservations he had expressed privately a year previously in the *Daily Telegraph*, calling for a compromise peace. At the front, Haig, who had at first planned to resume the Ypres battle when the weather improved in the spring, realised on 15 November that it would not be possible. However, he couched his decision in terms not of the losses caused by his own operations, but of those inflicted by the government. Initially two – and ultimately five – divisions, together with Plumer and six French divisions, were sent to reinforce the Italians.

Of all the three Entente powers in the west, Italy was the shakiest in its hold on liberalism. First, the extension of the franchise in 1912 was undermined by the fact that 38 per cent of the electorate was illiterate. Second, socialist extremism was stronger than moderate reformism, and the only counter seemed to be the card of nationalism. Third, although entry to the war divided the country rather than united it, parliament was not consulted. Fourth, the economy was still predominantly rural, and it required the war to industrialise it. Moreover, with the war under way, Cadorna treated politicians with a contempt which blocked any alternatives to his own inept, if dogged, generalship. When in January 1916 Salandra suggested the formation of a council of war, combining the wisdom of generals and politicians, Cadorna declared that he was answerable only to the King. Criticised by the minister of war in the following month, he managed to force him to resign. He believed that the individualism of the Italians made them 'morally unprepared for war', and therefore saw the war as an opportunity to make peasants into Italians. His tool for doing this was harsh discipline. One in every seventeen Italian soldiers faced a disciplinary charge in the war, and 61 per cent were found guilty. About 750 were executed, the highest number of any army in the war, and Cadorna reintroduced the Roman practice of decimation – the killing of every tenth man – for units which failed to perform in battle.

The four battles on the River Isonzo in 1915 were followed by five more in 1916, and two in 1917. The Austrians on the Italian front had coined the phrase 'the battle of material' by September 1915, a full year before it was current in Germany. Normally outnumbered two to one, and unable to trade space for time, they possessed in the Croatian general Svetozar Boroević a commander who never wavered in his determination to regain ground lost, an objective he generally achieved until the sixth battle of the Isonzo in August 1916. Thus they played into the hands of an enemy resolved on attrition as an operational method. And that is what Cadorna had resolved to do by the beginning of 1916. He knew that, with Austria-Hungary's army divided over three fronts, he must eventually wear it down. But the result was that he failed to recognise opportunities for breakthrough when they presented themselves. On 10 August 1916 the Italians at last captured Gorizia, on the eastern bank of the Isonzo, and in the same month a year later, in the eleventh battle, Cadorna gained control of the Bainsizza plateau, but in both cases reckless disregard for casualties was accompanied by operational caution. In twenty-seven months' fighting and eleven battles, the Italians had advanced less than seven miles, a third of the way to their stated preliminary objective, Trieste.[37]

Italian casualties in the eleventh battle of the Isonzo were 166,000, 25 per cent greater than those of Nivelle on the Aisne. In the month of the battle, August, 5,471 soldiers deserted, as opposed to 2,137 in April. The Ravenna Brigade had mutinied in March and the Catanzaro Brigade in July.[38] Even Cadorna recognised that his army needed time to rest and recuperate. But it did little to prepare its defences in depth, keeping its gun line well forward as though simply allowing the winter to pass before resuming the offensive. The Central Powers had no intention of waiting for what could be a devastating blow, and Germany transported seven divisions to reinforce the Austrians on the upper Isonzo. On 24 October, after a short but intense bombardment which targeted the Italian batteries, the German and Austrian infantry achieved a complete breakthrough. 'The farther we penetrated into the hostile zone of defence', wrote Lieutenant Erwin Rommel, 'the less prepared were the garrisons for our arrival, and the easier the fighting. I did not worry about contact to right or left. Six companies of the Württemberg Mountain Battalion were able to protect their own flanks. The attack order stated: "Without limiting the day's activities in space or time, continue the advance to the west, knowing that we have strong reserves near and behind us".' [39]

By mid-November the Germans and Austrians had driven the Italians back sixty miles to the River Piave. By following the valley floors, they had sustained the momentum of their advance until logistics and command confusion slowed it. Italian losses totalled almost 700,000, of whom only 40,000 were killed and wounded; 280,000 had been captured, many of them as intact units, and about 350,000 had deserted. Cadorna attributed his defeat not to tactical incompetence but to anti-militarism and defeatism in Italy as a whole. A year before, Senator Camporeale had reported after a visit to the south of the country that 'more than half the land is uncultivated and with us poverty and rebellion and revolt are synonymous . . . [The countryside] is swarming with thousands – 20 to 30 thousand – deserters'.[40] There were about 100,000 deserters at large before the disaster of Caporetto (as the Italians called the battle; it was Karfreit to the Germans); peasants were ready to give the stragglers protection and to use their labour. The possibility of military collapse leading to revolution seemed real enough.

Violent protest peaked in May 1917, especially in Milan. In August, outbursts over bread shortages in Turin developed into anti-war demonstrations, and the army killed 41 and wounded about 200 more in restoring order. Women were at the forefront of these riots. By the end of the war they formed 21 per cent of the workforce but in 1917 they were 64 per cent of those striking, evidence of the anxiety about food but also of working-class solidarity. They struck because the penalties for them were lighter than for men, who were more subject to military discipline, and they linked the old patterns of rural, peasant protest with the first generation of urban workers in new industries. Although the number of individual strikes fell in 1917 as against 1915 and 1916, those which occurred were bigger in scale.

But the revolutionary moment did not become revolution. Caporetto played its part: it turned an offensive war into a defensive one. Its nationalist imperative also consolidated liberalism. On 30 October Vittorio Orlando, a defender of civil liberties, formed a coalition government, but one which used its mandate to be firm in its suppression of defeatism. Cadorna, having refused to resign even at the behest of the King, was dismissed and replaced by Armando Diaz. Diaz was the Pétain of Italy: he cared for his men, extending leave, improving rations, rethinking tactics and eschewing reckless offensive action. On 15 December a war council was finally established. But even before Caporetto much was already in place. Italy had enough food to feed itself, and the ration card became (as it became in Britain) the symbol of equality of distribution and sacrifice. The Mobilitazione Industriale, the army-organised agency for the management of war industry, which controlled 903,250 workers and 1,976 firms by the war's end, was elevated to a full ministry in July 1917. Its chief, General Alfredo Dallolio, believed that better real wages and improved conditions of employment would dampen radicalism, and used his power to curb the powers of employers as well as to regiment the employees.

The boundaries of the state were thereby extended, but as in Britain and France they were seen as temporary interventions designed to protect the liberal nation, not subvert it. Moreover, by the end of the year government in all three nations was firmly vested in the hands of civilian politicians, not of soldiers. In Britain Haig's standing slumped in the aftermath of Passchendaele. Lloyd George now possessed the political authority to remove him, if he could find a credible alternative. He could not, but he was able to ensure the replacement of Haig's directors of intelligence and of operations. In February 1918, the prime minister exploited the latent split between Haig and Robertson to oust the latter. The new Chief of the Imperial General Staff was General Sir Henry Wilson, an Irish unionist and a man whose love of intrigue was so great that the sight of a politician was said to induce in him a state of sexual excitement. Haig both distrusted and disliked him.

In November the division in Paris, between those ready to explore options for peace and those determined not to, destroyed Painlevé's government. France stood poised between pacifism and *guerre à outrance*. Poincaré swallowed his personal dislike and asked the seventy-six-year-old Georges Clemenceau, radical and atheist, scourge of governments, to form a ministry. One of the new prime minister's first acts was to have Caillaux, the pacifist contender for the premiership, arrested on charges of treason. France had one simple, single duty, he told the chamber in his first speech: 'to cleave to the soldier, to live, to suffer, to fight with him'. Clemenceau's government was the first in the war to coin the phrase 'total war', and it did so in reference to the need to mobilise all France's resources for its prosecution. This was more totalitarian than democratic. Although the new prime minister was of the left, as were most of his ministers, he drew his parliamentary support from the right and he infuriated the socialists. He ruled less through his ministers than through two personal cabinets, one military and one civil. When challenged in the chamber on 8 March 1918, he explained that as the head of a republican government he was called on to defend two doctrines: 'the first of these doctrines . . . is the principle of liberty. . . . The second, in the current situation, is that we are at war, that it is necessary to wage war, to think only of war, that it is necessary to apply our minds to war and to sacrifice everything to the rules, which we shall put right in the future if we are able to succeed in securing the victory of France . . . Today, our duty is to make war while maintaining the rights of the citizen, so safeguarding not one liberty but all liberties. So let us wage war.'[41]

Clemenceau disagreed with Lansdowne: the war had first to be won before a lasting peace was possible. By the winter of 1917–18 most *poilus* seemed to share his views. 'My war aims are these', wrote a soldier of the 272nd Regiment of Infantry at the end of 1917. 'I fight 1. because there is a war and I am a soldier, 2. because this war was inevitable, 3. because I do not want to become a Boche, 4. because they are in our country and we must make them leave or at least stop them getting any further, 5. because they must pay for the damage that they have done.'[42]

The Bolsheviks Seize Power

In neither France nor Italy had mutiny and desertion coalesced with protests and riots in the rear. Despite the fact that these were armies of citizens, made up of soldiers who yearned to go home and resume their peacetime pursuits, and despite the mechanisms of leave and mail that kept alive the links between front and rear, the consequences of grievances in one were kept separate from those in the other. That was not true for Russia.

'One cannot but notice, that in letters from the army as well as, mainly, in letters to the army, discontent arising from [the] internal political situation of the country is beginning to grow.'[43] This report from the military censor in Petrograd was dated November 1916. In March 1917, the troops in the northern districts, including Petrograd, totalled 850,000. Under the influence of left Socialist Revolutionaries, they gave their primary loyalty not to the temporary commission set up by the Duma but to the Petrograd Soviet of Workers and Soldiers. On 14 March, the Soviet's Order Number 1 confirmed this arrangement, and required that all units form committees of elected representatives of the lower ranks. Order Number 1 did not of itself demand that officers be elected, but that was its outcome. Officers had to court popularity, and some of those who did not were lynched, while others were arrested. 'Between us and them is an impassable gulf', one officer wrote at the end of March. 'No matter how well they get on with individual officers, in their eyes we are all *barins*. When we talk about the *narod*, we mean the nation; when they talk about it, they understand it as meaning only the democratic lower classes. In their eyes, what has occurred is not a political but a social revolution, which in their opinion they have won and we have lost.'[44]

That revolution travelled along the railway lines to the front; it did not go from front to rear. It reached the combat zones furthest from Petrograd – Romania and the Caucasus – last. Although most Russian soldiers were fed up with the war, they were still committed to the defence of their country. Senior commanders recognised in March that the way to restore order was not to oppose the establishment of soldiers' committees but to endorse them – just as they had endorsed the fall of the Tsar – in the hope of then reuniting the army and the nation in the prosecution of the war. Aleksandr Kerensky, first as minister of war and then as head of the Provisional Government, supported their endeavours. He launched an offensive in July, which failed, and then appointed the youthful and heroic Lavr Kornilov commander-in-chief, with a mandate to restore discipline. But he now feared the threat of counter-revolution more than that of revolution. The Germans took Riga at the beginning of September, and when Kornilov began to push troops towards Petrograd for its defence they were seen to be the outriders for a counter-revolutionary coup, not the agents of the Provisional Government. Kerensky turned to the Petrograd Soviet and its militia, the Red Guard, under Leon Trotsky, to check Kornilov.

It was not only domestic events which separated the army's officers from their men. Kerensky hoped the war would unite the nation and the revolution, as it had done in France in 1792. But the decision of the All-Russian Conference of Soviets on 11 April to support a peace without annexations or indemnities made those who supported the war's continuation seem imperialist. Moreover, peace promised land reform and redistribution. Peasants wanted to be at home when that happened. The rise in desertions was not immediate, and its effects were more obvious on the lines of communication than in the trenches, but the process of disintegration, linking grievances at the front to concerns at home, was now under way.

German and Austro-Hungarian propaganda played on the worries about land redistribution. Thus the pressures on the Russian army came not just from the rear, but from the other side of the line as well. The spontaneous truce of Christmas 1914 on the western front had had its eastern-front counterpart, albeit at Easter and in every year up to and including 1917. OberOst now condoned such fraternisation. It was also supported by Russian revolutionaries, who hoped to spread the revolution westwards. German efforts to use revolution as a tool for the conduct of the war had not so far been particularly successful. The means they had used had been inadequate to the ends they had sought. Gun-running to Ireland had resulted in rebellion in 1916, and covert funding of pacifists and socialists had sown dissension in France in 1917. But in neither case had there been a popular response: the revolutionaries were themselves minor players. In Russia, too, the Bolsheviks were minor players, but in 1915 Alexander Helphand, code-named Parvus, a German agent whose business activities profited from the blockade-driven trade between Denmark and Germany, persuaded the German Foreign Ministry that they might engineer a mass strike in Russia. In March 1917, despite the obvious paradox and equally obvious dangers in Imperial Germany sponsoring Marxism, Arthur Zimmermann convinced the Kaiser and the army that the Bolsheviks' leader, Lenin, who was living in exile in Switzerland, should be smuggled back into Russia. On 16 April 1917 Lenin arrived in Petrograd at the Finland station, having crossed Germany in a 'sealed' train. This was one revolutionary effort which reaped spectacular returns, albeit in a situation where spontaneous revolution had already occurred.

In November 1917 the Bolsheviks, under Trotsky's direct leadership but orchestrated by Lenin, seized power in Petrograd, toppling the Provisional Government. The All-Russian Congress of Soviets embraced a programme which differed little from earlier ideas – including land to the peasants, bread to the cities, workers' control of the factories, and complete democratisation of the army. But on the next day Lenin demanded an immediate armistice. Peace would provide the key to delivering bread and land.

The entire complexion of the war changed. A decade after the war had ended, Daniel Halévy's brother Elie, the great French historian of modern Britain, delivered the Rhodes lectures in Oxford. His subject, 'The World Crisis of 1914–18', was, he said, 'not only a war – the war of 1914 – but a revolution – the revolution of 1917'.[45] The conflation of war and revolution had grave implications for the Entente at two levels. The first was military. Without an active eastern front, the basis of the alliance's strategy became meaningless. For the first time since August 1914 the Central Powers were free to concentrate all their efforts in the west. The second was political. Here was a new vision of the world order to challenge liberalism. The Bolsheviks published the secret agreements on war aims reached between the Entente powers: Britain, France and Italy stood convicted, it seemed, of annexationist ambitions comparable with those of the monster which they were pledged to extirpate, German militarism. Those who could envisage the war ending in the coming year could do so only on the basis of a German victory.

9

GERMANY'S LAST GAMBLE

Germany between Militarism and Liberalism

On 3 March 1918, in Brest-Litovsk, the Russians signed a peace treaty with the Central Powers. In the north-west they lost Poland, Lithuania, and the Baltic states of Estonia, Livonia and Courland. Finland took the opportunity of the Bolshevik revolution to cede from Russia. To the south Ukraine did the same. In the Caucasus the Turks regained their pre-1878 frontiers. In all Russia lost a million square miles of territory, together with almost all its coal and oil, three-quarters of its iron ore, and about half its industry. About a third of its population, 55 million people, and the same proportion of its agriculture were also forfeit. Lenin, who was not present for the final meeting with the representatives of the Central Powers, described the settlement as 'that abyss of defeat, dismemberment, enslavement, and humiliation'. Three months of negotiation and renewed fighting had followed the Bolsheviks' initial request for an armistice, and Lenin knew that further discussion was pointless. He had no army to speak of and he had a civil war to contend with: his leverage was minimal. He could do nothing but bank on the hope that the Treaty of Brest-Litovsk would be overthrown by the spread of revolution abroad. 'You must sign this shameful peace', he told the Congress of Soviets, 'in order to save the world revolution, in order to hold fast to . . . its only foothold – the Soviet Republic'.[1]

Two months later, on 7 May 1918, it was Romania's turn. Although largely overrun in the autumn and winter of 1916, Romania had stayed in the war in 1917, holding a territorial rump in

Moldavia with the aid of Russian reinforcements. France had sent a military mission, and, while the Russian army disintegrated, the Romanian was rebuilt. In July and August 1917, it successfully held off Mackensen's army on the River Sereth, but its position was fatally compromised by the collapse of its principal ally. On 9 December 1917 it sought an armistice. The terms of the peace treaty were delivered as an ultimatum on 27 February 1918. 'It was a disaster', the head of the French mission, Henri Berthelot, reported in his final despatch to Paris. 'Since Romania was deprived of its frontiers, of Dobrudja, of the products of its soil, of its army, since it was going without doubt to undergo enemy occupation for an indefinite period, what difference was there between these conditions and those which Romania would have undergone after a last disastrous battle, where it would at least have salvaged honour?'[2] Even the pro-German conservatives, including the prime minister who signed the treaty, Alexander Marghiloman, were staggered by the terms. The notion of a German-dominated customs union in Central Europe, adumbrated in 1915 in Friedrich Naumann's idea of *Mitteleuropa*, had been militarised into a form of indirect annexation. Germany took no territory solely for itself. It gave Wallachia to Austria-Hungary and southern Dobrudja to Bulgaria; as it intended to dominate both its allies, the concession was notional. The direct evidence of Germany's mastery was economic. It took a ninety-nine-year lease on Romania's oil deposits; it assumed control of the railways and the navigation of the Danube; it shared Romania's agricultural surplus with Austria-Hungary, but it established a monopoly over Romanian trade through a customs union.

The treaties of Brest-Litovsk and Bucharest defined what a German victory meant. 'For those who think Germany will be satisfied with a peace of conciliation', wrote a French gunner, the Russians' cowardice 'will have made them see what defeat would mean on our front. German militarism must be beaten for ever and that is what must reinvigorate us.'[3] Russia and Romania were not the only losers at Brest-Litovsk and Bucharest. So, too, were advocates everywhere of a negotiated peace, and they included liberals in Germany.

On 19 July 1917 the Reichstag had passed a resolution calling for a peace without annexations or indemnities. Its vocabulary deliberately invoked memories of the Kaiser's speech of 4 August 1914, suggesting that this was a defensive war, sustained by a domestic truce; it spoke of freedom of the seas, of the establishment of an international legal body, and of mutual understanding and economic cooperation. The work of a centre–left coalition, made up of the Catholic Centre Party, the Progressives and the Socialists, the peace resolution seemed to confirm the waxing strength of German liberalism. In his Easter message, the Kaiser had promised constitutional reform at the end of the war: his terms had been vague, but he had at least accepted Bethmann Hollweg's determination that the Prussian upper house should be reformed and that the three-class suffrage which guaranteed a conservative majority in the Prussian Diet should go.

The primary effect was to isolate the radical and revolutionary left. Germany, like other belligerents on both sides, experienced more strikes in 1917 than in the earlier years of the war – 561 as against 137 in 1915 and 240 in 1916. As elsewhere, too, falling real wages and food shortages, especially after the 'turnip' winter of 1916–17, were the principal explanations. But there were big variations in individual experiences. In all countries, both metal-workers and women proved vital to war production, and central to industrial unrest. In Germany female metal-workers' wages rose 324 per cent between 1914 and 1918. On the other hand, those on fixed incomes, civil servants and white-collar workers, the so-called '*Mittelstand*', found themselves losing status as well as earnings: in one association the average wage rose 18.2 per cent between the outbreak of the war and the end of 1917, while the cost of living soared 185 per cent.[4] The lower middle class was therefore radicalised by the war as much as the skilled male or the unskilled female. In January and February 1917 strikers in the Ruhr and in Berlin, female metal-workers at their head, demanded food or more wages to buy food. 'Any other people on earth would rise against a Government that had reduced it to such misery', Ethel Cooper wrote on 11 February 1917.[5] Two months later strikers in her home town of Leipzig did call for political change. But the demands were for reform, not revolution: equal and universal suffrage, the removal of military controls on political discourse, and a peace without annexations.

Elsewhere in Germany the strikes in April were not politicised, or at least not overtly so. In Berlin on the 16th 200,000 workers, half of them women, staged a one-day demonstration to demand food. The newspaper of the Social Democrats, *Vorwärts*, denied the motivations were political. But the denial in itself carried a message. The Social Democrats had voted for war credits in 1914, and had embraced the idea that support for the state in its time of trial would be the path to political reform after the war was over. But for a party still constitutionally committed to revolution a policy of reform carried penalties. Although the largest single grouping in the Reichstag, its individual membership had fallen from over a million in 1914 to a quarter of a million in 1917. A minority rejected the *Burgfrieden*, the domestic truce between parties of August 1914, and in April 1917 broke away from the majority Socialists to create an Independent Socialist Party. The new grouping shaped the demands of the Leipzig strikers, which in themselves suggest that the Independent Socialists were not a major threat. They looked back to the original programme of the German Socialists, adopted at Erfurt in 1890, not forward, and they were still ready to support a defensive war. However, they did possess an inner core, the Spartacists, headed by Karl Liebknecht and Rosa Luxemburg. In 1916, in Switzerland, Luxemburg, under the *nom de guerre* of Junius, had published a refutation of the notion that the war was defensive for Germany. Its purposes were imperialist and capitalist: 'The cannon fodder inflated with patriotism and carried off in August and September 1914 now rots in Belgium, in the Vosges, in the Masurian swamps, creating fertile plains of death on which profits can grow.'[6] She declared that social democracy had failed the working class, and that only international class action could bring peace. Inspired by the events in Russia, she and Liebknecht believed that a mass strike could be the trigger for revolution.

For Bethmann Hollweg, therefore, the message was clear: political reform would keep the majority Socialists tied to the state, would validate their position in the eyes of the working class they aspired to represent, and would divide social and economic grievances from the idea of revolution. Wilhelm Groener, appointed to head the war office, or *Kriegsamt*, within the Prussian Ministry of War, was committed to a parallel and complementary set of ideas. He was the principal architect of the Auxiliary Service Law, a deal between army, industry and labour on the management of German manpower in the war. For the first time in Germany, the trade unions were given an acknowledged role in the arbitration of disputes. Between 1916 and 1918 trade-union membership, which had been savaged by the consequences of conscription, recovered: that of the metal-workers' union in upper Silesia increased 154 per cent in 1917 alone.[7] But for many German socialists the Auxiliary Service Law was not an important step towards workers' rights but another compromise which weakened them. Workers were restricted in their ability to move between jobs, while industrialists' profits were not controlled. Groener wished the army to be the neutral representative of the state, the embodiment in some senses of Walther Rathenau's corporatist dream, an amalgam of the best of capitalism and collectivism. But many of his military colleagues preferred to align the army more closely with the interests of the industrialists. The war aims programme, which aspired to secure for Germany the iron ore and coalfields of Belgium and of Longwy-Briey in France, was one manifestation of this alliance. Another, in October 1917, was the dismissal of Groener, who tried to control both wages and profits, as labour and industry exploited the Hindenburg programme for their respective advantage.

The peace resolution and the emergence of a centre–left coalition may have weakened the right in parliamentary terms but it had not silenced its effectiveness outside the Reichstag. Here it had powerful allies in Hindenburg and Ludendorff. They, not the centre–left or Bethmann Hollweg, were the beneficiaries of the political crisis the peace resolution generated.

On 6 July 1917 Matthias Erzberger, the leader of the Catholic Centre Party, delivered a speech during the debate on the war credits for the coming year, in which he declared that 'all our calculations as regards the submarine war are false', that the idea of defensive war should be resuscitated, and that 'we must do everything possible to find a way which favours the conclusion of a peace this year'.[8] Erzberger thus began the process that concluded with the Reichstag peace resolution. However, his victim was not the Pan-German League and its annexationist war aims, which he specifically mentioned, but the chancellor. Bethmann Hollweg was tired, committed to a policy of unrestricted submarine war in which he did not believe but which Erzberger among others had once advocated. 'My position does not matter', he said when he rose to reply on 9 July. 'I myself am convinced of my own limitations ... I am considered weak because I seek to end the war. A leading statesman can receive support neither from the Left nor the Right in Germany.'[9]

But that was precisely the function of the chancellor in the Kaiser's eyes. Bethmann Hollweg resigned the following day, not because the army wanted him to go but because he could not manage the Reichstag. His policy of what he had called the 'diagonal' was no longer sustainable. In the minds of the centre and left the chancellor was now bracketed with the Pan-German League, and in the minds of the right and the army he was a reformer and liberal, insufficiently committed to the idea of a 'German peace'. The army's opportunity arose from its ability to strike out on a new diagonal of its own. Colonel Max Bauer, the army's most adroit intriguer, dined with Erzberger and Gustav Stresemann, leader of the National Liberals, and suggested that the chancellor had failed in his democratic duty by denying the Reichstag committee the opportunity to discuss the issues with the supreme command itself. The notion that Hindenburg and Ludendorff were the people's representatives was not as absurd as first appearances might suggest. Rathenau told Ludendorff that he was 'exercising an unconscious dictatorship and that, if he were to appeal to his real power-base, he would have the support not only of parliament, but the whole of public opinion.'[10] The rising talents in the war, such as Ludendorff and Groener, were not Junkers but bourgeois, and, although they had a traditional Prussian in Hindenburg at their head, even his authority rested on demagogic populism derived from the victory at Tannenberg.

On 12 July Bauer arranged a meeting between Crown Prince Wilhelm, the Kaiser's son, and selected representatives of the principal Reichstag parties. Bethmann Hollweg's fate was sealed and he resigned the next day. When the Reichstag formally adopted the peace resolution on 19 July, it did so not with the Kaiser's or the Reichstag's nominee installed as chancellor, but with the army's, Georg Michaelis. Political heavyweights were surprised and cynical: 'We have lost a statesman and have secured a functionary in his place', said a Social Democrat, Conrad Haussmann.[11] But Michaelis was a man for his times, a bureaucrat who was popular because he had run the wheat administration effectively. 'In my opinion, this is the only organization which has completely fulfilled its responsibilities without mismanagement', wrote Richard Stumpf, a seaman. 'He is Germany's first bourgeois chancellor.'[12] Michaelis's response to the peace resolution was to accept it as 'he understood it'.

The army's presence in the chamber as Michaelis spoke was unmistakable, but the 'silent dictatorship' was exactly that – silent. The army did not itself govern. Moreover, it was the navy which revealed the limits on military power in German politics. In August 1917 mutinies broke out on the capital ships moored at Wilhelmshaven. The grievances were in part professional. Relations between officers and men were poor, the ships had not put to sea since Jutland, and the crews were bored; those on U-boats, now fully engaged in the fighting, remained quiet. But the sailors also expressed themselves in terms similar to the workers with whom they consorted in their off-duty hours, complaining of war-weariness and poor food. The mutineers had made contact with the Independent Socialists, and Admiral Scheer – like Pétain and Cadorna – was quick to detect an external conspiracy. Two of the mutineers were executed after a summary court martial. Michaelis seized the opportunity to castigate the Independent Socialists in the Reichstag, hoping thereby to drive a wedge between them and the centre–left coalition. He had miscalculated. The Reichstag rallied to the Independent Socialists, and Michaelis fell. His successor was appointed without the army being consulted. Georg von Hertling, a Bavarian Catholic, was no democrat, but he was a member of the Centre Party and was clear on his constitutional responsibilities. He selected a Social Democrat, Friedrich von Payer, as his vice-chancellor and a liberal, Richard Kühlmann, as his foreign secretary. In January 1918 he reminded Hindenburg that the general staff's role was advisory.[13]

Hertling's difficulty was that he was claiming a responsibility which he did not have the tools to exercise. Germany was fighting what Ludendorff in later life called a 'total war', but with the administrative structures of a small nineteenth-century state. It had no equivalent of Britain's Ministry of Munitions; the Prussian Ministry of War did duty as a Reich economics ministry; it never collected its various propaganda agencies into a ministry of information. Therefore the general staff expanded to fill the gaps, and took over functions for which its structures and attitudes – geared to the conduct of war at operational level – were not fitted. By January 1918 2.3 million men had been released from military service for war production. But no checks were imposed to ensure that they were being efficiently used. Daimler, the manufacturer of automobiles and aero engines, employed 1.8 workers per machine in 1914, but 2.4 in 1918. At the beginning of 1917 the firm demanded a 50 per cent price increase after a year in which it had paid out a 35 per cent dividend and written off the entire book value of its plant.[14] No body existed to take an overview, to balance competing priorities, or to link the military conduct of the war to its economic and social imperatives.

The principal casualty of the army's arrogation of power was not the Reichstag but the Kaiser. Increasingly redundant, he went for walks in the woods, played *skat*, bickered with the Empress, and complained about his own irrelevance. 'Great indignation with the Kaiser who spends hours supervising the building of a fountain at Homburg, for which a war contractor has raised the money', wrote

Georg von Müller in his diary on 7 August 1916. While his soldiers slogged it out at Verdun and on the Somme, 'He went for an excursion to Saalburg and Friedrichshof this afternoon and refused to read a report from Hindenburg on the situation on the Eastern Front because "he had no time"'.[15]

In the people's eyes, Hindenburg, not the Kaiser, became the supreme warlord. The principal political vehicle for this idea was the Fatherland Party, formally launched on 2 September 1917, the anniversary of Prussia's defeat of France at Sedan in 1870. The purpose of its founders, Wolfgang Kapp (an advocate of extreme war aims) and Tirpitz (now out of office), was to rekindle the 'spirit of 1914' by appealing for national unity in order to achieve a German victory. In reality, its supporters were conservative – schoolteachers, clergy and the professional middle class conspicuous among them. Right-wing nationalism, with its anti-capitalist overtones and its rejection of constitutional reform, was elided with calls for conquest. Its policies were in reality more divisive than unifying, but it could still claim 1.25 million members by 1918.

The army supported the Fatherland Party through its own press agency and through the censorship of the party's political opponents. Formally speaking, soldiers could not be members, but Ludendorff was very conscious that mechanisms like mail and leave meant they could not be insulated from the effects of war-weariness at home. He tightened postal censorship, and at the end of July set up an organisation for patriotic instruction, to remind the army what it was fighting for. French intelligence reported mutinies on the western front between May and August 1917, a phenomenon which may explain why Ludendorff did not exploit the disturbances in the French army. By September and October morale was very low, particularly on the Ypres sector, with cases of desertion reaching a peak not surpassed until the following August. 'There must be an end,' Hans Spiess wrote to his mother from the front on 16 August 1917, 'even the 30 Years [War] came to an end'. Dispirited soldiers could depress those at home. 'When you go on leave, leave the muck and melancholy in the trenches', a leaflet of December 1917 enjoined;

'bring them a pinch of fresh air from the front and the humour of the front line'.[16]

In September 1916 the Prussian war minister ordered all letters to be written exclusively in German. The easy scapegoats in the event of defeat or disobedience were the non-German nationalities. As early as November 1914 there were reports of Poles in the German army surrendering to the French with cries of 'Catholics! Poles! Friends!'[17] In 1915 Danish soldiers were denied leave and had to serve for a year before being given civic rights. But the army's suspicions focused particularly on those from Alsace-Lorraine. A third of all orders concerning desertion were directed at them, a policy which might become a self-fulfilling prophecy.[18] Dominik Richert was in a unit ordered to go from the eastern front to the western at the beginning of 1917. All Alsatians (like Richert himself) and Lorrainers were told that they were to stay behind and be incorporated in other regiments. As they left their barracks on the morning of 2 January, calls of 'Vive la France!' and 'Vive l'Alsace!' rippled up and down the column.[19]

Germany's Allies under Strain

The nationality issue was even more emotive in the Austro-Hungarian army. In 1914 Czechs were blamed for the initial defeats in Serbia, earning a reputation which their brave conduct on the Italian front could not subsequently slough off. In Romanian units of the Honved, the Hungarian territorial army, 'A gulf of deadly hatred appeared between the officers and men', Octavian Tăslăuanu wrote. 'The Hungarian officers, mad to think that Roumania had not declared herself for them, vented their rage on our peasants. They knocked them about abominably, and boasted each night of their schemes of punishment.'[20] But the most significant tensions were those between Magyars and Austrians. Conrad von Hötzendorff blamed the inadequacy of the army's budget on Budapest before the war broke out. He was therefore particularly irked when Hungary resisted the authority of the War Surveillance Office in 1914. With parliamentary government in Austria suspended, the focus of open debate and press criticism shifted to Budapest. István Tisza, the Magyar prime minister, had good cause to be anxious: as the Russians fought to break through the Carpathians, Hungary was likely to be the first casualty of the army's incompetence. In 1916 Romania's declaration of war widened the gulf yet further, with Hungary blaming the Austro-Germans for Romania's decision and rightly fearful that chunks of Hungarian territory would be Bucharest's reward from the Entente.

Food was the most emotive aspect of the problem. Austria-Hungary was predominantly agricultural without being agriculturally self-sufficient. The direct effects of the blockade were not great, but the war shut off the empire's two principal sources of supplementary food, Russia and Romania (which although still neutral in 1914 imposed an embargo). By 1917 Austria's own output of wheat had fallen to 47 per cent of its 1913 total, of rye to 43 per cent and of oats to 29 per cent. Hungary's production also fell, in large part for the same reasons – the loss of labour, fertilisers and horses – although not to the same extent; it was also hit by the conquest of Galicia. It therefore had less to market. In 1912 Hungary had supplied 85 per cent of Austria's wheat and cattle, but in 1914 Hungary closed its frontier with Austria and ceased to regard its food as a common resource, preferring to sell its surplus to Germany and to the army. By 1917 Austrian imports of cereals and flour from Hungary were 2.5 per cent of their 1913 total.[21]

Lack of animal fodder led to meat shortages, and by 1917 the most obvious manifestations of the food problem were two or three meatless days a week in big cities. The shortages were not as severe as in Germany, and in some respects Hungary was taking the blame for Austrian maladministration. Throughout the war Austria-Hungary maintained the fiction that its currency, the crown, was not losing its value, despite an increase in circulation of 1,400 per cent. Excessive liquidity meant that money was translated into goods as quickly as possible, so forcing up prices. They doubled every year, and yet wages remained constant until 1917, and had only risen by a maximum of 100 per cent by the war's end. Thus the problem was less the production of food than the ability to buy it. Hyperinflation encouraged producers to opt out of the cash economy, either hoarding or bartering. Those in the cities, and consequently furthest from the sources of production, were worst hit. The problems of the railways compounded urban food shortages. Suffering from poor maintenance and overstrain, the trains could not deliver to the cities. Austria's stock of cows fell only 18.4 per cent between 1910 and 1918, yet milk deliveries to Vienna declined 69 per cent.[22] Finally, food supply was never brought under a single head. Austria-Hungary aped Rathenau's war raw-materials agencies, calling them 'centrals', but they established them for services as well as goods. The slaughter of an ox involved five centrals, those for leather, meat, bone, fat and procurement. In February 1917 a common food agency was established under General Ottokar Landwehr von Pragenau, but he lacked full executive powers, especially in Hungary.

There was irony in this: Landwehr had been appointed by the Emperor precisely to get round the constitutional trammels of the dual monarchy. Franz Josef died on 21 November 1916, and was succeeded by his great-nephew, Karl. Karl was aged twenty-nine, 'a sympathetic young man, who did not yet know how to begin what was right for him and who did not particularly seek to diminish his function as the fifth wheel'.[23] None the less he assumed the supreme command of the army, and dismissed Conrad von Hötzendorff as chief of the general staff. His antipathy was as much personal as professional: Conrad had fulfilled his pre-war ambition by marrying Gina von Reininghaus and had installed her at headquarters, a bitter affront to a Catholic as devout as the new monarch. Karl hoped to remobilise the peoples of the empire through consensus, but instead gave them the opportunity to vent their differences.

He was crowned King of Hungary, but refused to swear an oath of loyalty to the Austrian constitution, so giving notice that he planned to put in hand the reforms that had been so long postponed. Liberalisation was their hallmark. Press censorship was eased, and the remit of the army in domestic affairs curtailed. However, for some this spelt laxity, not progress: Karl Stürgkh, Austria's prime minister, was assassinated on 21 October 1916 by Friedrich Adler, son of the socialists' leader, but Adler was never brought to trial. Stürgkh had opposed the convening of Austria's parliament, and the combination of his death and Karl's accession opened the door to its recall. In May 1917, Karl told it that its task was 'the free national and cultural development of equally privileged peoples'.[24] The empire was being pointed in the direction of federalism, but in conditions where political change would be hard to direct.

Karl's reforms were also a direct challenge to Hungary. For a brief period Tisza had been able to pose as a liberal prime minister. The bluff had already been called by Mihály Károlyi, who in the summer of 1916 had formed the Party of Independence and 1848. The compromise between Austria and Hungary was due for renewal in 1917, and the aim of the Károlyi party was complete autonomy. Its programme combined domestic reform – a widening of the franchise, and land redistribution – with calls for an investigation into the army and a peace without annexations or indemnities. Károlyi attracted the support of socialists and revolutionaries, and orchestrated major demonstrations in Budapest on 1 May 1917. None the less it was he, rather than Tisza, whom Karl consulted. The prime minister resigned on 23 May at Karl's request, and was succeeded by Moritz Esterházy, who declared, 'I desire to work on democratic lines, but naturally democracy in Hungary can only be Hungarian democracy'.[25] When, in December 1917, Austria and Hungary brokered a new deal, it was set to last not twenty years, as had been originally intended, but two.

Developments in the Habsburg Empire worried its German ally. The pursuit of political change required conditions of peace, not war. On 3 April Karl and his foreign minister, Ottokar Czernin, visited the Kaiser, ostensibly to complain about the declaration of unrestricted U-boat war, on which their German ally had – with predictable high-handedness – failed to consult them. Their real mission was to press the need for peace. Arz von Straussenburg,

Conrad's successor as chief of the general staff, warned his German hosts that the empire could not last beyond the coming winter. Czernin was more alarmist: 'I'll tell you something', he said to Georg von Müller. 'Unless the war ends within three months the people will end it without their governments. I can't have a wager with you because should this happen it will be impossible to pay the debt.'[26]

Czernin's aim was to get Germany to accept the need for a negotiated peace rather than court revolution. In strategic terms, if not economic or social, Austria-Hungary's position was eminently satisfactory: Serbia had been crushed, Romania had been largely overrun, and the fall of the Tsar had put Russia on the back foot. Vienna had no immediate quarrel with Britain or France, both of whom would be satisfied if Germany agreed to the independence of Belgium and the return of Alsace-Lorraine. But that was the rub: Germany, and particularly Hindenburg and Ludendorff, refused to consider terms which did not conform to their idea of a 'German peace'. Czernin protested his loyalty to Berlin, but peace on Germany's terms implied Austria-Hungary's subordination to its overbearing ally for the foreseeable future. Although he probably did not know it, his monarch was already in separate negotiations with Britain and France. Karl's wife, Zita, was French, and his brother-in-law, Prince Sixte Bourbon-Parma, had served with distinction in the Belgian army, and was acting as an intermediary.

Tensions were also multiplying in Germany's relations with the Ottoman Empire. Turkey's value to Germany lay in the threat it could pose to Britain in the Middle East and in its ability to divert Russian troops from the European front to the Caucasus. In achieving the second of these objectives, the Turks lost eastern Anatolia. The Russians captured Erzurum by 15 February 1916 and reached Trabzon on the Black Sea coast on 18 April. With the British defeated at Gallipoli and Kut, the Turks were able to concentrate twenty-six of their fifty-two divisions on the Caucasus front by the summer of 1916. But as combat casualties (which peaked in the first two years of the war) fell, losses through desertion and disease rose. In September 1916, Enver Pasha restructured the army in the light of its real strength rather than its paper establishment: 'in general the old battalions became companies, the regiments battalions, the divisions regiments, the corps divisions'.[27] Despite this, Enver was able to be supportive when he visited the newly appointed Hindenburg: 'The decision of the war as a whole lies in Europe,' he declared on 11 September 1916, 'and I make all my forces available for the battle there.'[28]

He did not mean quite what he said. Four Turkish divisions were already deployed in Romania, a campaign whose success could clearly jeopardise the Russian position in the Caucasus, but when Ludendorff asked him for three more he prevaricated. The success of the Russians in pulling Turkish divisions to the north of the Ottoman Empire had reopened the British route to Baghdad. The city fell on 11 March 1917. This was no side-show for the Germans: Ludendorff had begun prodding Enver about measures for Baghdad's defence long before the Ottoman minister of war woke up to the threat. They immediately agreed to release a German commander for the theatre, none other than the former chief of the general staff, Falkenhayn, as well as 18,000 German and Austrian troops.

Falkenhayn planned an offensive campaign, codenamed 'Yilderim' (lightning), to recapture Baghdad. But when he arrived in the Middle East in May, it became clear that the British in Egypt were pushing into the Sinai desert, and might well advance into Palestine in the autumn. In that event the Turks, conscious of the strengths and weaknesses of their own army, and of the limits imposed by logistical considerations, favoured fighting a defensive battle on the line between Gaza and Beersheba. Falkenhayn feared that the Central Powers' forces would therefore be divided over two fronts and that a British breakthrough into Palestine would threaten his lines of communication in Iraq. He demanded that all the forces in the two theatres be combined under his command, creating what was essentially a German headquarters which not only marginalised the Turks but also was too far to the rear, in Aleppo. He proposed to strike first against the British in Sinai before turning back to Mesopotamia. His high-handed manner affronted the Turks, and it also antagonised Germans, who had been in the region much longer than he. Falkenhayn saw them as 'Turkified'; they saw him as 'commanding the Turkish army in the desert as one would lead a German army in civilised Europe'.[29]

Falkenhayn was not the only new commander in the Middle East with ideas derived from the war in Europe. Edmund Allenby, fresh from leading the British 3rd Army in the battle of Arras and the capture of Vimy Ridge, arrived to take over the British command in Egypt in June 1917. A cavalryman, 'he looks the sort of man whose hopes rapidly crystalise into a determination to carry all before it'.[30] In London Robertson supported the idea of an attack on the Gaza–Beersheba line, realising that it would take pressure off Baghdad. Here was no purblind westerner: Mesopotamia, Robertson declared on 1 August 1917, was not a 'side-show because as long as we keep up a good show there India and Persia will be more or less all right'.[31] Climatic considerations meant that the Palestine front would open up as that in France and Flanders closed down. When the battle of Gaza began on 27 October, the British mounted the war's heaviest artillery attack outside Europe, with as many heavy guns per yard of front as in the battle of the Somme. Furthermore, aerial supremacy meant that their fire was better directed and coordinated.

But while the guns and infantry pinned the Turks frontally, inland and to the east 'there grew a muttering that spread for miles – the pounding of ten thousand hooves'. This was a campaign in which cavalry still had a role to play: 'though most of us laughed when the first shells screamed towards us, other men smoked as we broke into a thundering canter holding back in the saddles to prevent the horses from breaking into a mad gallop'. Beersheba, with its water supply, was captured on 31 October. 'Men are remarking', noted one exultant trooper of the Australian Light Horse, 'how the Turk fights till the very last charge, until the pounding hooves are upon him, then he drops his rifle and runs screaming; while the Austrian artillerymen and German machine-gun teams often fight with their guns until they are bayoneted.'[32] Unable to hold the line, Falkenhayn pulled back to the hills north of Jerusalem, resting his right flank on Jaffa. In February 1918 he was recalled to Germany, but not before he had intervened to prevent the resettlement of the Jews; they were reckoned to be spying, but neither the Germans nor Talât, elevated to become Ottoman Grand Vizier in February 1917, wanted a repeat of the Armenian massacres.

Allenby's forces entered Jerusalem on 9 December, and prepared for the expected Turkish counterattack. On his right flank, across the River Jordan, he had the support of Arabs under the command of Feisal, son of Sherif Hussein of Mecca. The British were as ready as the Germans to use revolution as an instrument of war. The Government of India had pinned many of their initial hopes for the campaign in Mesopotamia on the possibility of Arab support. In reality, many Arabs remained loyal to the Turks, while others observed a form of neutrality, eyeing each other and ready to loot either army; as the British advanced up the Tigris in 1915–16, the rule was 'upstream of us hostile, downstream friendly'.[33] But to the west, in September 1914, before war with Turkey had even begun, Kitchener initiated contacts with Sherif Hussein. Initially Britain offered the Caliphate, which it understood in spiritual rather than temporal terms, but in October 1915 the high commissioner in Egypt, Sir Henry McMahon, also promised Arab independence. The India Office was appalled, because it hoped to annex Iraq for itself. Moreover, although the high commissioner had entered a caveat in relation to French interests in the region, his proposal was at odds with a deal struck in December 1915 between Mark Sykes and François Picot of France. Picot, who represented a small group determined to secure 'greater Syria' for France, acted on his own initiative. Sykes responded by setting British desiderata higher in order to off-set French influence in the region. As a result he neglected Arab nationalism. The two divided all Arabia into two spheres of influence, albeit one in which suzerainty would be indirect rather than direct. Sykes was concerned with the post-war settlement; McMahon's focus was on getting the Arabs into the war. Hussein remained undecided until June 1916. When he did at last declare his hand for revolt, he gave the Turks a scapegoat for defeat not unlike the subject nationalities exploited by the Germans and Austro-Hungarians.

The Foreign Office set up an Arab Bureau, staffed by such luminaries as the self-publicising T. E. Lawrence and the redoubtable explorer Gertrude Bell, in Cairo to liaise with Hussein and his sons. Its self-appointed role was to undo the Sykes–Picot agreement and to wrong-foot the India Office by making 'an efficient Arab empire'. In 1918, Lawrence was to claim that, 'The phrase "Arab Movement" was invented in Cairo as a common denomination for all the vague discontent against Turkey'.[34] The strength of the Arab forces in the field oscillated wildly, and the difficulty in military terms was holding the tribesmen together in any coherent body, especially as the Palestine campaign moved north away from their home territories. Since 1915 Syria had been ravaged by famine. Its coastal areas were victims of the allied blockade, and the problems were exacerbated by poor Ottoman administration, bad harvests and speculation. By 1918 the death toll may have reached half a million, and 'food was the commodity of political allegiance'.[35] As the Australian Light Horse advanced in the wake of the shattered Turkish army, 'swarms of Arabs, men, women and children, staggering under loads of loot' pillaged its abandoned baggage. 'Numbers of these Arab cut-throats carried sacks of little flat loaves of brown Turkish bread, looted from the still warm ovens.'[36] Lawrence's success as a guerrilla leader lay in his ability to harness plunder for the purposes of the war.

The allies' advance was amplified by the dissolution of the apparatus of the Ottoman state, at least in the southern half of the empire. Paper currency, if negotiable at all, was traded at eight to ten times its face value in Syria and Mesopotamia. For most Arabs, only gold was acceptable, and as the British disbursed it so they secured support. Even in Constantinople the cash economy collapsed. The price of bread rose fifty-fold between 1914 and 1918, and by February 1918 the cost of living had risen 1,970 per cent since the war began. An inadequate internal transport system had left Constantinople dependent

The United States enters the war, April 1917: the Stars and Stripes, borne alongside the Union Jack in a British tank, are paraded past the Flatiron in New York.

The soldiers of the Petrograd garrison pose for their photograph. On 14 March 1917 the Soviet of Workers and Soldiers Deputies issued its Order Number 1, instructing military units to obey only those orders that did not conflict with those of the Soviet.

37

The Germans too suffered at Ypres. Morale slumped in the autumn, and not just among those photographed, wounded and captured, at a dressing station near Zillebeke on 20 September 1917. The steel helmet began to replace the leather *Pickelhaube* early in 1916.

The village of Passchendaele was the furthest point of the British advance in the battle of Ypres, captured by the Canadian Corps on 6 November 1917.

40

The aftermath of Caporetto: Italian prisoners are collected at Udine.

On 15 July 1917 the Provisional Government in Russia collapsed, and the Bolsheviks tried to seize power in Petrograd. Street fighting peaks on 17 July. Kerensky took charge and Lenin went into hiding – for the moment.

41

42

A German field post office on the Western Front, March 1918. Mail was both vital to the maintenance of morale and the principal conduit linking front and rear. None the less, the German army did not tighten censorship of its post until 1917.

Kaiser Karl's young family broke up the stuffiness of the Habsburg court, but the influence exercised over him by his French wife, Zita, gave rise to rumours of treason and betrayal.

43

The Turks established a reputation for themselves as fierce fighters in defensive battles. Their lines around Gaza were strengthened in 1916 and 1917.

German troops maintained order in the Ukraine, establishing their authority along the axes of the railway lines.

German infantry enter a French village in 1918. The officer on the right is adjusting his map case, and looking to his bugler, still necessary for communications in the field. Unlike many German units, this one has sufficient transport.

The allied supreme command pose for the camera on 24 July 1918, the only occasion during the war when they all met. Left to right: Pétain, Haig, Foch and Pershing.

Equipped by their allies, from British helmets to French light tanks, the Americans go forward to the forest of Argonne, 26 September 1918.

Soldiers of the Devonshire Regiment, part of the British 62nd Division serving in the French sector, capture a German in the Bois de Reims during the battle of Tardenois in late July 1918.

British troops enter Lille on 17 October 1918, ending four years of occupation.

For many, allied victory meant not liberation but migration. Clutching their possessions, German nationals leave Alsace and cross the Rhine.

on imported food even in peacetime. In war the blockade increased the city's reliance on the hinterland, but its production was falling. Anatolia had been sucked dry of its principal resource, men. Total Turkish deaths in the war may have risen as high as 2.5 million, more than three times those of Britain, and in some villages only 10–20 per cent of those of military age returned. Agricultural production depended in large part on the enormous number of deserters, perhaps as many as half a million, who roamed the interior.[37] Turkey was bitterly disappointed to be excluded by its allies from the proceeds of Romania's surrender in May 1918.

The 'Bread' Peace

But if the treaty of Bucharest was a source of frustration for the Turks, that of Brest-Litovsk was an opportunity. The Caucasian front had been quiet since the overthrow of the Tsar, and a local armistice was brokered at Erzincan on 18 December 1917. In the negotiations at Brest-Litovsk, Richard Kühlmann was keen to make the German army's lust for eastern conquests look like national self-determination, principally to appease the centre–left bloc in the Reichstag. Russia's evacuation of eastern Anatolia and Turkey's claim to its pre-1878 frontiers could be rendered compatible with such notions. But in the Baltic states and Poland independence was a fig-leaf for German domination. On 9 February Trotsky walked out of the negotiations, declaring 'no peace, no war', rather than accept terms so humiliating. Three days later, the armies of the Central Powers crossed the armistice line. 'It is the most comical war I have ever known', the German chief of staff in the east, Major-General Max Hoffmann, wrote in his diary. 'We put a handful of infantrymen with machine guns and one gun on a train and push them off to the next station; they take it, make prisoners of the Bolsheviks, pick up a few more troops, and go on.'[38] To the south, the Ottoman army re-entered Trabzon on 17 February 1918 and Erzurum on 12 March. On 3 March, when the Russians signed the treaty, they accepted that

Kars, Ardahan and Batum would be restored to Turkey, and acknowledged the independence of Transcaucasia. By now, however, the Turks said they were advancing not to check Bolshevism but to protect Muslims under attack from Armenians. In oil-rich Baku Muslims clashed with Bolsheviks and Christians. While Turkish troops abandoned the southern half of the Ottoman Empire, falling back on Damascus and Mosul, in the northern half the pan-Turk ambitions that had led Enver to Sarikamish over three years before revived. 'You see that destiny draws Turkey from the West to the East', Vehib, the army commander in the Caucasus, explained to the Armenians. 'We left the Balkans, we are also leaving Africa, but we must extend toward the East. Our blood, our religion, our language is there. And this has an irresistible magnetism. Our brothers are in Baku, Daghestan, Turkestan, and Azerbaijan.'[39]

For Austria-Hungary, too, the treaty of Brest-Litovsk promised to reinvigorate flagging spirits. Czernin was caught between the wishes of Karl, who favoured a peace without annexations, and the pressure that Ludendorff was putting on his German counterpart, Kühlmann. The key issue for Vienna was not territory but food, and the settlement that mattered was therefore that with Ukraine, rather than that with Russia. On 15 January Czernin heard from the governor of Bohemia that food shortages threatened imminent disaster: 'we receive only small quantities from Hungary, thus far we have got 10,000 wagons of maize from Romania, and so there are at least 30,000 wagons of corn outstanding, without which we must simply be ruined. . . . In a few weeks our war industry, our transport network will come to a standstill, the supply of the army will become impossible, [and] they must collapse, and this catastrophe must lead to the collapse of Austria and as a result to that of Hungary.'[40]

Flour rations in Austria had been cut on the previous day. Workers at the Daimler factory in Wiener Neustadt immediately protested. By 17 January 200,000 were on strike in Vienna, and by the 19th, according to the reports received by Josef Redlich, 'the strike has become universal, and all mines in Ostrau, Brno, Pilsen, Prague and in Steiermark are at a standstill. . . . In Budapest, there is a general strike, and the trams are not running. Machine-guns have been erected everywhere.'[41] Trotsky was sufficiently heartened to hope that the spread of the Bolshevik revolution would usurp the Brest-Litovsk negotiations. 'In Russia', one Austrian poster declared, 'the land has been divided among the people, and factories and pits have been taken into collective ownership.'[42] Shop councils were elected on the lines of Soviets, and they stressed that the Central Powers' demands should not stand in the way of peace with the Bolsheviks. But the Social Democrats followed the crowd rather than led it; they joined the demonstrations in order not to lose credibility with the workers, and to moderate not foment their demands. The immediate government response was conciliatory: Czernin told the Social Democrats that peace with Russia was imminent and that food would come from Poland and Ukraine. The protests had begun in the core areas of the empire; they were not the work of the 'subject nationalities' seeking its disintegration. By the time the navy mutinied at Cattaro on the Adriatic coast at the beginning of February, order had returned around Vienna.

The Ukraine did not deliver as much as expected. The new government, the Rada, challenged by the Bolsheviks, could not impose its authority on the country, and was toppled by a counter-revolution at the end of April. Order depended on German and Austrian bayonets. Wilhelm Groener, now a corps commander in Kiev, reported to Ludendorff on 23 March: 'The administrative structure is in total disorder, completely incompetent and in no way ready for quick results. Austria-Hungary sees the situation in eminently practical terms; it would be in our interests to treat the Ukrainian government as a "cover", and for us to do the rest ourselves'.[43] All told, about 1.5 million soldiers, albeit older and less fit than those in the west, remained on the eastern front in 1918. They ate a great deal of the food that they were trying to procure for their civilian populations. Moreover, the root cause of food shortages in the Habsburg Empire, and a contributory factor in Germany itself, was transport. Food bound for Austria-Hungary had to be shipped across the Black Sea and up the Danube or brought across war-ravaged Galicia. For

Germany, bringing grain from the Ukraine, and moving troops to and from an eastern front which refused to be closed down even after Brest-Litovsk was signed, put strains on a railway network already operating way beyond its normal territorial range and cursed with worn-out locomotives, inadequate maintenance and insufficient fuel. The Germans occupied the Donets basin by the end of April, but it produced only 5 million tons of coal in the first half of 1918: they had to send 80,000 tons a month from Germany to keep the trains operational.[44] All four Central Powers imported only 113,421 tons of food from Ukraine in 1918: as Czernin acknowledged, 'the hopes, which the settlement at Brest-Litovsk had universally raised, were not remotely fulfilled.'[45]

In Germany the Vienna strikes, especially when they seemed to achieve their objectives with so much ease, inspired the workers to similar demonstrations. On 28 January 100,000 struck in Berlin, and within days 400,000 were out, with support in many major cities across Germany, including Dusseldorf, Kiel, Hamburg and Cologne. One estimate reckoned that about 4 million took to the streets. The leaders were radical shop stewards alienated from the official trade unions, but in most cases their objectives were still not revolutionary. As in Austria-Hungary, the majority Socialists responded to the initiative of the workers rather than prompted it. But in Germany the official reaction was very different. 'My old friend, the Commandant of Berlin, General Kessel', Princess Blücher noted, 'is doing his best to stir up the troubled waters by stamping with his heavy foot and rattling with his iron fist.'[46] The army believed that the workers were encouraging the Russians' intransigence at the negotiating table. On 31 January a state of siege was declared, and the ringleaders were rounded up and court-martialled. A hundred and fifty of them were imprisoned, and up to 50,000 were put into uniform. In the army they joined prisoners of war released from Russia and units which had been exposed to the two-way flow of fraternisation on the eastern front. Trains which carried them westwards bore slogans like 'Cannon fodder for Flanders'.

Germany's 1918 Offensives

The soldiers at the front showed little sympathy for those they called the 'rowdies'. 'We have to thank these Berlin whelps for lengthening the war by at least half a year', wrote one.[47] So far morale at the front remained distinct from feeling at home. But the army was breaking down the division by drafting all the men it could get. For the first time since February 1916, it was planning a major offensive on the western front. Success on the battlefield would fulfil a domestic objective: like Tannenberg it would give the military popular legitimacy. Many senior army officers were of the view that it was too late, that the German army could mount only limited offensives. General Hoffmann reckoned that Germany should seek a compromise peace without annexations, others that it should roll up like a hedgehog, and fight a defensive battle on shortened lines. But the collapse of Russia permitted Germany to shift forty-four divisions to the west between 1 November 1917 and 21 March 1918.[48] 'Our overall position', Ludendorff told a conference of army commanders on 11 November 1917, 'requires the earliest possible blow, if possible at the end of February, or the beginning of March, before the Americans can throw strong forces into the scales.'[49]

That was about as far as strategic logic went. German hopes for 1917 had been pinned on the U-boat offensive. Holtzendorff had calculated that, if Germany could sink 600,000 tons of British shipping a month for five months, Britain would have to make peace. The navy delivered: it sank 860,334 tons in April, and exceeded its target in May and June. Given that it had only about thirty submarines on station at any one time, that was a remarkable achievement: before the war it was thought 222 would be needed for an effective blockade of Britain.[50] But when Erzberger attacked the chancellor in July, he did so on the basis that the U-boat offensive had failed. British countermeasures were only part of the reason. By grouping merchantmen in convoys the Royal Navy made the best use of its destroyers, the bulk of which had hitherto been committed to escorting the Grand Fleet; this was also where the contribution of the

United States Navy came in. Destroyers, unlike most merchant vessels, carried wirelesses, and thus ensured that the most up-to-date signals intelligence from Room 40 was available in routing convoys away from U-boats. However, the essential point was that Holtzendorff had miscalculated. He had assumed that neutral tonnage would be frightened off the seas. It was not. Freight rates and London's control of the insurance market saw to that. Instead, less was imported into border neutrals for re-export to the Central Powers. In this respect the Germans shot themselves in the foot: the U-boat campaign tightened the allied blockade. Moreover, Britain's own food supplies were more elastic than Holtzendorff had imagined. Britain imported about 64 per cent of its food in 1914, but it had spare pasture which it could bring into cultivation. Output was promoted rather than retarded, especially since rationing, when it was eventually introduced, was exercised at the point of sale, not at the point of production. Wheat yields rose 40 per cent between 1914 and 1918, and those of most other foodstuffs were at least constant.[51] Imports emphasised commodities like grain which were more efficient than livestock in the ratio of weight to calorific value. Mortality rates among the working class declined, as diets became healthier and rationing guaranteed a minimum subsistence for the underprivileged.[52] By the time Britain moved to full-scale rationing, in 1918, the worst of the danger to its trade was over, and the benefits were largely psychological. With a minimal black market, state controls on food supply promoted social solidarity – rather than, as in Germany, undermining it. 'Look well at the loaf on your breakfast table and treat it as if it were real gold,' declared Kennedy Jones, director-general of food economy, in a speech in Edinburgh in May 1917, 'because the British loaf is going to beat the German.'[53]

By June 1917 the German navy was ordering new submarines for 1919, effectively acknowledging that Holtzendorff's assumptions had already been proven wrong. However, the total number of vessels available at any one time fell thereafter. It was symptomatic of the army's approach to the direction of the war that neither materials nor men were released for an even bigger construction programme.

Germany did not have the resources or the planning mechanisms to enable it to mount a major effort by land and sea simultaneously. In 1916 the land offensive in the west had not been accompanied by a U-boat campaign; in 1917, the year of the U-boat, there was no major offensive in France; and in 1918 the land option was pursued to the detriment of the naval. In January 1918 Hindenburg told the Kaiser that 'We have to defeat the Western Powers in order to secure the political and economic position in the world that we need'.[54] But even if the Germans got to Paris and Calais, as some optimists hoped, their victory would not knock out either Britain or the United States. Czernin believed that Britain might be persuaded to negotiate before the American presence was felt, so that it retained the upper hand in world politics, but that in turn implied a German readiness to compromise on Belgium and Alsace-Lorraine. Neither Hindenburg nor Ludendorff would do so, especially when they and others were increasingly thinking in terms of the 'Second Punic War'. If the current world war did not secure the full package of German war aims, it would have to be followed by another. In that case it would be even more important to conclude this one with gains which would enable the next to be fought to a victorious conclusion.

Planning at the operational level in the winter of 1917–18 was as confused as at that of overall strategy. If the aim was to knock out France, Verdun was still the sector that could be treated in isolation. But the battle of 1916 carried its own lesson: the French army would not easily give in. The British army was seen as a softer nut, less adroit and less committed to holding ground which was not its own. Therefore, the Army Group commanded by Crown Prince Rupprecht of Bavaria favoured an attack in Flanders, directed due west, and designed to cut off the British in the Ypres salient. But the boggy ground militated against an attack early in the year, and so the balance swung to objectives further south. The sector chosen, from Arras south to St Quentin, covered the old Somme battlefield, whose devastated terrain would slow the German advance just at the point where it might hope to achieve breakthrough. Moreover, the main thrust of the attack, mounted by the 2nd and 17th Armies, would have to go first to the south-west, to clear the salient at Cambrai, and then reorientate itself in mid-battle to go north-west towards Arras and Vimy. To their south, the 18th Army, originally given the task of protecting their left flank, had the limits on its objectives removed and so was encouraged to push south if it could. There was a distinct possibility that the Germans' effort would dissipate itself in divergent directions. Germany had sufficient resources for one major offensive, but seemed to be committing itself to a series of indecisive engagements. Crown Prince Rupprecht was not happy. This was the first offensive in the west that Hindenburg and Ludendorff had mounted, and he believed that they underestimated the difficulties. When, on 21 January 1918, he pointed out that the attack did 'not lead in any favourable operational direction', Ludendorff replied: 'In Russia we have always set ourselves a close objective and then seen how things develop'. Rupprecht responded with two observations: first, that tactical success could not be an end in itself but had to have an operational foundation, and, second, that fighting the Russians was not the same thing as taking on the British or French.[55]

Rupprecht was marginalised. The German principle of delegating command forward, which applied at the forward edge of the battlefield, was not applied at the level of higher command. Ludendorff used three armies for the offensive, code-named 'Michael', and divided them over two army groups, so that decisions had to work their way up the command chain, not down it. Only he could resolve disputes, and it was clear that his own conceptual grasp was limited. 'Ludendorff is a man of absolute determination,' Rupprecht noted, 'but determination alone is not enough, if it is not combined with clear-headed intelligence.'[56]

Ludendorff had decided that in the circumstances of trench warfare tactics were all. If a breakthrough could be effected, then strategy could follow. A sequence of battles in the second half of 1917, the capture of Riga, the breakthrough at Caporetto, and a counterattack at Cambrai, did indeed suggest that the Germans had cracked the conundrums of trench warfare. In January 1918 they promulgated a new manual, the 'attack in position warfare'. This was not as fresh in its thinking as is sometimes claimed. Its immediate origins lay in the manner in which the Germans had conducted their defensive battles of 1917, on the Chemin des Dames and at Ypres. By adopting defence in depth, with the front line only thinly held and the main position to the rear, the Germans had drawn the enemy attack away from its own artillery support, and been able to stress the counterattack even in defensive battles. They had also delegated command forward, to ensure that the response to any allied gains was immediate, and to enable lost ground to be recaptured before it had been consolidated. But the roots of the tactics of 1918 went even further back: to 1915, and Willy Rohr's first storm-troops. By 1918 squads or groups of seven to ten storm-troopers were trained to bypass strong points, maintaining the momentum of the advance by seeking soft spots. Supporting formations would mop up.

The other key to reintegrating fire and movement was the artillery, and here the principal innovator on the German side was a lieutenant-colonel who had retired before the war's outbreak and had still not been formally restored to the active list, Georg Bruchmüller. The bombardment on 21 March 1918 lasted only five hours, its aim being to stun and suppress, not to destroy and – above all – not to forfeit surprise. Its principal target was less the defensive positions of the enemy's infantry than his artillery batteries. Once armies had learnt countermeasures, gas was not a big killer in the First World War. However, gas shells meant that it could be used with precision. Bruchmüller fired tear-gas shells at the same time as phosgene, forcing enemy gun crews to take off their gas masks, to relieve the irritation to their eyes, and so expose their lungs. The sophisticated use of artillery meant that the battle, which had become linear because of the trenches, was also fought in depth. Effective counter-battery work enabled the German infantry to assemble without itself coming under fire. At 9.40 a.m. storm-troopers clambered out of their trenches, and crossed no man's land in groups rather than waves, staying close to the rolling barrage that preceded them.

Ludendorff's problem at the tactical level was less in the theory and more in the practice. He reckoned standards had sunk so low that the army was little better than a militia. In the winter of 1917–18 a total of fifty-six divisions were brought out of the line for training in the attack. But the real emphasis was laid less on the skills of the unit and more on the morale of the individual. The advent of new technology to the battlefield, the battle of matériel, had increased the strains to which the soldier was exposed. In seeking to motivate him the Germans returned to the principles of 1914: 'the troops must have dash if an assault is to be successful'.[57] The army was divided into mobile, attack and trench divisions, the first of these being given better rations and expected to lead the attack. Morale, which had slumped in late October 1917, did rise in the lead-up to the offensives in the west. 'Everywhere men are working feverishly', one soldier wrote home on 21 March, 'and the picture on the roads is as excited as in the first months of the war.'[58] But the enthusiasm was conditional: it assumed that the offensive would end the war. Going forward seemed to be the shortest and quickest way home.

The principal blow struck the British 5th Army, under General Sir Hubert Gough, astride the Somme. This was the most thinly defended of all British sectors of the line. It had been occupied only after the German retreat to the Hindenburg line a year before, and much of it had been held by the French until only a few weeks previously. Its defensive positions, although marked out, had not been fully prepared. Both Haig and Pétain knew that an attack was imminent but had not been able to decide where the main blow would fall. The fact that the Germans took so long to make up their minds helped the deception, as did raids and artillery preparations along the length of the front. But the biggest surprise was tactical. The British had underestimated the impact of the initial German assault. The latter was helped by the weather. Low-lying fog enabled the storm-troopers to get between the machine-gun nests in the British forward line. 'We honestly could not see each other, it was that thick with the German guns and the fog', recalled Corporal Ted Gale. British casualties on the first day were 38,512, of whom as many as 21,000 were captured. Gale was one of them: 'Jerry had broken through on right and left of us. This was a mopping-up party coming. They'd never attempted a frontal attack.'[59]

Panic spread down the command chain, as well as up. The Germans did not get as far on the first day as they hoped. But British corps commanders, unable to see what was happening, overreacted. 'As soon as telegraphic & telephone communications with Brigades ceased to exist, Divisional Headquarters in many cases became paralysed,' one staff officer recalled. 'They had become so welded to a set piece type of warfare, that, when open warfare occurred, they failed to appreciate the situation, and were unable to function independent of a fixed headquarters.'[60] Gough's own orders created confusion as to whether the second line was to be held or not. The result was that the Germans' gains on the second and third days were amplified as the British fell back. On the 23rd even the cautious Crown Prince Rupprecht was prompted to conclude that 'The progress of our offensive is so quick, that one cannot follow it with a pen'.[61]

Territorially the attacks of late March 1918 produced the most significant advances in the west since 1914. They reached almost forty miles, and threatened the vital railway junction of Amiens. But they followed the line of least enemy resistance. Consequently, the German advances were greatest to the south, where they had less strategic effect. To the north, the British 3rd Army (under General Sir Julian Byng) held its positions around the crucial Vimy Ridge. If the aim was to swing north, this was not where the Germans were going. Moreover, the Germans could not keep up with their own success. Deprived of horses, they lacked cavalry to exploit and transport to bring up artillery and supplies. German units in the front line were not relieved, but were expected to sustain the momentum of the advance. The best were killed, and those who survived stopped to plunder and loot: 'we are already in the English rest areas', Rudolph Binding wrote as his unit approached Albert on 27 March, 'a land flowing with milk and honey'.[62]

The 'Michael' offensive was formally closed down on 5 April. Ludendorff launched four more. On 9 April, in 'Georgette', he struck in Flanders, a far more sensible location if his strategic purpose was to roll the British up against the Channel ports. But by the same token the British defences here were better prepared and more dogged. When

'Georgette' was closed down, the greatest advance was twelve miles. Ludendorff now switched his attention to the Aisne and the French. Pétain had always feared he would, and so had urged the French to thin out their first defensive line and adopt defence in depth. But his army commanders could not bring themselves wantonly to lose more French territory, and the defences proved brittle when hit by the Germans in Operation 'Blücher' on 27 May 1918. Some unfortunate British divisions, taken out of the line to the north in the hope of a rest on a quiet sector, found themselves once again in the teeth of a German attack. The Chemin des Dames offensive buckled the French 7th Army, and reached Château-Thierry on the Marne, fifty-six miles from Paris. What was conceived of as a limited offensive to push the French away from the British now assumed its own importance. Paris itself came under fire from Germany artillery, and the panic in the civil population reproduced that of 1914. Ludendorff therefore renewed the attack against the French on 9 June, between Noyon and Montdidier, in Operation 'Gneisenau'. Gains were limited, and the French, supported by the Americans, counterattacked at Château-Thierry and Belleau Wood. Ludendorff's last offensive, in Champagne on 15 July, hit French units which had now mastered the defensive battle, and got nowhere.

In mid-July 1918 the German Empire stood at its greatest ever extent. It had pushed on Paris in the west; in the east it held the Ukraine; the Baltic states were under its control; in the Caucasus, the Russian collapse had reopened the route to Baku; and in Italy its Austrian ally had attacked on the Piave in June. For some civilians at home the army seemed poised to deliver the victory that would resolve all their domestic problems. But this time the soldiers knew that they had shot their bolt. The effort to mount the offensives had withdrawn too many troops from other fronts, threatening them with destabilisation. The attacks themselves had created great salients on the western front without achieving a breakthrough. On 20 March, the German army in the west held a front of 390 km; by 25 June 1918 that front extended 510 km. In the interim the army had lost over 800,000 men, with a disproportionate share borne by crack troops.[63] During the summer the first wave of the influenza epidemic that was to ravage Europe in 1918–19 hit the German army in the west. At home munitions production was throttled back for lack of men to use its output in the field. The German historian Gerhard Ritter, who was then a young officer serving at the front, called the offensives 'a crushing disappointment. Once again war's end had receded into the distant future, once again hecatombs had done no more than haplessly lengthen the front; and how could what had not been achieved in the first great blow, struck with every resource, full surprise, and tremendous artillery barrages, now be won with far weaker forces, consisting largely of decimated and exhausted divisions?'[64]

Despite being engaged in the most desperate fighting on the western front in a campaign which everybody else saw as Germany's last gasp, Ludendorff was still engaging in Napoleonic fantasies. On 21 May 1918, he wrote to Hans von Seeckt, now chief of staff on the Caucasian front: 'There is the hope that we will yet succeed in forcing France to the ground this year. But even if we are victorious in France, it is still in no way certain that we can force the English to a peace acceptable to us, if we are not able to threaten their most sensitive spot, in India. Therefore, we must now prepare ourselves as this necessity approaches.'[65] In June and July he planned operations for the Caucasus and Mesopotamia, largely using Turkish forces as though they were capable of such grandiose objectives and as though they were willing to fulfil Germany's objectives rather than their own. He had lost all grasp of strategic reality. The Turks were no longer willing to do Germany's bidding. Hindenburg asked Enver Pasha to withdraw the Ottoman 3rd Army from any points beyond the frontiers set by Brest-Litovsk, and concentrate against the British in Persia and Mesopotomia. Enver refused. He was bent not only on supporting the Muslim peoples of the north Caucasus but also in getting the oil of Baku. So were the Germans, but for themselves. Halil Pasha, the army group commander in the Caucasus, declared at the end of June that, 'If necessary I would not hold back from waging war on the Germans'.[66]

The alliance of the Central Powers was coming apart. The Germans had created a supreme military command in September

1916. On the suggestion of Enver, the Kaiser had been nominated as commander-in-chief, and the German general staff was installed as the supreme command's advisory body. 'In other words', as August von Cramon shrewdly observed, 'there would be a supreme council of war, but not a supreme command.'[67] Moreover, the inadequacies of Germany's own arrangements were extended to the alliance as a whole: the remit of the 'supreme war command' embraced only military matters narrowly defined, and in the circumstances of 'total war' that was clearly insufficient.

Enver had proposed the arrangement to obviate the tensions between Germany and Austria-Hungary. But it had not. The biggest alliance pressure on Austria-Hungary was fear. For Czernin, the rumours that it wanted peace forced it to disprove them by showing itself loyal, but in April 1918 the French published the Sixte negotiations of the previous year. Czernin felt that he had been betrayed by Karl, and resigned. In the eyes of the Entente his actions confirmed that the alliance between Austria-Hungary and Germany would be broken only by its complete defeat. At one level the Entente was right. Some Austrians, observing the impending disintegration of the empire, looked to Germany to hold it together – or, more realistically, to incorporate the German element within a greater Germany. The Germans themselves seized the moment to tie the bonds tighter in a meeting of the two emperors on 12 May. The reality, however, was that Austria-Hungary was caught in a situation where nothing added up any more. The army was divided against itself, with the chief of the general staff wanting every available man at the front, while the Ministry of War needed seven divisions at home to maintain order. General Landwehr, the Austrian food supremo in Vienna, seized Ukrainian grain bound for Germany as it was transported up the Danube. Food might bring domestic order, but the Germans' quid pro quo for more grain was six divisions for the western front. Vienna agreed to provide three. Austria-Hungary was truly shackled to Germany, but by the same token Germany was itself now too weak to survive without its ally.

10

WAR WITHOUT END

Coalition Warfare

The First World War was a coalition war. Its intensity, its scale and its length were all the products of the alliances that sustained it. In 1918 one, that of the Central Powers, began to fall apart, but the other, that of the Entente, achieved a fusion, albeit flawed, which enabled it to wield greater military and economic power than any unit previously seen in the history of the world. In liberalism, however imperfectly expressed and however compromised by the business of waging war, it had a common ideological focus. 'What we demand in this war', Woodrow Wilson told the United States Congress on 8 January 1918, 'is nothing peculiar to ourselves.'[1]

Wilson went on to give shape to that ambition, spelling out his Fourteen Points which he believed could deliver a 'peace without victory'. His aim was to keep Russia in the war, and, in providing a counterpoint to Bolshevism, he was sufficiently anti-imperialist to alarm both Britain and France. Freedom of the seas (his second point) challenged British maritime supremacy, and his fifth called for the recognition of the rights of colonial populations. But the specifics were ambiguous and negotiable. In the event the allies' responses were muted; the Fourteen Points embraced their fundamental territorial ambitions within Europe, and included the German evacuation of Belgium, the return to France of Alsace-Lorraine, and the settlement of Italy's frontier with Austria-Hungary on the basis of nationality. Wilson's key audience was not governments but peoples. Only three days previously Lloyd George had delivered a speech on war aims to the Trades Union Congress in London, which was couched in similar terms and in which he had embraced open diplomacy and the idea of a 'democratic peace'. 'The days of the Treaty of Vienna are long past. We can no longer submit the future of European civilisation to the arbitrary decisions of a few negotiators striving to secure by chicanery or persuasion the interests of this or that dynasty or nation. The settlement of the new Europe must be based on such grounds of reason and justice as will give some promise of stability. Therefore it is we feel that government with the consent of the governed must be the basis for any territorial settlement in this war.'[2]

Clemenceau may have entertained reservations about some of the things said by his British and American counterparts, but the French left did not. Publicly, he endorsed Lloyd George. Moreover, Wilson's fourteenth and best known point, the formation of 'a general association of nations', had British and French authors too – including Jan Christian Smuts and Lord Robert Cecil; the latter had drafted Lloyd George's speech. 'The programme of the world's peace', Wilson said, 'is our programme . . . the only possible programme.'[3] In the popular imagination he had captured the moral high ground for the Entente.

America's participation in the alliance, even if as a self-proclaimed associate rather than as a full ally, also brought in other powers to what was evidently a going concern. The states of South America either entered the war or severed relations with Germany. In Asia, China declared war on the Central Powers on 14 August 1917 and offered 300,000 men for service in Europe. In the Balkans, Greece joined the Entente on 2 July 1917. But, after Bulgaria did so in September 1915, no other power in the world sided with Germany.

The combined populations of the four Central Powers totalled 144 million in 1914; those of the principal Entente powers of 1918 (including their colonies) 690 million.[4] However, economic potential and military capability were not the same. Turkey, despite its backwardness, had twice defeated Britain in battle, and its military contribution to the war as a whole was greater than that of the United

States. By the same token, the Entente's comparative strength rested on more than the sum of its resources. First, its principals were to a greater extent equals than were the Central Powers. That did not mean there were not great disparities of wealth between them: by 1918 America had the money, but France still had the biggest army and Britain the biggest navy. Second, the allies had in 1915 begun a process of organic growth which, however fractious, had reached a maturity and breadth by 1918 which ensured that joint military command was the coping-stone of the whole – not, as in the case of the Central Powers, its only foundation. Third, many of the fronts, particularly the principal one in the west, were genuinely shared responsibilities. Germany shored up the western front single-handedly, but then on other fronts could expect its allies to act as virtual mercenaries, providing the cannon fodder for German commanders to use according to German priorities. There were Entente fronts, pre-eminently the Italian, which were largely sustained by the army of one nation, but that army sustained its legitimacy by acting in conformity with its own national objectives.

Indeed that was the Entente's recurring problem with Italy: it timed its offensives to suit its own needs, not those of achieving unity of effect in space and time. The collapse at Caporetto created the opportunity both to integrate Italy's efforts with those on other fronts and to complete the integration of the Entente by the establishment of a Supreme War Council. In July 1917 Robertson and Foch, as their countries' chiefs of staff, had met Generals Cadorna and Pershing, the commander of the American Expeditionary Force, to discuss the acceleration of the American military commitment to Europe in the light of Russia's collapse. They had broached the idea of amalgamating the Americans with more experienced British and French units. But Pershing's orders told him that 'the forces of the United States are a separate and distinct component of the combined forces, the identity of which must be preserved'. This was not just a matter of national pride or public opinion, it was also one of policy: an independent army would enable America to retain a free hand at the peace negotiations. Dogmatic and rigid, a teetotaller, 'Black Jack'

Pershing had lost his wife and three daughters in a fire in 1915; although he consoled himself with a mistress while in France, his men were banned access to brothels. He adhered to the principle of independence with similar vehemence. However, there was one major obstacle to its fulfilment: the lack of a sizeable body of proven American commanders and trained staff officers. The British experience had shown that it might be possible to improvise a mass army in comparatively short order, but that, as Haig's director of military intelligence put it, 'It will be a very difficult job for them [the Americans] to get a serviceable staff going even in a year's time'.[5] The allies' military representatives had therefore concluded that some form of inter-allied organisation would be required to facilitate this process.

The prime ministers of Britain and France, together with Robertson and Foch, met at Rapallo between 5 and 7 November 1917 to coordinate their response to Italy's plea for help. The Italians, according to their prime minister, Vittorio Orlando, 'were treated like servants'.[6] The problem was Cadorna, who not only failed to attend but also submitted such inflated and inaccurate calculations of the German and Austro-Hungarian forces opposing him as to confirm the doubts about his competence. Foch and Robertson were being asked to commit eleven French and British divisions to a command structure in which they had no faith. Both Foch and Pétain were adamant that the six French divisions should remain at the disposal of France, and should be handled in conjunction with those on the French front: in other words, that the line from the Somme to the Piave should be a unit.

The French divisions in Italy were placed under Foch as chief of the general staff, not Pétain as France's commander-in-chief: another step in the principle of dividing and ruling the military. Of the representatives at Rapallo, Foch was the only one whose motives in promoting the idea of a Supreme War Council smacked of altruism, and even he – having been tarred in 1916 with the brush of Joffre and of the Somme battle – had a career to resurrect. His prime minister, still Painlevé for a few days more, saw the creation of a Supreme War

Council as an interim step towards the promotion of Foch as allied commander-in-chief, but felt that he could not say so to the British: that was understandable after the Nivelle affair. Besides, Painlevé and Pétain thought the principal benefit in the creation of joint command would be that the British would take over more of the line from the battered French army. The French therefore proposed that Foch, being chief of the general staff, should also be their permanent military representative on the Supreme War Council. The corollary of such an arrangement would have been that Robertson would similarly exercise both functions for Britain. This was totally unacceptable to Lloyd George, who saw the Supreme War Council as an opportunity not only to subordinate Haig but also to break the axis between him and Robertson. He persuaded the French that Foch should not hold both appointments simultaneously and asked Henry Wilson, then languishing in a job at home, to be Britain's military representative on the Supreme War Council. Wilson, like his chum Foch, found his career reviving because of his usefulness to civilians as an alternative source of professional military advice.

The key issue facing the new body was the creation of a strategic reserve, not least in anticipation of a German offensive in the west in 1918. Robertson argued that British reserves should be under his control as it was his job as chief of staff to know their capabilities, and Haig and Pétain both said that they could not spare any divisions to create a reserve. Robertson resigned over the issue, and Wilson succeeded him, with Rawlinson moving into the Versailles post. Rawlinson backed Haig, and when the German offensive was unleashed between St Quentin and Arras on 21 March 1918 the Supreme War Council was no more than an advisory body, with no troops under its command and no ability to help General Gough's 5th Army.

It did not matter. Haig and Pétain had agreed a scheme for mutual assistance which the French fulfilled to the letter. On 20 January Pétain had undertaken to release up to twelve divisions immediately in the event of a German attack against the British, and up to half the French army if need be. By the end of 23 March, he had committed fourteen divisions to the battle, all of which were in action by the 28th. By then half the French army was on the move. The roads were jammed with troops and transport. Haig consistently underestimated his own requirements and the scale of French support. Before the blow fell he thought six French divisions would suffice, and on the 21st itself he asked for only three. He requested twenty divisions on the 25th, but by then he already had the support of twenty-one, with a further nineteen on the way. Pétain created a whole new army group, under Fayolle's command, to straddle the front between the Somme and Oise rivers. Of its front of thirty-six miles, fully two-thirds was held by British troops, the elements of the 5th Army, which Haig told General Byng, commander of its northern neighbour, the 3rd Army, was finished.

Normally calm and imperturbable, Haig was exhibiting the nearest to panic of which he was capable. He confronted a crisis with unfamiliar tools: his staff had been emasculated over the winter, and Wilson, his new spokesman in London, was 'our only military blackleg', seemingly determined to curb the powers of the individual commanders-in-chief. When Wilson came to France and saw him on 25 March, Haig 'said that "unless the whole French army came up we were beaten" and "it would be better to make peace on any terms we could"'.[7] Haig was convinced that the greater danger lay to the north, towards Flanders. Pétain disagreed: he correctly concluded that the thrust south of the Somme, spearheaded by Crown Prince Wilhelm's army group, constituted the major threat. Haig's desire to pull back to the north, using the British 3rd Army to guard his right flank, reflected the operational logic of what his enemy ought to have been doing, but not what he was actually doing. Ludendorff's offensive was being carried on the back of its own tactical opportunism, and Pétain, who had paid more attention than the British to the evolution of German tactics, recognised that. Haig's subsequent claim that the French failed to support him and were pulling back to defend Paris was the exact opposite of the truth.

That is not to say that there was not deep despondency in Entente circles by 23 March. Paris was shelled, and it was suggested that as in 1914 the French government should leave the city. The Australian corps commander, Lieutenant-General John Monash, an engineer in civilian life and a brigadier at Gallipoli, recalled from leave in the south of France, reached Doullens at about 3 pm on the 25th: 'Viewed from that particular locality it almost looked as if the whole British Army in this part of the world was in a state of rout'.[8] On the following day Poincaré, the president of France, arrived in the town to chair a meeting attended not only by the headquarters staffs of the British and French armies but also by Clemenceau and, for the British war cabinet, Lord Milner. Henry Wilson was also there. After seeing Haig the previous day, he had then met his friend Ferdinand Foch, the putative commander of the allied reserve if it had existed. Both of them were convinced advocates of a united command, both of them knew that Foch was the logical choice to exercise it, and they had little difficulty in persuading their political superiors at the meeting, Clemenceau and Milner, that that was the way forward. Haig's alleged role in the appointment of the allied generalissimo was little more than a face-saving exercise conducted for the benefit of his own dignity and posterity.

Some doubted Foch's mental faculties: his head had received a severe blow in a recent car accident. He was, in Clemenceau's words, 'not superabundant in nuances'.[9] Furthermore, he had been educated by Jesuits, a definite disqualification in the mind of the anti-clerical prime minister. But will-power and faith were precisely the attributes that the situation demanded. On 26 March Foch was given the task of coordinating the actions of the British and French armies on the western front. At Beauvais, on 3 April, his powers were extended to embrace 'the strategic direction' of all the armies, including that of the United States. Foch conveyed the sort of rhetorical determination that politicians like to hear. 'I shall fight without ceasing', he was reported to have said to a group of officers. 'I shall fight in front of Amiens. I shall fight in Amiens. I shall fight behind Amiens. I shall fight all the time.'[10] It could have been one of Clemenceau's own speeches. It meant nothing, but it conveyed an aura of command.

Foch visited Gough the same day. He 'said in a loud, excited manner, "There must be no more retreat, the line must now be held at all costs," and then walked out of the room back to his car'.[11] He offered no troops and no specifics. His role was to rally, not to plan. Haig grumbled that Foch 'spoke a lot of nonsense' and complained – with some reason – that he was 'unmethodical and takes a "short view" of the situation. For instance, he does not look ahead and make a forecast of what may be required in a week in a certain area and arrange accordingly'.[12] In late March and early April 1918, the only allied commander with that sort of vision was Pétain, whom Haig, like Clemenceau, had convinced himself was defeatist. The French commander-in-chief was bent not simply on stopping the Germans and on closing the gap between the two allied armies, but also on preparing the counterattack that would strike north-east into the salient created by the German advance. The effect of his taking the 'long view' was ironically to widen the gap in understanding between himself on the one hand and Haig and Foch on the other. Pétain's attacks were conceived within an overall context of mobile defence and of conserving lives. For Foch, there was only one sort of attack: 'Everything that will not be achieved rapidly will not be achieved at all. . . . Our offensive must therefore be mounted both with speed and force.'[13] He spoke in the accents of 1914, as did Haig. Haig may have been a Presbyterian, but his inner certainty meant that more united than separated him from Foch, and in the second half of the year the circumstances of the war swung their way, bringing events on the ground into harmony with their notions of warfare.

Pétain's credibility was further dented on 27 May 1918. He had long forecasted a German attack on the Chemin des Dames, but he had not anticipated its scale and his subordinates were reluctant to apply his defensive tactics: it was the most significant defeat suffered by the French on the western front since 1914. Five British divisions had been transferred to the sector to 'rest' after the spring offensives but Haig refused more, so showing the limits of reciprocity as well as of Foch's authority to bend the national commanders-in-chief to his will. By 1 June the Germans were held and Pétain turned his thoughts once more to the counterattack, rather than a step-by-step withdrawal. Foch rejected the idea, but the French were ready when the Germans attacked again, in Champagne on 15 July. Pétain's instructions on defence in depth were implemented as they had not been on 27 May. The French 'put up no resistance in front', a German officer, Rudolf Binding, wrote in his diary; 'they had neither infantry nor artillery in this forward battle-zone . . . Our guns bombarded empty trenches; our gas-shells gassed empty artillery positions; only in little hidden folds in the ground, sparsely distributed, lay machine gun posts, like lice in the seams and folds of a garment, to give the attacking force a warm reception. The barrage, which was to have preceded and pro-tected it, went right on somewhere over the enemy's rear positions, while in front the first real line of resistance was not yet carried.'[14] The Germans had walked into a sack. This time Foch, even more than Pétain, saw the opportunity for a successful counterattack. On 18 July, Crown Prince Wilhelm recalled, 'Without artillery preparation, simply following the sudden rolling barrage, supported by numerous deep-flying aircraft and with unprecedented masses of tanks, the enemy infantry – including a number of American divisions – unleashed the storm against the 9th and 7th Armies at 5.40 in the morning.'[15] Dubbed the second battle of the Marne, the blow drove the Germans back from Château-Thierry to Soissons on the River Aisne.

The Tools of Victory

There were now twenty-five American divisions in France. Pershing's insistence on independence seemed to have confirmed the Germans' expectation that the United States army would not make an effec-tive contribution until 1919. In the event, although it undoubtedly delayed the Americans' impact, it was moderated in practice. Elements of eight divisions took part in the Marne battle, and they did so under temporary French command. The Americans' arrival was speeded by the decision to provide them with British and particularly French equipment, including the 75mm field gun and the Renault light tank. The shipping space thus saved brought over men instead: 1.5 million US soldiers arrived in Europe in the last six months of the war, with the result that there were forty-two divisions in the field by the time of the armistice and twenty-nine of them had seen action. In the space of eighteen months the army had grown from 100,000 men to 4 million, and had sent over 2 million overseas. By then the American Expeditionary Force was comparable in size with both the British imperial forces, which totalled 1.8 million in France, and those of France itself, which had fallen from a peak of 2.2 million in July 1916 to 1.7 million.

The effect of these numbers, and the prodigious effort that had produced them, was above all psychological. In April 1918, when the British army was fighting its desperate defensive action against the second of Ludendorff's offensives, Vera Brittain, serving as a nurse in Étaples, saw a contingent of American soldiers march down the road. They looked like 'Tommies in heaven'. 'I pressed forward . . . to watch the United States physically entering the War, so god-like, so magnificent, so splendidly unimpaired in comparison with the tired, nerve-racked men of the British Army'.[16] That confidence and self-assurance both helped and hindered the American Expeditionary Force in its adaptation to European warfare. It bred a courage not yet dimmed by age, loss and experience, a product of ignorance and naivety. But what Pershing could not accept was that in losing that vigour, which they, too, had possessed in 1914, the British and French armies had also learnt tactical wisdom. He believed that mobile warfare was the path to victory, that battle should be fought in the open, and that the key to success was aimed rifle-fire. He rejected the views of those who urged that machinery could substitute for manpower. The American division consisted of 28,000 men, twice the size of those of its allies, which were being restructured as smaller units with fewer men but greater firepower. It was short of lorries and guns, and it proved cumbersome in manoeuvre and poor in its ability to coordinate infantry and artillery.

It also had few tanks. The French had attacked with 375 Renault light tanks on 18 July. These were the brainchild of Jean-Baptiste Estienne, a French artillery officer, whose service in an aviation unit before the war had awoken him to the possibilities of inter-arm tactical cooperation. He encountered his first caterpillar tractor, the key to the tank's cross-country capability, in service with the British army in 1915. On 28 December 1915 he wrote to Joffre urging the development of the tank as an armoured platform for a gun, so as to provide direct fire support for the infantry. Like those under development in Britain at the same time, the first French tanks were heavy machines which were also designed to cross trenches and crush wire. Excessive weight, the result of emphasising armour over mobility, often proved a false friend on the muddy battlefields of France. It also put great mechanical strain on the power-to-weight ratio of the tank. The British models of 1917 and 1918 weighed around 30 tons, and German tank production, based on British types, fell flat on its face because of its pursuit of excessive weight. The breakdown rate of tanks in the First World War was very high – the speed of most ranged between 2 and 4 mph across country – and their range was restricted. The argument that the British had forfeited their surprise value by using them prematurely on the Somme in September 1916 is nonsense: here was an imperfect but evolving weapon which needed the benefit of combat experience. In essence the tank was only just moving into full series production when the war ended. However, in December 1916 Estienne proposed that tank development move in a radically different direction. He favoured lightness and manoeuvrability over protection, designing a two-man tank, with a weight of 5 tons. Unlike British tanks, which were rhomboidal in shape and carried their main armament on the sides, the Renault had a turret in which was mounted either a machine-gun or a 37mm gun. British tanks required special trains to transport them: the Renault did not, and could therefore be shifted from one sector to another with greater ease and concentrated for the attack in greater secrecy. Over 3,000 entered French service in 1918. The French manufactured about 800 heavy tanks, and the British about 5,000 of all types; about 20 of the monster German A7V were produced, and the handful of tanks the Germans deployed on the western front were mostly captured British models.

The tank was the most striking evidence of a number of points: that the Entente tackled the integration of science, technology and tactics with greater success than the Germans; that the link between tactical experience and factory production was a continuous loop, involving fresh blueprints and the rejigging of machine-tools and plant, as well as feeding munitions into the battle; that by 1918 the Entente, not the Central Powers, derived greater benefit from the trade-off between the mass army and mass production; and that the ultimate benefit was on the battlefield, in the reintegration of fire and movement.

The exponential growth in the numbers of aircraft during the course of the war illustrated similar arguments. Aerial combat at the start of the war was an affair of individuals, and generated its own heroes, the aces so loved by propaganda and the press. By 1917–18 it was a matter of masses, and was therefore sustained as much by the capabilities of its industrial base as by the skills and courage of the pilots who flew the aircraft. In the last year of the war, Britain, France and the United States jointly produced an average of 11,200 machines and 14,500 aero engines per month; the German equivalents were each below 2,000. The corollary of this point was that the air forces were themselves being reshaped. At the start of the war, their role was reconnaissance; by the middle fighters were contesting control of the air above the battlefield; by the end bombers were targeting positions on the ground and interdicting lines of communication. The products of war industries themselves, heavy bombers were beginning to be used to target war production. In 1917 German Gotha heavy bombers raided Paris and London. Spurred to retaliate, the British established the world's first air force on 1 April 1918 and created an 'Independent Force' to target factories, railways and airfields. This strategy set missions which were beyond the capabilities of the existing aircraft, but its implications were already becoming clear: 'I would very much like it', Lord Weir, secretary of state for air, instructed the chief of the air staff, Hugh Trenchard, on 10 September 1918, 'if you could start up a really big fire in one of the German towns. If I were you, I would not be too exacting as regards accuracy in bombing railway stations in the middle of towns. The German is susceptible to bloodiness, and I would not mind a few accidents due to inaccuracy.'[17] In practice, bombing against civilian targets produced negligible results in the First World War, but ground attack on the battlefield played a crucial role in checking the German spring offensives in 1918 and in the combined arms offensives of the late summer and autumn. 'The whistling of the falling bombs was like the noise of a thousand door-keys used to hiss a bad play', wrote Rudolf Binding as he fell back to the Aisne on 30 July. 'On explosion they burst into millions of splinters, which flew out horizontally and caused hundreds of casualties.'[18] In the last year of the war the aeroplane as well as the tank embodied in one platform the ability both to manoeuvre and to deliver accurate fire on a target.

Neither of them, however, was the true artisan of victory: that was the artillery. The biggest single intellectual shift in making war between 1914 and 1918 was that the combined-arms battle was planned around the capabilities of the guns rather than of the infantry. On 20 November 1917 the British had attacked at Cambrai with 378 tanks; they achieved complete surprise, penetrating up to 4,000 yards on a six-mile front. British tank advocates, including their most effective spokesman after the war, J. F. C. Fuller, who was involved in the planning of the battle, later used the victory as evidence of the decisive independent use of armour. It was not. Fuller himself had written in February 1917: 'It must be remembered that the Creeping Barrage will usually be more effective than the Tank and that the Tank is in no way intended to replace this Barrage but to supplement it when it breaks down or becomes ineffective'.[19] By November the Royal Artillery had perfected the techniques of predicted fire. It used microphones to record from different points the low-frequency sound waves following the firing of a gun in order to take a cross-bearing and locate the position of an enemy battery. Unlike aerial observation or the visual spotting of gun flashes, both also methods of immense value in identifying targets, sound-ranging could be used in bad visibility. Consequently, artillery could register its guns in advance of an attack without the preliminary bombardment that had squandered surprise in the past, particularly when the tanks could themselves take on the tasks of crushing wire and destroying enemy machine-gun nests.

The success at Cambrai was the product of the short bombardment as much as of the massed use of tanks. These were the principles carried forward into 1918. In the last year of the war bombardments were short, but their effects were greater than those of the long bombardments of 1916 and early 1917. First, second and third lines of defence could be isolated from each other by curtains of fire, which moved forward or back according to plan, matching the type of shell to the nature of the target. Confronted with mortal danger, and cut off from resupply or relief, the defenders had to respond in the most unnatural way of all: 'In absolute darkness we simply lay and trembled from sheer nervous tension'. Industrialised war enforced passivity, as one of Pershing's officers, Hervey Allen, found out: 'There is a faraway moan that grows to a scream, then a roar like a train, followed by a ground-shaking smash and a diabolical red light. . . . Everybody simply shakes and crawls . . . A hunching of the shoulders and then another comes, and the thought – How long, how long? There is nothing to do. Whether you get through or not is just sheer chance and nothing more.'[20]

Accuracy of fire meant less wasted effort, but quantity still had a part to play. More guns were available, especially heavy ones. In 1918 France's holdings of field artillery, 5,000 guns, were comparable with those of 1914, but those of heavy artillery had risen from 300 to 5,700. Britain manufactured 3,226 guns in 1915 but 10,680 in 1918. Therefore as many shells could be fired in a short period as could be fired in a longer period two years previously. Shell production was now always ahead of shell consumption. Pétain focused on mobility to create concentrations of fire, but in the British case abundance meant that the guns did not necessarily have to be moved to create a local concentration, so attacks could be launched in rapid succession at different points of the line with minimum delay. At the end of the war, the French artillery constituted 37 per cent of the army, as opposed to 18 per cent in May 1915, and the Royal Artillery mustered half a million men, and constituted a quarter of the British army. Germany's artillery strength was greater than both Britain's and France's combined at the beginning of 1918, but by November was comparable with Britain's alone. Deliveries of new field guns fell from 3,000 per month in 1917 to 2,000 in February 1918 and 1,200 in September. Having had 7,130 guns at the front in February 1917, Germany had only 6,172 a year later. Lack of men and horses to provide gun crews was a more important reason for this decline than falling productivity, although this too had its impact: from July 1918 the monthly output of shells was half that of 1917. In a war in which 70 per cent of all casualties were attributed to artillery it was a fatal weakness.

The Entente's Victories

'The Boche holds firm,' wrote Charles Mangin, commander of the Soissons counterattack, to his wife on 28 July 1918.[21] That was not how it seemed on the German side of the line. Opposite him, Crown Prince Wilhelm said the whole position had changed. His fellow army group commander, Crown Prince Rupprecht, concluded on 20 July that 'we stand at the turning point of the war: what I expected first for the autumn, the necessity to go over to the defensive, is already on us, and in addition all the gains which we made in the spring – such as they were – have been lost again'. But Ludendorff refused to confront realities, defying the advice of his senior commanders that they pull back or even negotiate, and ignoring the evidence of the collapsing morale of his troops. 'Poor provisions, heavy losses and the deepening influenza have deeply depressed the spirits of the men in the III Infantry Division', Rupprecht wrote on 3 August. Postal censors told him that letters home complained of the mounting numbers of Americans and of British aerial domination, and – even more importantly – called for peace in ways which linked front and rear; war, they said, was the product of capitalism, and 'at home, they must strike and strike hard, and cause a revolution, and then peace must come'.[22]

Nobody on the allied side had yet realised that victory was possible this side of Christmas. In London the war cabinet was making preparations for 1919. In France Foch convened a conference of the national army commanders on 24 July. He appreciated that the opportunity to take the initiative had now arrived; morally, materially and numerically the allies were in the ascendant on the western front. But even he, ebullient spokesman of the offensive that he was, rejected a single decisive blow. Instead he envisaged a series of limited attacks. Their aims would be to free the principal railway lines radiating out from Paris, to regain the economic heartlands of France and above all to improve the armies' lines of communication for the next, more mobile, phase of operations. 'These movements should be executed with such rapidity as to inflict upon the enemy a succession of blows. This condition necessarily limits their extent . . . These actions must succeed each other at brief intervals, so as to embarrass the enemy in the utilization of his reserves and not allow him sufficient time to fill up his units.'[23] Here was a concept of operations which harnessed the Entente's superior resources to the constraints of trench war. Attacks would go no deeper into the enemy's positions than the reach of the artillery supporting them. By rapidly switching the axis of the advance, Foch would pull the enemy first in one direction and then in another. Most important of all, it was a framework to which Pershing, Pétain and Haig were prepared to subscribe. The first recognised that the inexperience of his army required him to go gently; the other two needed to husband their forces after the battering of the first half of 1918. Foch was being realistic: he himself had only a skeleton staff, and his powers extended little further than any consensus he could forge. Individual blows, coordinated in time and space, allowed each national army to do its own thing.

Haig had drawn up a plan for a limited offensive at Amiens, a direct consequence of his precipitate withdrawal in March. The German line here lacked deep defensive positions. Orchestrated by Rawlinson, who had been recalled to the command of the 4th Army, and supported by the French to the south, the attack maximised firepower and method. Each gun was allocated twenty-five yards of trench, and thanks in part to allied aerial superiority (1,800 British and French aircraft were assembled) 95 per cent of German batteries were located in advance. On the Somme British battalions had numbered 1,000 men and were equipped with four Lewis light machine-guns and one or two light trench mortars. At Amiens they numbered 500 men but had thirty Lewis guns, eight mortars and – if in the first line – were accompanied by six tanks.[24] In all over 400 tanks took part in the attack on 8 August; by the 9th only 145 were fit for action. Mechanical problems were their principal defect, but the Germans also learnt to overcome what Ludendorff called 'tank fright'. Stiffer anti-tank defences contributed to such high losses that never again in the war did more than 150 tanks go into action at any one time.

Ludendorff dubbed 8 August 'the black day of the German army'. Of 27,000 German casualties, fully 12,000 had surrendered, an unprecedentedly high proportion. But the German army did not cease fighting thereafter. Front-line resistance continued until the armistice; the problems of desertion and disobedience were more in its rear, on the lines of communication and at home. The significance of Amiens lay as much in its shock effect on Ludendorff, who at last woke up to what others had been saying for weeks. But, when the Kaiser summoned his principal political and military leaders to a council at Spa on 13 and 14 August, he failed to present a realistic appraisal of the military situation. Instead he blamed the mood at home. Over the next six weeks Ludendorff's mood showed alarming swings, as he oscillated between unfounded optimism and the search for scapegoats other than himself. A psychologist told him he needed to rest and to sing German folk songs on waking in the morning. At Spa, Wilhelm thought it sensible to seek an intermediary in order to open peace negotiations. But his foreign minister, Paul von Hintze, still made such an approach conditional on the next German victory, and could not resolve definitively to abandon Germany's claims to Belgium and Alsace-Lorraine. A week later, Hintze told the party leaders that the army believed that 'there was no reason to doubt ultimate victory. We shall be vanquished only when we doubt that we shall win'.[25]

The Austrians did doubt it. Karl, accompanied by Count Burian, Czernin's successor as foreign minister, and Arz, attended the Spa conference and said that direct negotiations were needed as soon as possible. The Entente had been cautious about the dismemberment of Austria-Hungary, which if united would at least provide a counter-weight to Germany in central Europe. In January 1918 Wilson's tenth point had allowed for the 'autonomous' development of the peoples of Austria-Hungary. But his thirteenth provided specifically for an independent Polish state, and, although he had been more cautious about Czechoslovakia, by the summer it, too, had received de facto recognition. With the coalescence of their war aims, the allies were able to coordinate their efforts in propaganda as in other spheres. This was an approach that appealed to the Italian high command. Throughout 1918 Armando Diaz resisted pressure from the Supreme War Council for an Italian offensive, and put his effort into the subversion of the Austro-Hungarian army instead. Ideas were less costly in lives than bullets, and so did not threaten the fragile morale of the Italian army after Caporetto. The Italians were not very successful: in June 1918 the Austro-Hungarian army attacked on the Piave, and the head of the British military mission reported that 'as a whole the enemy troops . . . are fighting with great determination'.[26] The attack failed, but not primarily because of desertion or nationalist sentiment. The men were exhausted, without equipment and, more importantly, food. They had dubbed the attack on the Piave the 'bread offensive'. The pressures to which they were succumbing came from behind them rather than from in front; as in the German army, grievances at home were merging with grievances in the army. Allied propaganda aimed at the subject nationalities was blamed for strikes and mutinies generated by other causes. In August malaria added to the woes of the Austro-Hungarian army in Italy: two-thirds of its divisions were below half strength. When Hintze told Karl and his advisers on 3 September that Ludendorff was predicting eventual success on the western front, they decided on unilateral action. On 14 September Burian asked for talks on peace terms. The allies rejected him: in a belated bid to save the Dual Monarchy the Austro-Hungarians had at last resolved to abandon the alliance with Germany, but as in 1914 the Entente leaders saw the two as indivisible.

Haig had been surprised by the scale of his success at Amiens and had had to hold Foch back from pushing the offensive beyond its limits. But both commanders now realised, as Haig told a sceptical Winston Churchill on 21 August, that 'we ought to do our utmost to get a decision this autumn'.[27] The American army was capable of independent operations, as it showed when it pinched out the St Mihiel salient south of Verdun between 12 and 16 September. It got the early success that Pershing had seen as essential to buoy the morale of his young army; it had done so in part because the Germans had taken the decision two days earlier not to hold the salient. But, rather than continue the advance, it was then re-deployed, with considerable logistical difficulty, to the west of Verdun, to form the right flank of a joint attack with the French, going north through the Argonne forest. Foch hoped to get into the guts of the German rear areas from below. Beginning on 26 September and continuing through October, the French and American armies punched their way through deep German defences, the Americans' right flank following the line of the Meuse valley.

The British attacked on the other side of the enormous salient that made up the German position in France. The 1st and 3rd Armies took over from Rawlinson's 4th in continuous fighting from late August into September. The battlefield was familiar from two years previously: 'Then we attacked *en masse* from the south-east, and fought for yards of ground thickly held by an enemy with no thought of retreat. Now the front in movement was wide and elastic, the fighting was open, and we were attacking positions from the flank.'[28] The Germans fell back to the Hindenburg line. Formidable obstacle though it was, it had been built at the end of 1916. It was an indication of the war's dynamism and the pace of its tactical innovation that its principles were now obsolescent. Made up of six defensive lines, it formed a zone 6,000 yards deep, with concrete emplacements and belts of barbed wire. But the southern part included the St Quentin canal, and did not therefore rest on a reverse slope out of artillery observation, and the whole was linear in design when more recent constructions had been made up of strongpoints, arranged in chequer-board fashion to create converging fields of fire. Unlike Amiens the Hindenburg line was strongly held, and unlike Cambrai it presented no opportunity for surprise. The answer was a 56-hour artillery bombardment, using 1,637 guns on a 10,000-yard front, twice the density of the Somme, and targeting the defences rather than the defenders. In the last twenty-four hours the British fired a record 945,052 shells. The capture of the canal by the 46th Division was one of the great feats of arms of the war, helped by heavy early-morning fog and a creeping barrage which rained down 126 shells for every 500 yards of German trench for eight hours.[29] The Hindenburg line was breached on 29 September.

For three days the entire western front had been under coordinated allied attack. To the north of the Hindenburg line the Canadians in the 1st Army, supported by the 3rd Army on their right, had crossed the Canal du Nord, and above them two more British armies and – for the first time since 1914 – the Belgians were pushing into Flanders. Paul von Hintze, briefed on the realities of the military situation by Ludendorff's subordinates, realised that defeat was likely to precipitate a revolution. To avert it, he proposed a 'revolution from above'. Germany's government should be reformed on more democratic lines as a preliminary to any peace negotiations. This might achieve two objectives: it would preserve the monarchy and it might channel the opprobrium for defeat on to the left and not the right.

These careful calculations needed time to be put into effect. They were wrong-footed by Ludendorff. On the night of 28 September his nerve cracked: he fell to the floor and according to some accounts foamed at the mouth. At a crown council convened at Spa on the following morning, he demanded an immediate armistice on the basis of Wilson's Fourteen Points. He had suddenly changed his assessment of the military situation, and as a result had at last usurped the political process. Georg von Hertling, who reached the meeting too late to play an active part, resigned the chancellorship. His successor, Max von Baden, arrived in Berlin to take up office at 4 a.m. on 1 October, and promptly made it clear that his whole policy depended on holding out for some while longer. He protested that Ludendorff was inverting the logical sequence: 'a request for an armistice makes any peace initiative impossible'.[30] Germany was in danger of forfeiting its long-term powers of negotiation because the army insisted it needed a short-term breathing space.

None the less, Ludendorff's erratic behaviour was not in any immediate sense the product of the situation on the western front. 'Deep but partial break-ins; on the whole the front still holds', one of his staff officers wrote in his diary on 28 September. 'I believe that we are still parrying the assault this time.'[31] The crisis was triggered by the news that Bulgaria had sought and been granted an armistice. In some respects the First World War ended where it began, in the Balkans. But the impact of Bulgaria's decision makes another more substantial point: that in the First World War no front stood in total isolation from another.

The Salonika front had been locked in stalemate for much of 1916 and 1917. For the French and British troops there it may have been a side-show, a theatre of war which exposed them to boredom, extremes of weather, and disease – above all malaria: British non-battle casualties in Macedonia exceeded battle casualties by twenty to one. But for their allies this was where the Third Balkan War now had its focus. The Serb army, evacuated from Albania via Corfu, represented the nation in exile and carried its hopes for a greater Serbia. To their left, at Valona on the Adriatic coast, were the Italians, harbouring ambitions of conquest in Dalmatia and so set to rival Serbia. To their right were the Greeks, who had failed to support Serbia in 1914 but who had been dragooned into joining the Entente in June 1917. King Constantine's pragmatic neutrality in 1915 had been undermined by his prime minister, Eleutherios Venizelos. Venizelos argued that joining the Entente would open the door to a greater Greece, and in 1916 secured the Entente's recognition for a provisional government in Thessalonica. In 1917, with a disregard for neutrality which accorded ill with their defence of Belgium, the British blockaded Greece and the French landed at Piraeus; Constantine abdicated.

The mountainous front that faced this multi-national force was naturally strong, but very hard to supply. Moreover, the occupants, the Bulgarians, had lost their reasons for fighting. Their war aims had been gained with the conquests of Serbia in 1915 and Romania in 1916. They were now fighting to meet German objectives, but the Germans showed them little generosity. They were not included in the deal cut at Brest-Litovsk. They hoped that the Treaty of Bucharest would give them all Dobrudja and its grain. It did not. The north was put under joint German–Austrian–Bulgarian administration. While the Bulgarians starved, the German troops in Bulgaria bought up supplies for transport to Germany. The withdrawal of German divisions for the western front prompted warnings that the Central Powers' position in the Balkans was now dangerously exposed. Hindenburg and Ludendorff were powerless to respond: they had not got the men and they refused to compromise on Dobrudja. On 17 September they simply signalled that 'it must be accepted that the decision of the whole war' rested on the western front.[32]

By then the Serbs were ten miles into the Bulgarian positions and about to prove them wrong. Entente forces under the French general, Louis Franchet d'Esperey, 'Desperate Frankie' to the British, had attacked on 15 September. By 22 September the campaign was mobile enough for the continuing value of horses to become evident in another theatre, as well as Palestine. A brigade of 3,000 French cavalry, Spahis from North Africa, covered sixty miles over terrain which rose to 5,000 feet above sea level, entering Skopje, inside Serbia, on 29 September, the day that Bulgaria agreed terms. Its commander, General F. L. Jouinot-Gambetta, recorded the delirium of a liberated people: 'The women kiss our hands while crying for joy'. But at the same time came retribution. He received reports that those who had been friendly with the Germans and Bulgarians were now seeking refuge in the Turkish quarter. His comment revealed the menace of shifting loyalties in the region: 'we shall pick them up soon'.[33]

Skopje was the southern railhead for the north–south Serbian railway. 'I can with 200,000 men cross Hungary and Austria, mass in Bohemia covered by Czechs and march immediately on Dresden', Franchet d'Esperey wrote to a friend on 2 October.[34] His orders were in fact to move on Romania and open contact with Russia from the south. On 1 November he reached the Danube, and the Serbs re-entered Belgrade. The victory had torn open the Central Powers' southern front, and gone straight to the heart of the coalition's communications network. The advantages they had so long enjoyed of operating on 'interior lines' had been overthrown. Germany's links to Constantinople were severed, Vienna's route to the Ukraine was cut, and the back door to the army in the west stood ajar. Ludendorff's alarm was none the less exaggerated; the advance through devastated Serbia had exceeded its logistic limits, and could not be renewed until 1919. What could not be saved was the alliance that had created the southern front in the first place.

As the bulk of the Entente forces pushed north up the Balkan peninsula, the British component swung east into Thrace and advanced on the Dardanelles and Constantinople from the landward side. In October 1918, while the Ottoman army pursued its pan-Turkish dream in the Caucasus, its empire folded on its other three fronts. On 19 September Allenby renewed the Palestine campaign in a classic manoeuvre at Megiddo. He directed a feint up the Jordan valley but then used the mobility of his cavalry, screened by his aerial supremacy, to switch the weight of his breakthrough to the west and up the coast. Damascus fell on 1 October; Faisal claimed it for the Arabs, and the British let him have it, ready now to exclude the French. In Mesopotamia, the British began a dash to secure territory and oil before an armistice should bring their advance to a halt. The Turkish 6th Army mustered only 3,500 men in July, and could offer no effective opposition. On 4 November the British entered Mosul, which according to the Sykes–Picot agreement lay in the French sphere of influence. The Turks had surrendered six days before, on a British Dreadnought in Mudros on the Aegean island of Lemnos, essentially unconditionally and to all intents and purposes to the British alone.

Franchet d'Esperey was concerned less by Anglo-French rivalry in the Middle East than by the prospects of reciprocal action with the Italians against Austria-Hungary. On 2 October Tullio Marchetti, the most effective of the Italian army's intelligence officers, had told his high command that the empire was 'like a pudding which has a crust of roasted almonds and is filled with cream. The crust which is the army in the front line is hard to break.'[35] But the cream was dissolving the crust. Karl had tried to implement his version of a revolution from above, announcing the adoption of a federal structure on 16 October. He exempted Hungary, and thereby abandoned the south Slavs under Magyar rule. Four days later Wilson said that the Fourteen Points were no longer relevant to the future of Austria-Hungary because of the commitments he had made to Czechoslovakia and now to Yugoslavia. He therefore rejected Karl's efforts at federalism and made clear to the subject nationalities that he, not the Emperor, was likely to be the effective arbiter of their futures. But at the same time he declined to deal with Austria-Hungary as a sovereign state: Wilson negotiated with Germany alone. On the 23rd, the Italians, conscious, as the other belligerents were, that gains made in the last weeks of the war might shape post-war settlements on the ground, struck on the Piave, at Vittorio-Veneto. Even now the Austro-Hungarian army held for five days. But then it collapsed, and began to go home. Revolutions broke out in Vienna and Budapest on 31 October. Austria secured an armistice on 3 November but Hungary did not do so until the 13th.

Kaiser Karl did not formally abdicate; Kaiser Wilhelm did. Max von Baden may have been both an aristocrat and the Kaiser's choice as chancellor, but he was also a liberal. He had formed a government which represented the Reichstag majority and on 5 October had declared his acceptance of its programme. The allies, however, did not recognise this shift towards parliamentary government. Wilson's responses to the German request for an armistice, and in particular his notes of 14 and 23 October, increasingly emphasised that they would only deal with a democratic Germany. They revealed, too, that Germany's ploy of trying to separate a conciliatory Wilson from his vengeful European partners was not working. It was evident that he and they were united in seeing the armistice not as a pause in the fighting in order to thrash out peace terms but as a means to bring the war to a definite end. The German army would be emasculated both as a fighting force and as a factor in domestic politics. Ludendorff's resolve returned. He said that Wilson's note of 23 October should be rejected and the war resumed. But the prospect of the armistice had opened 'enchanting celestial pictures' which neither army nor people would agree to again abandoning. At the front, 'There was no going back psychologically', a Catholic chaplain recalled. 'No power in the world could have induced the average soldier at the front to take part in fighting that was to last still longer.'[36] At home there was resignation, not resistance: 'They are acting almost like criminals who have broken into a neighbor's house, with no thought of defending themselves when caught red-handed. . . . The only fear they have is that peace might slip away at the last minute.'[37]

On the western front fighting continued with no mitigation in its ferocity. Its mobility once again put civilians and their property more at risk than they had been when the front was static. Germans looted and pillaged as they retreated. At sea U-boats still torpedoed neutral shipping, and at the end of October the navy planned to take the fleet to sea to fight one last climactic battle. Word of the proposed 'death ride' got out. By 3 and 4 November disturbances gripped the fleet in Kiel, with the sailors' demands focusing not on professional griev-ances but on issues like constitutional reform, peace, and the removal of the royal family. The mutiny spread to Wilhelmshaven, and then merged with spontaneous workers' risings elsewhere. On 9 November a general strike broke out in Berlin. The Reichstag was in danger of forfeiting its authority to the sailors', workers' and – increasingly – soldiers' councils that were being set up; the majority Socialists were fearful of losing control of the workers to the Independent Socialists; and the Spartacists wanted to ensure that the councils prepared for the next stage of the revolution that had now begun and which would establish a Soviet system in Germany. The army held the balance, and the Kaiser sought to use it to impose his authority in Berlin. At last it confronted the choice between the nation and the monarchy, which had been implicit in much of its behaviour throughout the war. But the man who had done most to marginalise the Kaiser did not see his actions through to their logical conclusion. Ludendorff had been forced to resign on 26 October. He had been replaced by Groener. On 8 November the new first quartermaster-general received thirty-nine reports on feeling in the army, only one of which said that the troops were ready to fight for Wilhelm. 'The army', Groener told its supreme commander, 'will march home in peace and order under its leaders and commanding generals, but not under the command of Your Majesty; for it no longer stands behind Your Majesty.'[38]

Victory Without Peace

The Germany that signed the armistice on 11 November 1918 was a republic, no longer an empire. Entente propaganda had vilified the Kaiser and castigated German militarism. It had distinguished between the rulers and the ruled. But the German people were not exempted from the humiliation of the defeat. For them the most direct consequence was the continuation of the blockade until the peace treaty was signed. Moreover, with no effective opposition and with unfettered access to the one sea that had remained a German enclave, the Baltic, the allies were able to apply it with a level of severity that had eluded them in the war. The winter of 1918–19, even more than the war years, determined the Germans' and Austrians' folk memories of hunger as an instrument of war.

More important in the eyes of the allies was the use of the armistice to define military victory. If the triumph of the Entente was the fruit of attrition, through the exhaustion of the enemy's resources as well as through the grinding down of armies, its implication was a compromise peace. In the autumn of 1918, the armies in the west were still reckoning on the wearing-out battle in which they were then engaged leading to breakthrough, as indeed happened so spectacularly on other fronts. The offer of an armistice before that point had been reached confronted them with a quandary. If the war ended while still in its attritional phase, the definite victory that the scale of the conflict and the issues which surrounded it demanded might elude them. Some French generals wanted to inflict on the Boche the hiding they felt he deserved, to re-divide Germany into separate states, and to make the German people conscious of invasion and defeat as the French had been in 1870 and 1914. Pétain had a scheme to regain Lorraine in 1919; 'We must go right into the heart of Germany', Charles Mangin, the victor of the second battle of the Marne, told all who would listen, or 'The Germans will not admit they were beaten'.[39]

Mangin's British colleagues did not agree. Their advance in September and October was so rapid that it created logistic strains, particularly for an army which had geared its supply arrangements to a less fluid operational situation. It was now slowing as a result, and the deteriorating weather was turning the roads to mud. Haig reckoned that the German army was capable of retiring to its own frontier, and both he and Henry Wilson still regarded it as an effective opponent in the field. They feared that, if an immediate armistice were rejected, the war would go on until 1919. In Haig's perhaps unduly harsh assessment, the French army was played out and the United States army, according even to Pershing, would still not be fully ready until autumn 1919. 'The British alone might bring the enemy to his knees', Haig commented. 'But why expend more British lives – and for what?'[40]

Foch therefore made the armistice terms do duty for the success in battle that the Entente would have gained in 1919; they turned the compromise that was the logical outcome of attrition into victory. The German army had to withdraw to its frontiers, and to hand over 5,000 artillery pieces, 25,000 machine-guns, 3,000 trench mortars and 1,700 aeroplanes. He insisted on possession of the Rhine bridge-heads in case hostilities were renewed: the left bank of the Rhine was to be demilitarised, the right neutralised. Once in Germany, the allied army of occupation would have the right to requisition what it required. Admiral Beatty and the British were equally uncompromising over the naval terms. Germany was to hand over six battle cruisers, ten battleships, eight light cruisers, and fifty destroyers; all submarines were to be surrendered. The armistice stripped Germany of its ability to fight.

What most people celebrated on 11 November was peace. In the quiet that hushed the front at 11 a.m., some soldiers wondered how they would adjust; the war was their job, their routine; it gave them a feeling of purpose. But for others there was a real awareness of victory. As in Skopje, liberation was its most obvious incarnation. Belgium had been stripped of its industrial plant and raw materials; 120,000 workers had been forcibly deported to the Reich; and civil liberties had been forfeit to military occupation. The soldiers of the Belgian army who advanced into Belgium in October were freeing their own nation; they were also going home for the first time in four years: 'Never has life been so dear to us as now, standing here facing home', was how J. G. Gheuens described it in a later novel *De Mis Kenden* (The Unsung). 'We can smell the stables; all we want . . . is to eat, to sleep and rest, and then to charge again, until we are there.' On 22 November King Albert entered Brussels. His reception was delirious: 'Nobody will ever experience such a thing again! In the trees, on the fences, everywhere, people!'[41]

Belgians did not need to ask what the purpose of the war was. Nor did the population of occupied France. The entry to Lille was celebrated by an enormous crowd in the Place de la Concorde on 18 October, and in Charleville, used by Hindenburg as his headquarters, 'what we wanted above all, was the victory of justice, liberty and civilisation'.[42] The *poilus* were greeted with peals of bells, fireworks and songs. The entry to Alsace and Lorraine was the most emotive of all; their wait had been over forty years, not four. 'We have just entered Château-Salins! What emotion, but also what joy, what bliss! Long before the town, the young girls adorned with ribbons in the colours of France came to meet us with flowers and much to our surprise we found the whole town bedecked with flags ... The former mayor with his great white beard cried tears of joy, veterans of [18]70 held out their hands to take ours. I was so moved that I could not speak. In the afternoon, our band gave a concert. The old mayor asked the bandmaster for his baton and conducted the "Marseillaise" with masterly skill and full of emotion.'[43]

Belgium and France had suffered; they wanted revenge for past wrongs and they wanted security for the future. The peace settlement had to do two things. It had to draw a line under the First World War, and it had to meet the expectations that from it a new world order would emerge. Woodrow Wilson was the popular focus for the latter, but his idealism did not blind him to the legitimacy of the former. In his mind, as in the minds of many pacifists and radicals, the Germans had caused the war and had waged it in a manner which defied the customs and conventions that governed relations between states. A successful settlement had to incorporate that reality, because, if it did not, it would poison the efforts to create something better.

Each of the Central Powers was subject to a separate peace treaty, and all had reason to feel aggrieved, given the expectations the Fourteen Points had generated. But that with Germany has carried the greatest weight because of its role in the causes of the Second World War. Despite its defeat, Germany manufactured its own feeling of victory out of the war. Ludendorff's determination in 1917 to separate the demoralisation at home from the motivation of those at the front fed directly into the post-war argument that the German army had not been defeated in the field. It still stood deep in enemy territory on all fronts when it laid down its arms; its front had been neither broken through nor enveloped; thus, none of the features of an operational defeat on the battlefield was present. The British blockade, and the claim that it had reduced the civilian population to starvation, fitted in with the argument that the army had been stabbed in the back by the revolution at home. On 28 November 1918 Herbert Sulzbach's division marched through the streets of Bonn, packed with civilians waving flags and throwing flowers: 'our home country', he wrote in his diary, 'really seems to have understood that we are undefeated and unconquerable'.[44] Two weeks later, on 11 December, the first troops marched down Unter den Linden in Berlin. 'The men wore green laurel wreaths over their steel helmets, each rifle bore its little spray of flowers, the machine-guns were garlanded with green branches, and children waving gaily-coloured flags sat by the side of them.'[45] They were greeted by Germany's new chancellor, the socialist Friedrich Ebert: 'I salute you who return unvanquished from the field of battle'.[46]

Those who could not quite swallow this used another tack. In the desperate defensive battles of 1916 and 1917, the German soldier had been venerated for his courage and his determination. To fight a good fight carried its own reward; to rise above the terrors of industrialised warfare and so to master the battlefield was itself a moral victory. Strains of this sort of thinking appeared in the war memorials and memoirs of soldiers other than in Germany. But in Germany it carried particular resonance precisely because this inner experience had to do duty for victory more conventionally defined. Ernst Jünger, a storm-troop officer awarded Germany's highest decoration, the *Pour le Mérite*, concluded his fictionalised diary, *Stahlgewittern* (The Storm of Steel): 'Hardened as scarcely another generation ever was in fire and flame, we could go into life as though from the anvil'. That conviction underpinned the writing of Germany's history of the war. Georg Soldan, general editor of a popular but official series on battles, declared his aim was not to deny the horrors of the war, but to glorify them, in the hope that, like the Bible, the books would enter every home and help rebuild the fatherland. 'The nation was no longer for me an empty thought veiled in symbols', Jünger wrote, 'and how could it have been otherwise when I had seen so many die for its sake, and been schooled myself to stake my life for its credit every minute, day and night, without a thought?'[47]

When Ulrich Brockdorff-Rantzau, the senior German delegate to the peace conference, was presented with the fat volume of Versailles demands on 7 May 1919, his shock was palpable. He summarised its contents: 'Germany renounces its existence'.[48] It was to lose 13 per cent of its territory and 10 per cent of its population. It was also required to pay reparations, which the allies themselves took turns to boost. The Americans refused to link them to the Entente's settlement of its war debt, and the British and French, unable to quantify loss of life in other terms, added the pension bill that the casualties of the war had generated. In the event, the actual amounts proved irrelevant; Germany ended up paying less than France had paid after 1871. What mattered was the rhetoric that accompanied the settlement. Before the peace treaty was signed one member of the British delegation, John Maynard Keynes, resigned in protest at the harshness of the terms, and then published a hugely successful popular book in order to damn its economic clauses. *The Economic Consequences of the Peace* prepared the way for liberal doubters, who were further exploited by the Germans' response to article 231 of the treaty. This asserted German war guilt, but for the sole purpose of justifying reparations. The Germans used it to attack the peace settlement as a whole. The allies' failure at Versailles was a failure of resolve in implementing its terms. There was no inevitable link between it and the outbreak of a second war twenty years later. The reality was that, given the enormity of the task that confronted the victors, they drew up a settlement which promised far more than it proved able to deliver in practice.

The only precedent the powers had when they convened in Paris in 1919 was the settlement whose ultimate failure caused them to be there in the first place. In 1815 the Congress of Vienna set about restoring order in Europe by looking back; in 1919 thirty-seven powers looked forward, and sought solutions which would regulate the affairs not just of Europe but of the whole world. They brought to that process vocabulary which still underpins notions of international relations: the rule of international law, the value of multilateral solutions, and the belief that liberal democracy should be the basis for progress. Their efforts were shaped by two key, if ill-defined, Wilsonian concepts. The first was national self-determination. Given that the United States was itself a community made up predominantly of immigrants, Wilson's presumption against multi-ethnic empires was arrogant and naive. In Europe about 30 million found themselves on the wrong sides of frontiers. In so far as he recognised they would generate problems, he relied on his other over-arching idea, the League of Nations, to sort things out.

The programme was ambitious, and in the long view of the twentieth century it failed. Clear ethnic divisions were particularly hard to draw in the Balkans. Italy felt aggrieved that the deal it had struck under the conditions of 'old diplomacy', as the price for its entry to the war in 1915, was not honoured by the spokesmen for 'new diplomacy' in 1919. Its frustration led it to flout the League in 1936. In Asia another power on the side of the victors, Japan, was incensed by the refusal to adopt its proposed clause on racial equality, that the members of the League would treat each other's citizens without discrimination. It secured compensation in the recognition of its claim to Tsingtao and Shantung despite China's membership of the Entente and despite the principle of national self-determination. In 1937 it, too, was to ignore the League as it used its gains as a platform to extend its claims to Asiatic hegemony. In the Middle East the Arabs did not get the nationhood they had been led to expect. The competition between France and Britain for influence in the region was further compounded by the latter's recognition of the Zionist movement in the Balfour Declaration of November 1917. But the series of settlements were not simply a charter for covert imperialism. The 'mandate' system adopted outside Europe gave the powers to whose charge territories were allocated responsibilities as well as privileges, and made clear that their occupation was temporary not permanent.

Britain's handling of many issues, particularly those raised by Japan, was the product less of London's wishes than of those of its dominions. Billy Hughes, Australia's prime minister, reflecting his white population's fear of the 'yellow peril', rejected Japan's summons for racial equality. In trying to act as broker between two Pacific powers, the prime minister of a third, Canada, had to grapple with his own uncertainties. Canada, Robert Borden said, was 'a nation that is not a nation'.[49] For those who had been at Vimy Ridge such reticence seemed ill-placed; the war had made Canada a nation, as it had made Australia, New Zealand and South Africa nations. These were developments the peace settlements were being asked to confirm. Within Europe, Poland, Czechoslovakia, Hungary, Yugoslavia, Finland and Lithuania had all achieved independence and a measure of definition before Woodrow Wilson even landed in Europe. The challenge he confronted was therefore a somewhat different one from that to which his speeches were directed. In Central and Eastern Europe war had effected change, and for those who sought such changes it continued to do so. Indeed, the United States's own decision to intervene was confirmation of the same point. War could work.

For that reason the First World War did not end as neatly on 11 November as the celebration of Armistice Day suggests. 'One year and three days' later, Henry Wilson wrote to Lord Esher, 'we have between 20 and 30 wars raging in different parts of the world'.[50] Russia was engaged in a civil war to define its revolution, a war in which the allies had intervened. It included war in and for Poland. To the south Turkey's war hero, Mustafa Kemal, was exploiting the support of the Bolsheviks to enable him to take on the Greeks and British in order to re-found the Turkish nation. And the example set by Europe spread. On 27 February 1919 the French pacifist Romain Rolland wrote to the socialist Jean-Richard Bloch, to tell him of a young Japanese friend who had just returned home after two years observing the war in Europe and America. 'My greatest surprise', the Japanese had said, 'has been that there are among you men who, *truly*, believe in the idealism that they profess. We others, we Japanese, think: "Idealism is for the Europeans a political means". And we do not blame them; we are now going to act like them.'[51]

The notion of war's utility was not just transmitted across continents. It spanned generations. Children who had grown up in the thrall of war had seen it permeate their schooling, their reading and their games: they, too, expected to defend their nations as their parents had done. Anna Eisenmenger, a Viennese grandmother, had three sons and a daughter. One son was killed, one blinded, and the third lost his reason; he killed his sister's husband. One day in March 1920, Anna found her grandson playing with a schoolfriend. Both 'were wearing soldiers' caps . . . made for them out of newspaper. They had pokers in their hands and were sitting behind the backs of armchairs "in the trenches". Wolfi was an "Austrian", his friend a "Frenchman". They were shooting at each other. Wolfi . . . was playing at war.'[52] Boys were told of an intensity of experience whose loss their fathers still regretted. From it came the adventures of Biggles, written by a pilot, W. E. Johns, and of Bulldog Drummond. The latter's creator, H. C. McNeile, wrote under a pseudonym, 'Sapper', which reflected what he had done in the war. 'Cementing everything, crowning everything, the spirit of camaraderie, of good fellowship', he wrote in the preface to the collected edition of his war stories: 'No nightmare that, but a dream one would only willingly repeat today.'[53]

The war memorials and the war literature that today can seem the war's most pervasive legacy in Western Europe did not necessarily carry the messages of waste and futility that are now associated with them. The biggest memorial in Germany, erected at Tannenberg in 1927, trumpeted a victory. For many Entente veterans, Armistice Day was a focus for reunions and drinking, for celebration as well as commemoration. Wives and mothers were scandalised, unable to comprehend any response except overwhelming grief. About 10 million soldiers died in the war. Twice that number bore the scars of wounds – some so mutilated in body or mind as to be unfit for further work and unable to lead fulfilled lives. Calculations of civilian dead remain inadequate, partly because so many deaths were indirect, the result of starvation or disease rather than of bullets or shells, and partly because they were forgotten in the war's immediate aftermath. Globally up to 20 million succumbed in the influenza epidemic which swept from Asia through Europe and on to America in 1918–19. But the bereaved were not forgotten, because one of the purposes of mourning was to remember. 'Every day one meets saddened women, with haggard faces and lethargic movements, and one dare not ask after husband or son', Beatrice Webb wrote in her diary on 17 November 1918.[54]

Those who mourned needed to find meaning in their loss. When the British struck their Victory Medal for issue to all those who had served, they provided one answer: 'For Civilisation', it said. It was a theme which linked the ideas of 1914 to the war's outcome, and it was repeated throughout the British Empire and in France. In Germany the city of Hamburg commissioned Ernst Barlach to design a memorial to its 40,000 'sons' killed in action. A stele, it has on one side another recurrent image in war memorials, the mother and child, equating the grieving mother with the Madonna. Five years later, in 1936, the 76th Infantry Regiment responded to Barlach's memorial with one of its own: erected near that commemorating Hamburg's dead of 1870, it linked the past to the future, declaring on its oblong block, 'Germany must live even if we must die.'

By then the allies' memories of victory were fading. 'Armistice Day ceased to exist as a restaurant orgy: the Two Minutes Silence took its place', as Ian Hay noted with irony. The trophies that had stood by the memorials, the captured guns and trench mortars symbolic of triumph, were removed, and only the memorials remained. The idea that the war had purpose languished. In 1926 Lance-Corporal John Jackson, who had served on the western front between 1915 and 1918, wrote his memoirs. 'Let it ever be remembered', he prefaced his story, that, but for British intervention, 'German "Kultur" would dominate us all, and only those who saw it in force, in parts of France and Belgium occupied by German forces, can understand the humiliation such a situation would have entailed.'[55] It was a plea which fell on increasingly deaf ears. A year later, in 1927, the dead of his regiment, the Cameron Highlanders, were commemorated with the opening of the Scottish National War

Memorial in Edinburgh Castle, in itself evidence of another nation which used the war to shape its identity. In the memorial's guide-book, Ian Hay noted with bemusement the change in attitudes over the years since the armistice. 'War has become a monstrous, unspeakable thing', he acknowledged. However, he insisted, there was more to its comprehension than that. 'Our reactions and emo-tions upon the subject of recent history are at present too fluid to have any lasting value. We must leave it to Time to crystallize them.'[56]

In 1929 Erich Maria Remarque published *Im Westen nichts Neues* (All Quiet on the Western Front), a book which at a stroke revived the by-then flagging market for war literature. Within a year Remarque's book was translated into twenty-eight languages, sold nearly 4 million copies, and became an academy-award winning film. And yet it was less about the war than about the problems of a gen-eration unable to reintegrate itself with post-war society. Its message was one of shattered illusions, a theme often echoed in what Ian Hay called 'the new style War novels'. In the 1920s there had been many interpretations of the war; thereafter one increasingly dominated over the others. It created a barrier between our understanding of the war and that of those who fought in it. Even those who survived came to see it in terms different from those which they embraced at the time. Hindsight bred arrogance, and – worse – misconception. Many of the ideologies which had given the war meaning became loaded, larded with later connotations.

The Second World War irrevocably demonstrated that the First World War was not, after all, the war to end all wars. But it also enabled posterity to have it both ways. It venerated the writers who condemned the war of 1914–18 but at the same time condemned those who embraced appeasement, the logical corollary. War liter-ature and appeasement both derived their appeal from the same basic liberalism which had underpinned the ideals of the peacemakers at Versailles. Liberalism's comparative failure in the inter-war years was in large part due to its own fundamental decency. It lost the deter-mination to enforce its own standards, a quality it possessed in 1914 and 1917, and it was reluctant to assert itself in the internal politics of states that deviated from democratic norms.

The issues of course did not present themselves in such clear-cut fashion. One reason why Adolf Hitler could appeal to the German people in 1933 was precisely because many genuinely convinced themselves that they had been wronged in 1919. But that of itself does not explain the Second World War. Hitler was able to play back some of the themes of German popular mobilisation in the First World War – the ideas of the *Burgfrieden* in 1914, the Fatherland Party's appeal to national unity over party loyalty, OberOst's notion of Germany's mission in the east, the expectation that a Second Punic War might be necessary to complete the agenda of the First. Above all, the Kaiser's failure as supreme warlord generated a belief that a real leader would have delivered a German victory. But by 1918 Germans had also learnt what modern war entailed. They did not take to the streets to show their enthusiasm when war broke out in 1939. The Second World War is inexplicable without knowledge of the First, but there is no inevitability linking Versailles and the ambitions of the peacemakers to its outbreak.

The First World War broke the empires of Germany, Russia, Austria-Hungary and Turkey. It triggered the Russian Revolution and provided the bedrock for the Soviet Union; it forced a reluctant United States on to the world stage and revivified liberalism. On Europe's edge, it provided a temporary but not a long-term solution to the ambitions of the Balkan nations. Outside Europe it laid the seeds for the conflict in the Middle East. In short it shaped not just Europe but the world in the twentieth century. It was emphatically not a war without meaning or purpose.

Acknowledgements

My first debt in writing this book is to a man whom I have never met, the father of Alan Clements. He had the good sense to give his son, on the occasion of his fortieth birthday, the first volume in my planned trilogy on the First World War. *To Arms* was published by Oxford University Press in 2001, and it prompted Alan to ask me whether I thought the First World War could be the subject of a new television documentary series. This is a book born in Glasgow: Alan's production company, Wark Clements, is based in the city, and Alan himself is a history graduate of its university, whose professor of modern history I then had the privilege to be.

Alan was not the first representative of a television production company to raise the idea with me, but he was the first to accept that it might be possible to do it as I felt it should be done. The problems that any documentary of the First World War confronts are uncertainty about the authenticity of footage and in particular the lack of sufficient surviving film from the first half of the war. The pioneering series made by the BBC in 1964, *The Great War*, often got round these two difficulties by ignoring them; forty years on we have more regard for the evidence. My solutions were threefold. First, we should not exaggerate the problem: there were fresh sources of film, particularly those in eastern Europe and Russia opened with the end of the Cold War, yet to be exploited. Secondly, we had to be ready to fill gaps by using the feature films made in the immediate aftermath of the war, provided we told the audience exactly what we were doing. In this way, the Gallipoli landings – for example – could be shown on screen. Thirdly, I argued that it was possible to go back to the battlefields today and to inter-cut freshly-shot film of the landscape with stills of the events that took place there in 1914–18. This was not an original idea: Ken Burns did it to great effect in his series on the American Civil War. He conveyed movement and action through the sound-track – which combined music and the noise of battle with the words of participants.

That final point carried a further consequence. As far as possible this series should convey the realities of war in phrases uttered at the time not in the memories of surviving veterans, however powerful. Mediated by the intervening events of the twentieth century, such testimony can create not an immediacy but a distance between us and the First World War. Those who fought in 1914–18 who still survived in 2001 no longer saw the world as they saw it as young men. Interviews of another sort too were banned. Television history has become addicted to a cult of the historian as personality: by contrast, this series would have no presenter and no debates between competing interpretations. It has a strong authorial line, but that is conveyed solely in its commentary.

Alan asked me how a series of ten parts should be divided. My opinion was that its framework should be a narrative provided by the military and political, not the social and cultural, history of the war. Thus somebody who viewed the entire ten programmes would have some grasp of the war's overall sweep and shape. There have been modifications, but in general terms the ten programmes reflect the ten topics that I suggested then. They have also been used as the basis of the ten chapters of this book. The titles of each are identical, the precise contents not so. In some cases ideas that worked well for one programme belonged in another chapter, and in others themes which could be explored in words made less sense visually – or vice versa.

Both the book and the series have been shaped by two overarching considerations. First, this war was a global war, even if it began as a local Balkan conflict. In particular the aim has been to offset the Anglophone emphasis on the western front and Britain's participation in it, so central to popular conceptions of the war. Second, we have sought to recover the views of the war that prevailed before it fell into the hands of the writers and novelists of the late 1920s. Much of the war was futile, and it was also wasteful – of treasure as well as of lives. But it was fought because big issues were at stake, some of them concepts that continue to shape our values and views of the world. Moreover, the fact that other ideas and ideologies now seem foreign to us does not deny their charge for those who went to war in 1914. Hindsight of this sort fosters arrogance, not understanding.

Readers of *To Arms* will recognise its role in shaping the first third of this book, but the remainder has had to anticipate in a brief compass what I plan to say in the subsequent two volumes in greater detail. Given the range of reading on which that study has been based, it seemed otiose to provide a bibliography for this book. Instead, I have used its notes not only to convey immediate sources but also to give guidance as to some of the best secondary reading.

Alan and Janice Hadlow of Channel 4 told me that the key to the project's success was the relationship I would forge with the series producer. They were right. Undoubtedly, the series is Jonathan Lewis's much more than it is mine, but it is one to which I remain proud to put my name. Not all historians can say as much. Jonathan told me at the outset that I must not go native, not compromise on my academic standards because I felt that the medium of television required me to do so. There was never a danger of this happening, principally because of Jonathan's own standards, which comfortably exceed those of even the most scrupulous historian. Script and footage were revisited scores of times. But what impressed me even more was Jonathan's ability to turn complex ideas, often involving the usual academic vice of spurning the simplistic generalisation for something more even-handed, into clear and arresting commentary. He put the humanity into the story, and made sure that the final product was not just military history for other military historians. If my prose style in this book is different from anything I have written before it is a consequence of late nights with Jonathan searching for forms of words that possess pace but retain veracity. I have been immensely fortunate to work with a man of intelligence, honesty, wisdom and wit.

Individual programme production was in the hands of a team of five producers, each of whom took charge of two films. Marcus Kiggell, Simon Rockell, Emma Wallace, Ben Steele and Corinna Sturmer, and their assistant producers, Milan Grba, Gregor Murbach, Andrea Laux, Martina Caviccholi and Ross Harper, prompted me to rethink some of my assumptions, and also turned up fresh sources. So too did Sarah Wallis and Svetlana Palmer, whose search for what the production team dubbed 'biscuits' (the testimony of participants), has resulted in their own book, *A War in Words*. Alison McAllan headed the film archive team and delivered on the promise of my first two solutions to the problem of footage. The illustrations for this book only occasionally duplicate those used in the series. The initial research for both was undertaken by Isobel Hinshelwood, whose rapid illness and sudden death left a huge hole. It might have been even bigger but for Gregor Murbach. Gregor is one of the principal creators of this book. He has located images that are fresh, and has brought an aesthetic as well as a historical judgement to bear as we have wrestled with the final selection.

Gregor has read and commented on the text, as have my other principal supporters, Andrew Gordon of Simon & Schuster, Anthony Goff of David Higham Associates, my agents, and of course Jonathan Lewis. Evan Mawdsley, Jürgen Förster, Donald Bloxham, Roy Foster, Michael Hochedlinger and John Gooch have helped with specific queries. Kath Steedman, Kate Cotter and Susanna Posnett, all of Wark Clements, have provided tremendous back-up over a hectic eighteen months.

The principal casualties of this particular war have been, once again, my family. My wife, Pamela, has provided unswerving love, and kept better track of my movements and papers than I have. She and Mungo, the only one of our children still at home, have had not one but two family holidays cancelled to meet the deadlines of series and book. My only response is love and gratitude.

Notes

Chapter 1: To Arms

1 Sidney Fay, *The Origins of the World War* (2 vols, New York, 1934), vol. 2, p. 31.
2 Imanuel Geiss, *July 1914* (London, 1967), p. 64.
3 Stanoje Stanojević, quoted in Samuel Williamson and Russel Van Wyk, *July 1914* (Boston, 2003), p. 20.
4 Kurt Peball, *Conrad von Hötzendorf. Private Aufzeichnungen* (Vienna, 1977), p. 148.
5 Gerhard Ritter, *The Sword and the Sceptre: the problem of militarism in Germany* (4 vols, London, 1971–73), vol. 2, p. 229.
6 Williamson and Van Wyk, *July 1914*, p. 57.
7 Ibid., p. 102.
8 Fay, vol. 2, p. 204.
9 Geiss, *July 1914*, p. 78.
10 Keith Wilson (ed.), *The Rasp of War: The Letters of H. A. Gwynne to the Countess Bathurst* (London, 1988), p. 15.
11 Williamson and Van Wyk, *July 1914*, p. 123.
12 Slavka Mihajlovic, *Oblaci nad gradom 1914–1918* (Belgrade, 1955).
13 Josef Redlich, *Schicksalsjahre Österreichs 1908–1919. Das politische Tagebuch Josef Redlichs*, ed. Fritz Fellner (2 vols, Graz, 1953), vol. 1, p. 240.
14 Geiss, *July 1914*, p. 289.
15 Graydon A. Tunstall, *Planning for War against Russia and Serbia: Austro-Hungarian and German Military Strategies, 1897–1914* (Boulder, CO, 1993), p. 221.
16 Rudolf Jerabek, *Potiorek* (Graz, 1991), p. 93.
17 R. A. Reiss, *How Austria-Hungary Waged War in Serbia: Personal Investigations of a Neutral* (Paris, 1915), p. 46.

18 Jerabek, *Potiorek*, p. 165.

19 John R. Schindler, 'Disaster on the Drina: The Austro-Hungarian Army in Serbia, 1914', *War in History*, vol. 9 (2002), p. 187.

20 A. A. Brusilov, *A Soldier's Note-book 1914–1918* (London, 1930), p. 96.

21 Manfred Rauchensteiner, *Der Tod des Doppeladlers. Österreich-Ungarn und der Erste Weltkrieg* (Graz, 1993), p. 136.

Chapter 2: Under the Eagle

1 Wolfgang Mommsen, *Max Weber in German politics* (Chicago, 1984), p. 69.

2 Lloyd George, *War Memoirs* (2 vols, London, n.d.), vol. 1, p. 26.

3 James Joll, *Second International* (London, 1975), p. 168.

4 John Röhl, 'An der Schwelle zum Weltkrieg: eine Dokumentation über den "Kriegsrat" vom 8.Dezember 1912', *Militärgeschichte Mitteilungen*, vol. 1 (1977), no. 21, p. 100.

5 Helmuth von Moltke, *Erinnerungen-Briefe-Dokumente, 1877–1916* (Stuttgart, 1922), p. 308.

6 Robert T. Foley, *Alfred von Schlieffen's Military Writings* (London, 2002), p. 198.

7 Gerhard Ritter, *The Schlieffen Plan* (London, 1958), p. 166.

8 Nicholas Stargardt, *The German Idea of Militarism* (Cambridge, 1994), p. 36.

9 John Horne and Alan Kramer, *German Atrocities 1914: A History of Denial* (London, 2001), pp. 145–6.

10 Joseph Bédier, *Les Crimes allemands d'après des témoignages allemands* (Paris, 1915), p. 12.

11 Ernst Röhm, *Die Geschichte eines Hochverräters* (Munich, 1933), p. 33, quoted by Dieter Storz in Wolfgang Michalka (ed.) *Der erste Weltkrieg* (Munich, 1994), p. 252.

12 Aubrey Herbert, *Mons, Anzac and Kut* (London, 1930), p. 45.

13 Pierre Rocolle, *L'hécatombe des généraux* (Paris, 1980), p. 98.

14 Dr Antoine, *Au village pendant la guerre* (Paris, 1924), p. 25.

15 Guy Pedroncinci, *Les Mutineries de 1917* (Paris, 1967), p. 23.

16 Shimon Naveh, *In pursuit of military excellence* (London, 1997), p. 76.

17 E. L. Spears, *Liaison 1914* (London, 1930), p. 417.

18 Henri Barbusse, *Under Fire* (London, 1929), p. 156.

19 'Correspondance entre Romain Rolland et Jean-Richard Bloch 1914–1919', *La Revue Europe*, nos. 95–103 (1953–4), pp. 4–5.

20 Romain Rolland, *Au-dessus de la mêlée* (Paris, 1915), pp. 39–42.

21 Hermann Lübbe, *Politische Philosophie in Deutschland* (Munich, 1974), p. 186.

22 Anna Woebcken (ed.), *Im Westen. Briefe eines Deutschen Frontsoldaten* (Oldenburg, 1929), p. 23.

23 Eric Labayle (ed.), *Carnets de guerre d'Alexis Callies (1914–1918)* (Château-Thierry, 1999), p. 185.

Chapter 3: Global War

1 Melvin Page, *The Chiwaya War* (Boulder, CO, 2000), p. 101.

2 Quoted in I. F. Clarke (ed.), *The Great War with Germany, 1890–1914* (Liverpool, 1997), p. 202.

3 Quoted in Michael Howard, *The Lessons of History* (Oxford, 1991), pp. 84–5.

4 Frederick R. Dickinson, *War and National Reinvention: Japan and the Great War, 1914–1919* (Cambridge, MA, 1999), p. 35.

5 The words of Tanaka Giichi, ibid., p. 51.

6 Hans Werner Neulen, *Feldgrau in Jerusalem. Das Levantekorps des kaiserlichen Deutschland* (Munich, 1991), p. 113.

7 Andrew Gordon, *The Rules of the Game* (London, 1996), p. 391.

8 Richard Hough, *The Great War at Sea* (Oxford, 1986), p. 96.

9 Hans Pochhammer, *Before Jutland* (London, 1931), p. 214.

10 Page, *The Chiwaya War*, p. 32.

11 Ludwig Deppe, *Mit Lettow-Vorbeck durch Afrika* (Berlin 1919), p. 393.

12 Richard Meinertzhagen, *Army Diary 1899–1926* (Edinburgh, 1960), p. 82.

13 Ibid., p. 166.

14 Joe Lunn, *Memoirs of the Maelstrom: a Senagalese oral history of the First World War* (Portsmouth, NH, 1999), p. 137.

Chapter 4: Jihad

1 Quoted in Geoffrey Lewis, 'The Ottoman Proclamation of Jihad in 1914', in *Arabic and Islamic Garland: Historical, Educational and Literary Papers Presented to Abdul-Latif Tibawi* (London, 1977), p. 164.

2 Ulrich Gehrke, *Persien in der deutschen Orientpolitik* (2 vols, Stuttgart, 1960), vol. 1, p. 1.

3 Carl Mühlmann, *Deutschland und die Türkei 1913–1914* (Berlin, 1929), p. 39.

4 Carl Mühlmann, *Oberste Heeresleitung und Balkan im Weltkrieg 1914–1918* (Berlin, 1942), pp. 22–3.

5   Henry Morgenthau, *Ambassador Morgenthau's Story* (New York, 1919), p. 32.

6   Yigal Sheffy, *British Military Intelligence in the Palestine Campaign 1914–1918* (London, 1998), p. 61.

7   Georges Kopp, trans. R. Jouan, *À bord du 'Goeben' 1914–1918* (Paris, 1931), p. 46.

8   Gotthard Jäschke, 'Der Turanismus der Jungtürken. Zur osmanischen Aussenpolitik im Weltkriege', *Die Welt des Islams*, vol. 22 (1941), p. 5.

9   Felix Guse, *Die Kaukasusfront im Weltkrieg* (Leipzig, 1940), p. 7.

10 Gérard Chaliand and Yves Ternon, *Le Génocide des Arméniens* (Brussels, 1984), p. 47.

11 Ibid., p. 54.

12 Martin Gilbert, *Winston S. Churchill 1874–1965*, (8 vols, plus companion vols, London, 1971–88), vol. 3: *Companion* part I, p. 361.

13 John Gooch, *The Plans of War: The General Staff and British Military Strategy, c. 1900–1916* (London, 1974), p. 259.

14 Robert Rhodes James, *Gallipoli* (Basingstoke, 1989), p. 4.

15 Wilhelm Groener, *Lebenserinnerungen* (Göttingen, 1957)), p. 224.

16 Morgenthau, *Ambassador Morgenthau's Story*, p. 210.

17 Kevin Fewster (ed.), *Gallipoli Correspondent* (Sydney, 1983), p. 70.

18 Jock Philips, Nicholas Boyack and E. P. Malone (eds), *The Great Adventure: New Zealand Soldiers Describe the First World War* (Wellington, 1988), p. 37.

19 Tim Travers, *Gallipoli 1915* (Stroud, 2001), p. 199.

20 Jean Giraudoux, *Carnet des Dardanelles* (Paris, 1969), p. 97.

21 Travers, *Gallipoli*, p. 229.

22 Fewster, *Gallipoli Correspondent*, p. 153.

23 David Omissi (ed.), *Indian Voices of the Great War: Soldiers' Letters, 1914–1918* (Basingstoke, 1999), p. 160.

24 Carl Mühlmann, *Das deutsch-türkische Waffenbündnis im Weltkriege* (Leipzig, 1940), p. 71.

25 Colmar von der Goltz, *Denkwürdigkeiten* (Berlin, 1932), pp. 421–2.

26 John Buchan, *Greenmantle* (London, 1917 edn.), p. 16.

Chapter 5: Shackled to a Corpse

1   Gustaf Steffen, *Weltkrieg und Imperialismus* (Jena, 1915), pp. 49–51.

2   Vladimir Littauer, *Russian Hussar* (London, 1965), pp. 138, 150.

3   Max Hoffmann, *War Diaries and other papers* (2 vols, London, 1929), vol. 1, p. 40.

4 Jeffrey Verhey, *The Spirit of 1914: Militarism, Myth and Mobilization in Germany* (Cambridge, 2000), p. 91.

5 Reichsarchiv, *Der Weltkrieg 1914 bis 1918*, vol. 2 (Berlin, 1925), p. 324.

6 Dennis Showalter, *Tannenberg* (Hamden, Conn., 1991), p. 143.

7 Karl Friedrich Nowak (ed.), *Die Aufzeichnungen des Generalmajors Max Hoffmann* (2 vols, Berlin, 1929), vol. 2, p. 29.

8 Hoffmann, *War Diaries*, vol. 1, p. 41.

9 Alfred Knox, *With the Russian Army, 1914–1917* (2 vols, London, 1921), vol. 1, p. 68.

10 Letter from Hauptmann Geisler, 1 September 1914, in Wolfgang Foerster and Helmuth Greiner (eds), *Wir Kämpfer im Weltkrieg* (Berlin, n.d.), pp. 159–60.

11 Prince A. Lobanov-Rostovsky, *The Grinding Mill: Reminiscences of War and Revolution in Russia, 1913–1920* (New York, 1935), p. 22.

12 Wolfgang Foerster (ed.), *Mackensen. Briefe und Aufzeichnungen* (Leipzig, 1938), pp. 73–4.

13 Holger Afflerbach, *Falkenhayn* (Munich, 1994), p. 217.

14 Norman Stone, *The Eastern Front 1914–1917* (London, 1975), p. 178.

15 Diary of Hauptmann von Loebell of 3rd Foot Guards, in Wolfgang Foerster and Helmuth Greiner (eds), *Wir Kämpfer im Weltkrieg* (Berlin, n.d.), pp. 168–9.

16 Lobanov-Rostovsky, *The Grinding Mill*, p. 20.

17 George Buchanan, *My Mission to Russia and Other Diplomatic Memories* (2 vols, London, 1923), vol. 1, p. 215.

18 Knox, *With the Russian Army*, vol. 1, p. 349.

19 A. A. Brusilov, *A Soldier's Note-book 1914–1918* (London, 1930), p. 151.

20 Lobanov-Rostovsky, *The Grinding Mill*, p. 160.

21 Peter Gatrell, *A Whole Empire Walking: Refugees in Russia during World War I* (Bloomington, IN, 1999), p. 15.

22 Ibid., p. 16.

23 Vejas Gabriel Liulevicius, *War Land on the Eastern Front: Culture, National Identity and German Occupation in World War I* (Cambridge, 2000), p. 192.

24 Ibid., p. 71.

25 Stone, *The Eastern Front*, p. 210.

26 David Stevenson, *The First World War and International Politics* (Oxford, 1988), p. 51.

27 John R. Schindler, *Isonzo: The Forgotten Sacrifice of the Great War* (Westport, CT, 2001), p. 18.

28 Holger Herwig, *The First World War: Germany and Austria-Hungary 1914–1918* (London, 1997), p. 151.

29 Fernanda Bellachioma (trans.), *Letters and Drawings of Enzo Valentini, Conte di Laviano, Italian Volunteer and Soldier* (London, 1917), p. 78; see also pp. 157–68.

30 C. E. J. Fryer, *The Destruction of Serbia in 1915* (New York, 1997), pp. 149, 159.

31 Misha Glenny, *The Balkans* (Harmondsworth, 1999), p. 331.

32 David French, *British Strategy and War Aims 1914–1916* (London, 1986), p. 141.

33 George Leon, *Greece and the Great Powers 1914–1917* (Thessaloniki, 1974), p. 282.

Chapter 6: Breaking the Deadlock

1 Alexander Murray, 'Remembrance', *Oxford Magazine*, no. 208 (2002), p. 10.

2 Jean Bernier, *La Percée* (Paris, 1920), quoted in Edmund Blunden (ed.) *Great Short Stories of the War* (London, 1933), p. 311.

3 Alexandre Arnoux, *Le Cabaret* (Paris, 1919), quoted in ibid., p. 127.

4 Charles Edmonds [Carrington], *A Subaltern's War* (London, 1930), p. 23.

5 George Coppard, *With a Machine Gun to Cambrai* (London, 1969), pp. 24–5.

6 J. C. Dunn, *The War the Infantry Knew, 1914–1919* (London, 1987; first published 1938), pp. 192, 195–6.

7 Gerd Hardach, *The First World War 1914–1918* (London, 1977), p. 80.

8 Arthur J. Marder, *Fear God and Dread Nought: The Correspondence of Admiral of the Fleet Lord Fisher of Kilverstone* (3 vols, London, 1952–9), vol. 3, p. 238.

9 Abel Ferry, *Les Carnets secrets (1914–1918)* (Paris, 1957), p. 88.

10 Description by Queen Marie of Romania, quoted in Glenn Torrey, *Henri Mathias Berthelot* (Iaşi, 2001), p. 191.

11 Margaret H. Darrow, *French Women and the First World War* (Oxford, 2000), p. 185.

12 Ute Daniel, *The War from Within: German Working-class Women in the First World War* (Oxford, 1997), pp. 46–7.

13 Angela Woollacott, *On Her Their Lives Depend: Munitions Workers in the Great War* (Berkeley, CA, 1994), p. 82.

14 Robert Blake (ed.), *The Private Papers of Douglas Haig* (London, 1952), p. 93.

15 Maréchal Fayolle, *Carnets secrets de la Grande Guerre*, ed. Henri Contamine (Paris, 1963), p. 169.

16 Robert Foley, *Alfred von Schlieffen's Military Writings* (London, 2003), p. 199.

17 Cyril Falls, 'Contact with Troops: Commanders and Staffs in the First World War', *Army Quarterly*, vol. 88, no. 2 (1964), p. 179.

18 David French, 'The Meaning of Attrition', *English Historical Review*, vol. 103 (1988), p. 395.

19 M. Daille, *Joffre et la guerre d'usure 1915–1916* (Paris, 1936), p. 170.

20 Pierre Miquel, *Les Poilus* (Paris, 2000), p. 228.

21 Karl von Einem, *Ein Armeeführer erlebt den Weltkrieg* (Leipzig, 1938), pp. 150–1.

22 Miquel, *Les Poilus*, p. 229.

23 Charles Mangin, *Lettres de guerre 1914–1918* (Paris, 1950), p. 59.

24 E. L. Spears, *Prelude to Victory* (London, 1939), p. 33.

25 David Woodward, *Lloyd George and the Generals* (Newark, 1983), p. 77.

26 French, 'The Meaning of Attrition', p. 398.

27 Daille, *Joffre et la guerre d'usure*, p. 256.

28 Elizabeth Greenhalgh, 'Why the British Were on the Somme in 1916', *War in History*, vol. 6 (1999), p. 156.

29 Jacques Péricard, *Verdun. Histoire des combats qui sont livrés de 1914 à 1918 sur les deux rives de La Meuse* (Paris, 1934), p. 80.

30 German Werth, *Verdun. Die Schlacht und der Mythos* (Bergisch Gladbach, 1979), p. 72.

31 Alistair Horne, *The Price of Glory: Verdun 1916* (London, 1962), p. 39.

32 Ian Ousby, *The Road to Verdun: France, Nationalism and the First World War* (London, 2002), p. 195.

33 Stephen Ryan, *Pétain the Soldier* (Cranbury, NJ, 1969), p. 74.

34 Philippe Pétain, *Verdun*, trans. Margaret MacVeagh (London, 1936), pp. 100–1.

35 Ousby, *The Road to Verdun*, p. 206.

36 Gerard De Groot, *Douglas Haig, 1861–1928* (London, 1988), p. 238.

37 Guy Chapman, *Vain Glory* (London, 1937), p. 320.

38 Tim Travers, *The Killing Ground: The British Army, the Western Front and the Emergence of Modern Warfare 1900–1918* (London, 1987), p. 178.

39 Fayolle, *Cahiers secrets*, p. 167.

40 P. Lucas, *L'Evolution des idées tactiques en France et en Allemagne pendant la guerre de 1914–1918* (Paris, 1924), p. 158.

41 David Woodward, 'Britain in a Continental War: The Civil–Military Debate over the Strategical Direction of the Great War of 1914–1918', *Albion*, vol. 12 (1980), pp. 37–65.

Chapter 7: Blockade

1 B. McL. Ranft (ed.), *The Beatty Papers*, (2 vols, Aldershot, 1989–92), vol. 1, pp. 145–6.

2 Ibid., pp. 36–7.

3 Patrick Beesley, *Room 40: British Naval Intelligence 1914–1918* (London, 1982), pp. 36–7.

4 Ranft, *The Beatty Papers*, p. 211.

5 Jon Sumida, *In Defence of Naval Supremacy: Finance, Technology and British Naval Policy, 1889–1914* (Boston, MA, 1989), pp. 297–9.

6 A. Temple Patterson, *The Jellicoe Papers* (2 vols, London, 1966–8), vol. 1, p. 76.

7 Andrew Gordon, *The Rules of the Game: Jutland and British Naval Command* (London, 1996), p. 112.

8 V. E. Tarrant, *Jutland: The German Perspective* (London, 1995), p. 107.

9 Geoffrey Bennett, *Naval Battles of the First World War* (London, 1968), p. 256.

10 Lord Hankey, *The Supreme Command 1914–1918* (2 vols, London, 1961), vol. 2, p. 858.

11 Anne Roerkohl, *Hungersblockade und Heimatfront. Die kommunale Lebensmittelversorgung in Westfalen während des Ersten Weltkrieges* (Stuttgart, 1991), p. 306.

12 A. C. Bell, *A History of the Blockade of Germany* (London, 1937), p. 672.

13 Charles Gilbert, *American Financing of World War I* (Westport, CT, 1970), pp. 33, 37.

14 M. W. W. P. Consett, *The Triumph of Unarmed Forces (1914–1918)* (London, 1923), p. 184.

15 Bell, *A History of the Blockade*, pp. 250–1.

16 Gerd Hardach, *The First World War 1914–1918* (London, 1977), pp. 32–3.

17 Avner Offer, *The First World War: An Agrarian Interpretation* (Oxford, 1989), pp. 33, 45–53.

18 Belinda J. Davis, *Home Fires Burning: Food, Politics, and Everyday Life in World War I Berlin* (Chapel Hill, NC, 2000), pp. 205–6.

19 Roerkohl, *Hungersblockade und Heimatfront*, pp. 95, 211–27.

20 Caroline Ethel Cooper, *Behind the Lines: One Woman's War 1914–1918*, ed. Decie Denholm (London, 1982), p. 165.

21 Joe Lee, 'Administrators and Agriculture: Aspects of German Agricultural Policy in the First World War', in J. M. Winter (ed.), *War and Economic Policy* (Cambridge, 1975), pp. 231–4.

22 Davis, *Home Fires Burning*, p. 162.

23 Roerkohl, *Hungersblockade and Heimatfront*, p. 33.

24 Cooper, *Behind the Lines*, p. 233.

25 Ibid., p. 270.

26 Paul Halpern, *A Naval History of World War I* (London, 1994), p. 296.

27 Charles Seymour, *The Intimate Papers of Colonel House* (2 vols, London, 1926), vol. 1, p. 437.

28 Thomas J. Knock, *To End All Wars: Woodrow Wilson and the Quest for a New World Order* (New York, 1992), p. 60.

29 Walter Görlitz (ed.), *The Kaiser and His Court: the diaries of Admiral Georg von Müller* (London, 1961), p. 229.

30 Hans Peter Hanssen, *Diary of a Dying Empire* (Port Washington, NY, 1973), p. 161.

31 John Whiteclay Chambers (ed.), *The Eagle and the Dove: The American Peace Movement and United States Foreign Policy 1900–1922* (Syracuse, NY, 1991), pp. 113–4.

32 Kathleen Burk, *Britain, America and the Sinews of War 1914–1918* (Boston, 1985), pp. 80–95.

33 William S. Sims, *The Victory at Sea* (London, 1920), p. 39.

Chapter 8: Revolution

1 Brock Millman, *Pessimism and British War Policy 1916–1918* (London, 2001), p. 30.

2 David Woodward (ed.), *The Military Correspondence of Field-Marshal Sir William Robertson* (London, 1989), p. 320.

3 *Lord Riddell's War Diary 1914–1918* (London, 1933), p. 220.

4 Bentley Brinkerhoff Gilbert, *David Lloyd George: A Political Life: The Organizer of Victory 1912–16* (London, 1992), p. 369.

5 Ibid., pp. 375–6.

6 Daniel Halévy, *L'Europe brisée* (Paris, 1998), pp. 233–8.

7 Jean-Baptiste Duroselle, *La Grande Guerre des français* (Paris, 1994), p. 157.

8 Gaëtan Gallieni (ed.), *Les Carnets de Gallieni* (Paris, 1932), p. 205.

9 Jere Clemens King, *Generals and Politicians* (Berkeley, CA, 1951), p. 108.

10 Richard Lambert, *The Parliamentary History of Conscription in Great Britain* (London, 1917), p. iv.

11 William Robert Scott, *Economic Problems of Peace after War* (Cambridge, 1917), pp. 12–13.

12 Gilbert, *David Lloyd George*, pp. 419, 424.

13 Raymond Pearson, *The Russian Moderates and the Crisis of Tsarism 1914–1917* (London, 1977), p. 51.

14 Dominic Lieven, *Nicholas II* (London, 1993), p. 211.

15 Joseph Furmann (ed.), *The Complete Wartime Correspondence of Tsar Nicholas II and the Empress Alexandra* (Westport, CT, 1999), p. 181.

16 George Buchanan, *My Mission to Russia and Other Diplomatic Memories* (2 vols, London, 1923), vol. 2, pp. 4, 31.

17 Robert McKean, *St Petersburg between the Revolutions* (New Haven, CT, 1990), pp. 327, 336–45.

18 W. Bruce Lincoln, *Passage through Armageddon: The Russians in War and Revolution 1914–1918* (New York, 1986), pp. 315, 318.

19 Furmann, *The Complete Wartime Correspondence*, p. 692.

20 Buchanan, *My Mission to Russia*, vol. 2, p. 48.

21 Keith Neilson, *Strategy and Supply: The Anglo-Russian Alliance 1914–17* (London, 1984), pp. 251–2.

22 Maurice Paléologue, *An Ambassador's Memoirs*, trans. F. A. Holt (3 vols, London, 1925), vol. 3, p. 228.

23 Guy Pedroncini, 'Les Rapports du gouvernement et du haut commandement en France en 1917', *Revue d'histoire moderne et contemporaine*, vol. 15 (1968), p. 128.

24 Trevor Wilson, *The Myriad Faces of War* (Cambridge, 1986), p. 453.

25 Reginald H. Roy (ed.), *The Journal of Private Fraser* (Victoria, BC, 1985), pp. 261, 263.

26 R. G. Nobécourt, *Les Fantassins du Chemin des Dames* (Paris, 1965), p. 220.

27 Jean-Jacques Becker, *The Great War and the French People*, trans. Arnold Pomerans (Leamington Spa, 1985), pp. 226–35.

28 Lionel Lemarchand, *Lettres censurées des tranchées 1917* (Paris, 2001), p. 144.

29 Guy Pedroncini, *Les Mutineries de 1917* (Paris, 1967), pp. 194, 211–2.

30 A. Temple Patterson, *The Jellicoe Papers* (2 vols, London 1966–8), vol. 2, p. 161; italics in the original.

31 Woodward, *Correspondence of Robertson*, p. 179.

32 Général Palat [Pierre Lehautcourt], *La Grande Guerre sur le front occidental*, (14 vols, Paris, 1917–29), vol. 12, pp. 400–1.

33 David Woodward, *Lloyd George and the Generals* (Newark, NJ, 1983), pp. 163–4.

34 John Terraine, *The Road to Passchendaele* (London, 1977), p. 119.

35 Robin Prior and Trevor Wilson, *Passchendaele: The Untold Story* (New Haven, CT, 1996), p. 160.

36 Ibid., p. 196.

37 John R. Schindler, *Isonzo: The Forgotten Sacrifice of the Great War* (Westport, CT, 2001), p. 242.

38 John Gooch, 'Morale and Discipline in the Italian Army', in Hugh Cecil and Peter Liddle (eds), *Facing Armageddon* (London, 1996), p. 441.

39 Erwin Rommel, *Attacks*, trans. J. R. Driscoll (Vienna, VA, 1979), p. 214.

40 Luigi Tomassini, 'The Home Front in Italy', in Hugh Cecil and Peter Liddle (eds), *Facing Armageddon* (London, 1996), p. 586. For what follows, see also Giovanna Procacci, 'Popular Protest and Labour Conflict in Italy, 1915–18', *Social History*, vol. 14 (1989), pp. 31–58.

41 Georges Clemenceau, *Discours de guerre* (Paris, 1968), pp. 166–7; see also p. 131.

42 Jean Nicot, *Les Poilus ont la parole: lettres du front: 1917–1918* (Brussels, 1998), p. 261.

43 Irina Davidian, 'The Russian Soldier's Morale from the Evidence of Tsarist Military Censorship', in Hugh Cecil and Peter Liddle (eds), *Facing Armageddon* (London, 1996), p. 432.

44 Allan K. Wildman, *The End of the Russian Imperial Army: The Old Army and the Soldiers' Revolt (March–April 1917)* (Princeton, NJ, 1980), p. 245.

45 Elie Halévy, *The World Crisis of 1914–1918* (Oxford, 1930), p. 5.

Chapter 9: Germany's Last Gamble

1 W. Bruce Lincoln, *Passage through Armageddon: The Russians in War and Revolution 1914–1918* (New York 1986), pp. 502–3.

2 Jean-Noël Grandhomme, Michel Roucaud and Thierry Sarmant (eds), *La Roumanie dans la Grande Guerre et l'effondrement de l'armée russe* (Paris, 2000), pp. 415, 423.

3 Jean Nicot, *Les Poilus ont la parole: lettres du front: 1917–1918* (Brussels, 1998), p. 333.

4 Jürgen Kocka, *Facing Total War: German Society 1914–1918*, trans. Barbara Weinberger (Leamington Spa, 1984), pp. 19, 85–6.

5 Caroline Ethel Cooper, *Behind the Lines: One Woman's War 1914–1918*, ed. Decie Denholm (London, 1982), p. 182.

6 J. P. Nettl, *Rosa Luxemburg* (Oxford, 1969), p. 387.

7 Gerald Feldman, *Army, Industry and Labor in Germany 1914–1918* (Princeton, NJ, 1966), p. 360.

8 R. H. Lutz (ed.), *Documents of the German Revolution: Fall of the German Empire* (2 vols, Stanford, CA, 1932), vol. 2, pp. 262–6.

9 Hans Peter Hanssen, *Diary of a Dying Empire* (Port Washington, NY, 1973), p. 225.

10 Holger Afflerbach, 'Wilhelm II as Supreme Warlord in the First World War', *War in History*, vol. 5 (1998), p. 445.

11 Hanssen, *Diary of a Dying Empire*, p. 231.

12 Daniel Horn (ed.), *The Private War of Seaman Stumpf* (London, 1969), p. 345.

13 Martin Kitchen, *The Silent Dictatorship: The Politics of the High Command under Hindenburg and Ludendorff 1916–1918* (London, 1976), pp. 170–1.

14 Bernard P. Bellon, *Mercedes in Peace and War: German Automobile Workers* (New York, 1990), pp. 89–92, 102–12.

15 Walter Görlitz (ed.), *The Kaiser and His Court: the diaries of Admiral Georg von Müller* (London, 1961), p. 190.

16 Bernd Ulrich and Benjamin Ziemann, *Frontalltag im Ersten Weltkrieg* (Frankfurt, 1994), pp. 184, 131.

17 Paul Christophe (ed.), *Les Carnets du Cardinal Alfred Baudrillart* (Paris, 1994), p. 94.

18 Christoph Jahr, *Gewöhnliche Soldaten* (Göttingen, 1998), p. 283.

19 Dominique Richert, *Cahiers d'un survivant* (Strasbourg, 1994), p. 156.

20 Octavian Tăslăuanu, *With the Austrian Army in Galicia* (London, 1918), p. 193.

21 Eduard März, *Austrian Banking and Financial Policy* (London, 1984), pp. 16, 113, 121–2, 164, 177–8.

22 Wilhelm Winkler, *Die Einkommensverschiebungen in Österreich während des Weltkrieges* (Vienna, 1930), pp. 47–8.

23 August von Cramon, *Unser Österreich-Ungarischer Bundesgenosse im Weltkriege* (Berlin, 1920), p. 89.

24 Arthur May, *The Passing of the Hapsburg Monarchy* (Philadelphia, PA, 1966), p. 642.

25 Ibid., p. 687.

26 Görlitz, *The Kaiser and His Court*, p. 252.

27 Felix Guse, *Die Kaukasusfront im Weltkrieg* (Leipzig, 1940), p. 93.

28 Carl Mühlmann, *Das deutsch-türkische Waffenbündnis im Weltkrieg* (Leipzig, 1940), p. 120.

29 Kress von Kressenstein, quoted in Jehuda Wallach, *Anatomie einer Militärhilfe* (Dusseldorf, 1976), p. 220.

30 Richard Meinertzhagen, *Army Diary 1899–1926* (Edinburgh, 1960), p. 219.

31 David French, *The Strategy of the Lloyd George Coalition* (Oxford, 1995), p. 133.

32 Ion Idriess, *The Desert Column* (Sydney, 1982), pp. 248, 261.

33 Briton C. Busch, *Britain, India and the Arabs* (Berkeley, CA, 1971), p. 52.

34 Elie Kedourie, *England and the Middle East* (London, 1956), p. 103.

35 L. Schatkowski Schilcher, 'The Famine of 1915–1918 in Greater Syria', in John Spagnolo (ed.), *Problems of the Modern Middle East in Historical Perspective* (Reading, 1992), p. 248.

36 Idriess, *The Desert Column*, pp. 271–2.

37 Ahmed Emin, *Turkey in the World War* (New Haven, CT, 1930), pp. 144–51, 253.

38 Max Hoffmann, *War Diaries and Other Papers* (2 vols, London, 1929), vol. 1, p. 207.

39 Richard G. Hovannisian, *Armenia on the Road to Independence 1918* (Berkeley, CA, 1967), p. 195.

40 Ottokar Czernin, *Im Weltkriege* (Berlin, 1919), pp. 322–3.

41 Josef Redlich, *Schicksalsjahre Österreichs 1908–1919. Das politische Tagebuch Josef Redlichs*, ed. Fritz Fellner (2 vols, Graz, 1953), vol. 2, p. 256.

42 Richard Plaschka, Horst Haselsteiner and Arnold Suppan, *Innere Front* (Munich, 1974), p. 60.

43 Dorothea Groener-Geyer, *General Groener* (Frankfurt am Main, 1955), p. 81.

44 Kitchen, *The Silent Dictatorship*, pp. 234–5.

45 Czernin, *Im Weltkriege*, pp. 344–5.

46 Evelyn, Princess Blücher, *An English Wife in Berlin* (London, 1920), p. 193.

47 Benjamin Ziemann, 'Enttäuschte Erwartung und kollektive Erschöpfung. Die deutsche Soldaten an der Westfront 1918 auf dem Weg zur Revolution', in Jörg Duppler and Gerhard P. Gross (eds), *Kriegsende 1918* (Munich, 1999), p. 170.

48 Giordan Fong, 'The Movement of German Divisions to the Western Front, Winter 1917–1918', *War in History*, vol. 7 (2000), pp. 225–35.

49 Gregory Martin, 'German Strategy and Military Assessments of the American Expeditionary Force', *War in History*, vol. 1 (1994), p. 179.

50 Holger Herwig, *The First World War: Germany and Austria-Hungary 1914–1918* (London, 1997), p. 319.

51 P. E. Dewey, *British Agriculture in the First World War* (London, 1989), p. 244.

52 J. M. Winter, *The Great War and the British People* (Basingstoke, 1985), pp. 104–24.

53 Cate Haste, *Keep the Home Fires Burning: propaganda in the First World War* (London, 1977), p. 43.

54 Martin Kitchen, *The German Offensives of 1918* (Stroud, 2001), p. 16.

55 Rupprecht, Kronprinz von Bayern, *Mein Kriegstagebuch* (3 vols, Berlin, 1929), vol. 2, p. 322.

56 Ibid., p. 320.
57 Lutz, *Fall of the German Empire*, vol. 1, pp. 642–3.
58 Ulrich and Ziemann, *Frontalltag im Ersten Weltkrieg*, p. 197.
59 Lyn Macdonald, *To the Last Man: Spring 1918* (London, 1998), pp. 92–3.
60 Tim Travers, *How the War Was Won* (London, 1992), p. 55.
61 Rupprecht, *Mein Kriegstagebuch*, vol. 2, p. 351.
62 Rudolph Binding, *A Fatalist at War* (London, 1929), p. 208.
63 Wilhelm Deist, 'The Military Collapse of the German Empire: The Reality behind the Stab-in-the-back Myth', *War in History*, vol. 3 (1996), pp. 199, 203.
64 Gerhard Ritter, *The Sword and the Sceptre: the problem of militarism in Germany* (4 vols, London, 1971–3), vol. 4, p. 232.
65 Mühlmann, *Das deutsch-türkische Waffenbündnis*, p. 197.
66 Ibid., p. 211.
67 Cramon, *Unser Österreich-Ungarischer Bundesgenosse*, p. 72.

Chapter 10: War Without End

1 John Whiteclay Chambers (ed.), *The Eagle and the Dove: The American Peace Movement and United States Foreign Policy 1900–1922* (Syracuse, NY, 1991), p. 131.
2 Lloyd George, *War Memoirs* (2 vols, London, 1938), vol. 2, p. 1513.
3 Chambers, *The Eagle and the Dove*, p. 131.
4 Niall Ferguson, *The Pity of War* (London, 1998), pp. 248–9.
5 David Trask, *The AEF and Coalition Warmaking 1917–1918* (Kansas, 1993), pp. 12, 16–17.
6 Mario Morselli, *Caporetto 1917: Victory or Defeat?* (London, 2001), p. 111.
7 Harald Høiback, *Command and Control in Military Crisis* (London, 2003), pp. 20, 44.
8 F. M. Cutlack (ed.), *War Letters of General Monash* (Sydney, 1935), p. 223.
9 Georges Clemenceau, *Grandeurs et misères d'une victoire* (Paris, 1930), p. 20.
10 Ibid., p. 22.
11 Hubert Gough, *The March Retreat* (London, 1934), pp. 154–5.
12 Robert Blake (ed.), *The Private Papers of Douglas Haig* (London, 1952), p. 303.
13 Guy Pedroncini, *Pétain: général-en-chef* (Paris, 1974), p. 360.
14 Rudolph Binding, *A Fatalist at War* (London, 1929), p. 234.
15 Wilhelm, Kronprinz von Preussen, *Meine Erinnerungen aus Deutschlands Heldenkampf* (Berlin, 1923), p. 338.

16 Vera Brittain, *Testament of Youth: An Autobiographical Study of the Years 1900–1925* (London, 1978), pp. 420–1.

17 John Morrow, *The Great War in the Air* (Shrewsbury, 1993), p. 322; for 1918 production, see also J. M. Spaight, *The Beginnings of Organised Air Power* (London, 1927), p. 293.

18 Binding, *A Fatalist at War*, p. 239.

19 J. P. Harris, *Men, Ideas and Tanks* (Manchester, 1995), p. 89.

20 James H. Hallas (ed.), *Doughboy War: The American Expeditionary Force in World War I* (Boulder, CO, 2000), p. 174.

21 Charles Mangin, *Lettres de guerre 1914–1918* (Paris, 1950), p. 284.

22 Rupprecht, Kronprinz von Bayern, *Mein Kriegstagebuch* (3 vols, Berlin, 1929), vol. 2, pp. 424–5, 430.

23 *Memoirs of Marshal Foch* (London, 1931), pp. 427–8.

24 Robin Prior and Trevor Wilson, *Command on the Western Front* (Oxford, 1992), p. 311.

25 Gerhard Ritter, *The Sword and the Sceptre: the problem of militarism in Germany* (4 vols, London, 1971–73), vol. 4, p. 331.

26 Mark Cornwall, *The Undermining of Austria-Hungary: the battle for hearts and minds* (Basingstoke, 2000), p. 305.

27 Blake, *The Private Papers of Douglas Haig*, p. 324.

28 J. C. Dunn, *The War the Infantry Knew, 1914–1919* (London, 1987; first published 1938), p. 516.

29 Prior and Wilson, *Command on the Western Front*, pp. 373–4.

30 Max von Baden, *Erinnerungen und Dokumente* (Stuttgart, 1968), p. 324.

31 Diary of Heinrich-Gottfried Vietinghoff, 28 September 1918, Bundes-Archiv Militär-Archiv, N574/2.

32 Carl Mühlmann, *Oberste Heeresleitung und Balkan* (Berlin, 1942), p. 230.

33 Général Jouinot-Gambetta, *Uskub* (Paris, 1920), p. 89.

34 Alan Palmer, *The Gardeners of Salonika* (New York, 1965), p. 229.

35 Cornwall, *The Undermining of Austria-Hungary*, p. 421.

36 R. H. Lutz, *The Causes of the German Collapse in 1918* (Stanford, CA, 1934), p. 268.

37 8 October 1918; Hans Peter Hanssen, *Diary of a Dying Empire* (Port Washington, NY, 1973), pp. 332–3.

38 R. H. Lutz (ed.), *The Fall of the German Empire* (Stanford, CA, 1932), vol. 2, pp. 541–2.

39 Stanley Weintraub, *A Stillness Heard Around the World* (Oxford, 1987), p. 175.

40 Blake, *The Private Papers of Douglas Haig*, p. 333.

41 Mark Derez, 'Belgium: A Soldier's Tale', in Hugh Cecil and Peter Liddle (eds), *At the Eleventh Hour* (Barnsley, 1998), pp. 109, 133.

42 Henri Domelier, *Au GQG allemand* (Paris, 1919), p. 370.

43 Jean Nicot, *Les Poilus ont la parole: lettres du front: 1917–1918* (Brussels, 1998), pp. 553–4.

44 Herbert Sulzbach, *With the German Guns: four years on the Western Front 1914–1918*, trans. Richard Thonger (London, 1973), p. 255.

45 Evelyn, Princess Blücher, *An English Wife in Berlin* (London, 1920), p. 305.

46 Heinz Hagenlücke, 'Germany and the Armistice', in Hugh Cecil and Peter Liddle (eds), *At the Eleventh Hour* (Barnsley, 1998), p. 40.

47 Ernst Jünger, *The Storm of Steel* (London, 1929), pp. 316–17.

48 Margaret Macmillan, *Peacemakers: the Paris Conference of 1919 and its attempt to end war* (London, 2001), p. 475.

49 Ibid., p. 52.

50 Keith Jeffery, *Military Correspondence of Field Marshal Sir Henry Wilson* (London, 1985), p. 133.

51 'Correspondance entre Romain Rolland et Jean-Richard Bloch 1914–1919', *La Revue Europe*, nos 95–103 (1953–4), p. 84.

52 Anna Eisenmenger, *Blockade: The Diary of an Austrian Middle-class Woman* (London, 1932), p. 265.

53 *Sapper's War Stories* (London, n.d.), p. 10.

54 Margaret Cole (ed.), *Beatrice Webb's Diaries* (London, 1952), p. 137.

55 John Jackson, unpublished memoir, quoted by permission of his family.

56 Ian Hay [John Beith], *Their Name Liveth* (London, 1931), pp. 2, 152, 154.

Index